The Economics of Brexit

Philip B. Whyman · Alina I. Petrescu

The Economics of Brexit

A Cost-Benefit Analysis of the UK's Economic Relationship with the EU

Philip B. Whyman
The Lancashire Institute for Economic
and Business Research
University of Central Lancashire
Preston, UK

Alina I. Petrescu
The Lancashire Institute for Economic
and Business Research
University of Central Lancashire
Preston, UK

ISBN 978-3-319-58282-5   ISBN 978-3-319-58283-2   (eBook)
DOI 10.1007/978-3-319-58283-2

Library of Congress Control Number: 2017943637

This Palgrave Macmillan imprint is published by Springer Nature
The registered company is Springer International Publishing AG
The registered company address is: Gewerbestrasse 11, 6330 Cham, Switzerland

Acknowledgements

There are a large number of people we wish to thank for their assistance, directly or indirectly, in the preparation of this book.

Firstly, we wish to thank our respective families for their forbearance during the countless hours we have been locked in our respective studies. For your patience and goodwill, we would like to dedicate this book to you: AP—my husband, child, mum and dad; PBW—Claire, Barbara and Boyd.

Secondly, we thank Laura Pacey and her colleagues at Palgrave for their support for this project and patience during the almost inevitable overruns. I hope you are pleased with the final product and agree that it was worth the wait!

Thirdly, we would like to thank our colleagues at the University of Central Lancashire, and research collaborators elsewhere (Mark, Brian, Tunde), since our single-minded dedication to this project has proven to be more than a tad distracting for our other work. Thanks for the comradeship.

Any remaining errors and omissions, we gladly attribute to each other!

Lancaster and Nether Edge, UK
January 2017

Summary European Integration Timeline

See Fig. 1

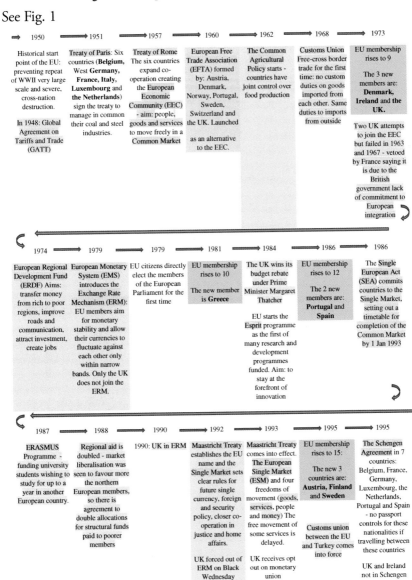

➡ 1950 ➡ 1951 ➡ 1957 ➡ 1960 ➡ 1962 ➡ 1968 ➡ 1973

1950 Historical start point of the EU: preventing repeat of WWII very large scale and severe, cross-nation destruction.

In 1948: Global Agreement on Tariffs and Trade (GATT)

1951 Treaty of Paris: Six countries (**Belgium**, West **Germany**, **France, Italy, Luxembourg** and **the Netherlands**) sign the treaty to manage in common their coal and steel industries.

1957 Treaty of Rome The six countries expand co-operation creating the European Economic Community (EEC) - aim: people, goods and services to move freely in a Common Market

1960 European Free Trade Association (EFTA) formed by: Austria, Denmark, Norway, Portugal, Sweden, Switzerland and the UK. Launched as an alternative to the EEC.

1962 The Common Agricultural Policy starts - countries have joint control over food production

1968 Customs Union Free-cross border trade for the first time: no custom duties on goods imported from each other. Same duties to imports from outside

1973 EU membership rises to 9

The 3 new members are: **Denmark, Ireland** and the **UK.**

Two UK attempts to join the EEC but failed in 1963 and 1967 - vetoed by France saying it is due to the British government lack of commitment to European integration

⟵

➡ 1974 ➡ 1979 ➡ 1979 ➡ 1981 ➡ 1984 ➡ 1986 ➡ 1986

1974 European Regional Development Fund (ERDF) Aims: transfer money from rich to poor regions, improve roads and communication, attract investment, create jobs

1979 European Monetary System (EMS) introduces the Exchange Rate Mechanism (ERM): EU members aim for monetary stability and allow their currencies to fluctuate against each other only within narrow bands. Only the UK does not join the ERM.

1979 EU citizens directly elect the members of the European Parliament for the first time

1981 EU membership rises to 10

The new member is **Greece**

1984 The UK wins its budget rebate under Prime Minister Margaret Thatcher

EU starts the Esprit programme as the first of many research and development programmes funded. Aim: to stay at the forefront of innovation

1986 EU membership rises to 12

The 2 new members are: **Portugal** and **Spain**

1986 The Single European Act (SEA) commits countries to the Single Market, setting out a timetable for completion of the Common Market by 1 Jan 1993

⟵

➡ 1987 ➡ 1988 ➡ 1990 ➡ 1992 ➡ 1993 ➡ 1995 ➡ 1995

1987 ERASMUS Programme - funding university students wishing to study for up to a year in another European country.

1988 Regional aid is doubled - market liberalisation was seen to favour more the northern European members, so there is agreement to double allocations for structural funds paid to poorer members

1990 1990: UK in ERM

1992 Maastricht Treaty establishes the EU name and the Single Market sets clear rules for future single currency, foreign and security policy, closer co-operation in justice and home affairs.

UK forced out of ERM on Black Wednesday

1993 Maastricht Treaty comes into effect. The European Single Market (ESM) and four freedoms of movement (goods, services, people and money) The free movement of some services is delayed.

UK receives opt out on monetary union

1995 EU membership rises to 15:

The new 3 countries are: **Austria, Finland** and **Sweden**

Customs union between the EU and Turkey comes into force

1995 The Schengen Agreement in 7 countries: Belgium, France, Germany, Luxembourg, the Netherlands, Portugal and Spain - no passport controls for these nationalities if travelling between these countries

UK and Ireland not in Schengen

vii

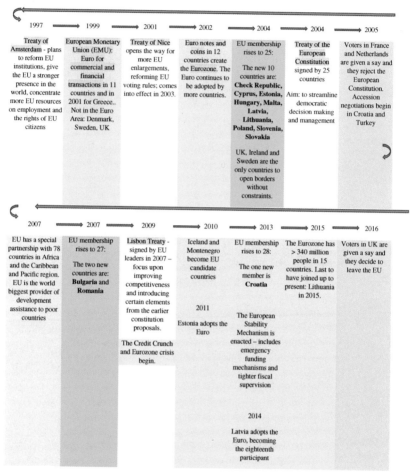

1997	1999	2001	2002	2004	2004	2005
Treaty of Amsterdam - plans to reform EU institutions, give the EU a stronger presence in the world, concentrate more EU resources on employment and the rights of EU citizens	European Monetary Union (EMU): Euro for commercial and financial transactions in 11 countries and in 2001 for Greece.. Not in the Euro Area: Denmark, Sweden, UK	Treaty of Nice opens the way for more EU enlargements, reforming EU voting rules; comes into effect in 2003.	Euro notes and coins in 12 countries create the Eurozone. The Euro continues to be adopted by more countries.	EU membership rises to 25: The new 10 countries are: Check Republic, Cyprus, Estonia, Hungary, Malta, Latvia, Lithuania, Poland, Slovenia, Slovakia UK, Ireland and Sweden are the only countries to open borders without constraints.	Treaty of the European Constitution signed by 25 countries Aim: to streamline democratic decision making and management	Voters in France and Netherlands are given a say and they reject the European Constitution. Accession negotiations begin in Croatia and Turkey

2007	2007	2009	2010	2013	2015	2016
EU has a special partnership with 78 countries in Africa and the Caribbean and Pacific region. EU is the world biggest provider of development assistance to poor countries	EU membership rises to 27: The two new countries are: **Bulgaria** and **Romania**	Lisbon Treaty - signed by EU leaders in 2007 – focus upon improving competitiveness and introducing certain elements from the earlier constitution proposals. The Credit Crunch and Eurozone crisis begin.	Iceland and Montenegro become EU candidate countries 2011 Estonia adopts the Euro	EU membership rises to 28: The one new member is **Croatia** The European Stability Mechanism is enacted – includes emergency funding mechanisms and tighter fiscal supervision 2014 Latvia adopts the Euro, becoming the eighteenth participant	The Eurozone has > 340 million people in 15 countries. Last to have joined up to present: Lithuania in 2015.	Voters in UK are given a say and they decide to leave the EU

Legend:
Uncoloured background - General events related to the EU
Yellow - Finance related events
Blue Trade-related events
Pink - EU enlargements (Pale pink - related events)
Grey - Most significant event/treaty
Bold font - Names of new member states

Fig. 1 Main European Union and selected UK events related to integration, finance and trade, 1950–present. *Note* see Panel B for continued part of the timeline. Legend: *Uncoloured background* general events related to the EU, *Yellow* finance related events, *Blue* trade-related events, *Pink* EU enlargements (*Pale pink* related events), *Grey* most significant event/treaty, *Bold font* names of new member states. *Source* Authors' selection of relevant events, using a variety of sources such as the Europa website: http://ec.europa.eu/consumers/europadi-ary/uk/about_eu/eu_timeline_en.htm (last accessed 27 September 2016)

Contents

Abbreviations

BBC	British Broadcasting Corporation
BCC	British Chambers of Commerce
BIS	Department for Business, Innovation and Skills
BoE	Bank of England
Brexit	Britain Exiting the European Union
CAP	Common Agricultural Policy
CBI	Confederation of Business Industry
CEP	Centre for Economic Performance
CET	Common External Tariff
CFP	Common Fisheries Policy
CGE	Computable General Equilibrium (econometrics modelling)
CIPD	Chartered Institute of Personnel and Development
CU	Customs Union
ECB	European Central Bank
EEA	European Economic Area
EEC	European Economic Community
EFTA	European Free Trade Association
EMS	European Monetary System
EMU	European Monetary Union
EP	European Parliament
EPA	Economic Partnership Agreement

ERM	Exchange Rate Mechanism
ESM	European Single Market
ESRC	Economic and Social Research Council
EU	European Union
FDI	Foreign Direct Investment
FTA	Free Trade Area
GATS	General Agreement on Trade in Services
GATT	Global Agreement on Tariffs and Trade
GDP	Gross Domestic Product
GNI	Gross National Income
HMG	Her Majesty's Government
HMRC	Her Majesty's Revenue and Customs
HoC	House of Commons
IMF	International Monetary Fund
IoD	Institute of Directors
IT	Information Technology
LSE	London School of Economics
M&A	Mergers and Acquisitions
MAC	Migration Advisory Committee
MEP	Member of the European Parliament
MFN	Most Favoured Nation
NAFTA	North American Free Trade Agreement
NIESR	National Institute of Economic and Social Research
NiGEM	National Institute's Global Econometric Model (a macroeconomic simulation model)
NTB	Non-Tariff Barriers
OBR	Office for Budget Responsibility
OECD	Organisation for Economic Cooperation and Development
ONS	Office of National Statistics
PAYE	Pay-as-you-earn tax
PTA	Preferential Trade Arrangements
PwC	PricewaterhouseCoopers
R&D	Research and Development
RES	Royal Economic Society
RIAs	Regulatory Impact Assessments
SBE	Society of Business Economists
SEA	Single European Act
SIM	Single Internal Market

SMEs	Small and Medium Sized Enterprise(s)
SOC	Standard Occupational Classification
TFEU	Treaty on the Functioning of the European Union
TPP	Trans-Pacific Partnership
TTIP	Transatlantic Trade and Investment Partnership
TUC	Trades Union Congress
UK	United Kingdom
UN	United Nations
UNCTAD	United Nations Conference for Trade and Development
USA	United States of America
USITC	United States International Trade Commission
VAR	Vector Autoregressive Model
VAT	Value Added Tax
WDI	World Development Indicators
WERS	Workplace Employment Relations Survey
WTD	Working Time Directive
WTO	World Trade Organisation
WWII	The Second World War

List of Figures

List of Tables

Introduction

The 2016 European referendum proved to be a decisive turning point for the UK as, despite the position adopted by the majority of the political and (big) business establishment, 51.9% of the population took the first opportunity they had been given in 41 years to vote to withdraw from the European Union; a margin of more than 1.2 million people. This decision will have a significant impact upon the lives of UK citizens, in a number of different areas, not the least of which being the economy.[1]

As the UK rediscovers its independence, it will necessitate a structural change in its economy and a reconfiguring of economic policy to facilitate this process, by magnifying the advantages arising from withdrawal from the EU whilst mitigating as many of the costs as possible. Brexit will inevitably pose challenges and opportunities for UK exporters and those engaged in trade more widely, both in terms of seeking to maintain existing trading links with consumers and supply chains within other EU member states, whilst simultaneously seeking to take advantage of new and more rapidly expanding markets elsewhere in the world. There will be challenges for government seeking to rebuild the UK's industrial base and increasing both the productivity and international competitiveness of UK businesses. The continued attraction of inward investment will be a key part of this approach, but so will attempt to increase R&D and technological innovation within UK companies. It will involve the repatriation of a significant element of regulation and its redesign with a greater focus on UK rather than EU needs. Similarly, it will encompass a new approach to the inward migration of labour and, were this to be restricted in the future, a strategy to ensure a re-skilling of the existing UK labour force to meet business requirements. Finally, it will require government to reject the economic orthodoxy of the past half-century, and ensure a sufficient level of aggregate demand to provide sufficient incentives for businesses to invest and produce, and hence to increase employment and be willing to invest in increasing the productivity of their activities.

Therefore, the first objective of this book is to outline a number of the options available to policy makers, in how the UK economy might be better adapted to the challenges and opportunities presented by Brexit.

It is vital that policy makers and indeed other economic actors as well (e.g. business leaders, consumers and workers) have reasonably accurate information on which to formulate their future strategies, whether for the management of the economy, future investment decisions in productive capacity or whether it is preferable to increase or restrain individual consumption. Similarly, for journalists and other commentators, it is important that their perceptions about the economic news items of the day are based upon solid foundations. Yet there is a problem here, since there is no single definitive study which satisfactorily deals with all of the relevant costs and benefits arising from Brexit (Portes 2013: F4–5; Webb et al. 2015: 4; Miller et al. 2016: 5,12). Moreover, those studies which have been produced have relied upon a range of simplifying assumptions to deal with difficult analytical problems, not the least of which is that there is no comparable historical precedent to Brexit against which to calibrate economic models, except perhaps for Greenland, which is the only country to have withdrawn from the EU, but is a much smaller country than the UK. Therefore, all predictions are subject to considerable uncertainty (Harari and Thompson 2013; HM Treasury 2016: 124).

It is perhaps not surprising that so many of the studies thus produced have been criticised as being inaccurate (Capital Economics 2016: 3). Moreover, the admittedly limited economic evidence, drawn from the post-referendum period, has not been in line with some of the more negative predictions made by these studies. Each time the Bank of England and other economic agencies raise their growth forecasts for the UK economy, this increases scepticism about the accuracy of mainstream studies. Furthermore, it has led to *The Times* newspaper to suggest that the reputations of economists, or at least those working with mathematical models, is on the line over this issue.[2]

Hence, the second objective of this book is to evaluate the available evidence relating to how Brexit might have an economic impact upon the UK, in order to assess the rigour of the studies and hence likely accuracy of their conclusions.

It is too easy, when writing a book of this type, for the prior convictions of the authors to dominate over an objective review of the evidence (Harari and Thompson 2013). In this volume, we have sought to avoid this temptation and the fact that the authors have rather different initial degrees of enthusiasm or scepticism for the EU has perhaps helped in this respect. However, we leave it to the reader to decide how ultimately successful we have been in this respect.

The book is constituted of nine chapters.

Chapter 1 provides a detailed examination of the mainstream 'consensus' economic studies, which have formed the basis for many of the comments made during and after the European referendum, but which also form the basis for much of the advice currently being presented to policy makers. To the extent that the predictions made by these studies are inaccurate, then not only were the electorate presented with flawed information upon which to make their decision during the recent referendum, but policy makers and businesses are basing their current decisions upon this imprecise foundation.

The following five chapters explore key elements that should form the basis of any economic impact study. Chapter 2 examines the fiscal benefit that should accrue to the UK following Brexit, as payments to the EU budget will either be eliminated entirely, as would be the case in a Free Trade Agreement (FTA) or reliance upon World Trade

Organisation (WTO) rules, or else these payments would be substantially reduced in the case of other forms of preferential trade association. Chapter 3 examines the potential impact upon UK trade with the EU following Brexit, whilst Chap. 4 does likewise with the inflow of Foreign Direct Investment (FDI). These are the two areas where theorists anticipate that Brexit will incur the most significant costs. In contrast, Chap. 5 assesses the potential for regulation to provide a significant benefit to the UK economy, once regulations are repatriated and redesigned for national rather than super-national economic requirements. Finally, Chap. 6 explores the issue of inward migration and the economic consequences of net EU migration being restricted following withdrawal.

Chapter 7 evaluates the potential economic impact that may occur due to dynamic rather than static factors. These range from the extent that the degree of openness has upon productivity, to evaluating the evidence relating EU membership to economic growth.

Chapter 8 is concerned with a range of options that the UK may wish to incorporate in any post-Brexit economic strategy. This area is, for the authors, potentially *the* most significant means of influencing the economic impact of Brexit.

Finally, Chap. 9 outlines the range of options available for the UK to consider in its negotiation of a new trade relationship with the EU, but, perhaps just as (if not more) importantly in the long term, how the UK might seek to build upon existing historical and cultural ties to forge new preferential trade relationships with the rest of the world.

Notes

1. If you want to read further generalist material on the debate leading up to the EU Referendum, Gill (2015) provides a good introductory reading list.
2. https://www.ft.com/content/e66852f0-3249-11e6-ad39-3fee5ffe5b5b; http://researchbriefings.parliament.uk/ResearchBriefing/Summary/CBP-7893.

References

Capital Economics. (2016). *The Economics Impact of 'Brexit': A paper discussing the United Kingdom' relationship with Europe and the impact of 'Brexit' on the British economy*. Oxford: Woodford Investment Management LLP. Available via: https://woodfordfunds.com/economic-impact-brexit-report/.

Gill, J. (2015). The UK and the EU: Reform, renegotiation, withdrawal? A reading list. *House of Commons Library Briefing Paper*, No. HC07229. Available via: http://researchbriefings.parliament.uk/ResearchBriefing/Summary/CBP-7220#fullreport.

HM Treasury. (2016). *HM Treasury Analysis: The long term economic impact of EU membership and the alternatives*, Cm 9250. London: The Stationary Office. Available via: https://www.gov.uk/government/uploads/system/uploads/attachment_data/file/517415/treasury_analysis_economic_impact_of_eu_membership_web.pdf.

Miller, V., Lang, A., Smith, B., Webb, D., Harari, D., Keep, M, et al. (2016). Exiting the EU: UK reform proposals, legal impact and alternatives to membership. *House of Commons Library Briefing Paper*, No. HC 07214. Available via: http://researchbriefings.parliament.uk/ResearchBriefing/Summary/CBP-7214#fullreport.

Portes, J. (2013). Commentary: The economic implications for the UK of leaving the European Union. *National Institute Economic Review*, No. 266, F4–9. Available via: http://www.niesr.ac.uk/sites/default/files/commentary.pdf.

Thompson, G, & Harari, D. (2013). The Economic Impact of EU Membership on the UK. *House of Commons Library Briefing Paper*, SN/EP/6730. Available via: http://researchbriefings.parliament.uk/ResearchBriefing/Summary/SN06730#fullreport.

Webb, D., Keep, M, & Wilton, M. (2015). In Brief: UK-EU economic relations. *House of Commons Library Briefing Paper (HC 06091)*. London: The Stationary Office. Available via: http://researchbriefings.parliament.uk/ResearchBriefing/Summary/SN06091.

1

Was There Really an Economic Consensus on Brexit?

One of the most notable claims made during the recent referendum campaign was that there was a broad consensus amongst economists, that Brexit would prove damaging to the UK economy.[1] This was a view seized upon by the then Chancellor of the Exchequer, George Osborne, citing similar sentiments expressed by made by the Governor of the Bank of England, Mark Carney, and the head of the IMF, Christine Lagarde.[2] A number of reports were published, during the campaign, by organisations such as the Treasury, the IMF, the OECD, the IFS, the LSE/CEP, the NIESR and the TUC, all forecasting that Brexit would inflict significant damage upon the UK economy. There was, in addition, a survey of economists which was widely reported as demonstrating an overwhelming consensus amongst economists; a view repeated by then Prime Minister, David Cameron.[3] Thus, the Institute for Fiscal Studies felt able to suggest that the 'only significant exception' to this 'overwhelming consensus' came from Economists for Brexit.[4]

Simultaneously, the CBI made the case that the UK business community was overwhelmingly in favour of the UK remaining within the EU, because the costs were outweighed by the benefits of membership

© The Author(s) 2017
P.B. Whyman and A.I. Petrescu, *The Economics of Brexit*,
DOI 10.1007/978-3-319-58283-2_1

(CBI 2015). Indeed, John Cridland, Director-General of the CBI, could not have expressed this view more clearly (CBI 2013: 6):

For British business, large and small, the response to this is unequivocal: we should remain in a reformed EU.

This case was a little more difficult to justify, given that the head of the British Chambers of Commerce, John Longworth, was first suspended and later resigned over his support for Brexit,[5] whilst a Federation of Small Businesses (FSB 2015) internal survey indicated that its membership was fairly evenly split, with 47% preferring the UK to remain a member of the EU, whilst 41% supported Brexit and the remainder undecided.

The purpose of this emphasis upon an economic consensus was the attempt, by the 'Remain' campaign, to 'frame' the referendum debate in terms of its impact upon the economy. Thus, by suggesting that a consensus amongst economists and business leaders existed, voters would be more likely to support continued EU membership.[6] This resulted in a vociferous reaction from those supporting the Brexit position,[7] with Economists for Brexit (2016) describing this as the 'Great Brexit Consensus Deceit' and 'a lot of economic nonsense'. Most memorably, it also led the then Secretary of State for Justice, Michael Gove, to declare that 'people in this country have had enough of experts from organisations... with acronyms saying that they know what is best and getting it consistently wrong'.[8] In the 'rough and tumble' of political discourse, it is perhaps inevitable that Gove was characterised as denouncing experts in general,[9] rather than focusing his comments upon those organisations he also described as 'distant, unaccountable and elitist'. Nevertheless, this opinion was clearly held as Gove has repeated these criticisms in the immediate aftermath of the referendum, where the predictions made by his target organisations had not (yet) occurred.[10]

Survey of Economists

A survey conducted of members of the Royal Economic Society (RES) and the Society of Business Economists (SBE), was undertaken by Ipsos-MORI for *The Observer* newspaper in May 2016.[11] Of the 639 responses, representing a response rate of approximately 17%, approximately 57% of respondents were academic economists, with 43% represented by economists working in the private, public or third sectors. Most interestingly, only a minority of respondents (311 against 328) were British citizens living in the UK at the time of the survey (Ipsos-MORI 2016). This is significant because it might be assumed that European citizens working in the UK might have a more negative perception of Brexit than amongst all members of these organisations.

The results of the survey indicated an overwhelming majority opinion amongst respondents that Brexit would be likely to have a detrimental impact on the UK economy in the short to medium term. Fully 88% of respondents predicted negative impact over a five year period following a vote for Brexit, with 72% forecasting a continued negative impact extending beyond a decade. The primary reasons cited were a potential loss of trade with the EU, should the UK lose full access to the SIM, and the detrimental impact upon business investment caused by uncertainty (Ipsos-MORI 2016). Given that the survey was undertaken shortly after the publication of reports undertaken by the Centre for Economic Performance (LSE), the Treasury and the OECD, together with commentaries from Bank of England and IMF officials, it is plausible that these results were influenced by the conclusions reached by these pieces of work, rather than representing the independently formulated evaluations of the evidence from amongst the academic and business economist community. It is also plausible that the composition of the respondents skewed the result somewhat. Nevertheless, it still represents an impressive finding that a large majority of those responding to the survey accepted the findings of these official and semi-official economic studies.

The survey was followed-up by a letter sent to *The Times* newspaper, where 171 academic and 25 non-academic economist signatories argued that Brexit would produce both a 'short-term shock to confidence' and 'entail significant long-term costs' as negative consequences arising from uncertainty about future trading relationships with the EU would 'weigh heavily for many years'.[12] Writing in an economics blog, one of the originators of the letter, Wren-Lewis, claimed, that:

'There is therefore a huge disparity between the overwhelming majority of economists that say we would be worse off with Brexit and the handful that say otherwise. That is as near to unanimity among economists as you will ever get'.[13]

This, however, raises an interesting question, first pondered in *The Times* newspaper, that the emphasis placed upon a consensus amongst economists means that:

"...economics itself is on the line. If leaving the EU turns out to be beneficial, the profession will enter a crisis that will dwarf its inability to see the global financial crisis coming."[14]

Difficulties in Reaching Firm Conclusions

The difficulty in reaching firm conclusions, in relation to the economic impact of Brexit, was noted in repeated reports from the House of Commons library, given that many of the costs and benefits are subjective and the analysis is heavily dependent upon a range of assumptions (Thompson and Harari 2013: 5; Webb et al. 2015: 4; Miller et al. 2016: 5, 12). Hence, reaching firm conclusions was described as a 'formidably difficult exercise' (Miller et al. 2016: 12) and that there existed:

...no definitive study of the economic impact of the UK's EU membership, or equivalently, the costs and benefits of withdrawal (Thompson and Harari 2013:5; Miller et al. 2016: 5).   .

Similarly, the former Director of the NIESR, Portes (2013:F5), noted that:

......there is no single 'right' answer, because there is no single counter-factual. We simply do not know what the broad parameters of the relationship between the UK and the EU would be after British exit, nor do we know how the British economy would change and adapt to its new status outside the EU. This suggests that, rather than producing point estimates of the economic impact of exit, it is more sensible and informative to try to identify plausible alternative scenarios, which can then be used to model potential impacts on different assumptions about the post-exit economic environment.

The synthetic counterfactual analysis, completed by Campos et al. (2014), illustrates the difficulty inherent in seeking to contrast the historical record with a hypothetical comparator of what might have happened if different decisions had been taken. The method adopted is to select a baseline of similar countries who did not make the change under investigation—in this circumstance, they did not join the EU—and to compare the development paths for accession economies against this baseline. Clearly, the validity of this analysis depends upon the selection of baseline comparator countries. In this case, the Campos et al. paper utilised a previous selection of countries used in a study by Bower and Turrini (2009: 6), which comprised 10 OECD and 16 developing or emergent nations. Given that the Bower and Turrini study focused upon the impact of accession for the ten new member states who joined the EU in 2004, there was a strong argument to include developing or emergent nations in the baseline, since eight of the ten accession nations were undergoing their own transition from command to market economies. However, it is harder to justify this selection of comparator nations if investigating the impact of EU membership upon the UK. For example, whilst it may be argued that Australia, Canada, Japan, Norway and New Zealand may form a potential comparator group for the UK, it is much harder to justify the inclusion of Brazil, Columbia, China, Morocco, Russia, Thailand, Tunisia, Ukraine and Uruguay. As a result, the fact that the Campos et al. (2014: 36) study produced an estimated benefit for the UK after its four decades of EU membership of approximately 23.7%, which is by far the largest estimated impact from all of the studies examined in this book, makes its conclusions more than a little questionable in the context of seeking to understand how withdrawing from the EU might affect the UK economy.

Five of the Most Influential Studies
1. Centre for Economic Performance at the London School of Economics (CEP-LSE)—this analysis forms the basis for the various reports published by Ottaviano et al. (2014a, b) and Dhingra et al. (2015a, b, 2016).
2. The Treasury report (HM Treasury 2016).
3. OECD (2016).
4. IMF (2016).
5. NIESR (Baker et al. 2016; Ebell and Warren 2016).

The main findings from these five key reports are summarised in Table 1.1.

CEP-LSE

The first of the five studies focuses upon the trade implications of Brexit.[15] It utilised a computable general equilibrium (CGE) model[16] to develop two counterfactual scenarios. In the first, an 'optimistic' case was developed in which the UK was able to negotiate tariff free trade with the EU, either in the form of (i) a Free Trade Agreement (FTA), (ii) bilateral negotiations such as in the example of Switzerland, or (iii) through participation in the European Economic Area (EEA) as is currently the case for EFTA nations such as Iceland and Norway. An alternative 'pessimistic' option was developed, in which the UK proved unable or unwilling to secure tariff free trade with the EU, and therefore has to rely upon 'most favoured nation' tariffs under World Trade Organisation (WTO) rules. These options are discussed in more detail in Chap. 9 of this book.

The immediate or static trade costs of Brexit are presumed to arise from a combination of direct tariff costs, increased non-tariff barriers (NTBs), together with any loss from potential future reductions in NTBs that the EU may secure between its members, but which the UK, as a result of its withdrawal, would no longer gain. The impact of NTBs were drawn from previous work which examined NTBs between the

Table 1.1 Assessments of 2030 economic impact of Brexit in five most influential studies

	Organisation	Scenario	Estimate (% GDP)	Range	Impacts modelled
1	CEP-LSE	Dynamic EEA/FTA	−7.9	(−6.3 to −9.5)	Budget, trade, productivity
		Static EEA	−1.3	N/A	Trade only
		Static WTO	−2.6	N/A	Trade only
2	HM Treasury	EEA	−3.8	(−3.4 to −4.3)	Budget, trade, FDI, productivity
		FTA	−6.2	(−4.6 to −7.8)	
		WTO	−7.5	(−5.4 to −9.5)	
3	OECD	WTO/FTA	−5.1	(−2.7 to −7.7)	Budget, trade, FDI, productivity, migration, regulation
4	IMF	EEA	−1.4 by 2021	(0 to −1.4)	Trade, FDI, fiscal benefits, migration from the EU, productivity
		WTO	−4.5 by 2021	(0 to −5.5)	Unlike other studies, the UK is predicted to experience a recession in 2017
5	NIESR	EEA	−1.8	(−1.5 to −2.1)	Budget, trade, FDI
		FTA	−2.1	(−1.9 to −2.3)	
		WTO	−3.2	(−2.7 to −3.7)	
		WTO+	−7.8	N/A	Adds productivity

Notes Estimates are for the impact on GDP are for 2030 unless otherwise specified

Sources Baker et al. (2016); Dhingra et al. (2015a, b, 2016); Ebell and Warren (2016); HM Treasury (2016); IMF (2016); OECD (2016); and Ottaviano et al. (2014a, b). Authors' assessment of impacts modelled

EU and USA, with the CEP-LSE study making the assumption that the UK would face around one quarter of equivalent costs in its 'optimistic' scenario, and two-thirds in the 'pessimistic' alternative (Ottaviano et al. 2014a: 6–7). Future NTBs are assumed to be reduced faster than occurs in the rest of the world; in the pessimistic case, 40% faster, compared to 20% faster in the optimistic scenario (Ottaviano et al. 2014a: 7).

Both of these assumptions are questionable. The former, because the UK would begin with an identical set of regulations and standards as the remainder of the EU. Thus, whilst a divergence may appear and widen in time, it is unlikely to be as large as the CEP-LSE studies suggest. Whereas the latter is equally unlikely because past performance does not necessarily infer future performance. Indeed, since the EU had a disproportionate success in reducing NTBs in the past, this is likely to make it more difficult to reduce barriers further in the future, as the easiest gains to achieve will already have been made and only more difficult NTBs remaining. If those 'low hanging fruit' of NTB reductions had already been picked, an alternative hypothesis might have been entertained, namely that the EU is only able to reduce future barriers at the same speed, or slower, than the world at large.

Nevertheless, on the basis of this analysis, the CEP-LSE analysis predicted that Brexit is likely to produce a negative net impact on the UK economy of around 1.13% if a form of free trade agreement is negotiated, or 3.09% if reliance upon WTO rules (see Table 1.2). It is worth noting, however, that the bulk of these negative effects, in both scenarios, relate to the inability to reap possible future reductions in NTBs, if indeed these continue to occur at the previous rate. If it were assumed that the EU were only able to reduce NTBs in line with the rest of the world, then these negative findings would be considerably smaller, as direct and indirect static trade effects are found to be barely higher than fiscal savings accruing to the UK through not having to pay into the EU budget; indeed, fiscal effects would be higher than immediate trade costs if a FTA were negotiated.

The CEP-LSE analysis does not model beyond immediate (static) effects of Brexit, however, it does note that dynamic effects may significantly increase potential economic losses, if Brexit leads to a reduction in competition, a slower adoption of new technology and/or declining

Table 1.2 Estimated welfare changes due to UK withdrawal from the EU

	Multiple Sector Intermediates
Panel A: Optimistic Scenario	
Due to Increase in EU/UK Tradable Tariffs (0%)	0%
Doe to Increase in EU/UK Non-Tariff Barriers (+2.01%)	−0.40%
Due to Future Falls in EU/UK Non-Tariff Barriers (−5.68%)	−1.26%
Due to Fiscal Benefit	0.53%
Total Welfare Change	*−1.13%*
Panel B: Pessimistic Scenario	
Due to Increase in EU/UK Tradable Tariffs (MFN EU Tariffs)	−0.14%
Due to Increase in EU/UK Non-Tariff Barriers (+5.37%)	−0.93%
Due to Future Falls in EU/UK Non-Tariff Barriers (−10.54%)	−2.55%
Due to Fiscal Benefit	0.53%
Total Welfare Change	*−3.09%*

Source Ottaviano (2014a)
Notes Counterfactuals changes in welfare, measured by changes in real GDP. Methodology based on Costinot and Rodriguez-Clare (2013). Fiscal benefit information comes from Treasury (2013). EU is defined as EU 28 minus the UK and Croatia. Panel A shows an optimistic scenario: tariff on goods remain zero, non-tariff barriers are equal to 1/4 of the reducible barriers faced by USA exporters to the EU (2.01% increase), and that in the next ten years the intra-EU non-tariff barriers will fall 20% faster than in the rest of the world (fall of 5.68%). Panel B shows a pessimistic scenario: tariff on goods are the MFN tariffs imposed by the EU, non-tariff barriers are equal to 2/3 of the reducible barriers faced by USA exporters to the EU (5.37% increase), and that in the next ten years the intra-EU non-tariff barriers will fall 40% faster than in the rest of the world (fall of 10.54%).

productivity (Dhingra et al. 2015a:4, 2015b: 16–17). Their stated expectation is that such dynamic effects could produce a negative effect equivalent to double that of their modelled static effects which, if accurate, would indicate that the cost of Brexit could be as high as 3.5% of GDP with a FTA or 9.3% of GDP in the absence of a FTA (Ottaviano et al. 2014b: 4).

The CEP-LSE analysis is important because it highlights the strengths and weaknesses of seeking to forecast the impact of Brexit using modelling techniques. Their static analysis produced only very small direct (tariff) effects of around 0.14% UK GDP, even in the 'pessimistic' WTO scenario, where the UK is expected to face MFN tariffs levied upon its traded goods. NTBs are likely to be higher, although one might question the magnitude of the predicted effects produced by the CEP-LSE model due to its unrealistic assumptions that UK firms would suffer from a significant proportion of the same indirect trade costs applying to US competitors, despite the UK sharing (at least initially) common standards and regulations with the EU. Thus, it is only assumptions as to future savings realised by EU nations in further reducing NTBs faster than the global average, and further assumptions linking any reduction in trade with the EU as leading to eventual falls in competition, technological change and resultant productivity effects (see Chap. 5 for further discussion on this point), that the CEP-LSE study predicts any sizeable negative economic impact at all.

The more economic analysis is influenced by the assumptions made by the team of academics devising the analytical model, the less robust the findings. Thus, the most reliable aspects of this study relate to the direct tariff effects, which appear to be relatively insignificant even in the 'pessimistic' WTO scenario, and the suggestion that NTBs are likely to be higher, although the extent of these, certainly in the short term, are likely to be lower than suggested in this study. Forecasts for future changes in NTBs and possible dynamic effects, are conditional upon future reductions in UK-EU trade being larger than any equivalent increase in UK trade with the rest of the world, *and if* this leads to less competition or slower adoption of technology. Were any of these chains of predicted causality to be weaker than expected, or indeed fail to occur, then predictions for future NTB reductions and/or dynamic effects may not be realised.

The Treasury Report

Unlike the CEP-LSE study, which focused more narrowly upon the possible trade impact of Brexit, the 200 page report produced by the Treasury stated its intention to produce a comprehensive analysis of all major costs and benefits arising from Brexit. Consequently, it was widely used a reference point for many of the claims made in the European referendum campaign. As a result, it is worth looking in a little more detail about how it reaches its predictions.

The Treasury analysis utilises three different economic models. In the short run, the Treasury uses a vector autoregressive (VAR) model to estimate the potential impact arising from Brexit. This is intended to extend existing trends forward in time, and examine how historical evidence can be utilised to predict how similar changes may impact upon future economic developments. Beyond this initial two year transition period, the Treasury uses a gravity model to compare the historical development of trade in the UK with a group of comparator countries, whilst seeking to isolate other determinants such as distance, historical ties, relative national income and the size of the national population (HM Treasury 2016: 130). In this way, the gravity model can estimate the net beneficial impact upon trade and inward FDI flows from the UK joining the EU. These results are then fed into the NiGEM macroeconomic simulation model, developed by the National Institute of Economic and Social Research (NIESR). This simulation model was also used by the IMF, OECD and NIESR in their own studies, discussed later in this chapter (HM Treasury 2016: 153–155).

The resultant forecast is that Brexit would impose substantial and *permanent* costs upon the UK, totalling between 3.4 and 9.5% of its GDP, depending upon the type of trade arrangement subsequently negotiated (see Table 1.3).[17] These forecasts led the former Chancellor of the Exchequer, Osborne, to claim that it proved that leaving the EU would be the 'most extraordinary self-inflicted wound' and that those supporting 'Brexit' were 'economically illiterate'.[18]

There are, however, a number of weaknesses with the Treasury model which undermines the rigour of its forecasts. The first pertains to methodological weaknesses in the range of models selected. For example, the VAR approach operates by projecting forward existing trends in a series of economic variables, and historical evidence can be used to identify the likely impact of a reoccurrence of previous historical phenomena. However, there is no equivalent to Brexit. Only one country has previously left the EU, namely Greenland, and this occurred as part of a process of independence from its former status as a Danish

Table 1.3 Annual impact of leaving the EU on the UK (difference from being in the EU after 15 years)

	EEA	Negotiated bilateral agreement	WTO
GDP level (%)-central	−3.8	−6.2	−7.5
GDP level (%)	−3.4 to −4.3	−4.6 to −7.8	−5.4 to -9.5
GDP per capita-central[a]	−£1,100	−£1,800	−£2,100
GDP per capita	−£1,000 to −£1,200	−£1,300 to −£2,200	−£1,500 to −£2,700
GDP per capita-central[a]	−£2,600	−£4,300	−£5,200
GDP per household	−£2,400 to −£2,900	−£3,200 to −£5,400	−£3,700 to −£6,600

Source HM Treasury (2016:186)
Notes [a]Expressed in terms of 2015 GDP in 2015 prices, rounded to the nearest £100

province. Consequently, there is little direct comparability with the current position of the UK, although, it might be worth noting in passing, that in the five years following withdrawal from the EU in 1985, the Greenland economy grew by an average of 5.7% (Blake 2016: 5). In the absence of comparable historical precedent, the VAR model was calibrated by reference to a sample period between 1989 and 2016, thus impairing its ability to satisfactorily forecast the likely impact of any post Brexit shock upon the UK economy (Blake 2016: 5).

The second economic model used in the Treasury study, namely the gravity model, predicts the levels of trade well in a statistical sense, as long as their assumption of *ceteris paribus* remains true. However, Brexit would involve changes in far more than a few trade barriers; potentially including changes in regulations, different preferential trade relationships being formed with other countries outside of the EU, whilst national economic policy will shift to accommodate these changes and hopefully to magnify potential economic benefits derived from Brexit. Thus, there are insufficient data points to allow the proper calibration of the gravity model, leading to problems of selection bias (Minford 2016: 5–6). As a result, the Treasury resorts to assuming that the consequences of leaving the EU will be the mirror opposite of joining it (HM

Treasury 2016: 129, 166). Yet, this is inaccurate as, once trade has been established between nations and firms have formed established supply chains, it is unlikely that there would be a sharp and immediate reversal to pre-accession trade patterns following 'Brexit'. It is possible that non-tariff barriers could make such existing links more time consuming and costly to continue, and that, over time, reductions in trade may occur, but it unlikely to be instantaneous.

Gravity models rely upon historical data as to how trade relationships, such as EU membership, have facilitated the growth in trade between nations. As such, they are likely to inflate the benefits of current preferential trade relationships, when tariff rates are historically low, because part of the dataset on which the gravity model calculations are based relates to a time period when tariffs were considerably higher and therefore the advantage for being inside a tariff wall was greater than today. Moreover, the Treasury report claims to have found only trade creation, and not trade diversion, when examining why trade grows when countries join the EU (HM Treasury 2016: 157–164). This is very surprising, because economic theory suggests that both are likely to occur. A customs union or single market makes it cheaper to shift trade within the trade zone. This is not trade creation but diversion. Early studies of the UK's initial accession to the EU found considerable trade diversion, as the imposition of the EU's CET caused the switching of a significant proportion of trade from commonwealth nations previously benefiting from the 'Empire Preference' preferential trade relationship with the UK (Miller and Spencer 1977: 82–90; Portes 2013: F5–6). To have found none of this would suggest a fault with the modelling. To the extent that trade diversion occurs, Brexit opens up the possibility of securing greater efficiencies and lowering costs for UK consumers by trading globally, and, to this extent at least, the Treasury predictions are exaggerated.

Because the Treasury analysis does not consider how trade might develop with the rest of the world, following Brexit, it models its predicted reductions in trade with the EU as a form of protectionism shock, which it then anticipates will feed into lowering technological adaptation and depress future productivity (HM Treasury 2016: 185). Yet, if trade with the rest of the world were to increase as a result of the UK being able to negotiate future preferential trade agreements with other nations and/or as a result of a depreciation in sterling or any lowering of the former EU-imposed CET upon non-EU goods, then this would offset (partially or in full) any restriction of trade with the EU member states. Over the longer term, it is plausible that a redistribution of trade interests from regional to global markets might result in an expansion in net UK trade. In which case, presumably the Treasury model would predict that greater openness would result from Brexit, which would, according to the earlier chain of logic, lead to higher technological adaptation and higher productivity levels. The problem with this element of the analysis, therefore, is the decision not to consider what impact Brexit might have upon the 56% of UK exports that are sold outside the EU's SIM.

It is a pity that the Treasury economists did not attempt to model potential trade implications for the formation of FTAs with various nations or non-EU trade blocs, because this is the type of analysis that would be of particular assistance to those government departments currently considering how best to maximise future trade opportunities for the UK economy. Moreover, had the Treasury instead used a gravity model focused upon the UK's relationship with the rest of the world, rather than more narrowly upon the EU, then its predictions may have been reversed (Blake 2016: 32).

The forecasts made by the gravity model would also appear to be inconsistent with the fact that the share of UK exports to EU member states has been in decline over the past decade, since its predictions would suggest that this trade should have grown in importance over this time period (Blake 2016: 4). Hence, the gravity model is likely to over-estimate the trade-related costs of Brexit and that its predictions of an instantaneous fall in UK-EU trade of perhaps 45–50% would seem unlikely (Blake 2016: 3, 16; HM Treasury 2016: 129).

In addition to methodological weaknesses with the Treasury study, like all such analytical studies seeking to predict future events, the Treasury model is only as robust or as flawed as the assumptions upon which its models and calculations are based. Some of these are simple factual inaccuracies, such as the Treasury estimate of EU 'most favoured nation' (MFN) (non-weighted) tariffs of 5% (HM Treasury 2016:

99), which would be levied against UK exports in the WTO scenario. However, this is more than double the equivalent rates cited by the World Trade Organisation (WTO 2015: 75) and significantly higher than the 1–2% the average EU *trade-weighted* 'MFN' tariffs calculated by the House of Commons library when calculating trade-related average tariffs (Thompson and Harari 2013: 8).

Other assumptions relate to the composition of those variables included in the Treasury model itself, and those that it determined to exclude; what economists term as missing variable bias. For example, migration was excluded as an independent variable, despite its prominence in the European referendum campaign (HM Treasury 2016: 136). The report does make the assumption that net migration will fall by about 40% following 'Brexit' (HM Treasury 2016: 136), and therefore it adjusts population forecasts accordingly in order to calculate GDP per capita effects, but it does not seek to include the potential impact of this shift in the quantity of migrant labour in its various models. There are two obvious problems with this stance. The first is that migration is likely to have potentially significant economic effects, if indeed there is a 40% reduction in flows coming from other EU member states. The second is that the 40% reduction is an arbitrary figure, and that a greater or lesser change would clearly impact upon the results of the study. Moreover, there would appear to be a priori no greater difficulty in estimating future developments in migration flows than trade or investment flows, which are included in the Treasury analysis. Given that results are presented in terms of different models of future relationships with the EU (i.e. EEA, FTA and WTO), then the point made about this increasing the difficulty of modelling related effects would seem rather tenuous at best.

The Treasury also omitted regulation as an independent variable in its model, on the grounds that it is indistinguishable from broader trade effects, due to its integral nature as part of the single market (HM Treasury 2016: 59, 137, 139). This is despite claims made by other theorists that regulatory savings might provide one of the more significant benefits arising from Brexit (Congdon 2014: 30; Business for Britain 2015: 122–123; Capital Economics 2016: 13). It moreover, ignores research which suggests that national (UK) regulation has a better benefit-to-cost ratio than EU regulation (Gaskell and Persson 2010: 10; HMG 2013: 41–42). In other words, this research suggests that, were the UK to leave the EU and even if the UK introduced regulation on all of the same issues as the EU, the fact that this could be better tailored for the needs of its own economy would produce a net gain to the UK. In such circumstances, it is surprising that the Treasury did not seek to test these claims within its own model, in order to establish their veracity.

A further set of assumptions were made, in the Treasury report, ostensibly in order to simplify the model. Two sets of assumptions relate to the treatment of inward flows of FDI. The first is that, because of what the Treasury describes as a shortage of data, their gravity analysis did not work as anticipated in respect of FDI, and therefore the report makes the perhaps surprising assumption that FDI flows react to exactly the same degree as trade effects (HM Treasury 2016: 130). This is disappointing, because there is no real shortage of data relating to FDI flows over a number of decades. It is true that the definitions relating to FDI changed a little more than a decade ago, thus making longitudinal comparisons more difficult. However, similar adjustments are regularly made by statisticians, from the Office for National Statistics (ONS) and elsewhere, in order to facilitate the comparability of data, and could have been done in this case, particularly with the weight of the state apparatus behind the study. The decision to link FDI flows with predicted developments in trade is problematical because trade and FDI can act as substitutes rather than compliments, as firms which previously export goods and services from their home location may set up foreign subsidiaries to satisfy local demand, with the result of a drop in the previous volume of trade. This decision also implies that any errors in calculating trade effects will be magnified by applying the same logic to FDI. Finally, the Treasury further assumed that non-EU FDI flows would react to Brexit in the same way as FDI flows originating in EU member states (HM Treasury 2016: 130). Yet, this is hardly credible.

Another set of assumptions relate to future developments and dynamic effects. For example, whilst the Treasury report emphasises the significance of Brexit causing 'a decade or more of uncertainty' (HM Treasury 2016: 132, 153), it neglects to consider whether future developments within the EU might result in other forms of uncertainty. The refugee crisis, for example, or the need to expand the supportive infrastructure designed to assist Eurozone countries, might be two sources of uncertainty. The Treasury report, unlike the CEP-LSE study, does not include forecasts for future reforms across the SIM within its analysis. However, it does note that, should these occur, costs arising from Brexit may rise by an additional 4% of UK GDP (HM Treasury 2016: 8). However, like the CEP-LSE study, this additional prediction is based upon suspect assumptions of the degree to which the EU is capable of realising significant future reductions in already low barriers to trade. Again, as with the CEP-LSE study, the Treasury report emphasises dynamic effects which link the degree of trade openness and living standards (HM Treasury 2016: 13–14). The report expresses the expectation that openness may facilitate increased competition, innovation and adaptation (HM Treasury 2016: 15, 176–177). To build this effect into the Treasury model, it borrows a multiplier estimate of 0.2–0.3 from trade to GDP from an earlier study undertaken by Frankel and Rose (2000: 22). Given that this study was completed using data from the last century, and that its focus was examining potential economic impacts from the establishment of currency unions, the estimates are not entirely applicable to an investigation of the impact of Brexit upon the UK economy. Moreover, as will be discussed in more detail in Chap. 7, the theoretical causal link between the degree of openness and productivity is not as unambiguous as its advocates would like to admit. Nevertheless, on this basis, the Treasury report predicted reductions in UK productivity of between 2–2.8% if the UK were to join the EEA, a 3–6% reduction if a FTA was negotiated, and a reduction of between 3.7–7.7% if relying upon WTO rules (HM Treasury 2016: 131).

The Treasury report made a further assumption, namely that the government would remain passive for a period of at least two years and not respond to accommodate or mitigate the consequences of Brexit during this period. This was presumably adopted to simplify the analysis. However, it is not realistic. Given the nature of the Treasury's responsibility in managing UK economic policy, and particularly in light of the Treasury report's own conclusions that Brexit may have negative consequences for the UK economy if corrective action was not taken, it is inconceivable that the UK government would do nothing for two years. The assumption is not credible as it would mean the Treasury negating its own core function of managing the UK economy (Blake 2016: 2). However, by adopting this assumption, the Treasury report magnified its critical conclusions by not allowing for an appropriate policy response which would reduce uncertainty and thereby mitigate against any resultant negative impact upon the UK economy (Blake 2016: 5).

To take one illustrative example, if the UK were to operate under WTO rules and the EU were accordingly to impose an 8–10% tariff on UK car exports, the assumption of *ceteris paribus* (all relevant things remaining the same) would lead the Treasury report to predict a commensurate fall in trade. However, this prediction would fail to consider whether, freed from the rules and constraints imposed by EU membership, the UK government might either compensate UK car manufacturers indirectly to offset any increase in costs, perhaps through providing a more generous R&D tax allowance. Or this might be accomplished by allowing the value of the pound to fall by an equivalent amount. If they did either, then the net effect would be closer to zero. Yet the fact that the Treasury report excluded this possibility from their analysis, effectively precludes one of the largest potential benefits that may arise if the UK left the EU, namely, that a greater range of policy options and instruments would be available for the use of policy makers in managing the economy. To take one example, discussed in more detail in Chap. 8, within the EU, active industrial policy is hampered because any measures seem as disproportionately benefitting one's own industry would be viewed as 'discriminatory' within a single European market. Yet, outside, there is no such restriction. Hence, it would be more likely that the UK might be able to rejuvenate its manufacturing sector and achieve more of the re-balancing of the economy that the Chancellor states is an official objective, but, within the constraints imposed by the EU, has done relatively little to achieve this goal.

The Treasury Report, therefore, is an interesting document, but it has to be judged as unreliable in its predictions because it leaves too much out of its calculations. It focuses primarily upon trade with the EU and FDI, both of which are more likely to have some sort of extra costs following Brexit, but ignores trade with the rest of the world, migration, regulation and economic policy options, which are more likely to deliver benefits. The decision on what variables to include and which to omit has resulted in what economists term selection bias, and has skewed the results unnecessarily towards forecasting negative results arising from Brexit, rather than providing a comprehensive analysis of the problem. This is perhaps one reason why the Treasury report appears to be too politicised and its results having to be treated with caution. It is a pity that the Treasury were not able to evade their organisational imperatives to deliver an independent analysis, which could have informed the public during the referendum campaign. But perhaps equally importantly, a less problematic analysis could have provided a firmer basis for advising policy makers in the aftermath of the referendum result, as they seek to design a new economic strategy for an independent nation. They would certainly have welcomed a more complete set of simulations which were able to more accurately indicate the relative merits of the various options available to them.

Organisation for Economic Cooperation and Development (OECD)

The OECD analysis used a combination of its METRO (CGE) model, to estimate trade effects arising from Brexit, combined with the NiGEM model to simulate macroeconomic impact (OECD 2016: 19, 21, 32). One distinguishing feature, relates to the assumption that any withdrawal process would be so lengthy that it precluded the agreement of either EEA membership or a FTA being ratified before the termination of the two year Article 50 process, and therefore, for the first four years following formal withdrawal from the EU, the UK would revert to trading under WTO rules. Variance would occur thereafter, with an optimistic scenario holding that a subsequent FTA would reduce some of these initial trade barriers, whilst an inability or unwillingness to ratify such an agreement would result in a pessimistic scenario, where the UK continues to trade according to WTO rules into the medium and longer term (OECD 2016: 19).

On the basis of these assumptions, the OECD study forecast that the UK economy would suffer a short term decline in economic growth potential equating to 3.3% of UK GDP by the year 2020. Thereafter, predictions diverged. By 2030, under the optimistic scenario, a degree of this loss would be regained, with the UK economy being 2.7% smaller than when compared to the baseline scenario of remaining an EU member, whereas continued trading under WTO rules in the pessimistic scenario would result in a maintenance of a slower rate of growth and thereby a cumulative loss of 7.7% of potential UK GDP over this 15 year period (OECD 2016: 6–7). Short term effects were related primarily to financial market shocks, together with a degree of uncertainty about the Brexit process reducing confidence and deferring investment. Longer term effects were more concerned with an estimated reduction in trade with the EU, a drop in the value of inward FDI and more limited migration reducing growth (OECD 2016: 7). An exchange rate depreciation is perceived as moderating negative trade effects to a degree (OECD 2016: 21), thereby helping to improve the balance of trade. However, the OECD simulation still maintains that private investment would be likely to decline by 10% by 2030, and FDI *stock* by up to a surprisingly large 45% (OECD 2016: 31). The OECD further considers that the refinancing of UK debt might prove problematic in the medium term, if, as it predicts, inward FDI flows no longer offset the UK's very large trade deficit, and the report postulates the possibility of capital flight (OECD 2016: 23). This does seem to be a little alarmist, although it is certainly the case that financial speculation and sudden shifts in 'hot money' can prove disruptive to the economic policy plans of even the most well managed nation.

The OECD approach is arguably more comprehensive (Armstrong and Portes 2016: 4) in its selection of variables than the Treasury, given that it includes estimates of the impact on migration flows, and includes certain estimates of regulatory benefit in its calculations (OECD 2016: 28–29). However, it still suffers from similar problems to the other 'consensus' studies, in terms of the assumptions it feeds into its models. For example, whilst inclusion of regulatory savings is an advance over other studies that tend to ignore the variable, the OECD proceeds to minimise its potential significance by assuming that there would appear to be only limited scope for future deregulation to benefit UK businesses because of the already comparatively low rates of regulation pertaining in the UK (OECD 2016: 29–30). Unfortunately, that confuses the point that regulatory savings may occur if national regulation is found to be more focused and effective than supra-national regulation. To the extent that this is true, then a shift from EU to UK regulation, even if the total scope of regulations remained unchanged, would still deliver a positive effect.

A second assumption, made in the OECD study, is that trade negotiations with the EU are likely to take six years from triggering Article 50 (OECD 2016: 18). This is the cause of the uncertainty which the OECD model predicts will cause a deterioration in investment and hence growth potential. The report seeks to justify this assumption by citing evidence from previous FTAs, negotiated by a variety of nations with the EU, where agreements with Australia took three years, Korea and Mexico four years and Canada five years (OECD 2016: 17). Yet, there are two problems with the OECD employing this assumption within their model. The first is that there is no reason why trade negotiations cannot be commenced before the UK formally withdraws from the EU, at the commencement of the two year Article 50 process. Withdrawal negotiations and future trade relationships would appear to be mutually reinforcing. Thus, the OECD's presumption that a FTA will take four years, and this time period can only begin upon formal withdrawal once the Article 50 process has been completed, is inaccurate.

There is every reason to assume that trade negotiations between the UK and the EU might be concluded over a much shorter timescale than with other countries, because the UK is starting from the position of sharing common rules, regulations and standards with the EU member states. Whilst the UK may wish to vary some of these upon withdrawal, the starting point for negotiations is a much closer initial relationship than for third party countries with very different regulations and standards. Moreover, since one option is for the UK to seek EEA membership, this could be achieved relatively seamlessly, without the need for six years of uncertainty and the need to trade under WTO rules until completed.

A third assumption is that, like the IMF (2016: 22), the OECD uses a figure for fiscal savings for the UK not having to pay into the EU budget of 0.3% of UK GDP per annum. Yet, this is significantly lower than the probably more accurate figure, developed in Chap. 2 of this book, of 0.53% of UK annual GDP. The OECD study makes a further assertion that, due to its predicted reduction in GDP growth rates, the UK's fiscal position would deteriorate and this would limit the ability for the government to use any potential budgetary savings from exiting the EU to relax fiscal policy (OECD 2016: 7). It is certainly correct to state that any increase in a fiscal deficit will limit discretionary policy action; however, it certainly does not prevent such action. To the extent that the OECD theorists appear to treat both as equivalent, this merely highlights the orthodox economic assumptions at the heart of their work.

A fourth assumption concerns the reliance upon neoclassical growth modelling to evaluate the likely impact of any reduction in migration from EU nations (HM Treasury 2016: 66). This employs simplifying assumptions derived from standard neo-classical theory, including that labour is homogenous and hence, if there are assumed to be no differences in skills or productivity between individual workers, then the matter of enlarging the labour force will inevitably increase economic growth if they are all employed. The assumption of Say's Law, where supply creates its own demand, ensures that the economy will always tend towards full employment. To the extent that these assumptions are accurate, the neo-classical growth theory argues that it is the quantity of capital and labour, together with technological change, that determines economic growth rates (see Chap. 7 for further discussion).

Accordingly, the OECD (2016: 6) feels able to assert that fully half of all economic growth achieved by the UK, over the past decade, was due to inward migration; around half of which from the EU member states. There are a number of problems with this simplistic argument. The first is that there is no a priori reason why migration should necessarily fall following Brexit. The stated aim of managing migration was primarily aimed at preventing unregulated flows into the UK from the EU, and this does not necessarily preclude the substitution of more qualified (and perhaps more productive) migrant labour from outside the EU within constant inward migratory flows.

Even if this is not the case, however, and indeed migration levels do decline following Brexit, there is a theoretical problem with the OECD's analysis, in that the neo-classical growth model doesn't work very well as there is a large difference between what it is capable of explaining and actual growth rates. In economic terminology, it has a large residual that it does not satisfactorily explain in its econometric modelling. As a result, a new set of models seeking to explain the determinants of economic growth have been advanced, including the endogenous growth theory, which accepts differences between the skills, education, motivations and productivity of workers (i.e. heterogeneous labour). However, this has an important implication for future migration flows. If, for example, the UK restricts the inward flow of former low-skilled migrant labour from EU member states, but attracts highly skilled labour from elsewhere in the world, even if total net migration levels decline, it is not automatic that it will have a detrimental impact upon economic growth. A greater proportion of more highly skilled labour would be expected to raise UK productivity, *ceteris paribus*, so whilst the quantity of labour may fall, the quality would rise, with the ultimate impact on growth depending upon which of these effects were the stronger.

Finally, the OECD study follows the CEP-LSE study in its inclusion of dynamic effects, whereby a reduction in trade openness is assumed to cause a decline in investment and productivity (Armstrong and Portes 2016: 4). Specifically, the OECD model predicts that a decline in trade openness of 4% reduces total factor productivity (TFP) by 1.17% after a decade (OECD 2016: 32). Further assumptions are made that research and development (R&D) expenditure will subsequently decline alongside management quality, thus having a further detrimental effect upon the UK economy (OECD 2016: 31). Yet, this all stems from a rather fragile theoretical chain, namely predictions of a fall in trade between the UK and the EU and that this decline will reduce the openness of the UK economy. However, this is based in part upon unrealistic estimates for average tariff rates, and the further assumption that FTAs cannot be negotiated within the Article 50 timescale. Moreover, it additionally ignores any potential growth in trade with the rest of the world and subsequently assumes that openness has a causal relationship with investment and productivity. As discussed in Chap. 7, all parts of this theoretical chain are questionable.

International Monetary Fund

The IMF analysis of Brexit impact examined the effect of changes through the medium of an uncertainty index, fed into a VAR model, to estimate the impact of short term economic impacts upon the economy (IMF 2016: 55), together with broader effects forecast through a dynamic stochastic general equilibrium model, similar to the NiGEM approach used by other studies. The trade impact of EU membership is calculated using a gravity model, in a similar manner to the other 'consensus' studies. It included five key variables, specifically; trade, FDI, fiscal benefits, migration from the EU and productivity effects arising from the combination of migration, trade openness and regulation (IMF 2016: 9). It focused primarily upon the short and medium terms, and hence less upon potential dynamic effects (IMF 2016: 30).

The study calculates two scenarios: (i) a 'limited' option, whereby the UK participated within the European Economic Area (EEA), and (ii) an 'adverse' scenario involving reliance upon WTO rules (IMF 2016: 30). In the limited case, uncertainty is relatively weak and of short duration, as economic actors (firms, workers and consumers) adjust quickly to what is the closest to the status quo relationship with the EU. Certain costs do remain, however, because, although part of the SIM, EEA members are not members of the EU customs union, in that they operate their own external trade policy and consequently must implement 'rules of origin' technical requirements for exports into the EU.[19] Nevertheless, the forecasts for the EEA option are quite limited in their magnitude, certainly when compared to other 'consensus' studies, with GDP declining compared to the model's baseline by only −1.4% of UK GDP by the year 2021 (IMF 2016: 32).

In the 'adverse' scenario, the IMF study assumes that the UK is unable or unwilling to negotiate a FTA with the EU and trade between

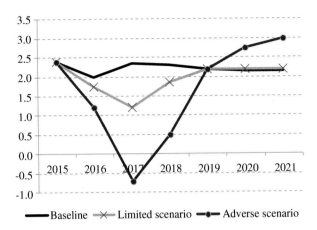

Fig. 1.1 IMF Study Predicted Impact on UK GDP growth (%), 2015–2021 *Source* IMF (2016: 31). Authors' best replication of IMF staff calculations

the two parties defaults to reliance upon WTO rules. In this scenario, uncertainty is assumed to be much greater and there are larger increases in risk premia, thereby increasing the cost of capital. Hence, there is a sharper reduction in economic growth forecasts, from which rates take longer to recover. The IMF model therefore predicts a steeper initial fall in UK growth compared to the baseline scenario, initially taking the UK economy into a short period of recession in 2017. This forecasted lost growth potential is modelled as peaking in 2019, relative to the baseline, before recovering slightly thereafter, but still leaving the economy 4.5% worse off than the baseline scenario by 2021(IMF 2016: 30, 32).These predictions are illustrated in Fig. 1.1.

Disaggregating the overall macroeconomic effect upon the UK economy, the IMF model predicted that the short term impact would derive almost equally from heightened uncertainty and a tightening of financial conditions on the one hand, and a decline in trade with the EU. This is slightly surprising, because for a minimum period of two years following the triggering of Article 50, which itself would not necessarily follow immediately upon the referendum decision, the UK would remain a member of the EU and retain full participation in the SIM. Therefore, during this period, it would be unlikely that significant trade losses would occur. Thereafter, the IMF predicted that trade and, to a far lesser degree, FDI inflows would represent the majority of Brexit costs (IMF 2016: 58).

There are four interesting features that are particularly notable about the predictions made by this study. Firstly, the UK economy is predicted to experience a short period of recession in the WTO scenario, whereas most other studies forecast a slowing of economic growth but where this still remains positive.

Secondly, over the long run, the economic impacts arising from Brexit are estimated to derive 'almost entirely' by trade effects, with the impact on inward FDI flows and any dynamic productivity effects considered to be of only marginal significance (IMF 2016: 58). This is interesting, because the CEP-LSE study found that there were only relatively marginal trade effects, particularly if a FTA were negotiated with the EU, and they emphasised dynamic productivity effects are their primary concern, whilst a potential decline in FDI flows forms a significant part of the forecasts made by the NIESR and Treasury studies. Yet, the IMF downplays the importance of these factors.

Thirdly, in both scenarios, it would appear that any negative economic consequences experienced by the UK economy would peak after two years, presumably due to the uncertainty arising from the Article 50 process and as the UK negotiates its future relationship with the EU. Thereafter, the IMF simulation suggests that any further negative economic impacts quickly decline and disappear after a total of four years. Thus, in contrast to other studies in the 'consensus' group, where longer term dynamic effects are postulated and economic uncertainty effects are assumed to last for almost an entire decade. The IMF considers that Brexit may indeed have a short term cost, as the UK economy adjusts to its new independent status, but after 4 years these effects are spent and thereafter there are few significant longer term effects.

Finally, and related to the previous point, the study forecasts that growth rates are likely to rebound, in the WTO scenario, to exceed the baseline comparator after two years of under-performance. Despite appearances, this is not due to the IMF predicting that Brexit will lead to an improvement in the economic performance of the UK economy. Rather, the study acknowledges that economic growth may temporarily exceed the baseline scenario as the economy begins to 'catch-up' some of the productive potential lost during the two years in which growth rates are depressed under the WTO scenario. Output is still predicted to remain below the baseline scenario for the whole of this period even allowing for the gap narrowing over time (IMF 2016: 31).

The IMF study acknowledges the limitations of their analysis by stating that the scenarios are meant to be illustrative and not firm predictions of the future (IMF 2016: 30). That is to their credit. However, this acknowledgement has not prevented the IMF results being used (or perhaps misused) alongside the other 'consensus' studies to infer a misleading degree of certainty about the future economic impact for the UK economy post-Brexit. As with the other studies examined in this chapter, the IMF analysis is based upon a set of assumptions which are often of questionable validity. For example, the IMF study utilised a similar figure of 5.3% for average tariff costs as the OECD and Treasury studies (IMF 2016: 16), even though, as previously indicated, this figure would seem rather excessive (e.g. WTO 2015: 75). It also uses the lower figure of 0.3% of UK GDP for the estimate of fiscal savings from exiting the EU (IMF 2016: 22), despite the fact that, as demonstrated in Chap. 2, the official UK statistical evidence indicates a higher figure. The study also assumes that economic policy remains constant for a minimum of two years, even though the document itself notes that this is simply a matter of simplifying the model rather than being particularly likely to occur (IMF 2016: 30).

The IMF study additionally includes an exchange rate variable, which allows it to model the beneficial effect that a depreciation of sterling might provide to the UK economy. The result is an improvement in the trade balance. However, perhaps surprisingly, the study argues that this is primarily due to an increase in import prices and a corresponding fall in imported goods, rather than any stimulative effect arising from an increase in UK exports (IMF 2016: 31). This conclusion clearly reflects an assumption, built into the model, that devaluation is ineffective and that any increase in international competitiveness is rapidly depleted through higher levels of inflation. Intriguingly, this is despite a recent report, produced by the IMF (2016: 105) itself, finding that a 10% devaluation led, on average, to an increase of around 1.5% of the nation's GDP over the medium term, and that suggestions that global supply chains had weakened this relationship were exaggerated.

National Institute for Economic and Social Research (NIESR)

The NIESR set of studies used its NiGEM macroeconomic model to suggest that Brexit would result in an immediate short term 0.8% reduction in growth in 2017; an effect compounded to lower growth potential by between 1.5 and 7.8% by 2030, compared to a hypothetical baseline where the UK remained within the EU.[20] In the short term, the NIESR emphasises the significance of uncertainty in raising the risk premia and hence cost of capital, thereby causing a predicted drop in investment of some 15% in 2017 (Baker et al. 2016: 116). In the medium and long run, broader effects predominate, including a reduction in trade (due to what is described as a 'modest' increase in trade barriers), together with a decline in inward FDI and a fall in the number of migrants from the EU, partially offset by a reduction in fiscal contributions to the EU budget (Ebell and Warren 2016).

The NIESR study can be differentiated from the Treasury and OECD analyses, which also use the NiGEM model, in that no attempt was made to incorporate any imputed productivity effects arising from a fall in openness, because of a concern over the robustness of this supposed relationship and a desire to focus upon better understood economic relationships (Ebell and Warren 2016: 122). The study also assumed a smaller reduction in GDP resulting from a given fall in the total volume of trade with the EU; whereas the CEP-LSE study assumed that GDP falls by 0.5% for every 1% drop in total trade, whilst the OECD and Treasury studies used an equivalent figure of 0.3%, the NIESR study adopted a more conservative value of 0.1% (Ebell and Warren 2016: 121).

Trade effects arising from Brexit were estimated from gravity model analysis of the different patterns of trade developments for each of the different scenarios, namely Norway (EEA), Switzerland (bilateral trade

Table 1.4 Summary of NIESR Simulation Predictions

	EEA	FTA	WTO
% GDP (2020)	−1.9	−2.1	−2.9
% GDP (2030)	−1.8	−2.1	−3.2

Source Armstrong and Portes (2016: 4)

agreements) and reliance upon WTO trade rules. Differences in trade between EU member states, EEA participants, nations having negotiated bilateral or FTAs with the EU and nations with no preferential trade arrangements, were taken as representing the trade effect of the different scenarios. These observed effects were then fed into the NiGEM model in order to estimate the total trade reductions arising from the replacement of EU with EEA membership. This produces the following forecasts (see Table 1.4).

There are, however, three problems with utilising these estimates as the basis for the simulation analysis.

Firstly, because the studies have typically relied upon panel data going back to the 1960s, when the common external tariff (CET) was significantly higher, this exaggerates the current importance of EU membership. The current position is less disadvantageous for EFTA members. The fact that their trade with the EU still lags in relative terms behind EU member states who have utilised their longer period of preferential access to the SIM is not surprising, but there is every expectation that this gap would narrow in the future. Therefore backward-looking analysis of this type probably over-states the impact of EU membership.

A similar problem with the analysis is that EFTA membership is equated with the EEA option available to the UK. Yet, the EEA only became operational in 1994. Thus, the majority of EFTA trade data, fed into the gravity model, does not adequately predict what might be expected should the UK shift from full EU membership to participation in the EEA.

A third issue concerns the point, previously made elsewhere in this chapter, that joining and leaving a trade bloc are not equivalent actions. Established trading links and supply chains are unlikely to be immediately fractured and reversed upon withdrawal from the EU.

There are, moreover, an additional set of assumptions built into the NIESR study which have a significant impact upon its predictions. For example, like the IMF, it simplifies its analysis by assuming that there will be no changes in economic policy for the first two years of the Brexit transitionary period (Baker et al. 2016: 117). This was never going to be a realistic assumption and, indeed, the measures taken by the Bank of England (see Chap. 8 for further discussion) had invalidated it within a matter of hours of the result of the European referendum. Consequently, the NIESR forecasts were almost immediately at least partly weakened.

A second feature is the estimate of MFN WTO tariffs of 5% to be levied on UK exports, used by the NIESR in its WTO scenario (Ebell and Warren 2016: 125). This is the same level of tariffs as were used by the Treasury in their analysis, and it suffers from the same criticism, namely that the WTO (2015: 75) cites a figure half this level, whilst the House of Commons Library notes that trade-related average tariffs are even lower than WTO un-weighted figures (Thompson and Harari 2013: 8).

The NIESR analysis additionally incorporates predicted changes in the exchange rate of around 20% against a basket of currencies, which is a much greater depreciation of sterling than accepted by other comparable studies. The initial stimulus to exports was modelled as an increase of 0.3 for every 1% fall in the value of sterling. Thus, a 20% devaluation would, according to the NIESR, be expected to boost exports by around 6%. This beneficial effect was considered to decline, over time, as rising prices reduced the competitive boost provided by the initial devaluation (Ebell and Warren 2016: 133). Nevertheless, the NIESR analysis contends that currency devaluation is an effective means of offsetting at least part of any negative consequences arising from Brexit reducing trade with the EU.[21] This is in sharp contrast to the assumption made by the IMF, namely that the export expansion arising from devaluation would be of little consequence.

Finally, migration effects are assumed to boost UK economic growth rates, by raising the average skills level inherent in the UK labour force, whilst simultaneously improving the matching of heterogeneous labour to varied job opportunities (Portes 2016: 18). Whilst it is accepted that migration may have negative effects upon the wages of unskilled and semi-skilled workers, these effects are regarded to be relatively small (Nickell and Salaheen 2015; Portes 2016: 17).

Other Studies

There are a number of additional reports commenting upon the economic impact of Brexit upon the UK economy that have utilised the 'consensus' studies as the basis for their own work rather than themselves producing their own independent analysis. The Trades Union Congress (TUC 2016: 1, 3, 9), for example, relied upon the results generated by the Treasury, CEP-LSE, OECD and NIESR studies, to substantiate their claim that withdrawal from the EU would have a negative impact upon wages, living standards, high skilled employment opportunities and pensions. Similarly, the Institute for Fiscal Studies (IFS) based its prediction of a shortfall in UK fiscal balances upon the forecasts made by the 'consensus' studies (Emmerson and Pope 2016: 14; Emmerson et al 2016: 18, 46–9). Again, the Office for Budget Responsibility (OBR) forecast for the UK economy, which intimately informs the economic policy strategy of the government, was based upon the conclusions reached by the NIESR, IMF, OECD and Treasury reports, rather than undertaking its own independent analysis (OBR 2016: 9, 47). Its predictions are summarised in Table 1.5. Hence, the OBR predictions are not independent of these earlier 'consensus' studies. Yet, they are not presented as being dependent upon this earlier body of work.[22] This is troubling because it both reinforces the approach undertaken, and predictions made, by the 'consensus' analysis, despite the weaknesses identified with this prior body of work, identified in this chapter.

Interestingly, the OBR predictions are more modest than earlier studies, in that they anticipate Brexit reducing UK growth potential by around 2.4%, after 5 years, once the impact of a more competitive exchange rate is factored into the analysis. Once again, in its analysis of Brexit impact, the OBR study does not include the impact from government policy, which is perhaps slightly more understandable in this case, as the report is intended to inform the government in finalising

Table 1.5 OBR Disaggregated Predicted Impact upon UK Public Sector Net Borrowing, 2016–2021

	Forecast (£ billion)				
	2016–2017	2017–2018	2012–2019	2019–2020	2020–2021
Changes related to the referendum result and exiting the EU of which:	3.5	9.9	15.4	14.7	15.2
Lower migration	0.6	1.9	3.0	4.4	5.9
Lower trend in productivity growth	0.0	1.2	4.2	5.5	7.2
Cyclical slow-down	2.3	7.6	8.6	5.4	2.3
Higher inflation	0.9	2.7	2.3	2.0	2.2
Lower interest rates	−0.5	−1.1	−1.3	−1.6	−1.8
Other factors	0.5	−2.5	−1.5	−1.1	−0.6

Source Author replication of analytical results reported in OBR (2015: 249), Table 8.1. Please note, in this table, a negative figure in the table refers to a reduction in public sector net borrowing (PSNB), achieved through either an increase in receipts or a fall in expenditure

its economic policy measures to be included in the Autumn Statement. Yet, this of course gives a misleading prediction of the likely future development of the UK economy once these measures have been implemented.

The narrow range of highly cited 'consensus' studies does not, however, fully reflect the range of economic reports that have sought to examine the potential impact of Brexit. A flavour of this broader set of studies, and their divergent findings, can be seen in the summary Table 1.8.

One such study derives from the Confederation of British Industry (CBI) commissioned report from PricewaterhouseCoopers (PwC), which used a computable general equilibrium (CGE) model to analyse the effects of uncertainty, trade barriers, migration, regulation and fiscal costs. There are two interesting results derived from this study. The first is that, as indicated in Table 1.6, regulatory savings were included in

Table 1.6 PwC Forecasted Economic Impact of Brexit in Comparison with a Counterfactual Baseline

Impacts	FTA scenario (%)			WTO scenario (%)		
	2020	2030	2040	2020	2030	2040
Uncertainty	−1.9	−0.1	−0.1	−2.6	−0.9	−0.1
Trade	−0.5	−0.5	−0.5	−1.7	−1.9	−2.1
Migration	−0.8	−0.8	−1.0	−1.3	−1.6	−1.6
Regulations	0.0	0.3	0.3	0.0	0.3	0.3
Fiscal	0.1	0.0	0.0	0.1	0.0	0.0
Total impact on GDP	−3.1	−1.1	−1.2	−5.5	−4.1	−3.5
Change in population	0.0	−0.2	−0.4	−0.1	−0.5	−0.9
Impact on GDP per capita	−3.0	−0.9	−0.8	−5.4	−3.6	−2.7

Source PwC (2016: 8), Table 2.1
Note Numbers in columns may not add up exactly, which is due to rounding

this model and, according to PwC, would partially (but not fully) mitigate against negative effects anticipated to derive from a fall in the levels of migration and a reduction in FDI (PwC 2016: 8, 20–21). This is an important innovation because the 'consensus' studies, examined thus far in this chapter, did not adequately account for regulation as a key variable in their analyses, either through choosing to omit the variable entirely or assuming that it would have only marginal effects. Yet, had they treated regulation more robustly in their models, and found similar results to PwC, their overall results would have been less negative, as regulatory savings would have offset some of the other predicted effects contained within these studies.

The second interesting result is that, in either scenario produced by PwC, the most significant negative impact was forecast to derive from a fall in private sector investment, whether through reduction in FDI or a more general deferral of investment due to the uncertainty caused by the Brexit process (PwC 2016: 21, 30). Assuming that a FTA could be negotiated with the EU, the PwC study predicted an initial drop of around 3% of UK GDP, which is gradually recovered by 2030, resulting in a marginal 1% loss in potential GDP over this period. If, however, the UK relied upon WTO rules, the initial loss of potential GDP would

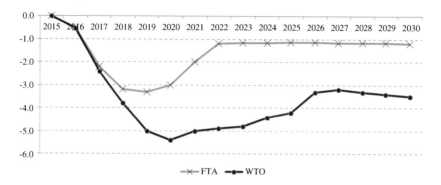

Fig. 1.2 PwC Difference from baseline GDP growth (%). *Source* Authors' best replication of PwC analysis, completed for the CBI (Fairbairn and Newton-Smith 2016: 20)

Table 1.7 Exit scenario results measured in percentage difference from counter-factual levels of expenditure categories

	FTA scenario (%)			WTO scenario (%)		
	2020	2030	2040	2020	2030	2040
Consumption	−2.8	−1.8	−1.8	−5.5	−5.3	−5.2
Investment	−16.4	−4.7	−1.7	−25.8	−14.8	−9.9
Government Expenditure	0.6	0.6	0.6	0.6	0.6	0.6
Exports	−3.6	0.4	0.7	−9.8	−8.4	−6.0
Imports	−4.8	−0.6	−0.3	−11.9	−10.5	−7.8
Total impact on GDP	−3.1	−1.1	−1.2	−5.5	−4.1	−3.5

Source PwC (2016: 30), Table 5.7

be larger (circa 5%) and, whilst half of this would be recovered by 2030, the UK economy would still have suffered around a 3% loss in potential GDP by the end of this time period (see Fig. 1.2).

In both scenarios, it is the deferral of investment due to the uncertainty caused by Brexit, compounded by an initial drop in FDI, which cause the short term negative impact (see Table 1.7). The gradual recovery in domestic investment and FDI flows result from the dissipation of uncertainty and as businesses reflect upon the fundamental strengths of the UK economy and future market opportunities in the new post-EU business environment. These effects could be potentially offset through application of policy interventions. For example, the maintenance of a high level of aggregate demand could reduce uncertainty, whilst the provision of fiscal investment incentives during this transition period could mitigate predicted deferral of business investment. If effective, these measures could cause this short term effect to be shallower than predicted and the longer term impact less problematic.

Part of the difference in predicted outcomes derives from the assumptions made as the basis for the two scenarios. For example, uncertainty is assumed to last for five years in the FTA option, presumably because PwC anticipates that negotiating and ratifying a FTA may take this period of time, whereas under the WTO alternative, uncertainty is expected to last for nine years, and during all of this time, credit risk raises the cost of capital and therefore increases the price of investment (PwC 2016: 19, 43–44). However, as stated previously in this chapter, there is no plausible reason given for either of these assumptions. It is quite possible that, given the starting point where the UK and EU share common regulations and standards, that a FTA might be fairly swiftly negotiated, whilst trading under WTO rules may conceivably raise the costs of trade but there is no a priori reason why uncertainty would last

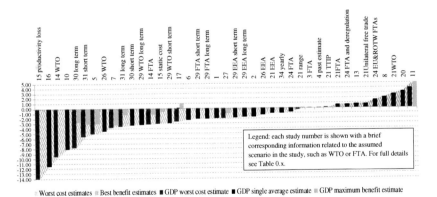

Fig. 1.3 Estimated net costs and net benefits of EU membership (% GDP), based on significant studies derived from Table 1.8. *Source* Authors' review of significant studies quantifying net costs and benefits. *Notes* Negative numbers show estimates of net costs, positive numbers show estimated net benefits. Please see Table 0.x for correspondence between number of study shown on the axis and more detail on estimates

much longer than the end of the two year Article 50 period where, if no FTA was forthcoming, WTO MFN tariffs would be imposed and the new environment settled. Yet, by adopting these key assumptions, the PwC study ensures that its results show a larger potential cost associated with the WTO option that persists for longer than might be otherwise anticipated.

There are, in addition, a number of studies which have been undertaken which forecast net positive impact arising from withdrawal from the EU. For example, Milne (2004) concluded that the recurring annual direct cost to the UK of EU membership was between 3–5% of GDP, and therefore, presumably a similar amount could be saved following completion of withdrawal. Similarly, the study completed by Open Europe predicts that the potential impact arising from Brexit would vary from a net cost of around 2.2% of UK GDP if trading under WTO rules, to a more positive net benefit of 0.64% of UK GDP if the UK was able to negotiate a comprehensive FTA with the EU, which would be extended to a net 1.55% net gain if this FTA was combined with an ambitious programme of deregulation (Booth et al. 2015: 5). The Economists for Brexit (2016b: 31) estimate is that UK GDP would be approximately 1.7% higher after Brexit, due largely to regulatory and fiscal savings, combined with supply side effects driven by a reduction in consumer prices following a drop in tariffs levied against the rest of the world. Business for Britain (2015: 55, 827) have estimated that, outside the EU, each UK household could be £933 better off per year. Given that the Office for National Statistics calculates that there are 27 million households in the UK at present,[23] then this equates to a net benefit from Brexit approximating £25.2 billion or 1.35% UK GDP. Finally, in a new study published just as this book was being finalised, a report from the Centre for Business Research (CBR) of the University of Cambridge used an alternative (post-Keynesian) model of the UK economy to predict that Brexit would be likely to have a mild dampening effect upon the UK economy, reducing future UK GDP by perhaps 1.5% compared to pre-referendum forecasts (Gudgin et al. 2017: 38–39).

These latter findings are not without their critics (e.g. Armstrong and Portes 2016: 5), and, indeed, they are correct to highlight the imprecision of modelling regulatory savings, which are broadly derived from Minford et al. (2015: 26–35), as equivalent to an equivalent cut in National Insurance. Nevertheless, it is important to note that different studies, using different methodologies, have produced a range of forecasts for the impact of Brexit. Indeed, in a broader summary of findings from a more comprehensive range of studies (see Fig. 1.3 and Table 1.8), it becomes clearer that there was never really a complete consensus amongst economists concerning the likely impact arising from Brexit for the UK economy. The fact that the CEP-LSE, IMF, OECD, Treasury and NIESR studies generally utilised similar models means that their conclusions were always likely to be rather similar to each other and this does not meet the test of utilising completely independent evidence to reinforce the conclusions reached by each study (Blake 2016: 40).

The Need for More Comprehensive Analysis

This chapter has highlighted the limitations of the suggestion that there was ever a consensus amongst economists on the predicted impact of Brexit. There are certainly areas of agreement between all economists in the various studies, for example that any increase in barriers to trade between the EU and the UK would be likely to reduce UK exports to the continent, and that a reduction in the regulatory burden placed on (particularly small) business may provide a boost to the economy. Nevertheless, there is considerable divergence in the magnitude of the predicted effects.

Given that most of the 'consensus' studies have used rather similar models and methodologies, it is perhaps unsurprising that the nature of these differences lie in the range of assumptions that the theorists use to construct the models and the choice of data with which to populate the calculations. Moreover, theoretical weaknesses inherent in the studies–whether ranging from their neo-classical foundations, the tenuous assumptions underpinning the inclusion of dynamic costs, the length of time it takes to negotiate a FTA or the issues relating to the applicability of historical data in gravity modelling—weaken the robustness of the

Table 1.8 Meta-analysis of the summary of net costs or net benefits, and of competences in significant cost–benefit studies

Study	Study number and scenario	GDP estimate			Trade				Macro				Policy			Conclusions
		%GDP min estimate	%GDP (single) estimate	%GDP max estimate	Budget	SIM	FDI	Sector	Growth & product'y	BOP	Macro policy	Exch Rate	Labour, migration	Regul'n	Industrial policy	
Burkett et al, 1996	1		-2		✓			✓	✓	✓	✓	✓			✓	Early study, focused more on costs of EU membership than benefits
Leach [IOD], 2000	2		-1.75		✓			✓	✓					✓	✓	Net cost of EU membership (hence net benefit of Brexit) = 1.75% GDP
USITC, 2000	3 FTA		-0.02			✓	✓	✓	✓				✓			Using a Global Trade Analysis Project (GTAP) general equilibrium trade model, the study concludes that UK withdrawal from the EU, combined with a subsequent FTA with NAFTA countries, would result in a 0.02% decline in UK GDP.
Gasiorek et al, 2002	4 past estimate		2		✓	✓	✓	✓	✓						✓	Using a CGE model, this study estimated the gains to the UK from EU membership to be net +2% UK GDP, between 1973 and 1985.
Milne, 2004	5	-5		-3	✓	✓	✓	✓	✓	✓	✓					Net Cost 3-5% GDP
Pain & Young, 2004	6		-2.25		✓	✓	✓		✓					✓		Simulation utilising the NIESR macroeconomic model of the UK economy. Net cost of Brexit = 2.25% GDP in the long run
Minford et al, 2005	7	-3.7		-3.2		✓	✓	✓					✓			EU membership net cost: 3.2-3.7% UK GDP
Ilkowitz et al, 2007	8		2.1			✓	✓									European Commission study examining the benefits for the EU as a whole (no figures for the UK in isolation) arising from the SIM, 1992-2006. Estimated EU GDP 2.1% higher.
Eichengreen and Bolitho, 2008	9				✓	✓			✓						✓	Historical literature review approach, focusing primarily on trade (SIM) and competition. Estimated net benefit of approximately 5% EU(15) GDP.
Gaskell and Persson, 2010	10		-8											✓	✓	Narrow focus on the cost of EU regulation. Estimate: costs UK economy £32.8bn p.a. (or approx. 8% of 2009 UK GDP). The benefit-cost ratio is *positive*, however, albeit significantly smaller than the net benefits of national regulation (1.02/1.58).
CBI, 2013	11	4		5	✓	✓			✓							Conclusion: net benefit arising from EU membership is in the region of 4-5% of UK GDP p.a. (p.11)
Drew and Bond (Eds) [Regents Report], 2013	12		N/A		✓	✓							✓	✓		A series of individual case studies. No summary conclusions reached.
Campos et al, 2014	13		0.7		✓				✓							Synthetical counterfactual approach estimates that the UK growth rate was 0.7% GDP p.a. higher due to EU membership
CEP-LSE studies [Ottaviano et al, 2014a and 2014b; Dhingra et al, 2015a and 2015b]	14 FTA / 14 WTO	-3.1 / -9.5	-1.1 / -3.3		✓	✓		✓	✓						✓	Use a standard quantitative static general equilibrium model with multiple sectors, countries and intermediates. Conclusion: Static losses lie between -1.1% UK GDP in the optimistic (FTA) scenario, and -3.1% UK GDP in the pessimistic (WTO) scenario; dynamic losses, although not explored in detail in the analysis, are reported as increasing potential losses from Brexit to between -3.3% UK GDP (FTA) and -9.5% UK GDP (WTO option).

(continued)

Table 1.8 (continued)

Study	Ref	Value	Value	Value	Description
BertelsmannStiftung, 2015	15 static cost / 15 productivity loss	-3 / -14	-11.5	-0.6	Depending on the degree of trade policy isolation, UK real GDP could fall by between 0.6 and 3.0% by 2030 (static costs), whilst lower investment and innovation may lower productivity and increase losses to 14% of UK GDP (dynamic costs) in the longer term.
Congdon, 2014	16		-11.5		Focused upon cost of EU membership – estimated at 11.5% of UK GDP (£185bn p.a.)
Mansfield, 2014	17	-2.6	0.1	1.1	Long-term impact between -2.6% and +1.1% of GDP, with, in the author's view, a best estimate of +0.1%.
Springford and Tilford 2014	18		N/A		Focusing on trade effects. Conclusion: "The UK has very little to gain by quitting the EU and much to lose".
Bank of England, 2015	19		N/A		Focused on policy consequences of EU membership leading to economic openness
Business for Britain 2015	20		3.2		Net cost of EU membership (and hence benefit from Brexit): £12.6bn (3.2% UK GDP) or £933 per household
Ciuriac et al. 2015	21 range	-2.76	0.03		Estimated impact of Brexit, ranged from: (a) -2.76% UK GDP (WTO option) by 2030 (b) -1.03% UK GDP (EEA option) (c) Participation in the TTIP would only boost UK GDP by 0.02-0.04%. (d) FTA with EU combined with further FTAs with other leading economies, such as Australian FTA with China, Japan, India and ASIEN, would boost the UK economy by around 0.6% of UK GDP (e) Unilateral free trade (Hong Kong) option would boost UK GDP by 0.75% of UK GDP. Depending upon the combination of options adopted, the UK could therefore face a net cost of -2.76% GDP to a small net gain of perhaps +0.03% UK GDP if combining FTAs with trade liberalisation.
	21 WTO		2.76		
	21 EEA		-1.03		
	21 TTIP	0.02		0.04	
	21 FTA		0.06		
	21 Unilateral free trade		0.075		
Irwin, 2015	22		N/A		Net costs (unquantified). Impact of Brexit is "severe".
McFadden and Tarrant 2015	23		N/A		Primarily a critique of other studies, the report nevertheless concludes that Brexit is likely to prove negative for the UK, particularly due to trade effects.
Booth et al. 2015	24 WTO		-2.2		Utilising a GTAP computable general equilibrium model (CGE), the study generates a range of possible scenarios: the worst case (WTO) scenario reduces UK GDP by -2.2% by 2030, a FTA option has only a modest reduction in UK GDP of -0.8% whilst a FTA accompanied by significant deregulation would result in a small net gain of 0.64%, compared to the best case scenario, where the Uk negotiates comprehensive FTAs with both the EU and elsewhere in the world, combined with significant deregulation, producing a net benefit to of 1.55% of UK GDP. The most feasible range, produced by the report, is assumed to lie between -0.81 to +0.64% of UK GDP.
	24 FTA		-0.8		
	24 FTA		0.64		
	24 and deregulation				
	24 EU&RO TW FTAs		1.55		

(continued)

Table 1.8   (continued)

Study															Notes
Webb et al [HoC Library], 2015	25	N/A											✓	✓	No conclusions reached
IMF, 2016	26 EEA	-1.4			✓							✓		✓	Utilising a combination of VAR, gravity and NiGEM simulation models, the IMF predicted that Brexit would lead to a loss of around -1.4% UK GDP in its limited (EEA) scenario by 2021, whereas in a more adverse (WTO) scenario, this potential loss compared to the baseline was -4.5% UK GDP.
	26 WTO	-4.5													
Punhani and Hill, 2016 Credit Suisse Report	27	-2	-1		✓										Predicts Brexit causing uncertainty and declining business investment and GDP falling by 1-2%
Miller, 2016 [HoC Library]	28	N/A			✓									✓	No conclusions reached
NIESR, 2016	29 WTO short term	-2.9			✓						✓				Analysis using the NiGEM general equilibrium econometric model. In the short term (2020), the net cost of Brexit was predicted to vary from -1.9% (EEA option), -2.1% (FTA) to -2.9% (WTO). In the longer term (2030), the net cost of Brexit declined slightly in the case of the EEA option to -1.8%, remained constant for the FTA option at -2.1% but increased slightly in the case of the WTO option at -3.2% of UK GDP.
	29 FTA short term	-2.1			✓										
	29 EEA short term	-1.9			✓										
	29 WTO long term	-3.2			✓										
	29 FTA long term	-2.1			✓										
	29 EEA long term	-1.8			✓										
OECD, 2016	30 short term	-3.3	-2.7		✓						✓				Using CGE and NiGEM models, the OECD forecast that Brexit would result in a shortfall of -3.3% UK GDP by 2020, whereas longer term effects would range from -2.7% UK GDP (FTA option) to -7.7% (WTO option) by 2030.
	30 long term	-7.7													
PwC, 2016	31 short term	-5.5	-3.0		✓						✓			✓	Utilised CGE model. Short term costs (by 2020) between 3-5.5% GDP; longer term costs are lower, at 1.2-3.5% UK GDP by 2030, as uncertainty resolved. However, average GDP per capita in 2030 would be similar after 'Brexit', being around 25-28% higher than in 2015 in the two exit scenarios, compared to an estimated 29% with continued EU membership
	31 long term	-3.5	-1.2												
Capital Economics [Woodford Report], 2016	32	N/A			✓						✓			✓	Slightly more plausible that the net impact of 'Brexit' will be modestly positive
TUC, 2016	33	N/A									✓				Report takes growth predictions from Treasury, IFS, LSE and IMF studies. Using this data, the TUC predict that Brexit will result in average wages falling by between £28 and £48 per week by 2030
JP Morgan, 2016	34 yearly	-1			✓										Reports views of 12 financial institutions and the HM Treasury (2016) report – predicting that GDP would be reduced by 1% GDP for every year that uncertainty persists, thus 2-3 years of negotiations would reduce GDP by up to 3% of GDP.

predicted outcomes. At their most basic, VAR, CGE and NiGEM simulation models operate by comparing predicted outcomes against a baseline projection of current trends and, as such, they must make a number of assumptions upon which the analysis is based. Yet, it is important that this simplification does not deviate too far from reality or else the predictive power of the forecasts will be significantly weakened.

The first fundamental assumption made is that identified historical trends will continue into the future (*ceteris paribus*), to establish the baseline comparator. Yet, this must, by definition, preclude unanticipated events. In economics, these are known as 'black swan' effects—it is known that they exist, but they are observed so infrequently that, when they do arrive, they are unexpected. Thus, although systematic financial crises do occur throughout the world on a far more frequent basis than financiers would like to admit, they are relatively infrequent amongst the leading developed nations, and therefore when such crises do occur, they provide a considerable shock to the economy.

Yet, assumptions built into economic models go beyond this starting point and, indeed, influence calculations at all levels. One issue relates to interpretation of the data. Whilst certain models use an estimate of potential fiscal savings from withdrawal of approximately 0.3% of GDP, others use a figure of 0.8%. Some models use a 2015 population baseline when estimating productivity figures in 2030, whereas others may use predictions for population levels in 2030. These choices make a significant difference to the outcomes of otherwise rather mechanistic calculations. Most studies use an figure to represent average tariffs that the EU would levy upon UK exports of 5% even though the WTO published statistic is less than half of this rate, and the House of Commons own research department trade-weighted estimated figure is even lower.

Other types of assumptions involve the choice of microeconomic foundations that are assumed to exist and whose influence permeates how the models operate. For example, it would appear that one reason why the small range of studies which have included migration as a variable within their simulation modelling found that a reduction in migration had a negative impact upon the UK economy was because they used a neo-classical model of growth. Yet, assumptions of homogenous capital and labour are meaningless in the real world and hence predictions relating to the economic impact of migration must include the quality or skill levels of migrant labour in addition to quantity. Doing so removes the automatic assumption that higher levels of migration will necessarily result in higher levels of growth, because the net effect will depend upon whether skill and productivity levels may rise to offset some or all of this effect. Thus, the choice of which theory of economic growth to incorporate within the modelling framework may have a significant impact upon its results.

Lord David Owen, the former Foreign Secretary, explained his concern in this way:

> You rig the [economic] model by what you put into it. If the Chancellor tells the Treasury to put in the following parameters, you get one kind of result. They have admitted they have not seen it necessary to present a model of what would be the benefits of going out of the EU. So we hear a lot about the risks of leaving, but nothing about the risks of remaining, which I believe are infinitely greater.[24]

In essence, Lord Owen is reiterating the critical effect of assumptions skewing the results of the model, but also suggesting that the comparison with the baseline projection is flawed because it is based upon the assumption that, were the UK to remain a full member of the EU, its current situation would remain essentially unchanged in the future. This is unlikely for a number of reasons, whether the desire on behalf of many within the EU to pursue ever-closer integration, or because the Eurozone will require additional measures taken for its long term sustainability which will inevitably change the nature of EU membership even for those countries which do not currently wish to participate in the single currency. As Business for Britain (2015: 712) so amusingly explain the difficulty with this status quo assumption, 'one might as well produce a weather forecast for Manchester on the assumption that it is never going to rain'.

A second area where most of the consensus models are flawed is in what they do, and do not, contain in their models. Portes (2013: F5) suggests that this should include examination of the impact upon trade, fiscal savings (from not having to contribute to the EU budget), investment, regulation, migration and the impact upon the financial sector. To this list should be added the effect upon the balance of payments, and through this whether growth is constrained, together with the impact of changes in the exchange rate and the effect of government policy. Other studies have sought to introduce what they term a dynamic analysis, where the association between openness, competition and productivity is hypothesised as generating a causal link whereby the former influences the development of the latter. This is not universally accepted, however (see the discussion in Chap. 7), and therefore its inclusion should be treated with a degree of caution.

A final flaw with the 'consensus' results is not necessarily in the construction of the models themselves, but rather in their interpretation. There were frequent examples, during the recent referendum campaign, where the former Prime Minister (Cameron) and the former Chancellor of the Exchequer (Osborne) cited the results of this handful of economic studies as though they were objective 'facts' rather than economic simulations based upon a range of often questionable assumptions (Blake 2016: 44–51). Moreover, studies by the IFS subsequent to the 'consensus' studies, but utilising their basic models and conclusions as the foundations for their own analysis, merely compound existing problems with the current analysis rather than offering a new interpretation of the data.

Notes

1. https://mainlymacro.blogspot.co.uk/2016/05/economists-say-no-to-brexit.html; https://www.theguardian.com/politics/2016/may/28/economists-reject-brexit-boost-cameron; https://www.ft.com/content/e66852f0-3249-11e6-ad39-3fee5ffe5b5b; http://www.niesr.ac.uk/blog/consensus-modelling-brexit.
2. http://www.politico.eu/article/george-osborne-economic-case-against-brexit-not-a-conspiracy-eu-referendum-date-june-23/; https://www.politicshome.com/news/europe/eu-policy-agenda/brexit/news/75047/george-osborne-tells-brexit-campaign-economic.
3. https://www.ipsos-mori.com/researchpublications/researcharchive/3739/Economists-Views-on-Brexit.aspx.

4. https://www.ifs.org.uk/publications/8296.
5. http://www.bbc.co.uk/news/business-35741715.
6. http://blogs.lse.ac.uk/brexitvote/2016/06/21/which-argument-will-win-the-referendum-immigration-or-the-economy/.
7. http://www.spectator.co.uk/2016/05/chancellor-this-eu-referendum-spin-just-wont-fly/.
8. https://www.youtube.com/watch?v=GGgiGtJk7MA.
9. http://www.ft.com/cms/s/0/3be49734-29cb-11e6-83e4-abc22d5d108c.html#ixzz4ExYoJJNI; http://www.telegraph.co.uk/business/2016/06/21/in-defence-of-experts-whether-they-support-leave-or-remain/; https://www.theguardian.com/commentisfree/2016/jun/09/michael-gove-experts-academics-vote; http://www.huffingtonpost.co.uk/entry/professor-brian-cox-michael-gove-experts_uk_5777dceee4b073366f0f20b5.
10. http://business-reporter.co.uk/2016/09/06/experts-predicted-brexit-gloom-egg-face-says-michael-gove/.
11. https://www.ipsos-mori.com/researchpublications/researcharchive/3739/Economists-Views-on-Brexit.aspx.
12. http://www.thetimes.co.uk/article/economists-warn-against-brexit-vote-bh07fdx0t.
13. https://mainlymacro.blogspot.co.uk/2016/05/economists-say-no-to-brexit.html.
14. https://www.ft.com/content/e66852f0-3249-11e6-ad39-3fee5ffe5b5b.
15. The research design of these studies is discussed, in more detail, in Chap. 3.
16. CGE models utilise input-output tables, which seek to establish the linkages between different sectors in the national economy and, when extended to study international trade, they attempt to predict the trade and income effects of different trade relationships between countries or regions. Their advantage is that, once the input-output relationships are established, repeated simulations can be undertaken, to test different scenarios, based upon different assumptions and policy changes. Their weaknesses relate to the quality of data on which they must rely (i.e. 'rubbish in, rubbish out') and the fact that they are founded upon Walrasian (neo-classical) assumptions of continuous market clearing and perfect competition, which certainly simplifies the model for the researchers, but which have little approximation to the real world. This implies that CGE results are potentially less useful than they might have been with less restrictive assumptions as to how the economy actually works at the heart of their models. For further reading on CGE

modelling, you may wish to read Piermartini and The (2005). For a critique of CGE modelling, Ackerman (2002) would be a good starting point. It is possible to modify CGE models to incorporate a more realistic (Keynesian) set of assumptions about how the economy works, but most CGE models do not choose to avail themselves of this option.

17. https://www.gov.uk/government/uploads/system/uploads/attachment_data/file/517415/treasury_analysis_economic_impact_of_eu_membership_web.pdf.
18. http://www.theguardian.com/politics/2016/apr/18/george-osborne-brexit-campaigners-case-is-economically-illiterate.
19. http://www.publications.parliament.uk/pa/cm201314/cmselect/cmfaff/87/8709.htm.
20. http://www.niesr.ac.uk/sites/default/files/NIESR%20Brexit%20Press%20Release%20-%20May%202016%20fin.pdf.
21. http://www.niesr.ac.uk/sites/default/files/NIESR%20Brexit%20Press%20Release%20-%20May%202016%20fin.pdf.
22. https://www.theguardian.com/politics/live/2016/nov/23/autumn-statement-2016-philip-hammond-brexit-growth-deficit-housing-jams-universal-credit-minimum-wage-live?page=with%3Ablock-5835a138e4b-0da4920d6b495; https://www.theguardian.com/uk-news/2016/nov/23/philip-hammonds-autumn-statement-welcome-reality-check-brexit; https://www.theguardian.com/commentisfree/2016/nov/23/the-guardian-view-on-the-autumn-statement-half-right-half-wrong.
23. http://www.ons.gov.uk/peoplepopulationandcommunity/birthsdeathsandmarriages/families/bulletins/familiesandhouseholds/2015-11-05.
24. Lord Owen: 'There is no need to be afraid of leaving the EU', *The Daily Telegraph*, 28 May 2016. Available via: http://www.telegraph.co.uk/news/2016/05/28/lord-owen-there-is-no-need-to-be-afraid-of-leaving-the-eu/.

References

Armstrong, A., & Portes, J. (2016). Commentary: The Economic Consequences of Leaving the EU. *National Institute Economic Review, 236*, 2–6.
Ackerman, F. (2002). Still dead after all of these years: Interpreting the failure of general equilibrium theory. *Journal of Economic Methodology, 9*(2), 119–139.

Baker, J., Carreras, O., Ebell, M., Hurst, I., Kirby, S., Meaning, J., et al. (2016). The Short-Term Economic Impact of Leaving the EU. *National Institute Economic Review, 236*, 108–120.

Bank of England. (2015). *EU Membership and the Bank of England*, Bank of England, London. http://www.bankofengland.co.uk/publications/Documents/speeches/2015/euboe211015.pdf.

BertelsmannStifung. (2015). *Brexit—potential economic consequences if the UK exits the EU*, Future Social Market Policy Brief 2015/05, Gütersloh. https://www.bertelsmann-stiftung.de/fileadmin/files/BSt/Publikationen/GrauePublikationen/Policy-Brief-Brexit-en_NW_05_2015.pdf.

Blake, D. (2016). *Measurement without Theory: On the extraordinary abuse of economic models in the EU referendum debate*, Cass Business School, London. http://www.cass.city.ac.uk/__data/assets/pdf_file/0007/320758/BlakeReviewsTreasuryModels.pdf.

Booth, S., Howarth, C., Persson, M., Ruparel, R., & Swidlicki, P. (2015). *What if…? The Consequences, challenges and opportunities facing Britain outside EU*, Open Europe Report 03/2015, London. http://openeurope.org.uk/intelligence/britain-and-the-eu/what-if-there-were-a-brexit/.

Burkitt, B., Baimbridge, M., & Whyman, P. B. (1996). *Thereis an Alternative: Britain and its Relationship with the EU*. Oxford: CIB/Nelson and Pollard.

Bower and Turrini (2009). *EU Accession: A road to fast track convergence? European Economy Economic Papers 393, European Commission, Brussels.* Available via: http://ec.europa.eu/economy_finance/publications/pages/publication16470_en.pdf.

Business for Britain. (2015). *Change or Go: How Britain would gain influence and prosper outside an unreformed EU*, Business for Britain, London. https://forbritain.org/cogwholebook.pdf.

Campos, N.F., Coricelli, F., & Moretti, L. (2014). *Economic Growth from Political Integration: Estimating the benefits from membership in the European Union using the synthetic counterfactuals method* (IZA Discussion Paper Series 8162), Bonn. http://anon-ftp.iza.org/dp8162.pdf.

Capital Economics. (2016). *The Economics Impact of 'Brexit': A paper discussing the United Kingdom' relationship with Europe and the impact of 'Brexit' on the British economy*, Woodford Investment Management LLP, Oxford. https://woodfordfunds.com/economic-impact-brexit-report/.

CBI [Confederation of British Industry]. (2013). *Our Global Future: The Business Vision for a Reformed EU*, CBI, London. http://www.cbi.org.uk/media/2451423/our_global_future.pdf#page=1&zoom=auto,-119,842.

CBI [Confederation of British Industry]. (2015). *Choosing Our Future: Why the European Union is good for business, but how it should be better*, CBI, London. http://news.cbi.org.uk/news/cbi-makes-case-for-being-in-a-reformed-eu/choosing-our-future/.

Congdon, T. (2014). *How much does the European Union cost Britain?* UKIP, London. http://www.timcongdon4ukip.com/docs/EU2014.pdf.

Dhingra, S., Ottaviano, G. I. P., & Sampson, T. (2015a). *Should we stay or should we go? The economic consequences of leaving the EU*, Centre for Economic Performance, LSE. https://ideas.repec.org/e/pot15.html.

Dhingra, S., Ottaviano, G., & Sampson, T. (2015b). *Britain's Future in Europe*, LSE, London. http://www.sdhingra.com/brexitwriteup.pdf.

Dhingra, S., Ottaviano, G., Sampson, T., & Van Reenen, J. (2016). *The Consequences of Brexit for UK Trade and Living Standards*, Centre for Economic Performance (CEP) and London School of Economics and Political Science (LSE). http://cep.lse.ac.uk/pubs/download/brexit02.pdf.

Drew, J., & Bond, M. (Eds.). (2013). *The UK and Europe: Costs, Benefits, Options – The Regents Report 2013*, Regents University London and Belmont Press, London. http://www.regents.ac.uk/files/regentsreport2013.pdf.

Ebell, M., & Warren, J. (2016). The Long-Term Economic Impact of Leaving the EU. *National Institute Economic Review, 236*, 121–138.

Eichengreen, B., & Boltho, A. (2008). *The Economic Impact of European Integration* (CEPR Discussion Paper No. 6820), CEPR, London. http://eml.berkeley.edu/~eichengr/econ_impact_euro_integ.pdf.

Emmerson, C., & Pope, T. (2016). Winter is Coming: The outlook for the public finances in the 2016 Autumn Statement, *IFS Briefing NoteBN188*, Institute for Fiscal Studies, London. https://www.ifs.org.uk/uploads/publications/bns/BN188.pdf.

Emmerson, C., Johnson, P., & Mitchell, I. (2016). *The EU single market: The value of membership versus access to the UK*. London: Institute for Fiscal Studies. Available via: http://www.ifs.org.uk/uploads/publications/comms/R119%20-%20The%20EU%20Single%20market%20-%20Final.pdf.

Fairbairn, C., & Newton-Smith, R. (2016). *Brexit – the Business View*, Lecture at London Business School, Monday 21st March. http://news.cbi.org.uk/business-issues/uk-and-the-european-union/eu-business-facts/brexit-the-business-view-pdf/.

Frankel, J. A., & Rose, A. K. (2000). *Estimating the Effect of Currency Unions on Trade and Output* (NBER Working Paper No. 7857). http://www.nber.org/papers/w7857.pdf.

FSB. (2015). A Study of FSB Members' Views on the UK's Membership of the European Union, Federation of Small Businesses, Blackpool. http://www.

fsb.org.uk/LegacySitePath/policy/assets/fsb%20eu%20research%20project%20-%20september%202015.pdf.

Gasiorek, M., Smith, A., & Venables, A. J. (2002). The Accession of the UK to the EC: A welfare analysis. *Journal of Common Market Studies, 40*(3), 425–447.

Gaskell, S., & Persson, M. (2010). *Still Out of Control? Measuring eleven years of EU regulation*, second edition, Open Europe, London. http://archive.openeurope.org.uk/Content/documents/Pdfs/stilloutofcontrol.pdf.

Gudgin, G., Coutts, K. & Gibson, N. (2017), The Macro-economic Impact of Brexit: Using the CBR Macroeconomic model of the UK economy (UKMOD), *Centre for Business Research Working Paper* No. 483. http://www.cbr.cam.ac.uk/fileadmin/user_upload/centre-for-business-research/downloads/working-papers/wp483revised.pdf.

HM Government (HMG). (2013). *Review of the balance of competencesbetween the United Kingdom and the European Union—The single market.*London: The Stationary Office. Available via: https://www.gov.uk/government/uploads/system/uploads/attachment_data/file/227069/2901084_SingleMarket_acc.pdf.

HM Treasury. (2016). *HM Treasury Analysis: The long term economic impact of EU membership and the alternatives*, Cm 9250, The Stationary Office, London. https://www.gov.uk/government/uploads/system/uploads/attachment_data/file/517415/treasury_analysis_economic_impact_of_eu_membership_web.pdf.

Ilzkovitz, F., Dierx, A., Kovacs, V., & Sousa, N. (2007). *Steps towards a deeper economic integration: The Internal Market in the 21st Century – A contribution to the Single Market Review*, European Economy – Economic Papers No. 271, European Commission, Brussels. http://ec.europa.eu/economy_finance/publications/publication784_en.pdf.

IMF (2016). *United Kingdom: IMF Country Report*, No. 16/169, IMF, Washington DC. https://www.imf.org/external/pubs/ft/scr/2016/cr16169.pdf.

Ipsos-MORI. (2016). *Economists Views on Brexit.* https://www.ipsos-mori.com/Assets/Docs/Polls/economists-views-on-brexit-2016-charts.pdf and https://www.ipsos-mori.com/Assets/Docs/Polls/economists-views-on-brexit-2016-tables.pdf.

Irwin, G. (2015). *Brexit: The impact on the UK and the EU*, Global Counsel, London. http://www.global-counsel.co.uk/system/files/publications/Global_Counsel_Impact_of_Brexit_June_2015.pdf.

JP Morgan. (2016). *Brexit Carries a Recessionary Risk.* https://am.jpmorgan.com/gb/en/asset-management/gim/adv/insights/brexit-february-update.

Leach, G. (2000). *EU Membership – What's the bottom line?* Institute of Directors Policy Paper, London. https://www.iod.com/MainWebSite/Resources/Document/europe_publications_eumembership.pdf.

Mansfield, I. (2014). *A Blueprint for Britain: Openness not isolation*, Institute for Economic Affairs, London. http://www.iea.org.uk/sites/default/files/publications/files/Brexit%20Entry%20170_final_bio_web.pdf.

McFadden, P., & Tarrant, A. (2015). *What Would 'Out' Look Like? Testing Eurosceptic alternatives to EU membership*, Policy Network, London. http://www.policy-network.net/publications/4995/What-would-out-look-like.

Miller, M., & Spencer, J. (1977). The Static Economic Effects of the UK Joining the EEC: A General Equilibrium Approach. *Review of Economic Studies, 44*(1), 71–93.

Miller, V. (Ed.). (2016). Exiting the EU: Impact in key UK policy areas, *House of Commons Library Briefing Paper* No. HC 07213. http://researchbriefings.parliament.uk/ResearchBriefing/Summary/CBP-7213#fullreport.

Miller, V., Lang, A., Smith, B., Webb, D., Harari, D., Keep, M., & Bowers, P. (2016). Exiting the EU: UK reform proposals, legal impact and alternatives to membership, *House of Commons Library Briefing Paper* No. HC 07214. http://research-briefings.parliament.uk/ResearchBriefing/Summary/CBP-7214#fullreport.

Milne, I. (2004). *A Cost Too Far? An Analysis of the net economic costs and benefits for the UK of EU membership*, Civitas, London. http://www.civitas.org.uk/pdf/cs37.pdf.

Minford, P. (2016). *The Treasury Report on Brexit: A Critique*, Economists for Brexit, London. http://static1.squarespace.com/static/570a10a460b5e93378a26ac5/t/5731a5a486db439545bf2eda/1462871465520/Economists+for+Brexit+-+The+Treasury+Report+on+Brexit+A+Critique.pdf.

Minford, P., Mahambare, V., & Nowell, E. (2005). *Should Britain Leave the EU? An Economic Analysis of a Troubled Relationship*. Cheltenham: IEA and Edward Elgar.

Minford, P., Gupta, S., Le, V.P.M., Mahambare, V. and Xu, Y. (2015). *Should Britain Leave the EU? An Economic Analysis of a Troubled Relationship – Second Edition*. Cheltenham: IEA and Edward Elgar.

Nickell, S. J., & Salaheen, J. (2015). *The Impact of Immigration on Occupational Wages: Evidence from Britain* (Bank of England Staff Working Paper No. 574). http://www.bankofengland.co.uk/research/Documents/workingpapers/2015/swp574.pdf.

OBR (Office for Budget Responsibility). (2016). Economic and Fiscal Outlook – November 2016, Cm 9346, The Stationary Office, London. http://cdn.budgetresponsibility.org.uk/Nov2016EFO.pdf.

OECD. (2016). *The Economic Consequences of Brexit: A taxing decision* (OECD Economic Policy Paper, No. 16). http://www.oecd.org/eco/The-Economic-consequences-of-Brexit-27-april-2016.pdf.

Ottaviano, G., Pessoa, J. P. & Sampson, T. (2014a). The Costs and Benefits of Leaving the EU, CEP mimeo. http://cep.lse.ac.uk/pubs/download/pa016_tech.pdf.

Ottaviano, G. I. P., Pessoa, J. P., Sampson, T., & Van Reenen, J. (2014b). *Brexit of Fixit? The trade and welfare effects of leaving the European Union*, Centre for Economic Performance 016, LSE. https://ideas.repec.org/p/cep/ceppap/016.html.

Portes, J. (2013). Commentary: The economic implications for the UK of leaving the European Union, *National Institute Economic Review*, No. 266, F4–9. http://www.niesr.ac.uk/sites/default/files/commentary.pdf.

Portes, J. (2016). Immigration, Free Movement and the EU Referendum. *National Institute Economic Review, 236*, 14–22.

Punhani, S., & Hill, N. (Credit Suisse Report). (2016). *Brexit: Breaking up is never easy, or cheap*, Credit Suisse, Zurich. https://doc.research-and-analytics.csfb.com/docView?language=ENG&format=PDF&document_id=806936650&source_id=emrna&serialid=lPu6YfMSDd9toXKa9EPxf5HiNBEoWX2fYou5bZ6jJhA%3D.

PwC [PricewaterhouseCoopers LLP]. (2016). *Leaving the EU: Implications for the UK economy*, PricewaterhouseCoopers LLP, London. http://news.cbi.org.uk/news/leaving-eu-would-cause-a-serious-shock-to-uk-economy-new-pwc-analysis/leaving-the-eu-implications-for-the-uk-economy/.

Springford, J., & Tilford, S. (2014). *The Great British Trade-Off: The impact of leaving the EU on the UK's trade and investment*, Centre for European Reform, London. http://www.cer.org.uk/publications/archive/policy-brief/2014/great-british-trade-impact-leaving-eu-uks-trade-and-investmen.

Thompson, G., & Harari, D. (2013). The Economic Impact of EU Membership on the UK, *House of Commons Library Briefing Paper* SN/EP/6730. http://researchbriefings.parliament.uk/ResearchBriefing/Summary/SN06730#fullreport.

TUC (2016), *Better Off In – Working people and the case for remaining in the EU*, TUC, London. https://www.tuc.org.uk/sites/default/files/BetteroffIN.pdf.

USITC [United States International Trade Commission]. (2000). *The Impact on the US Economy of Including the United Kingdom in a Free Trade Agreement with the United States, Canada and Mexico*, Investigation No. 332–409, USITC, Washington DC.

Webb, D., Keep, M., & Wilton, M. (2015). In Brief: UK-EU economic relations, *House of Commons Library Briefing Paper (HC 06091)*, The Stationary Office, London. http://researchbriefings.parliament.uk/ResearchBriefing/Summary/SN06091.

WTO [World Trade Organisation]. (2015). *World Tariff Profiles 2015*, WTO, Geneva. https://www.wto.org/english/res_e/booksp_e/tariff_profiles15_e.pdf.

2

The Fiscal Impact of Brexit

One of the main areas where even detractors of Brexit concede that the UK will benefit from withdrawal from the EU, concerns the saving of the annual contributions (sometimes described as the membership fee) paid to that organisation.[1] However, estimates of the potential savings vary considerably.[2] Thus, now that the UK is committed to negotiate its withdrawal from the EU, it is necessary to clarify the likely budgetary savings which will accrue to the UK Treasury.

The calculation of net budgetary contributions to the EU is not quite as straightforward as it might appear, however, for a number of different reasons, including:

1. The composition of the EU budgetary process is itself slightly opaque, due to the way in which budget payments are set, the resources over which the EU lays claim and the fact that contributions depend to a large extent upon the relative national income of member states. Thus, should the UK achieve a higher (lower) growth rate relative to other member states, it will incur higher (lower) demands for contributions to the EU budget than were initially anticipated. Retrospective adjustments are, therefore, common.

© The Author(s) 2017
P.B. Whyman and A.I. Petrescu, *The Economics of Brexit*,
DOI 10.1007/978-3-319-58283-2_2

2. When considering net payments to the EU budget, studies use different assumptions about the UK rebate, and how this may change over time, and also the range of payments received from the EU. For example, whilst it is relatively easy to justify payments made directly to the UK government, such as structural or rural development fund payments, and, moreover, payments made to farmers as part of the CAP, since these are administered by UK government departments, it is perhaps more difficult to justify the inclusion of funding achieved by private sector organisations (including UK universities) in research and/or training programmes, secured through competitive bidding.

3. The timing of calculating the payments is different when comparing Treasury and EU Commission estimates of net payments, with the result that they often present quite different estimates. Hence, there will be some discrepancy between different studies, depending upon which data sources they have chosen (Browne et al. 2016: 40). To take one example, the IFS typically use figures from the EU Commission, whereas, for this chapter, data has been drawn from HM Treasury.

4. The actual net fiscal savings, from withdrawal from the EU, will depend upon whether the type of trading arrangement, established with the EU, involves an element of fiscal contribution. However, discussion of this final element is postponed until Chap. 9, where the various models of multilateral and preferential trade arrangements are discussed in more detail.

There are two further reasons why estimates of budgetary savings, forecast during the referendum campaign, were problematic, namely: (i) the assumptions that were made relating to the future growth of the EU budget (if any); and, (ii) how potential changes to the composition of that budget were factored into the calculations. The latter, for example, could impact significantly upon the UK if additional low-income countries were to join the EU, with the consequences of regional development funds being redistributed away from poorer UK regions towards these new member states. Or, alternatively, whether those proportions allocated to CAP or research funding expenditure were to shift over time. Whilst these questions are less relevant for the UK once the withdrawal process has been completed, it is necessary to examine how effectively the different economic studies internalised these factors in their models in order to forecast likely economic consequences arising from Brexit.

For something as apparently clear-cut as UK budgetary contributions to the EU, therefore, estimating the likely fiscal benefit arising from Brexit is a little more complicated than might be expected.

Composition and Size of the EU Budget

The EU budget has increased, over time, from 0.5% of community Gross national income (GNI) in 1973, to its present 1% level (Browne et al. 2016: 6). It is set by a 5–7-year Multiannual Financial Framework, which was introduced in 1988 to provide a more stable funding platform than had previously applied. For 2014–2020, the budget was set at €960 billion, which implies an average of €137.14 billion per year during this 7-year framework period. This, in turn, equates to 1% of EU Gross National Income. This settlement represents a cash increase over the previous financial period, but a real terms (after inflation) decrease, which represents the first such real terms reduction in the EU budget (HM treasury 2014: 5). Thus, budgetary appropriations declined from the previous 1.12% of GNI (Keep 2015: 3).[3]

In practice, however, it is a little more complicated for two reasons. Firstly, the EU budget fails to include additional elements which are essentially off balance sheet (HMG 2014: 26). These include €36.8 billion worth of allocations to an Emergency Aid Reserve, a European Globalisation Fund, a Solidarity Fund, a Flexibility Instrument and the European Development Fund. If included in the core EU budget, this would represent an increase of 0.04% of total EU GNI, taking the total to 1.17% of EU GNI in 2015.[4] Secondly, the appropriation commitments are increased by what is described as a 'margin' of around 0.28% of EU GNI, presumably in order to provide a degree of flexibility to EU expenditures intended to cover a relatively long time period. Hence, the total appropriations (payments made into the EU budget) necessary to cover this total sum (i.e. core budget + margin) represents 1.23% of EU GNI up until 2020 (see Table 2.1).

Having established the magnitude of EU budgetary expenditures, the contributions can be established for each member state. This primarily derives from what the EU has established as its 'own resources', namely (HM Treasury 2014: 9–10):

i. Gross National Income (GNI)-based contributions (currently representing approximately 74% of total EU revenue) vary according to the relative affluence of member states. It is calculated that the UK's share of this revenue category was 14.5% in 2014;

ii. VAT contributions (13% of EU revenue) are based upon a slightly complicated set of assumptions and capped to limit excessive variations. The pertinent point is that the UK's share of contributions to the EU budget under this category was 16% in 2014;

iii. Customs duties (12% of EU revenue) levied on goods imported from non-member states. It is estimated that the UK contributed 16.1% of the revenue under this category;

iv. Sugar levies (less than 1% of EU revenue) are charged on the production of sugar;

v. A small proportion (approximately 1%) of EU revenue lies outside of the 'own resources' and includes contributions from non-EU member states to participate in certain programmes, taxes paid on EU staff salaries, interest on late payments and fines levied upon companies breaching competition law.

Customs duties and sugar levies comprised the initial basis for EU funding, reflecting its early focus upon agricultural production and its establishment of a customs union (described as a 'common market' in UK discourse), later augmented by VAT contributions and, more latterly, the rising importance of revenues calculated according to the relative affluence of member states. The volatility in calculating net payments to the EU budget is largely due to the inherent nature of the 'own resources' system (HM Treasury 2014: 13–14). Moreover,

Table 2.1 Multiannual financial framework EU 28 for 2014–2020, adjusted for 2017 (€m, 2017 prices)

Commitment appropriations	2014	2015	2016	2017	2018	2019	2020	Total 2014–2019
1. Smart and inclusive Growth	52 756	77 986	69 304	73 512	76 420	79 924	83 661	513 563
1a. Competitiveness for growth and jobs	16 560	17 666	18 467	19 925	21 239	23 082	25 191	142 130
1b. Economic, social and territorial cohesion	36 196	60 320	50 837	53 587	55 181	56 842	58 470	371 433
2. Sustainable growth: Natural resources	49 857	64 692	64 262	60 191	60 267	60 344	60 421	420 034
of which Market-related expenditure and direct payments	43 779	44 190	43 951	44 146	44 163	44 241	44 264	308 734
3. Security and citizenship	1 737	2 456	2 546	2 578	2 656	2 801	2 951	17 725
4. Global Europe	8 335	8 749	9 143	9 432	9 825	10268	10 510	66 262
5. Administration	8 721	9 076	9 483	9 918	10 346	10 786	11 254	69 584
of which administrative expenditure of the institution	7 056	7 351	7 679	8 007	8 360	8 700	9 071	56 224
6. Compensation	29	0	0	0	0	0	0	29
Total commitment appropriations	121 435	162 959	154 738	155 631	159 514	164 123	168 797	1 087 197
as a percentage of GNI (%)	0.90	1.17	1.05	1.04	1.04	1.04	1.03	1.04
Total payment appropriations	135 762	140 719	144 685	142 906	149 713	154 286	157 358	1 025 429
as a percentage of GNI (%)	1.01	1.02	0.98	0.95	0.97	0.97	0.96	0.98
Margin available (%)	0.22	0.21	0.25	0.28	0.26	0.26	0.27	0.25
Own Resources Ceiling as a percentage of GNI (%)	1.23	1.23	1.23	1.23	1.23	1.23	1.23	1.23

Source Europa EU (2016)

the complexity inherent in the 'own resources' approach therefore partly reflects the historical development of the EU and the difficulty in securing a more streamlined approach, when this would inherently involve individual nations who benefit from any changes and others who are required to make larger contributions as a result. The evolution and significance of each source of EU revenue are illustrated in Fig. 2.1.

In terms of EU expenditure, the initial dominance of the Common Agricultural Policy (CAP), which can be noted in the Fig. 2.2, has been reduced somewhat due to the dramatic expansion of cohesion and structural funds to promote regional development across all member

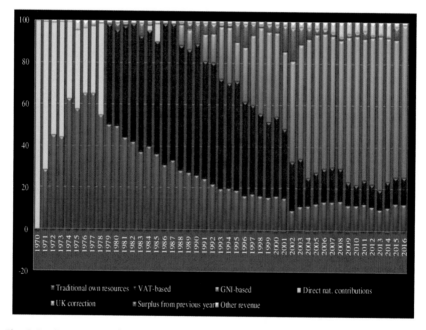

Fig. 2.1 Structure of EU financing, 1958–2015. *Sources* For 1970–2008: European Commission (2009). Financial Report EU budget 2008.Publication and accompanying dataset. Last accessed 15 August 2016. For 2009–2014: European Commission (2015). Financial Report EU budget 2014. Publication and accompanying dataset. Last accessed 15 August 2016. For 2015–2016: European Commission (2016). Definitive Adoption (EU, Euratom) 2016/150 of the European Union's general budget for the financial year 2016. Last accessed 15 Aug 2016

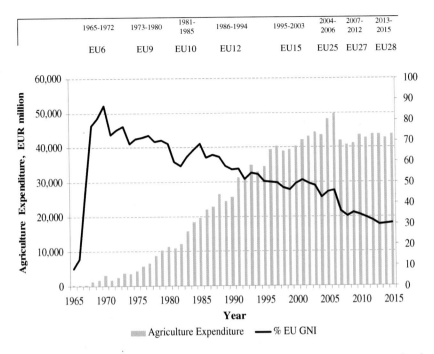

1965-1972	1973-1980	1981-1985	1986-1994	1995-2003	2004-2006	2007-2012	2013-2015
EU6	EU9	EU10	EU12	EU15	EU25	EU27	EU28

Fig. 2.2 Agriculture expenditure as part of the EU GNI, 1965–2015 (€m). *Sources* Author-collated data from various reports on CAP expenditure (European Commission, DG Agriculture and Rural Development, Financial Reports 2008 and 2013–2015)

states. Thus, in the current budgetary framework, 47% of total spending commitments relate to regional policy, 39% for CAP and sustainable development, with the balance incorporating administration (6%), external policy (6%) and issues relating to migration, public health, consumer protection, culture and youth policy (2%) (Keep 2015: 6–7).

Financial Management and Fraud

One issue which typically arises, when considering the EU budget, concerns accusations of financial mismanagement and/or fraud. This criticism derives from the annual reports produced by the European Court of Auditors (ECA), which assess the financial management of the EU's finances. In its opinion, the latest set of accounts to be assessed, in

2012, were found to be legal and regular, but that 4.8% of EU expenditure was subject to 'material error'—in essence, this means that spending did not conform to the rules established to guide EU expenditure. Data collected through monitoring sampling, undertaken across different categories of EU expenditure, indicate that errors were not confined to specific sectors, with agricultural support estimated to have a material error of perhaps 3.8% of total expenditure, rural development 7.9%, regional policy, energy and transport 6.8%, employment and social affairs 3.2%, external relations 3.3%, and research 3.9%.

The auditors emphasise that these findings do not necessarily equate to fraud, and nor do they necessarily imply that almost 5% of the total EU budget was wasted. Indeed, there is some evidence for this equivocation, as there were 1194 cases of suspected fraud reported in 2012, compared to 12,137 cases of non-fraudulent error noted in the same year (HM Treasury 2014: 27). Moreover, in mitigation, it has to be more difficult dealing with the complexity inherent in management a series of programmes across a large number of nations, each at different levels of development, and with different previous approaches to the administration and monitoring of public expenditure programmes. Indeed, the ECA themselves recognise this difficulty in setting an error ceiling of 2% as acceptable for EU spending programmes—a rate that would be difficult to justify in public spending programmes within a single nation (HMG 2014: 30). Nevertheless, the failure to meet even this generous target, together with the estimated irregularities and errors catalogued by the ECA, certainly create cause for concern about deficiencies in eligibility assessment and compliance monitoring which require corrective action. Consequently, for the nineteenth consecutive year, the ECA provided only partial assurance as to the accuracy of the EU's accounts (HM Treasury 2014: 21–24).

UK Contributions to the EU Budget

The UK has been an almost continuous net contributor to the EU's budget; the one exception being in 1975 (see Table 2.2).

The UK is currently the second largest net contributor to the EU, after Germany, but only the third largest when these payments are averaged per capita (per person) (see Table 2.3 and Fig. 2.3).

Table 2.2 UK net contributions to the EU/EC Budget (£m), 1973–2020

	Gross contribution	Negotiated refunds	Rebate	Total contribution (after rebate and refunds)	Public sector receipts	Net contribution (Gross contribution—rebate and refunds—public sector receipts)	GDP, chained volume measures, seasonally adjusted (£m)	Net contribution as % GDP
1973	181			181	79	102	781,583	0.013
1974	181			181	150	31	762,257	0.004
1975	342			342	398	−56	750,912	−0.007
1976	463			463	296	167	772,852	0.022
1977	737			737	368	369	791,889	0.047
1978	1348			1348	526	822	825,111	0.100
1979	1606			1606	659	947	855,933	0.111
1980	1767	98		1669	963	706	838,462	0.084
1981	2174	693		1481	1084	397	831,931	0.048
1982	2863	1019		1844	1238	606	848,700	0.071
1983	2976	807		2169	1522	647	884,520	0.073
1984	3204	528		2676	2020	656	904,639	0.073
1985	3940	61	166	3713	1905	1808	942,519	0.192
1986	4493		1701	2792	2220	572	972,239	0.059
1987	5202		1153	4049	2328	1721	1,024,346	0.168
1988	5138		1594	3544	2182	1362	1,083,629	0.126
1989	5585		1154	4431	2116	2315	1,111,618	0.208
1990	6355		1697	4658	2183	2475	1,119,587	0.221
1991	5807		2497	3309	2765	544	1,107,059	0.049
1992	6738		1881	4857	2827	2030	1,111,043	0.183

(continued)

Table 2.2 (continued)

	Gross contribution	Negotiated refunds	Rebate	Total contribution (after rebate and refunds)	Public sector receipts	Net contribution (Gross contribution—rebate and refunds—public sector receipts)	GDP, chained volume measures, seasonally adjusted (£m)	Net contribution as % GDP
1993	7985		2539	5446	3291	2155	1,138,897	0.189
1994	7189		1726	5463	3253	2211	1,183,144	0.187
1995	8889		1207	7682	3665	4017	1,212,798	0.331
1996	9133		2412	6721	4373	2348	1,243,709	0.189
1997	7991		1733	6258	4661	1597	1,282,602	0.125
1998	10,090		1378	8712	4115	4597	1,323,527	0.347
1999	10,287		3171	7117	3479	3638	1,366,983	0.266
2000	10,517		2085	8433	4241	4192	1,418,176	0.296
2001	9379		4560	4819	3430	1389	1,456,837	0.095
2002	9439		3099	6340	3201	3139	1,491,761	0.210
2003	10,966		3559	7407	3728	3679	1,543,468	0.238
2004	10,895		3593	7302	4294	3008	1,582,486	0.190
2005	12,567		3656	8911	5329	3582	1,629,519	0.220
2006	12,426		3569	8857	4948	3909	1,670,306	0.234
2007	12,456		3523	8933	4332	4601	1,712,996	0.269
2008	12,653		4862	7791	4497	3294	1,702,252	0.194
2009	14,129		5392	8737	4401	4336	1,628,583	0.266
2010	15,197		3047	12,150	4768	7382	1,659,772	0.445
2011	15,357		3143	12,214	4132	8082	1,684,820	0.480
2012	15,746		3110	12,636	4169	8467	1,706,942	0.496

(continued)

Table 2.2 (continued)

	Gross contribution	Negotiated refunds	Rebate	Total contribution (after rebate and refunds)	Public sector receipts	Net contribution (Gross contribution—rebate and refunds—public sector receipts)	GDP, chained volume measures, seasonally adjusted (£m)	Net contribution as % GDP
2013	18,135		3674	14,461	3996	10,465	1,739,563	0.602
2014	18,777		4416	14,361	4576	9785	1,792,976	0.546
2015[a]	17,779		4861	12,918	4445	8473	1,833,233	0.462
2016[b]	20,500		4800	15,700	4500	11,200		
2017[b]	18,000		6100	11,900	4600	7300		
2018[b]	18,600		4400	14,100	4800	9400		
2019[b]	19,800		4700	15,000	5200	9800		
2020[b]	20,300		5100	15,200	5400	9800		

Sources HM Treasury (2016), ONS, UK National Accounts (2016)
Note [a]2015 are estimates, [b]figures for 2016–2020 are forecasts rounded to the nearest £100 million

Table 2.3 EU budgetary balances by member state (€m), 2013–2015

	Expenditure			Contributions			Net contributions			Net contribution per head (in €), 2015
	2013	2014	2015	2013	2014	2015	2013	2014	2015	
Netherlands	2264	2014	2359	6552	8373	7947	4288	6358	5588	331
Sweden	1661	1691	1468	4211	4294	4019	2550	2603	2552	262
UK	6308	6985	7458	17,068	14,072	21,409	10,760	7088	13,952	215
Germany	13,056	11,484	11,013	29,376	29,143	28,125	16,320	17,659	17,112	211
Denmark	1435	1512	1529	2899	2508	2521	1465	996	993	175
Austria	1862	1573	1787	3191	2870	2726	1329	1297	939	109
Finland	1497	1062	1330	2159	1904	1854	662	842	524	96
France	14,239	13,479	14,468	23,292	20,968	20,606	9052	7489	6138	92
Italy	12,554	10,695	12,338	17,168	15,889	15,920	4614	5193	3582	59
Cyprus	227	273	203	185	161	230	−42	−112	27	32
Ireland	1874	1563	2009	1731	1651	1839	−143	87	−169	−37
Croatia	290	584	605	238	430	397	−52	−155	−207	−49
Malta	174	255	134	86	76	104	−87	−179	−30	−70
Spain	13,752	11,539	13,696	11,369	11,111	10,089	−2383	−428	−3606	−78
Portugal	6163	4943	2595	1793	1748	1646	−4370	−3195	−949	−91
Belgium	7209	7044	6952	5291	5233	5471	−1919	−1812	−1481	−132
Lithuania	1881	1886	877	405	385	390	−1476	−1501	−488	−167
Estonia	973	668	443	212	200	210	−761	−467	−233	−177
Poland	16,179	17,436	13,358	4214	3955	4236	−11,965	−13,481	−9121	−240
Romania	5561	5944	6538	1474	1459	1446	−4086	−4485	−5092	−256
Slovenia	814	1142	940	426	385	403	−388	−758	−537	−260
Bulgaria	1977	2255	2730	478	461	484	−1499	−1795	−2246	−312
Latvia	1063	1062	982	269	270	236	−794	−792	−746	−376

(continued)

Table 2.3 (continued)

	Expenditure			Contributions			Net contributions			Net contribution per head (in €), 2015
	2013	2014	2015	2013	2014	2015	2013	2014	2015	
Greece	7215	7095	6210	1906	1950	1343	−5308	−5145	−4867	−448
Hungary	5910	6620	5629	1011	996	1074	−4899	−5624	4556	−462
Czech Republic	4893	4377	7075	1617	1507	1542	−3276	−2871	−5532	−525
Slovakia	2026	1669	3735	799	720	697	−1227	−949	−3038	−560
Luxembourg	1598	1714	1649	322	246	367	−1276	−1468	−1283	−2278
Total	126,349	134,656	128,565	129,430	139,744	132,961				

Source European Commission, interactive graph on EU expenditure and revenue, Available at: http://ec.europa.eu/budget/figures/interactive/index_en.cfmEurostat (population data). *Notes* Negative net contribution denotes a member state being a net recipient

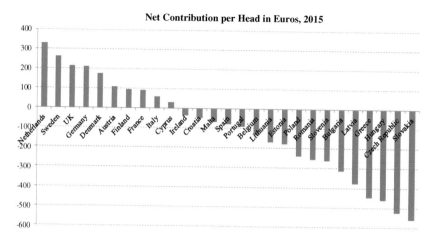

Fig. 2.3 EU member states net contribution to EU budget (in €), 2015. *Source* European Commission, interactive graph on EU expenditure and revenue, Available at: http://ec.europa.eu/budget/figures/interactive/index_en.cfmEurostat (population data)

Gross Contributions

One of the more controversial statements, made by the *Vote Leave* campaign in the recent referendum, concerned the claim, painted on the side of its campaign bus, which stated:

We send the EU £350 million a week – let's fund the NHS instead.

Critics of this claim have taken issue with two elements of this statement. Firstly, the apparent pledge that this £350 million would be spent on the National Health Service (NHS), albeit that leading members of the campaign stated that this was 'an aspiration' rather than a firm promise.[5] Certainly, the *Vote Leave* website makes the claim that the UK's EU contributions are of a sufficient magnitude to construct a 'new, fully-staffed NHS hospital every week'.[6] However, one problem faced by campaigners in a referendum is that, with a few exceptions such as the role played by Prime Minister Cameron in the *Remain* campaign, they do not control executive office and, therefore, cannot make firm commitments to future government action. Thus, it is difficult to criticise the *Vote Leave* campaign for highlighting the magnitude of budgetary transfers to the EU by comparing them to the cost of an NHS hospital, which appears to be factually accurate, even though certain voters might (and, indeed, were probably intended to) have inferred from this that the campaign was making a spending commitment for a future post-referendum government, which it was incapable of doing.

Secondly, the statement is criticised for using the word 'send',[7] given that gross contributions to the EU are not actually dispatched until the UK's rebate is deducted, which would give a figure of £275 million per week (Emmerson et al. 2016: 1). The *Vote Leave* website carried a more accurate, although less 'headline grabbing' description of the £350 million figure as representing the gross cost of EU membership.[8] This statement is accurate but has also been found to be 'misleading' by the UK Statistics Authority, given the failure to mention rebate deductions and on the basis that gross figures were being discussed in terms that they implied net payments.[9]

A second headline, during the referendum campaign, has been criticised on similar grounds, namely the claim that the UK contribution to the EU budget has exceeded half a trillion pounds over the period of UK membership.[10] This study re-calculated those figures given in Table 2.3, by inflating values to transfer historical fiscal transfers into 2014 prices, and then aggregating all adjusted contributions. Once again, this calculation is accurate but is not particularly helpful, because it ignores the rebate, which, when the calculations are repeated to include the rebate, over-state the gross contributions after rebate by £108.9 billion at 2014 prices, or around 29% of the reported total (Begg 2016: 46–47). The resultant figure of £375.1 billion (i.e. £484bn–£108.9bn) is still a very large number, but it does not make such attractive headlines.

The UK Rebate

One early acknowledgement of distributional concerns raised by the 'own resource' system resulted in the adjustment of the UK's net contributions paid into the EU budget by means of a correction or abatement—normally described as a 'rebate'. Given that the UK had a relatively efficient and small agricultural sector, and that CAP expenditures were a majority of EU spending at the time of its accession to the EU, the UK received relatively small expenditures from the EU budget. At the same time, as a trading nation, the UK's share of customs duties and VAT receipts were disproportionately large, thereby requiring a disproportionately high contribution to the EU budget. In 1984, the UK was the third-poorest EU member state, in terms of GNI per capita, and yet making the second largest net contribution to the EU budget (HMG 2014: 15). Unsurprisingly, this led to political tensions within the EU, and the rebate was negotiated to provide an *ex post facto* adjustment to reduce net contributions to a more equitable position.

The initial 1985 rebate lowered UK contributions by 66%, yet more recent increases in various elements of the EU budget that are excluded from this deduction have reduced its scope, thus significantly increasing UK net payments (Webb et al. 2015: 11–12). The rebate is calculated by subtracting the UK's percentage share of expenditure from the UK's percentage share of VAT contributions, then multiplying this by 0.66 and finally multiplying this sum by the total amount of EU expenditure.[11]This rebate is valuable to the UK (see Fig. 2.4), amounting to £4.9 billion in 2014 and signifying that the UK's net contribution would have been just under 50% larger had the rebate not been applied (see Table 2.4).

It should be noted that the UK is not the only member state to benefit from a budgetary correction mechanism. For example, Austria, Denmark, Germany, the Netherlands and Sweden are all net contributors to the EU budget who receive one or more forms of contribution adjustments, to prevent what might otherwise be termed an 'excessive' budgetary burden (HMG 2014: 27; Business for Britain 2015: 369–370). Thus, the UK is certainly not unique in the EU for having

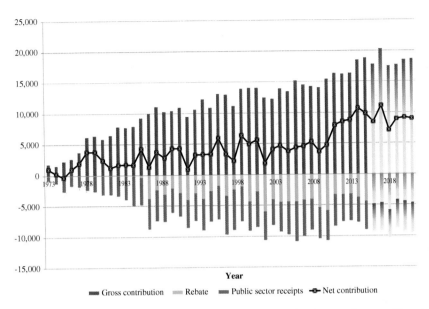

Fig. 2.4   UK contributions to and receipts from the EU budget real terms (£m at 2015 prices), 1973–2020. *Sources* HM Treasury (2016), ONS, UK National Accounts (2016). *Note* 2015 are estimates, figures for 2016–2020 are forecasts rounded to the nearest £100 million

Table 2.4   Percentage of UK rebate lost due to 2005 changes

Year	Actual size of UK rebate in nominal prices (€m)	Value of UK rebate had 2005 changes not been made in nominal prices (€m)	Lost value of the UK rebate (%)
2008	6114	6416	4.7
2009	6057	7407	18.2
2010	3553	5670	37.3
2011	3623	5978	39.4
2012	3835	6726	43.0
2013	4073 (est)	7480 (est)	45.5

Source Lewis (2014: 4)

what are regarded as disproportionate and inequitable funding burdens ameliorated. Despite this fact, the UK abatement has been subject to periodic criticism from the Commission and other member states (Business for Britain 2015: 182; Capital Economics 2016: 28).

Given that this is a fiscal matter, any decision to remove or reform the rebate would require unanimity in the Council of Ministers, and thus the UK, whilst a member of the EU, would have a veto over proposals to reform or remove the rebate. Yet, this is by itself no guarantee that a UK government, seeking other concessions, might bargain away part of the rebate. Indeed, this is precisely what happened in December 2005, when the UK conceded certain exemptions from the rebate in an attempt to negotiate a substantial fall in CAP expenditure. These exemptions included EU overseas aid and non-agricultural expenditure in the post-2004 new member states, and the effect was to significantly reduce the value of the rebate (Keep 2015: 15; Webb et al. 2015: 9; Begg 2016: 44). Unfortunately, CAP expenditure was not reduced as a quid pro quo, thus reinforcing the importance of securing formal agreements rather than less distinct 'understandings' in international negotiations (Business for Britain 2015: 182).[12] The budgetary impact, arising from this reduction in the effectiveness of the rebate, is illustrated in Table 2.4.

Net Contributions

One issue raised, during the referendum campaign, is whether it is more appropriate to use gross contributions to the EU budget rather than net figures—i.e. after all deductions. This is an interesting question to consider, because the answer partly depends upon circumstances. In regular conversation, if an individual is asked about their income, they will most likely reply giving their gross income, rather than what they actually receive into their bank accounts after tax. Nor will it be very likely that they will think to add back into the calculation of their income what they might receive in tax credits or social security benefits, and even less the net benefit they might personally receive through the provision of those public services which their tax payments help to fund, less any additional fees or charges involved in utilising these public services. The more complex net income calculation may provide the more accurate answer, but it is unlikely to be the one given, even if the individual concerned was an economics professor! Nevertheless, given that the issue under consideration is a matter of public policy, then it would seem reasonable that the net contribution figure is the one that should be preferred for giving a more useful understanding of the budgetary impact of EU membership upon the UK. Certainly, when seeking to estimate any likely budgetary savings from Brexit, the net figure is the more useful.

Utilising official figures from Table 2.2, and as illustrated in Fig. 2.4, the current UK net contribution to the EU budget is around £10 billion per annum. This figure relates to total contributions transferred to the EU by the UK government after the rebate has been deducted and after taking account of the receipts received back *by the public sector* from the EU for participation in various programmes, such as the CAP or regional development funding. It does not, however, include a further amount received by the private sector, in the UK, relating to their participation in EU programmes. These most notably include research funding won by UK universities, through a competitive process, from the Horizon 2020 research programme, and the Erasmus student mobility scheme. The Treasury estimates that, in 2013, these payments to private organisations totalled in the region of £1.4 billion (HM Treasury 2015: 14). If this is subtracted from the net public sector receipts, it gives a final net financial impact upon the UK economy from the EU budget of around £8.6 billion per year. This latter figure does not give an estimate of fiscal savings for the UK government arising from Brexit, however, but rather it begins to consider impacts upon the UK economy beyond the confines of national public expenditure.

The range of different estimates of UK contributions to the EU budget, therefore, range from around £19.2 billion gross payments, to £10 billion net contributions for the UK government and public sector, and around £8.6 billion for both public and private sectors. Each of these figures can be used for certain circumstances.

The gross figure is useful if the intent was to indicate what potential future transfers might be required if the UK rebate were eliminated by future reform of EU finances, or, alternatively, if considering whether any divergence between the efficiency of nationally, as opposed to supra-nationally, determined forms of expenditure may affect the economic impact experienced by the UK economy (Congdon 2014: 19–22). For example, if it were proven that UK expenditure was more (or less) effective than EU expenditure, then there would be an argument to deflate (or inflate) the anticipated economic impact accordingly, rather than simply focus on aggregate receipts and net budgetary contributions. However, in the absence of robust evidence on this point, it would be unwise to seek to manipulate fiscal estimates due to suspicions as to their effectiveness.

The net contribution estimate would, however, be preferable particularly when seeking to estimate the impact of withdrawal from the EU upon the UK economy. In this circumstance, the most accurate estimate of the fiscal savings to government following Brexit, *ceteris paribus*, would be a value around £10 billion per annum, representing around 0.53% of UK GDP, which is the figure that most studies tend to use in their calculations (e.g. HM Treasury 2015: 14; Ottaviano et al. 2014: 2; Dhingra et al. 2015: 3; Capital Economics 2016: 3).

The Uncertainty of Future Budgetary Developments

The estimates produced, above, do not, however, take into account possible future developments which may impact upon the level of potential budgetary savings. These may include:

a. future growth of the EU budget and consequent increase in UK fiscal contributions;
b. the macroeconomic impact arising from Brexit and consequences for the national budget;
c. which model of trade relationship the UK negotiates with the EU following Brexit.

For the first factor, it can be noted that the historical development of UK budgetary contributions has been variable, but following

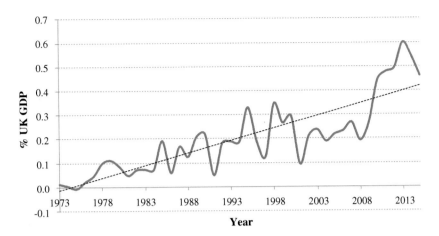

Fig. 2.5   UK net contributions to the EU budget (% of UK GDP), 1973–2015. *Sources* HM Treasury (2016), ONS, UK National Accounts (2016)

a steadily increasing trend (see Fig. 2.5). There are many causes to this phenomenon, including: (i) the natural growth in a budget fixed at a certain percentage of EU GDP; (ii) UK growth rates being faster than the EU average over recent years, partly because of problems with the Eurozone economies, and therefore the UK has to pay an increasing share of EU expenditure; (iii) the EU budget as a whole being expanded over time, from 0.5% of EU GDP in the 1970s to a little over 1% of GDP today; and (iv) the UK rebate being eroded through negotiating exemptions as a means to leverage additional change within the organisation. There is every expectation that the EU budget will increase further during the next budgetary period. This may arise out of the need to provide further support to the single currency (MacDougall 1977: 20; HMG 2014: 37–38) or to enable the EU to provide a sufficient fiscal stimulus in future economic crises (Begg 2016: 41). Whatever the reason, were this to occur before the UK formally completed the Brexit procedure, it would further exacerbate the UK's budgetary transfers to the EU and, therefore, fiscal savings post-Brexit would be larger than predicted.

A second factor concerns the impact of Brexit upon the UK economy and consequent affect upon the national government's fiscal position. The range of economic studies, produced over the past two decades, have put forward a range of predicted effects, ranging from large economic benefits to equally large economic costs, with the majority of the studies suggesting a more moderate impact of between plus or minus 2–3% of UK GDP (see Table 1.8). The most recent commentary on the likely impact of Brexit, produced by the Bank of England in its August 2016 inflation report, infers a slowing of UK growth by perhaps around 2.5% from what was previously forecast, despite active monetary policy measures (Bank of England 2016a, b). It may be questionable as to what proportion of this predicted economic slowdown is due to the uncertainty centring upon Brexit or whether the previous forecast was too optimistic. Nevertheless, *if* this proves to be accurate, and given the Office for Budget Responsibility rule of thumb that as little as a 0.8% permanent reduction in the level of output would be sufficient to eliminate Brexit's £10 billion budgetary saving, then the net fiscal impact may be negative (Capital Economics 2016: 29; Emmerson et al. 2016: 2).

The final factor concerns the future trade relationship that the UK negotiates with the EU, and whether this includes an element of financial contribution towards EU programmes. Around half of the preferential trade options, available to the UK and discussed in more detail in Chap. 9, would involve varying degrees of fiscal transfers to the EU (see Table 2.5). The closest forms of trade relationship would be likely to carry the most significant fiscal costs, whereas the more independent and less intimate the relationship, the less of a fiscal burden

Table 2.5 Estimated fiscal impact from different future trading relationships with the EU

	Gross		Net		UK net	
	£m	% GDP	£m	% GDP	£bn	% GDP
Norway—EEA	620	0.76	310	0.38	4.4	0.22
Turkey—Customs Union	n/a	n/a	n/a	n/a	3[a]	0.14[a]
Swiss—Bilateral	420	0.13	410	0.13	2.1	0.09
South Korea—FTA	0	0	0	0	0	0
Greenland—WTO	0	0	0	0	0	0
Hong Kong—Unilateral Free Trade	0	0	0	0	0	0

[a]Author estimate

may be required, if, indeed, any contribution is necessitated at all. Consequently, any financial contribution necessitated by the eventual model selected by the UK will have to be subtracted from the potential net £10 billion in UK budgetary savings in order to reach the final budgetary saving once any trade arrangement is operational. Thus, should the UK participate in the EEA on the same terms as Norway, the overall net savings to the UK from Brexit might be as low as £5.6 billion, whereas if the UK negotiated a Free Trade Agreement (FTA) on a similar basis to the deal offered to Canada, there would be no fiscal cost involved, and therefore the final budgetary saving for the UK would remain at around £10 billion.

Notes

1. This is not the only area where savings could occur, as the UK government would no longer have to contribute towards the cost of representation in the EU, and, although there would still be the need for trade and diplomatic missions following withdrawal, this is unlikely to incur a similar magnitude of expenditure.
2. The EU's own calculations of the net budgetary balance with the UK can be found via http://ec.europa.eu/budget/financialreport/2014/lib/financial_report_2014_en.pdf. This estimate records around half of the net contribution that the UK makes to the EU budget as calculated by the ONS or the HM Treasury. The ONS explains some of the reasons for differences in calculation via http://visual.ons.gov.uk/uk-perspectives-2016-the-uk-contribution-to-the-eu-budget/. The Treasury and Office for Budgetary Responsibility (OBR) estimates are to be found via https://www.gov.uk/government/uploads/system/uploads/attachment_data/file/483344/EU_finances_2015_final_web_09122015.pdf.
3. http://www.consilium.europa.eu/uedocs/cms_data/docs/pressdata/en/ecofin/139831.pdf.
4. *Op cit.*
5. http://www.independent.co.uk/news/uk/politics/brexit-350-million-a-week-extra-for-the-nhs-only-an-aspiration-says-vote-leave-campaigner-chris-a7105246.html.
6. http://www.voteleavetakecontrol.org/briefing_cost.

7. http://www.theguardian.com/politics/reality-check/2016/may/23/does-the-eu-really-cost-the-uk-350m-a-week.
8. http://www.voteleavetakecontrol.org/briefing_cost.
9. https://www.statisticsauthority.gov.uk/news/uk-statistics-authority-statement-on-the-use-of-official-statistics-on-contributions-to-the-european-union/.
10. http://www.voteleavetakecontrol.org/britain_has_paid_more_than_half_a_trillion_pounds_to_the_eu; http://www.voteleavetakecontrol.org/briefing_cost.
11. http://register.consilium.europa.eu/doc/srv?l=EN&f=ST%20 5602%202014%20INIT.
12. https://www.theguardian.com/world/2005/jun/21/eu.politics.

References

Bank of England. (2016a). *Inflation report—August 2016*. London: Bank of England. Available via: http://www.bankofengland.co.uk/publications/Documents/inflationreport/2016/aug.pdf.

Bank of England. (2016b). *Monetary policy summary* London: Bank of England. Available via: http://www.bankofengland.co.uk/publications/minutes/Documents/mpc/mps/2016/mpsaug.pdf.

Begg, I. (2016). The EU budget and UK contribution. *National Institute Economic Review, 236*, 39–47.

Browne, J., Johnson, P., & Phillips, D. (2016). *The budget of the European Union: A guide, IFS Briefing Note BN181*. London: Institute for Fiscal Studies.

Business for Britain. (2015). *Change or go: How Britain would gain influence and prosper outside an unreformed EU*. London: Business for Britain. Available via: https://forbritain.org/cogwholebook.pdf.

Capital Economics. (2016). *The Economics impact of 'Brexit': A paper discussing the United Kingdom' relationship with Europe and the impact of 'Brexit' on the British economy*. Oxford: Woodford Investment Management LLP. Available via: https://woodfordfunds.com/economic-impact-brexit-report/.

Congdon, T. (2014). *How much does the European Union cost Britain?* London: UKIP. Available via: http://www.timcongdon4ukip.com/docs/EU2014.pdf.

Dhingra, S., Ottaviano, G. I. P., & Sampson, T. (2015). *Should we stay or should we go? The economic consequences of leaving the EU*, Centre for Economic Performance, LSE. https://ideas.repec.org/e/pot15.html.

Emmerson, C., Johnson, P., Mitchell, I., & Phillips, D. (2016). *Brexit and the UK's public finances* (IFS Report 116). Institute for Fiscal Studies, London. Available via: http://www.ifs.org.uk/uploads/publications/comms/r116.pdf.

European Commission (EC). (2009). *Financial Report EU budget 2008*. Publication and accompanying dataset. Last accessed 15 August 2016.

European Commission (EC). (2015). *Financial Report EU budget 2014*. Publication and accompanying dataset. Last accessed 15 August 2016.

European Commission (EC). (2016). *Definitive Adoption (EU, Euratom) 2016/150 of the European Union's general budget for the financial year 2016*. Last accessed 15 Aug 2016.

Europa EU. (2016). *Budget figures and documents*. Available via: http://ec.europa.eu/budget/mff/figures/index_en.cfm.

HM Government (HMG). (2014). *Review of the balance of competences between the United Kingdom and the European union—EU budget*. London: The Stationary Office. Available via: https://www.gov.uk/government/uploads/system/uploads/attachment_data/file/332762/2902399_BoC_EU_Budget_acc.pdf.

HM Treasury. (2014). *European union finances 2014: Statement on the 2014 EU budget and measures to counter fraud and financial mismanagement*, Cm 8974. London: The Stationary Office. Available via: https://www.gov.uk/government/uploads/system/uploads/attachment_data/file/388882/EU_finances_2014_final.pdf.

HM Treasury. (2015). *European union finances, 2015: Statement on the 2015 EU budget and measures to counter fraud and financial mismanagement*, Cm 9167. London: The Stationary Office. Available via: https://www.gov.uk/government/uploads/system/uploads/attachment_data/file/483344/EU_finances_2015_final_web_09122015.pdf.

HM Treasury. (2016). *HM treasury analysis: The long term economic impact of EU membership and the alternatives*, Cm 9250. London: The Stationary Office. Available via: https://www.gov.uk/government/uploads/system/uploads/attachment_data/file/517415/treasury_analysis_economic_impact_of_eu_membership_web.pdf.

Keep, M. (2015). EU Budget 2014–2020, *house of Commons Library briefing paper (HC 06455)*. London: The Stationary Office. Available via: http://researchbriefings.files.parliament.uk/documents/SN06455/SN06455.pdf.

Lewis, D. (2014). *The UK's EU Rebate: How much did Tony Blair give away?* Business for Britain, Briefing Note 4.

MacDougall, D. (1977). *The Role of public finance in the European Communities.* Luxembourg: Office for the official publications of the European Communities.

ONS (Office of National Statistics) UK National Accounts. (2016). *Gross domestic product, chained volume measures: Seasonally adjusted.* Available via: https://www.ons.gov.uk/economy/grossdomesticproductgdp/timeseries/abmi/bb.

Ottaviano, G. I. P., Pessoa, J. P., Sampson, T., & Van Reenen, J. (2014). *Brexit of Fixit? The trade and welfare effects of leaving the European Union.* Centre for Economic Performance 016, LSE. Available via: https://ideas.repec.org/p/cep/ceppap/016.html.

Webb, D., Keep, M., & Wilton, M. (2015). In brief: UK-EU economic relations. In *House of commons library briefing paper (HC 06091).* London: The Stationary Office. Available via: http://researchbriefings.parliament.uk/ResearchBriefing/Summary/SN06091.

3

Brexit and Trade

The economic impact upon trade was the primary concern expressed by the opponents of Brexit during the recent referendum campaign. The CBI (2013: 11) argued that access to European markets has delivered the largest positive benefit from UK membership of the EU. This is not surprising, because the early EU initiatives were focused upon the promotion of trade integration amongst member states through lowering barriers to trade, with the anticipated result that trade would increase, thereby promoting faster economic growth. Hence, reversing this logic would infer that withdrawal from the EU might reduce trade and hence lower UK GDP. This chapter, therefore, seeks to examine this issue.

The Economic Theory of Trade

Long established theories of international trade tend to explain the flow of goods and services between countries in terms of comparative advantage derived from differences in the opportunity costs of production. This could arise because of differences in productivity, which is often termed 'Ricardian' comparative advantage, or due to differences in factor abundance and/or intensity, known as 'Heckschler-Ohlin'

© The Author(s) 2017   **77**
P.B. Whyman and A.I. Petrescu, *The Economics of Brexit*,
DOI 10.1007/978-3-319-58283-2_3

comparative advantage. The hypothesis is that countries will possess a relative advantage in one industry, from which it will export, and be less competitive in another, from which it will import. To the extent that these competitive advantages exist, and are relatively evenly distributed between nations, then the potential benefits from specialisation and trade between these nations is self-evident (Portes 2013: F9).

The theory of international trade is, however, complicated by three factors. The first is that when considering the costs and benefits arising from trade agreements, standard economic trade theory predicts that specialisation in areas of relative advantage, combined with the lowering of trade barriers, should benefit the free trade area *as a whole*. It does not, however, unambiguously follow that *all* participating nations benefit equally. Indeed, it is quite conceivable that some may lose from the process. The distribution of gains and losses, within and between individual participant nations, means that interpretation of trade flows in the absence of considering these additional impacts becomes problematic. For example, if, by joining a free trade area, a nation experienced lower prices paid by consumers, but simultaneously experienced a growing trade deficit and consequently lower future employment and growth potential, would that nation be said to have benefitted from the trade arrangement? A superficial reading of a study which examined the trade liberalisation in isolation from other economic impacts would suggest so, but if the productive potential of the nation shrank as a result, the macroeconomic consequences would be negative. Hence, there is a danger inherent in focusing upon one aspect of a general assessment as to the consequences of UK withdrawal from the EU, without placing this in context.

Secondly, standard Ricardian theory tends to discuss trade in terms of two nations, with very different factor endowments and specialising in very different product ranges—i.e. textiles and wine, or cheese and cars. Yet, even a cursory inspection of trade flows will highlight the fact that a large proportion of international trade occurs between countries with relatively similar profiles. Thus, whilst it might have once been the case that the UK exported manufactured goods (perhaps textiles) and imported non-manufactured items (perhaps food and wine), the majority of current UK trade is with other developed nations with broadly similar factor endowments and industrial structures. The UK imports cars from Germany, for example, yet there is also a thriving car industry in the UK which exports to continental Europe and across the globe. To account for this apparent paradox, new trade theories have sought to explain these trading patterns by emphasising differences in consumer tastes and economies of scale within different industries, as determining specialisation of production and trade between nations (Bernard et al. 2007: 106–108).

The third factor concerns the distribution of industries in which competitive advantage occurs, reinforced by the terms of trade pertaining to each industry. If one economy has a greater number of industries which possess competitive advantages over another economy, and/or the terms of trade are such to maintain or reinforce this beneficial position, then it is likely that the former economy will generate a trade surplus and the latter a trade deficit. The consumers in the deficit nation may have an initial benefit of lower prices for their imported goods, but the nation will have to sell assets or borrow to meet its trade obligations. Unless this situation is ultimately resolved and brought back into balance, the deficit nation may suffer growth constraints, and those same consumers, even if all of them remain in employment, are likely to have slower growing incomes than in the surplus nation (McCombie and Thirwall 1994).

In a simplified economic model of the world, where the relative exchange values of currencies are primarily determined by international trade and FDI, then the exchange rate might resolve differences in competitive advantage over time. However, the vast majority of foreign exchange trading today is related to financial speculation rather than financing international trade in goods and services. Indeed, one estimate is that the global value of all traded goods and services equates to a mere 4 days-worth of global foreign exchange trading (Singh 2000: 16). Hence, this equilibrating mechanism may not act in a smooth and timely fashion. Moreover, the principle of cumulative causation would suggest that those firms or countries which have an initial competitive advantage have the potential to retain and bolster this over time (Myrdal 1957: 12–13). Consequently, whilst the economic textbook theory of growth would indicate that it should be to everyone's advantage to encourage specialisation and free trade, the reality is not always so clear cut. The gains from trade are certainly not evenly distributed.

Theoretical Effects of Trade Integration

There are a number of reasons to expect that trade integration may result in increased trade flows, greater specialisation and hence efficiency. Adam Smith noted that the size of the market limited the degree of specialisation of labour, and therefore an expansion of the marketplace, through the creation of a customs union or a single market, should encourage a greater division of labour and specialisation (Baldwin 1989: 260). Endogenous growth theory allows for economic growth to be positively influenced through increased competition arising from an expanded market, together with increasing returns to scale and scope due to increased specialisation of inputs and technology spillovers (Baldwin 1989: 7–8, 36). Moreover, trade policy might also have growth effects (Baldwin and Seghezza 1996).

There have been a number of studies which have found a positive relationship between international trade and national income (Edwards 1998; Frankel and Romer 1999; Rodriguez and Rodrik 2000; Feyer, 2009). The inference is that increasing trade boosts national income. However, it is equally plausible that the direction of causality could run the other way—i.e. richer countries tend to engage in more trade. In order to seek to identify causality, economic models have shifted from cross sectional to time series data, and gravity models have gained in prominence, as will be seen later in the chapter.

Economic theory does not, however, form a consensus on the issue. For example, neo-classical growth theory suggests that trade integration can have only a minor impact upon economic development. The more competitive are existing markets, the smaller the impact of trade integration upon competition and prices, although there will remain the potential for the realisation of greater economies of scale (Allen et al. 1998: 447). Furthermore, when considering the impact of establishing a customs union, Viner (1950) noted that the expected boost to intra-EU trade ('trade creation') is, to some degree, offset as former trade with the rest of the world is disadvantaged by the erection of the common external tariff ('trade diversion'). Whilst trade creation should be welfare-enhancing, as domestic production is replaced by more efficient (cheaper) goods imported from other EU member states, trade diversion involves replacing more efficient production from non-EU nations with less efficient (higher cost) production from within the customs union. The economic impact of trade integration will therefore depend upon the balance of these two effects (Europe Economics 2013: 11).

The so-called Washington consensus asserts that trade liberalisation will improve performance. However, it has been criticised for basing its conclusions upon what is fundamentally a neoclassical, supply-side set of economic policies (Gnos and Rochon 2004: 188). Moreover, it appears to produce poor macroeconomic outcomes—i.e. low growth, repeated economic crises, a failure to produce full employment, secure current account balance and distributional inequalities (Arestis 2005: 252; Davidson 2005: 209). Even the architect of the Washington Consensus, John Williamson (2004), has acknowledged omissions in the original model and suggested a reformed version which includes institutional reform and counter-cyclical macroeconomic policy. Consequently, when viewed in a broader context, the evidence that trade openness has predictable, robust and systematic impact upon economic growth rates is quite weak (Rodrik 2006: 975).

Trends in Trade Development

International trade has, over a long time period, grown faster than total global output. For example, since the mid-1800s, whilst global population has increased by six-fold, and global output by 60-fold, the total value of international trade has expanded by more than 140-fold (Maddison 2008; WTO 2013: 46). During the period since 1950, the value of exports has risen as a share of global GDP from 5.5 to 17.2% in 1999 (WTO 2013: 47). Similarly, the 5.6% average growth in world trade, between 1985 and 2011, was almost twice as fast as the average 3.1% increase in global GDP during the same time period (WTO 2013: 56). This rapid expansion in trade has been facilitated by reduced costs of trade, as tariff and transport costs have fallen, together with a general catching-up effect arising from renewed trade activity in formerly more restricted economies in China and the former Soviet Union. Moreover, technological advances have in effect 'shrunk' the size of the globe as far as trade is concerned or, as Feyrer (2009: 31) explains the process, 'technology changes the nature of distance over time'.

UK Trade Development

The UK is the eleventh largest exporter in the world and is second only to the USA in the export of commercial services. However, this performance represents a decline in the UK's export ranking, as it was the eighth largest exporter in the world in 1980 (WTO 2013: 60–63).

UK trade with the EU has grown during the period of its membership. Part of this increase in trade volumes has occurred due to the EU's expansion in membership over this period. However, trade with the EU(8) member states, comprising the founder members and those nations joining at the same time as the UK, increased from around 28%

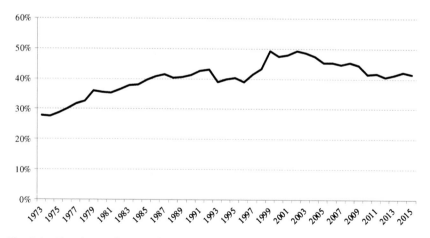

Fig. 3.1 The share of UK trade with the EU(8), measured as % of total UK trade, 1973–2015. *Source* OECD (2016b). *Notes* EU(8) economies comprise the eight EU member states of 1973 apart from the UK, namely Belgium, Netherlands, Luxembourg, France, Italy, Germany, Ireland and Denmark

prior to UK accession to the EU, to a peak of almost 50% around the turn of the century, before falling back again to just over 40% in 2015 (OECD 2016b). Thus, the share of trade increased amongst these established members of the union during the first half of the UK's membership, but decreased in importance thereafter (see Fig. 3.1).

Part of this increase in trade mirrors a gradual increase in the importance of trade as a share of national income, as can be seen in the Fig. 3.2, which traces the rising value of trade relative to GDP in leading OECD nations. Interestingly, trade was relatively more significant for the UK than other selected nations prior to accession to the EU than subsequently, whilst trade shares of GDP in Canada and Germany have grown more rapidly during the period of UK membership of the EU, to become relatively more significant.

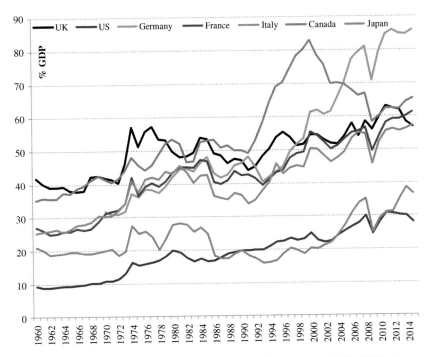

Fig. 3.2 Total trade relative to GDP in selected countries, 1960–2015. *Source* World Bank (2016b)

Precise figures for the share of UK trade with the EU are exaggerated by the 'Rotterdam effect', whereby UK exports destined for the rest of the world may first be shipped to Rotterdam, due to its position as a major shipping hub, and are therefore recorded as trade with the Netherlands rather than their ultimate destination of China or

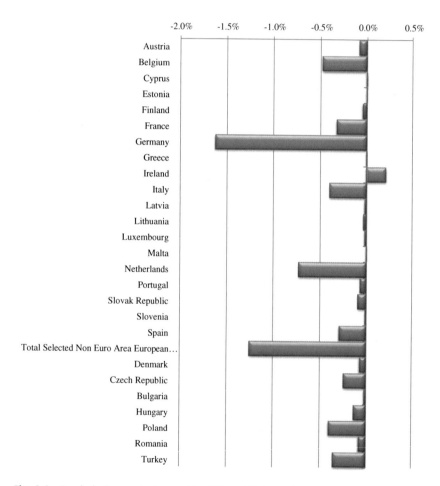

Fig. 3.3 Trade balances between the UK and EU member states in 2015, as % of UK GDP. *Source* IMF (2016). *Note* Negative (respectively positive) value numbers show that the respective country or area has a trade surplus (respectively deficit) with the UK, which is the equivalent of the UK having a trade deficit (respectively trade surplus) with the respective country or area

India. Similarly, oil imports from the Middle East may be shipped to Rotterdam before being transferred on to the UK, and will therefore be recorded as an EU import. The ONS is uncertain about the distortion in trade figures caused by the Rotterdam effect, but when using what it terms as a 'realistic assumption' that half of all UK trade with the Netherlands masks non-EU origination (for imports) or destination (for exports), then excluding this would produce an estimate that the EU purchases 46.5% of UK exports and sells the UK 50.6% of its imports (Webb et al. 2015: 7–8).

Aggregate trade figures obscure the fact that the UK runs a significant trade deficit with the rest of the EU, equivalent to 4.55% of UK GDP in 2015; the Euro Area accounts for the majority of this trade deficit, standing at 3.87% of UK GDP according to 2015 figures (IMF 2016). Indeed, the UK runs a trade deficit with the majority of EU member states except for Ireland, Cyprus, Greece, Malta

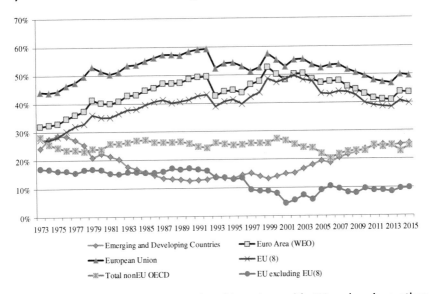

Fig. 3.4 The percentage of UK trade taking place with EU and various other nations, 1973–2015. *Source* IMF (2016). *Notes* Unless otherwise stated, EU means EU(28), whilst EU(8) member states comprise the nine members of the EU in 1973, less the UK—i.e. Belgium, Netherlands, Luxembourg, France, Italy, Germany, Ireland and Denmark. Percentages do not add to 100 due to various non-mutually exclusive ways in which European countries are shown

and Estonia; in all cases except Ireland, this surplus is marginal (see Fig. 3.3). For a number of member states, this trade surplus with the UK exceeds 1% of their national incomes—i.e. the Netherlands, Poland, Czech Republic, Belgium, Hungary, Latvia, Lithuania and Slovakia (Irwin 2015: 11). Whilst for the EU(27) as a whole, the EU's trade surplus with the UK is equivalent to around 0.6% of their GDP per annum (Irwin 2015: 11).

Furthermore, the trade deficit is not just an unwelcome sign of the weakness of UK international competitiveness, but it has a depressive effect upon the UK economy. Given that exports equated to 27.4% of UK GDP whilst imports represented 29.4% (World Bank 2016b), the trade deficit is equivalent to reducing UK GDP by 2% from what it would otherwise have been had trade balance been achieved.

As can be seen in Fig. 3.4, the EU is a declining market for UK trade (imports and exports). Moreover, the EU is likely to become less important over time. Part of this reason could be due to continued after-effects of the Eurozone crisis (Springford and Tilford 2014: 7), and

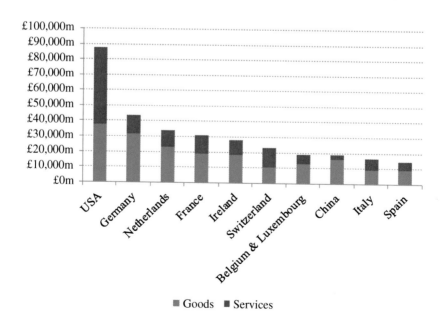

Fig. 3.5   The UK's top 10 export markets in 2014 (£m). *Source* ONS (2015), Chap. 9

the damaging policy response implemented by the leading EU nations (Baimbridge et al. 2012). Alternatively, it could reflect the rising share of trade currently being undertaken with emerging and developing nations, and because they are forecast to provide the majority of global growth in the medium term (CBI 2013: 9). Nevertheless, despite this relative decline, EU member states remain amongst the UK's largest export markets (see Fig. 3.5) and are likely to remain so into the medium term, even as trade links with nations outside the EU are strengthened and greater attention is given to export potential in these fast growing markets (Springford and Tilford 2014: 3; HMG 2016: 21).

Figure 3.6 highlights how the UK trade deficit has been temporarily financed through net inflows of FDI. Portfolio investment, although occasionally enhancing inward flows of capital, more often worsens the balance of payments position and hence make it more difficult to finance the trade deficit.

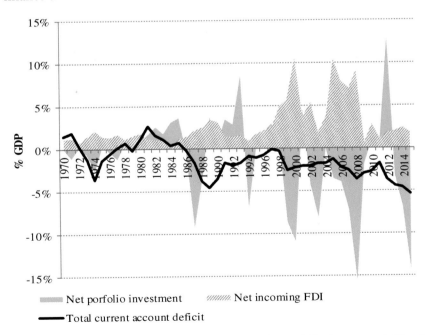

Fig. 3.6 UK current account deficit, net FDI and portfolio investment (% of GDP), 1970–2015. *Source* World Data Bank series on Portfolio investment and FDI (2016)

European Trade Integration

The promotion of European economic integration, through the creation of a common internal market, was a fundamental objective of the 1957 Treaty of Rome. Initially, this involved the creation of a customs union, involving the removal of internal customs barriers and the erection of a common external tariff with regard to non-member nations, and which came fully into force in 1968 (Europe Economics 2013: 9; HMG 2013: 22). This was intended to apply to both goods and services, although the rules relating to the latter has remained more fragmented and partial in operation (HMG 2013: 25–26). This process of trade integration was taken further by the introduction of the Single European Act, which established the creation of the Single Internal Market (SIM) by 31 December 1992, albeit that, in many key respects, the SIM remains incomplete to this day (HMG 2013: 16). Nevertheless, it certainly created a more integrated market, whilst strengthening competition policy and extending EU competence to areas of a research and development, social and environmental policy, alongside measures taken to enhance economic and social cohesion within the union.

A fundamental aspect of this approach was outlined in Article 7A, which necessitated the abolition of restrictions upon the free movement of people and capital (inputs), in addition to goods and services (outputs); known more popularly as the 'four freedoms' (EC 1996: 15; Europe Economics 2013) (see Fig. 3.7). These principles were more recently formulised in Article 3 of the Treaty on the EU and Articles 28–66 of the Treaty on the Functioning of the EU (TFEU) (Bank of England 2015: 17). The freedom of movement of economically active EU nationals was included in the Treaty of Rome, but this principle was extended through the creation of European citizenship via the Maastricht Treaty. Article 45 of the TFEU includes the right to move and reside freely within the territory of the EU member states without discrimination (HMG 2013: 24). Articles 63–66 of the TFEU further provide for the free movement of capital between EU member states and also between EU member states and outside nations, subject to certain restrictions intended to protect national tax systems, outlaw transactions related to criminal or terrorist activity, and where temporary

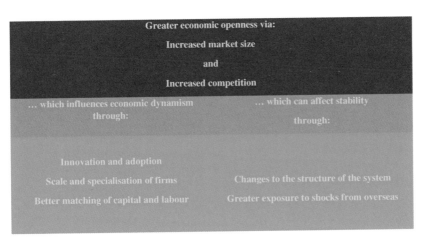

Custom duties (Arts. 28-30 TFEU)	Internal taxation (Art. 110 TFEU)	Free movement of imports (Art. 34 TFEU)	Free movement of exports (Art. 35 TFEU)	Free movement of citizens (Arts. 20-21 TFEU)	Free movement of workers (Art. 45 TFEU)	Freedom of establishment (Art. 49 TFEU)	Freedom to provide, receive services (Art. 56 TFEU)	Free movement of capital (Art. 63(1) TFEU)	Free movement of payments (Art. 63(2) TFEU)

As a member of the EU the UK has free movement of goods, services, capital and labour

THIS SUPPORTS

Greater economic openness via:

Increased market size

and

Increased competition

... which influences economic dynamism through:

... which can affect stability through:

Innovation and adoption

Scale and specialisation of firms

Better matching of capital and labour

Changes to the structure of the system

Greater exposure to shocks from overseas

Fig. 3.7 Four freedoms according to the Treaty of Rome—Overview and theoretical means of achieving dynamic effects. *Source* Authors' compilation of EU information based on material developed by the Bank of England (2015: 11). *Notes* TFEU stands for Treaty on the Functioning of the European Union (2007); Art(s) stands for Article(s)

capital controls might be required to protect the single currency (HMG 2013: 26; Bank of England 2015: 20). These temporary exchange controls have been used to protect the Cypriot and Greek economies during the recent Eurocrisis.

Empirical Studies—Initial Impact of EU Membership

For the six founding members of the EU, studies indicate that trade creation dominated trade diversion (Eicher et al. 2012; Allen et al. 1998; Magee 2008). For example, one such study estimated that the formation of the EU customs union raised intra-EU trade by 20%, whereas trade diversion only amounted to an average 3.8% (Badinger and Breuss 2011: 290). This is perhaps not particularly surprising, as the common external tariff (CET) set by the EU(6) was in line with rates previously pertaining in Germany and France, and lower than that of Italy, albeit higher than prior rates in the three Benelux nations. Therefore, the creation of free trade between the EU(6) member states would be likely to create additional trade, whilst the common tariff they employed was not sufficiently higher than previous rates to cause trade to be diverted to less efficient producers within this trade barrier.

The success of the establishment of the initial EU customs union, for its six founder member nations, led many commentators to anticipate that UK accession to the EU would result in 'dynamic gains', arising from the more intensive competition and potential for realising economies of scale that membership of a larger European market would deliver (HMG 1970: 26). Indeed, the 1970 White Paper *Britain and the European Communities* predicted that a combination of these dynamic factors, together with membership of a fast-growing European market, should result in a significant improvement to the UK's balance of payments (HMG 1970: 37).

Unfortunately, the UK's accession to the EU did not deliver such positive results. For example, when the UK joined the EU, the CET stood at an average of 17% (Badinger 2005: 50), which meant an increase in the UK's external tariff barrier. The result was a dramatic reorientation of UK trade towards other EU member states, shifting from around 20 to 40% within a decade and a half from accession

(Gasiorek et al. 2002: 425–426). However, far from this reflecting an unambiguous welfare gain, most studies, undertaken at the time, pointed to a large part of this comprising trade diversion, and that there were only negligible net trade benefits arising from EU membership. The Treasury's own calculations would suggest that, whilst the initial benefit derived from EU membership for most EU nations was an increase in inter-EU trade of around 38%, this was only 7% for the UK and, moreover, accession diverted trade from non-member states by 4% (Portes 2013: F5–6). Thus, the net benefit was only a mere 3% increase in trade. Given the Treasury's estimate that a 1% increase in trade share of GDP leads to an increase in growth of around 0.2%, then this would suggest that the trade effects arising from the UK's accession to the EU were likely to have been in the region of only 0.6% of UK GDP. Furthermore, if the loss of previous tariff revenue is included in the calculation, then accession to the EU may have had a negative impact on the UK economy (Miller and Spencer 1977: 82–85, 90).

UK accession was a little more favourable for the other EU(6) nations, as they were able to expand exports to the UK, thus producing a small 0.05% net boost to EU GDP per annum (Miller and Spencer 1977: 90). The UK suffered from a substantial increase in import penetration of the home market, as a result of eliminating tariffs with other EU member states, whilst the UK's export share of world trade contracted, as a result of the imposition of the EU's CET on former UK export markets (CEPG 1979: 31–32). Hence, the UK's trade balance deteriorated with respect to other EU member states (Winters 1985: 352). Whilst the macroeconomic impact upon the UK economy was partially obscured by the 1974 global recession, the impact can be inferred by the fact that the loss of output in the UK was more pronounced than in other developed nations (CEPG 1979: 32). One estimate suggests that, by 1977, net UK exports were around £2bn lower than would have been expected on the basis of trends prior to EU membership (Fetherston et al. 1979: 405). Moreover, this negative trade impact has never been corrected, and the UK has suffered an almost continuous trade deficit with the EU from the point of accession to the present period.[1] This has imposed a depressing effect on the UK economy (CEPG 1979: 28; Fetherston et al. 1979: 400).

A secondary effect of UK membership of the EU concerned the negative consequences of the Common Agricultural Policy (CAP) for the UK economy (CEPG 1979; Fetherston et al. 1979: 399). The CAP, combined with the effect of imposing the CET upon former sources of inexpensive food imports from Commonwealth nations, resulted in a 20% increase in food prices in the UK, which in turn caused a 0.67% adverse shift in the terms of trade (Miller and Spencer 1977: 77). This outcome was predicted in advance by the 1970 White Paper, which estimated that retail food prices were likely to increase by between 18 and 26% upon entry to the EU, with a resultant increase in the cost of living index by between 4 and 5% (HMG 1970: 42). The White Paper also predicted the UK balance of payments worsening by between £0.1bn and £1bn per annum (Wall 2012: 350).

A third negative consequence resulted from high net fiscal transfers to the EU, which were calculated to have depressed UK production by 1–2% compared to a steady-state position, with unemployment 100,000 to 200,000 higher, inflation 2–3% higher and national income 2–3.5% lower than necessary (CEPG 1979: 28–29).

Taking into account the deterioration in the UK balance of payments and the constraint imposed upon economic growth, together with the drain imposed by fiscal transfers to the EU budget and the cost of the CAP, one estimate has suggested that UK national income was fully 15% lower in 1977/1978 than it would have been had the UK not joined the EU (Fetherston et al. 1979: 405–406). Even should part of this analysis be flawed, it would seem reasonable to conclude that the initial shock, resulting from the UK joining the EU, had a negative impact upon the UK economy. This does not, of course, mean that membership of the EU has proven necessarily negative for the UK across the whole period of membership. Yet it would appear that the initial transition to membership did prove to be particularly painful for the UK, in contrast to the expectations of advocates at the time.

Empirical Studies—Medium Term Impact of EU Membership

There have been a number of studies which have sought to estimate the impact of EU membership for its member states, and a separate but related set of studies which have sought to calculate the economic impact arising from the evolution of the customs union into the Single Internal Market (SIM). These typically comprise a combination of static and dynamic gains. The former are more immediate, and derive primarily from the removal of barriers to trade, whereas the latter are more medium or long term, and may arise from the impact of competition, the realisation of economies of scale and restructuring of markets. Static effects are likely to be smaller than dynamic effects, but are more certain to calculate, as the latter depend upon longer term theoretical estimations which may or may not come to pass.

Prior to the establishment of the SIM, the European Commission produced the Cecchini Report, which attempted to quantify the predicted benefits which would arise from the SIM. These were forecast to be in the region of 4¼–6½% of EU GDP (Cecchini et al. 1988). Given the existence of the customs union, predicted benefits from further reductions in trade barriers were considered to be minor (perhaps 0.2 or 0.3% of EU GDP), whereas medium term dynamic effects, such as enhancing competition and realising economies of scale, were expected to provide the majority of forecast benefits (Emerson et al. 1998; HMG 2013: 63). A subsequent study, undertaken by Baldwin (1989: 249), suggested that these forecasts were likely to be too conservative, since they did not take into consideration additional dynamic benefits such as productivity gains. Using Romer's growth model, Baldwin argued that the Cecchini Report underestimated potential economic effects by between 40 and 250% (HMG 2013: 65). However, subsequent ex post facto (after the event) studies found that these predictions were overoptimistic; a fact that has demonstrated the difficulty inherent in *ex ante* (before the event) forecasts, but has also undermined confidence in later predictions made by the European Commission.

There have been a number of reports commissioned by the European Commission to study the impact of the SIM. For example, Monti and Buchan (1996) estimated its introduction to have increased EU output by between 1.1 and 1.5% by 1994. A second study, completed on the tenth anniversary of the foundation of the SIM, concluded that real GDP would have been an average of between 0.8 and 2.1% lower across participant nations had this measure not been implemented. Moreover, the Commission predicted further modest gains of 0.5%

by 2022 (Roeger and Sekkat 2002). A more recent study calculated that the introduction of the SIM may have raised EU GDP by around 2.18% between 1992 and 2006, thereby reducing the aggregate price-cost mark-up by 9% and boosted total factor productivity by 0.5% (Ilzkovitz et al. 2007). These predictions were subsequently slightly reduced, when extending the period under examination to 2008, with the revised economic boost being calculated to be approximately 2.13% (HMG 2013: 68–70). Most of these effects were from static analysis, with the dynamic effects proving to be much weaker than anticipated. Harrison et al. (1994) produced a slightly higher estimated gain for the EU of approximately 2.6% of EU GDP, whilst. Straathof et al. (2008) produced a slightly higher estimate of 3%.

These effects should have resulted in demonstrable improvements in the growth record of EU member states when compared to reference nations such as the USA, yet this was not the case (Badinger and Breuss 2011: 296, 308). This either suggests that the study's conclusions were over-optimistic or else that other factors (perhaps the depressing effect of the single currency and supportive economic framework) predominated any such trade effect upon economic growth.

Assessing trade impact over a longer time period, 1956–1973, and utilising a counterfactual analysis, Bayoumi and Eichengreen (1997) estimated that the annualised impact of the formation of the EU customs union for the six founder members was around 3.2% over the period. Viewing the impact of trade integration over a longer, 50 year period since 1958, Boltho and Eichengreen (2008) estimated that the whole period of European integration, from the Treaty of Rome to the date of their study, had boosted EU GDP by perhaps 5%, although SIM effects were relatively small. Conducting a similar exercise over a similar timescale, however, Straathof et al. (2008) estimated that European trade integration had increased EU GDP by only between 2 and 3%.

Other studies have found that European integration has succeeded in reducing trade barriers to a level lower than for other equivalent trading blocs (De Sousa et al. 2012), whilst competitive pressures have increased (Europe Economics 2013) and average mark-up over costs in manufacturing have been reduced by around 32% by the end of the

1990s (Badinger 2007). However, not all findings in the various studies were unambiguously positive. For example, the establishment of the SIM was noted to have encouraged a spate of cross-border mergers and acquisitions, as the EU's global share of such deals rose from just under 10% in 1985 to 28.8% 2 years later (EC 1996). Yet, whilst stimulating the development of pan-national supply chains, this development was also found to reduce the domestic share of home markets by an average of 5.4% in the 15 sectors examined in the study, inferring depressed opportunities for domestic firms in their home markets (Allen et al. 1998: 453).

Gravity models can be used to estimate differences between predicted and actual trade patterns with other nations, whilst taking account of other factors such as their relative size, wealth and spatial location relative to their trading partner(s). Declining transportation (particularly air freight) and communications costs have facilitated a general expansion in international trade and capital mobility, whilst the size of markets and levels of economic growth provide further export opportunities for domestic firms (Eichengreen and Bolitho 2008: 4–5). Hence, gravity models seek to take these factors into account and assessing whether increases in trade between nations has risen more quickly or more slowly than might have been expected, once allowing for these effects.

The gravity model approach is certainly a useful additional approach to analysing trade questions, but the importance of proximity can be over-exaggerated. For example, it remains the case that Britain's largest single trading partner remains the USA, despite its geographical distance from the UK. It would appear that cultural, linguistic and historical ties are also significant factors for a maritime trading nation such as the UK. Moreover, given the fact that new technology has significantly reduced the cost of long distance transportation, and the importance of service sector exports for the UK which typically have lower transportation costs than heavy industry, it is an open question as to whether spatial factors will decline in significance in the future and these other cultural ties will become even more important (Business for Britain 2015: 714). Brexit may, for example, reverse part of the trade diversion away from commonwealth nations which occurred upon the UK's accession to the EU. In addition, gravity models depend upon the assumption that observed elasticities remain constant even when the change in commercial relationships is rather large, such as would be the case with Brexit and the 'pessimistic' scenario of the imposition of tariff barriers. This is thought unlikely by Minford et al. (2015: 10–11).

Early gravity model analysis found, like the earlier *ex post* studies, only limited trade effects arising from European integration. Yet, this was later criticised as underestimating the true effects (Baier et al. 2008: 464, 493). The argument is a little technical, as it relates to the inclusion of the GDP of trade partners skewing the results because these variables are too closely related (correlated), thereby creating what is known as a multicollinearity effect. If the GDP of all trading partners is omitted from the analysis, it does show a much higher rate of trade creation (Europe Economics 2013: 55–56). However, the fact that this 'solution' omits key predictive variables from the model, namely the affluence of each of the trading nations, would appear equally problematic for an analysis seeking to investigate factors which influence the development of trade, given that the wealth and growth of individual economies are certainly two such key factors.

Turning from the impact of European integration on the whole of the EU, and focusing upon the specific impact upon the UK economy, the evidence would suggest that European trade integration has produced considerably less benefit for the UK than for the majority of EU member states. For example, the Treasury estimated that the creation of the SIM increased inter-EU trade by 9% for the UK, resulting in the Treasury ready-reckoner predicting a benefit to UK GDP of around 1.8% of GDP (HM Treasury 2005: 1–2). These conclusions are supported by evidence that the UK gained less than the EU average from the establishment of the SIM, as smaller economies recorded the largest gains, due to their proportionally greater exposure to trade as a share of their economy (Allen et al. 1998: 468; Deutsche Bank 2013: 5). Harrison et al. (1994: 23) produced similar findings, suggesting that the UK's benefit from the SIM was a lowly 0.8% of UK GDP, rising to 1.49% in the medium term as a result of dynamic effects, whereas comparable benefits to Belgium and the Netherlands were in excess of 6.39 and 7.73% of their national incomes, respectively.

Adopting a broader approach, which moves beyond a narrow focus upon trade integration to incorporate regulatory effects associated with the SIM and misallocation of resources resulting from the impact of the CAP, a study by Minford et al. (2005) estimated that UK GDP was between 2 and 3% lower than it might otherwise have been because of EU membership. There is some supportive evidence for this conclusion that can be drawn from work examining the trade diversion caused by the high tariff walls protecting agriculture within the EU. Indeed, Sapir (1992) found that this negative impact was larger than more positive trade creation effects created by the formation of the EU's customs union.

The SIM has not, therefore, produced the unambiguous positive economic benefits that its advocates predicted. Intra-EU trade effects have certainly occurred, although these were far lower for the UK than for the EU as a whole. Given the Treasury's ready-reckoner calculation, this would suggest that the UK has received a boost to GDP, over the period since the SIM was established, of perhaps 1.8% of GDP. This is a welcome boost, but hardly of the magnitude that would be disastrous for the UK economy were the UK to exit the SIM when it withdraws from the EU. Moreover, trade diversion risks increase when the rest of the world is growing faster than the nations within the SIM, which has been the case over the past few decades (Europe Economics 2013: 71). Furthermore, these trade effects do not appear to have translated into a reduction in unit costs in the UK, nor having stimulated an increase in research and development investment. Indeed, the SIM period has coincided with a 0.4% fall in annual R&D expenditure (Europe Economics 2013: 62–66).

The Predicted Trade-Related Impact from Brexit

The reason for outlining the evidence relating to the past impact of different phases of European integration upon international trade is because one way of viewing Brexit is to hypothesise that it involves a winding-back of this process. Thus, if the advent of the EU customs union increased intra-EU trade in the UK by 7%, or 3% after trade diversion effects are included, and the SIM by a further 9%, then were

Brexit to culminate in the UK withdrawing from the SIM and customs union in their entirety, then this may reverse the previous process and result in a decrease in intra-EU trade of around 12%.

This simplistic conclusion is, of course, dependent upon the assumption of a symmetric relationship—i.e. that exiting the EU is an exact mirror image of entry—which is unlikely to be accurate (Portes 2013: F5–6). Yet it is the simplest starting point for seeking to predict possible trade impact. Using the Treasury's ready-reckoner, that a 1% change in trade leads to an approximate 0.2% change in GDP, then an assumption of a simple reversal of former European integration effects would be expected to result in a 2.4% drop in UK GDP over time. This conclusion is, of course, rather simplistic. It ignores the potential for trade expansion for an independent UK, free to negotiate its own trade deals with the rest of the world. It also ignores the fact that trade barriers were much higher when the UK joined the EU than now prevail, and therefore the benefit of accession would be much larger than the cost of leaving.

One estimate of the cost to the UK of complete withdrawal from the EU (the so-called WTO option), was estimated at around 1.5% of value-added in manufacturing in the UK, and 0.12% for the EU(6) founder nations. If this results in a reduction in competition in UK manufacturing, the loss in value-added rises to 7.7%, with a corresponding reduction in GDP of 2.1% (Gasiorek et al. 2002: 438–439). Consequently, for this study, the direct trade effects of Brexit are predicted to be rather small, whereas *if* this subsequently led to a reduction in competition within UK industry, then dynamic effects would have a more significant potential impact (Gasiorek et al. 2002: 442).

In other studies, it is suggested that UK GDP could decline by around 2% by 2030, if relying upon WTO MFN trade rules, but only around 0.5% over the same period if a FTA was negotiated between the UK and the EU (PwC 2016: 9). Similarly, a CEPR (2013a) analysis suggested that the reduction in UK exports, resulting from the 'WTO option', would reduce UK GDP by around 1.77%, or alternatively 1.24% of UK GDP if the UK were able to use its independent status to force a new trade agreement of the TTIP type. Finally, analysis produced by Pain and Young (2004) suggested that Brexit would result in a reduction in UK GDP of around 2.5%, spread over the two decades following withdrawal.

CEP-LSE Analysis

One of the more important pieces of research, seeking to estimate the potential trade-related impact of Brexit, was conducted by a team of economists from the Centre for Economic Performance at the London School of Economics (CEP-LSE). They utilised an approach developed by Costinot and Rodriguez-Clare (2013), based upon neo-classical assumptions of perfect competition, whereby trade openness should facilitate an outward expansion of the production possibility frontier and hence boost economic welfare (Ottaviano et al. 2014b). As outlined in Chap. 1, the study constructs an 'optimistic' scenario, assuming the continuation of zero tariff trade through the European Economic Area (EEA) or a FTA, and a 'pessimistic' alternative when trade occurs under the auspices of WTO MFN rules. The study draws MFN tariff rates from WTO datasets and calculates the impact upon 35 industries across 40 countries by using United Nations Comtrade data (Ottaviano et al. 2014b: 4).

Evidence on non-tariff barriers (NTBs), such as differences in language and culture, legal barriers, currency exchange, transport and search costs, is drawn from a previous study conducted by Berden et al. (2009) examining trade between the EU and the USA. However, it is accepted that the UK is unlikely to experience similar levels of NTBs as the USA, since, at least initially, UK standards and regulations will be identical to those across the rest of the EU. Hence, the study makes the assumption that the UK incurs one quarter of the NTB costs as the USA in the 'optimistic' case and two thirds in the 'pessimistic' scenario (Dhingra et al. 2015a: 4). It is uncertain how the study arrives at such values, as there would seem to be no a priori reason why the authors should assume that UK standards would deviate considerably more from those pertaining across the rest of the SIM in the 'pessimistic' case than if a FTA was agreed, and nor why there would necessarily be any NTBs if the UK participated in the EEA.

The CEP-LSE calculations were based upon a number of other simplifying assumptions, including that the UK's withdrawal from the EU would not affect the UK's trade with the rest of the world (Dhingra et al. 2015a: 4; Ottaviano et al. 2014b: 10). It is, however, highly improbable that the UK would passively ignore the potential inherent gains from negotiating future preferential trade relationships with other nations outside the EU. Should non-EU global trade increase after Brexit, it would offset any diminution of trade with the EU and thereby lessen the impact of the conclusions reached by this study. Indeed, the NIESR analysis concedes this point (Armstrong and Portes 2016: 5).

The CEP-LSE study additionally appears to treat all trade as equally advantageous for the domestic economy (Ottaviano et al. 2014b: 4). Yet, the principle of comparative advantage does not always infer that all nations benefit from an expansion of trade, particularly when that results in their incurring a large and growing trade deficit, which will ultimately require correction or will constrain the future growth potential of the economy. An increase in the trade ratio of a nation, achieved through increasing import penetration of its economy, does not have the same macroeconomic impact as an export-led expansion. Thus, an economy with a high trade ratio, as a result of a large trade deficit, is unlikely to benefit by the same degree as if the trade ratio is slightly lower but the deficit has been eliminated and trade balance being restored.

Finally, the study relies upon the estimate made by Feyrer (2009), namely that the elasticity of income to trade is between 0.5 and 0.75. This relationship is generally in line with the findings of Frankel and Romer (1999: 394), who estimated a relationship between trade and standards of living of around 0.5, although in this case, the authors caution against over-reliance on their findings as their models only narrowly rejected the alternative hypothesis that trade has no impact on income. This is considerably larger than the 0.2 elasticity used by the UK Treasury, as reported previously in this chapter. These estimates are difficult to make, and indeed, the Feyrer (2009: 31) paper acknowledges that some of the effects that it ascribes to trade flows could be proxies for other economic integration variables, such as labour mobility or Foreign Direct Investment flows. Moreover, the model from which these estimates are drawn only explains 17% of the variation in growth rates between countries. Nevertheless, the choice of this elasticity estimate will have a significant impact upon the final predictions of the model.

The CEP-LSE analysis estimated that there would be only marginal impact upon the UK economy arising from direct tariff costs, with higher but still relatively small NTB effects (see Table 3.1). The latter is dependent upon the assumptions made that the UK would experience a relatively significant proportion of NTB costs faced by the USA, despite moving from a current position of total compliance with EU norms. However, even with these questionable assumptions, the static analysis would suggest that trade costs would be lower than fiscal savings were the UK to agree a FTA with the EU, and be only marginally higher (0.4% UK GDP) under the 'WTO option'. Consequently, the primary static economic impact, arising from Brexit, depends almost entirely upon the predictions made for *future* reductions in NTBs that the EU *plans* to make, but which may never be fully realised.

This is justified on the basis of the observation that intra-EU trade costs have fallen more rapidly than the OECD norm for a period of time, and therefore the study makes that assumption that this will continue over the following decade, resulting in a 10% decline in intra-EU trade costs which the UK would not realise if it were to withdraw (Ottaviano et al. 2014a: 3). This is questionable both because the potential for future reductions in trade barriers might be lower precisely because of previous successes in this area, but also because previous improvements occurred at a time of substantial institutional reform

Table 3.1   CEP–LSE study predicted impact of Brexit

	'Optimistic' scenario (%)	'Pessimistic' scenario (%)
Increase in Tariffs	0	−0.14
Increase in NTBs	−0.4	−0.93
Loss of benefit from any future falls in NTBs	−1.26	−2.55
Fiscal benefit	0.53	0.53
Total welfare effect (impact on real consumption)	−1.13	−3.09

Sources Ottaviano et al. (2014b): 8, Dhingra et al. (2015a): 5, (2015b): 17, (2016): 5

within the EU alongside the WTO simultaneously reducing global trade barriers, yet there are no similar substantial reforms planned in the near future. It is likely, therefore, that this element of the analysis over-states its predictions.

The CEP-LSE authors do suggest that dynamic effects may signifi-cantly increase potential economic losses, if Brexit leads to a reduction in competition, the adoption of new technology and/or productivity (Dhingra et al. 2015a: 4, 2015b: 16–17). The CEP-LSE model does not itself seek to test potential dynamic effects, but rather the authors draw this conclusion from previous studies which have suggested that dynamic effects could lie in the magnitude of double static effects. If accurate, this would indicate that the cost of Brexit could be as high as 3.5% of GDP with a FTA or 9.3% of GDP in the absence of a FTA (Ottaviano et al. 2014a: 4). However, by not testing any of this in their own analysis, these conclusions are more tentative and less rigorous than the static predictions made in this body of work.

Business for Britain Study

A study undertaken by Business for Britain examined 128,488 sub-cat-egories of export with the 27 other EU member states and an additional 29 countries in which the EU had negotiated a trade treaty by 2013. The resulting analysis suggested that UK exporters would be subject to an average tariff of 4.4% following Brexit if the UK failed to negotiate a FTA with any of the 56 nations included in the analysis, and 4.3% with the EU member states themselves. This 'WTO option' would represent the worst case scenario. Moreover, this additional tariff cost to export-ers was disproportionately concentrated upon a narrow range of export markets, such that less than 15% of UK exports were bore almost three quarters of these additional costs (Business for Britain 2015: 770–771). This fact actually makes it easier for the UK government to seek to off-set additional costs faced by those producers most adversely affected by any new tariff regime. The study calculates that around £2.8 billion of assistance would be required to offset additional export costs within the agricultural sector and a further £2 billion to non-agricultural indus-tries (Business for Britain 2015: 793–799). Given the approximately

£10 billion net savings as a result of no longer contributing to the EU budget, the report suggests that this would be easily affordable(Business for Britain 2015: 53, 772, 785–788).

Any such programme of state assistance would be subject to WTO rules, and accordingly, direct compensation for increased tariff costs would be prohibited by Article 3 of the WTO Agreement on Subsidies and Countervailing Measures of 1994. However, support for research and development, as long as this did not exceed 75% of the total cost of the R&D investment, would be allowed as would payments made to assist businesses in adapting to new environmental standards. Or, indeed, the provision of support for disadvantaged areas of the country. There would be fewer problems in relation to the food and agricultural sectors, as the rules are less specific and any assistance could be integrated within the design of agricultural and environmental support provided to the former, thus replacing the former CAP and CFP upon final withdrawal from the EU.

Minford et al.

The analysis produced by Minford et al. (2005), and latterly revised by Minford et al. (2015), highlights the significance of any misallocation of resources arising primarily from the deviation of EU trade and industry policy from the principles of free trade and neo-classical principles. In essence, the case is made that EU protectionism, through the operation of the CET, results in consumers and firms having to pay higher prices for goods than would otherwise be the case, thereby reducing economic welfare. The very high tariffs levied on agricultural products, for example, prevent the UK from consuming food at much lower world prices, and this in turn prevents the UK taking advantage of lower costs, and potentially compensatory lower wages, to boost its own competitive position as occurred with the repeal of the Corn Laws in 1846. Minford et al. (2015: 116) argue that the total cost of the CAP to the EU as a whole is around 0.9% of its GDP, whilst the earlier study placed the cost of the CAP for the UK at around 0.5% UK GDP (Minford et al. 2005: 27).

Combined with the impact of trade diversion upon the manufactured sector, Minford et al. (2015: 9) estimates that the total cost to the UK from EU trade protectionism is around 4% of GDP, when compared to the alternative of unilateral free trade which could be pursued after Brexit. This would involve the UK unilaterally dropping all tariff barriers against the rest of the world, irrespective of whether other nations maintained them against UK exports, as this would allow the UK to focus on areas of production where it has a genuine competitive advantage and import goods and services at lower global prices where this does not occur (Minford et al. 2015: 16–20). This option is discussed in a little more detail in Chap. 9.

BIS Study

In 2011, the Department for Business Innovation and Skills (BIS) undertook an analysis of the economic consequences for the UK were the EU to complete the SIM and remove all remaining barriers to trade, particularly in services (Assilloux et al. 2011). As part of this exercise, the research considered alternative economic relationships between the UK and the EU. These loosely correspond to joining the EEA, the 'WTO option' and the 'WTO option' combined with the UK joining NAFTA. The results were fairly clear. If the UK remained a full member of the EU and if the SIM was completed in full, the UK could anticipate benefits calculated at perhaps 7.1% of GDP over a 10 year period (Assilloux et al. 2011: 10). Whereas the UK would lose out on these potential gains should it leave the EU, with an additional loss of 0.3% of GDP if it joined the EEA, and a slightly smaller loss of 0.2% GDP if tariffs were reintroduced under the 'WTO option' (Assilloux et al. 2011: 14, 18). The latter is a much smaller estimate of the likely impact of introducing MFN tariffs upon UK exports, by the EU, than other studies cited in this chapter. Moreover, when examining whether joining NAFTA would have any positive benefit, the BIS analysis suggests not, as precisely the same magnitude of losses would occur as in the 'WTO option', namely 0.2% UK GDP (Assilloux et al. 2011: 18).

One difficulty with these results is that the analysis is automatically skewed by the decision to compare different Brexit scenarios with the option whereby the EU was able to fulfil what it has not thus far achieved, namely to complete the SIM in both goods and services. But what if the EU fails to achieve this objective? Thus, it would have been better to compare potential Brexit scenarios with the status quo first, and only subsequently with possible future losses that may or may not be realised. Had this been the focus of the exercise, then the BIS study would have concluded that any or all of the Brexit options that it examined—EEA membership, WTO and WTO plus NAFTA—would have generated only minor losses to the UK economy, not exceeding 0.3% of UK GDP after 10 years. This contrasts quite markedly with the results that another UK government department, the Treasury, produced during the European referendum campaign.

OECD

A study undertaken by the OECD (2016a: 20) suggested that UK exports would fall by 8.4% following Brexit, if the UK relied upon WTO MFN trade rules, and 6.4% if it negotiated a FTA with the EU but was unable to do so with the various nations where the EU had negotiated various trade agreements (OECD 2016: 19) (see Table 3.2).

These results are interesting for a number of reasons. Unlike the CEP-LSE study, where the negotiation of a FTA with the EU was estimated to cause only marginal immediate or static short term loss to the UK, the OECD assumes that the UK will be unable to negotiate a FTA with the EU by the time the withdrawal process is completed (OECD 2016a: 19). As a result, even if a FTA is agreed at a later stage, this interim period where the UK is subject to WTO MFN has a persistent negative impact upon levels of trade that are higher (at—3.1%) than in other comparable studies. It is further assumed that, even when the UK manages to negotiate a FTA with the EU, it remains unable to do so with those nations with which the EU has preferential trade agreements, and therefore trade with these third parties will be subject to WTO MFN rules. There is, however, no evidential basis to justify the OECD framing their analysis in this way.

It might, for example, take the UK longer to negotiate a FTA with the EU than the 2 year period specified in Article 50, yet this could be

Table 3.2 Predictions of UK trade changes post-Brexit - two scenarios

	Scenario 1: MFN rules for trade with the EU and other countries (%)	Scenario 2: FTA with the EU and MFN rules for trade with other countries (%)
Total UK exports	−8.1	−6.4
Intermediates		
UK exports	−8.4	−6.4
UK exports to the EU	−5.8	−3.1
UK imports from the EU	−9.4	−6.3
Final private consumption goods		
UK exports	−8.2	−6.9
UK exports to the EU	0.9	−5.9
UK imports from the EU	−9.7	−5.6
Capital goods		
UK exports	−6.1	−5.6
UK exports to the EU	6.4	0.3
UK imports from the EU	−1.1	2.2

Source Author amended table replicating OECD (2016a: 20) results
Notes MFN—Most Favorite Nation; FTA—Free Trade Area

extended by agreement between all the parties. It is also quite plausible that mutual benefits could facilitate a new trade relationship, within the 2 year period, particularly when the OECD's own predictions indicate that, in its absence, the economies of the remaining EU member states would suffer a reduction in growth rates as a result of trade turbulence following Brexit, (OECD 2016a: 22). Moreover, it has been argued, that the UK may be able to forge satisfactory trade agreements with many of these nations by the simple device of both parties agreeing to abide by the substantive terms of the agreement, based upon the principle of continuity under international law.[2]

The Loss of Future Trade Benefits from EU Membership

One regular feature of studies examining the trade impact of Brexit concerns the EU's ability to realise additional future trade benefits, through either a further reduction in trade barriers more rapidly than that achieved by the world as a whole, or the negotiation of preferential trade agreements with other nations on terms that are more favourable than those the UK as an independent nation could achieve. The inference is that, not only would the UK suffer the consequences of lower current trade benefits as a result of Brexit, but that it would miss out on these future predicted benefits.

It is difficult to assess the viability of these hypothetical scenarios. It is worthy of note that, to date, the SIM has been established for a quarter of a century and has not been very successful in securing completely unfettered trade in services. This, however, can be take either as evidence of the probability of it achieving significant future success in this area to be rather slight, or that, should it occur, there would be significant gains that could be realised and this would benefit the UK given its competitive advantage in financial and business services (Monteagudo et al. 2012; Portes 2013: F6).

Many studies utilising this argument have included in their calculations potential future benefits that could arise from the EU's negotiation of two major new FTAs, namely the Transatlantic Trade and Investment Partnership (TTIP) with the USA and the Economic Partnership Agreement (EPA) with Japan. Noting historical precedence, these trade deals are predicted to lower consumer prices within the EU, through reducing or removing trade barriers on a range of goods and thereby increasing competitive pressures (Dhingra et al. 2015a: 6; Dhingra et al. 2015b: 18). The Commission's own analysis predicts that the TTIP would result in a significant increase in trade volumes between the EU and the USA, with a permanent boost to the EU economy of 0.5% of GDP and a similar 0.4% benefit to the USA (CEPR 2013a; EC 2013: 2, 6–7). This analysis has, however, been undermined by more recent events, as the election of the new US administration, which would seem to have deferred, if not permanently derailed, the TTIP. Consequently, whilst Brexit would mean that the UK does not benefit from any of these potential benefits, they are unlikely to prove to be as significant as presented in many of these studies, because of difficulties inherent in actually securing future intra-EU reductions in barriers and because the TTIP in particular seems moribund for the foreseeable future.

Focusing upon potential lost opportunities is, of course, only one side of the balance sheet, as independence from the EU would mean that the UK could negotiate its own FTAs or EPAs with other countries. This subject is dealt with in more detail in Chap. 9, however, for now, it is reasonable to assume that the current close links between the UK and both the USA and Japan might facilitate future trade deals that should benefit all signatories. Certainly the comments made by the previous US President appear to have been superseded by a more favourable attitude, announced by his predecessor and leading members of Congress, towards a US–UK FTA.[3]

There are, furthermore, a number of other uncertainties relating to the future development of the EU, which may impact upon the UK in the future. For example, the Greek economic tragedy continues and there is the risk of further turbulence within the Eurozone, as it struggles with the after-effects of the financial crisis[4], having only barely recovered to the level of economic activity recorded at the start of 2008 (HMG 2013: 52–53). In addition, future EU enlargement offers the possibility of trade gains, although the political feasibility of Turkey gaining full access to the SIM is particularly uncertain (HMG 2013: 53–54).

Tariffs Under the 'WTO Option'

The World Trade Organisation (WTO) is the successor to the previous General Agreement on Tariffs and Trade (GATT), and it seeks to apply the principle of non-discrimination to international trade, such that one member does not treat another member less advantageously, with the exceptions of regional free trade agreements (FTAs) and customs unions such as the EU. Outside of these derogations, each nation should apply the same level of tariffs applied to its 'most favoured nation' (MFN) to all trading partners. This would preclude any punitive tariffs being imposed by a disgruntled EU, should withdrawal negotiations with the UK not proceed as it anticipates.

There has been a global trend towards falling tariff barriers, over the past three decades (CBI 2013: 51). This can be seen in Fig. 3.8.

The EU has moved broadly in line with this general trend, such that the current EU trade-weighted average MFN tariff has been estimated to be a mere 2.3% for non-agricultural products in 2015 (WTO 2015: 75) compared to an average rate of 17% in 1968 (Badinger 2005: 50). Thus, the CET has declined substantially over time (see Fig. 3.9), meaning that the cost of withdrawal from the EU in the absence of a FTA has also fallen significantly. To place this average level of tariffs into context, there has only been 1 year in which the Euro has not experienced a more than 5% fluctuation in its value from its average rate, since its establishment in 1999, yet this has had seemingly little noticeable impact upon the ability of UK companies to trade in the SIM (Business for Britain 2015: 54; Capital Economics 2016: 15). Moreover, it is the generally accepted conclusion, amongst economists, that tariff rates of 5% or below have relatively little impact upon trade (WTO 2015: 179). Thus, it is likely that, overall, the impact upon UK–EU trade is not likely to be particularly significant (Portes 2013: F5–6).

Using an augmented variant of a Solow growth model, Estevadeordal and Taylor (2008: 9–10) estimated that a 1% reduction in a tariff would produce 0.1% additional growth per annum over a period of perhaps 15 years. Hence, reversing this logic would indicate that an

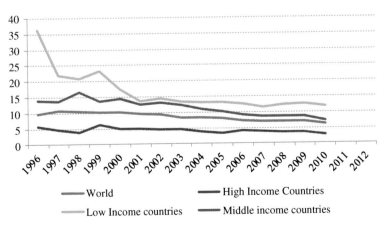

Fig. 3.8 Declining global tariff barriers (%), 1996–2011. *Source* World Data Bank (2016)

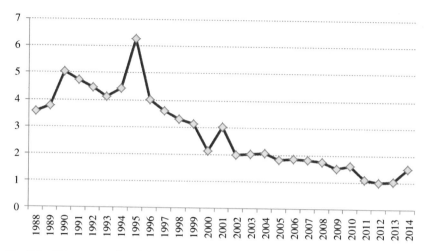

Fig. 3.9 EU average (trade-weighted) MFN tariff (%), 1988–2014. *Source* World Bank (2015)

increase in tariffs with the EU to an average trade-weighted level of around 2.3% for non-agricultural goods would indicate, *ceteris paribus*, a reduction in annual growth of around 0.23% per annum, over the short and medium term. This would equate to a reduction in UK GDP potential of perhaps 3.5–4% at the end of the 15 year timeframe, assuming that the abolition of the EU CET did not have any positive effect on UK trade with the rest of the world, which is unlikely.

The low average level of tariffs obscures the fact that tariff rates are likely to be significantly higher in certain sectors (Thompson and Harari 2013: 8; Booth et al. 2015: 27). The highest tariff rates currently levied by the EU are concentrated upon agricultural produce, such as meat and dairy produce, with effective tariff rates of around 48–49%, tobacco (44.4%), sugar (28.3%) bread and biscuits (15%) and fresh fish (9.1%). Fortunately, these industries only compose around 2.8% of UK exports, with an estimated cost of around £1.7bn, meaning that it should be relatively straightforward to build an equivalent level of support into the replacement to the CAP and CFP. The beverage industry is slightly more significant, representing a little over 2% of total UK exports, and its likely tariff rate of 8.8% is estimated to incur an additional industry cost of around £316m. Outside of the food and drink sector, other industries likely to incur a reasonably high tariff rate include clothing and footwear, which represent around 2.6% of UK exports and are likely to face tariffs ranging between 11.3 and 11.8%. Vehicle manufacture is of greater economic significance, representing around 9.5% of UK exports, such that its likely 8.5% tariff rate has been estimated to cost the industry around £1.4bn. Other significant export sectors incurring tariff rates over 5% include plastics, which represent around 3.4% of UK exports, and are likely to incur a tariff rate of 5.9% (Business for Britain 2015: 777–778).

Low levels of MFN tariffs for finished products are not, however, the only concern for UK industry. The growth of global supply chains means that around half of trade in non-fuel products is in intermediate rather than finished goods. Indeed, if financial services are included in the calculation, the intermediates share of exports increases (CBI 2013: 61) and hence the imposition of tariffs upon these intermediate products, as well as the final exported product, can amplify the impact of any tariff regime. Fortunately, for most industries, the average MFN tariffs payable upon intermediate inputs are relatively low. WTO (2015: 179, 184) data suggests that average MFN duties paid upon intermediate inputs lie at or below 2% for the majority of export sectors—i.e. petroleum, mining, office equipment, media, metals and metal products, medical equipment, chemicals and electrical machinery. Most other manufacturing, plastics and transport equipment received tariff rates of around 3%, with wood products and vehicles levied at a little over 4%, textiles around 5%, and with only agriculture and food products receiving significant tariffs of around 7 and 9% respectively.

One point that is worth noting, however, is that the UK has a current trade deficit with the EU in the majority of these markets, and therefore, were the UK to impose equivalent tariffs upon those goods imported from the EU, it would have a greater impact upon the sales of EU produce. This should reduce import penetration, given the higher prices for EU imports, and may result in a shift in focus to satisfying the demands of the domestic market for some of these producers. Higher tariff rates would have a negative impact upon consumers, who would pay higher prices for produce as a result of the imposition of tariffs, and it may impose upward pressure upon inflation.

Consequently, some economists have suggested that the UK should eliminate tariffs altogether, irrespective of whatever the EU decides to levy on UK exports, and take advantage of low global prices to enhance consumer welfare and reduce the cost of intermediate imports, thereby potentially providing some industries with a competitive advantage. This would have the consequence of promoting considerable structural change, as certain industries became less viable once exposed to global competition whilst others could expand their activities due to cheaper inputs. Another alternative would be to maintain equivalent tariff barriers against the EU, but to negotiate a series of FTAs with other nations, which would allow the importation of cheaper produce from third countries whilst providing a new market opportunity for UK companies disadvantaged by EU tariffs. An obvious option would be to re-establish the type of trading relationships that existed with Commonwealth nations prior to the UK joining the EU.[5]

Tariff barriers are not the only form of protectionism, and as they have declined, non-tariff barriers (NTBs) have become more prominent, albeit that the available evidence is that these are also being steadily reduced over time (De Sousa et al. 2012). NTBs can include (Europe Economics 2013: 12; UNCTAD 2013: 14–15; Miller 2016: 18–20):

1. Physical barriers—including customs controls.
2. Technical barriers—including different production or environmental standards, subsidies paid to domestic producers, health and safety regulation, together with public procurement restrictions.
3. Fiscal barriers—including differing rates of excise duties and VAT, alongside state aid for specific domestic industries.
4. Legal barriers—including poor protection of intellectual property rights and restrictions on foreign ownership or access to raw materials.
5. Anti-dumping measures—preventing goods being exported at a price below production costs.

Many of these NTBs are not necessarily problematic. For example, anti-dumping measures have been used by the EU against countries such as

China, most recently, in relation to the Steel industry. Moreover, many countries impose greater protection against foreign ownership in certain sectors, if these are deemed to be of particular national interest (i.e. energy, transportation, defence and security). Similarly, if the UK wishes to assert greater control over its borders, increased customs controls will be an essential part of any initiatives in this area. Yet, however justified in terms of national policy objectives, NTBs can be misused and will impose additional costs upon firms that wish to export into their markets.

Conclusions

The future of trade with the EU depends upon the type of relationship agreed following the withdrawal process. Yet, most studies suggest that even those options securing the closest market access to the SIM will incur additional costs and may result in a decline in trade between the UK and the EU. It is difficult to estimate precise cost implications for the UK, partly because of the uncertainty inherent in any counterfactual predictive analysis of this type. This is magnified by the diverse implications inherent within each of the multiple alternative future trading relationships that the UK might choose to pursue with the EU and rest of the world. Nevertheless, the CEP–LSE analysis suggests that the UK may experience only insignificant static costs, if able to negotiate a FTA with the EU, which will be more than compensated for by the depreciation of sterling. Reliance upon WTO rules is predicted to have a more substantial cost, even though trade-weighted average MFN tariffs would be only around 2.3% (WTO 2015: 75).

Most studies, however, ignored the other side of the balance sheet, which concerns the potential for trade expansion in the rest of the world, which after all purchases 56% of UK exports. If this were to expand, it would have the potential to compensate, in full or in part, for any loss of trade with the EU.

Were all of these factors taken into account by the studies cited in this chapter, it is probable that their forecasts for negative trade consequences arising from Brexit would be reduced somewhat, but it is unlikely that these effects would disappear. There is some evidence to suggest that trade linkages are highly persistent once they are established (McCallum 1995; Anderson and Van Wincoop 2003), which would suggest that UK trade patterns with the EU might be fairly robust irrespective of any impact from Brexit. However, confusingly there also appears to be evidence that suggests that once trade becomes interrupted for any reason, it may take a long time to recover (Beestermöller and Rauch 2014), which might infer a fragility in trade relationships.

Taking all of this into account, it would seem reasonable to conclude that UK withdrawal from the EU is likely to result in a short term reduction in trade with EU member states, whilst trade expansion in the rest of the world is indeterminate given the reluctance of the current set of studies to assess this potential. Longer term dynamic effects will depend upon the interplay of competitive and industrial policy effects that are not fully explored in the studies examined in this chapter. Consequently, given the very low levels of MFN tariffs, and the declining importance of NTBs, it is quite possible that Capital Economics (2016: 2) are accurate in their summation that even should the UK fail to secure a FTA with the EU, and revert to trading under WTO rules, this would be 'an inconvenience rather than a major barrier to trade'.

Notes

1. This topic is explored in more detail in Chap. 7.
2. http://www.lawyersforbritain.org/int-trade.shtml; https://www.chatham-house.org/publications/twt/preparing-uks-brexit-negotiation.
3. https://www.theguardian.com/politics/2016/apr/22/barack-obama-brexit-uk-back-of-queue-for-trade-talks; http://www.wsj.com/articles/a-new-american-deal-for-europe-1466974978?mod=wsj_review_&_out look&cb=logged0.1996315843048233; http://www.politico.com/story/2016/06/brexit-us-britain-trade-deal-224776; http://www.tel-egraph.co.uk/news/2017/01/27/congress-pushes-donald-trump-form-bilateral-trade-deal-uk/.
4. https://www.theguardian.com/business/2016/sep/27/deutsche-bank-how-did-a-beast-of-the-banking-world-get-into-this-mess.
5. These issues are dealt with in more detail in Chap. 9.

References

Allen, C., Gasiorek, M., & Smith, A. (1998). The competition effects of the single market in Europe. *Economic Policy, 27,* 439–486.

Anderson, J. E., & van Wincoop, E. (2004). Gravity with gravitas: A solution to the border puzzle. *American Economic Review, 93*(1), 170–192.

Arestis, P. (2005). Washington consensus and financial liberalisation. *Journal of Post Keynesian Economics, 27*(2), 251–270.

Armstrong, A., & Portes, J. (2016). Commentary: The economic consequences of leaving the EU. *National Institute Economic Review, 236,* 2–6.

Aussilloux, V., Boumellassa, H., Emlinger, C., & Fontagné, L. (2011). *The economic consequences for the UK and the EU of completing the single market* (BIS Economics Paper No. 11). London: Department for Business Innovation and Skills. Available via: https://www.gov.uk/government/uploads/system/uploads/attachment_data/file/83815/economic_consequences_for_the_UK_and_the_EU_of_completing_the_Single_Market.pdf.

Badinger, H. (2005). Growth effects of economic integration: Evidence from the EU member states. *Review of World Economics/Weltwirtschaftliches Archiv, 141*(1), 50–78.

Badinger, H. (2007). Has the EU's single market programme fostered competition? Testing for a decrease in mark-up ratios in EU industries. *Oxford Bulletin of Economics and Statistics, 69*(4), 497–519.

Badinger, H., & Breuss, F. (2011). The Quantitative effects of European Post-War economic integration. In M. Jovanovic (Ed.), *International handbook on the economics of integration* (pp. 285–315). Cheltenham: Edward Elgar.

Baier, S. L., Bergstrand, J. H., Egger, P., & McLaughlin, P. A. (2008). Do economic integration agreements actually work? Issues in understanding the causes and consequences of the growth of regionalism. *The World Economy, 31*(4), 461–497.

Baimbridge, M., Burkitt, B., & Whyman, P. B. (2012). The Eurozone as a flawed currency area. *Political Quarterly, 83*(1), 96–107.

Baldwin, R. E. (1989). *On the growth effects of 1992* (NBER Working Paper No. 3119). NBER: Cambridge, MA. Available via: http://www.nber.org/papers/w3119.pdf.

Baldwin, R. E., & Seghezza, E. (1996). *Testing for trade-induced investment-led growth* (NBER Working Paper No. 5416). Available via: http://www.nber.org/papers/w5416.

Bank of England. (2015). *EU Membership and the Bank of England*. London: Bank of England. Available via: http://www.bankofengland.co.uk/publications/Documents/speeches/2015/euboe211015.pdf.

Bayoumi, T., & Eichengreen, B. (1997). Is regionalism simply a diversion? Evidence from the evolution of the EC and EFTA. In T. Ito & A. O. Krueger (Eds.), *Regionalism vs. multilateral arrangements*. Chicago: University of Chicago Press.

Beestmöller, M., & Rauch, F. (2014). *A dissection of trading captial: Cultural persistence of trade in the aftermath of the fall of the iron curtain* (Working Papers No. 697). FREIT [Forum for Research on Empirical International Trade]. Available via: http://www.freit.org/WorkingPapers/Papers/TradePatterns/FREIT697.pdf.

Berden, K. G., Francois, J., Tamminen, S., Thelle, M., & Wymenga, P. (2009). *Non-tariff measures in EU-US trade and investment: An economic analysis*. Rotterdam: ECORYS. Available via: http://trade.ec.europa.eu/doclib/docs/2009/december/tradoc_145613.pdf.

Bernard, A. B., Jensen, J. B., Redding, S. J., & Schott, P. K. (2007). Firms in international trade. *Journal of Economic Perspectives, 21*(3), 105–130.

Boltho, A., & Eichengreen. B. (2008). *The economic impact of European integration* (CEPR Discussion Paper No. 6820). Available via: http://eml.berkeley.edu/~eichengr/econ_impact_euro_integ.pdf.

Booth, S., Howarth, C., Persson, M., Ruparel, R., & Swidlicki, P. (2015). *What if …? The consequences, challenges and opportunities facing Britain outside EU* (Open Europe Report 03/2015). London. Available via: http://openeurope.org.uk/intelligence/britain-and-the-eu/what-if-there-were-a-brexit/.

Business for Britain. (2015). *Change or go: How Britain would gain influence and prosper outside an unreformed EU*. London: Business for Britain. Available via: https://forbritain.org/cogwholebook.pdf.

Capital Economics. (2016). *The economics impact of 'Brexit': A paper discussing the United Kingdom' relationship with Europe and the impact of 'Brexit' on the British economy*. Oxford: Woodford Investment Management LLP. Available via: https://woodfordfunds.com/economic-impact-brexit-report/.

Confederation of British Industry (CBI). (2013). *Our global future: The business vision for a reformed EU*. London: CBI. Available via: http://www.cbi.org.uk/media/2451423/our_global_future.pdf#page=1&zoom=a uto,-119,842.

Cecchini, P., Catinat, M., & Jacquemin, A. (1988). *The European challenge 1992: The benefits of a single market*, prepared for the commission of the European communities. Aldershot: Gower.

CEPG (Cambridge Economic Policy Group). (1979). *Cambridge economic policy review* No. 5, London: Gower Press. Available via: http://cpes.org.uk/om/cambridge-economic-policy-review-volume-5.

CEPR. (2013a). *Estimating the economic impact on the UK of a transatlantic trade and investment partnership (TTIP) Agreement between the European Union and the United States*, Ref. 2BIS120020, London: Department of Business Innovation and Skills. Avalable via: https://www.gov.uk/government/uploads/system/uploads/attachment_data/file/198115/bis-13-869-economic-impact-on-uk-of-tranatlantic-trade-and-investment-partnership-between-eu-and-us.pdf.

CEPR. (2013b). *Trade and investment balance of competence review*. London: Department for Business Innovation and Skills. Available via: https://www.gov.uk/government/uploads/system/uploads/attachment_data/file/271784/bis-14-512-trade-and-investment-balance-of-competence-review-project-report.pdf.

Costinot, A., & Rodriguez-Clare, A. (2013). *Trade theory with numbers: Quantifying the consequences of globalisation*. CEPR Discussion Paper No 9398. Available via: http://www.cepr.org/pubs/dps/DP9398.asp.

Davidson, P. (2005). A post Keynesian view of the Washington consensus and how to improve it. *Journal of Post Keynesian Economics, 27*(2), 207–230.

De Sousa, J., Mayer, T., & Zignago, S. (2012). Market access in global and regional trade. *Regional Science and Urban Economics, 42*(6): 1037–1052. Available via: http://econ.sciences-po.fr/sites/default/files/file/tmayer/MA_revisionRSUE_jul2012.pdf.

Deutsche Bank. (2013). *The Single European Market—20 Years On*. Frankfurt: Deutsche Bank. Available via: https://www.dbresearch.com/PROD/DBR_INTERNET_EN-PROD/PROD0000000000322897/The+Single+European+Market+20+years+on%3A+Achievements,+unfulfilled+expectations+%26+further+potential.pdf.

Dhingra, S., Ottaviano, G. I. P., & Sampson, T. (2015a). *Should we stay or should we go? The economic consequences of leaving the EU*, Centre for Economic Performance, LSE. https://ideas.repec.org/e/pot15.html.

Dhingra, S., Ottaviano, G., & Sampson, T. (2015b). *Britain's future in Europe*. London: LSE. Available via: http://www.sdhingra.com/brexitwriteup.pdf.

Dhingra, S., Ottaviano, G., Sampson, T., & Van Reenen, J. (2016). *The consequences of Brexit for UK trade and living standards*. Centre for Economic Performance (CEP) and London School of Economics and Political Science (LSE). Available via: http://cep.lse.ac.uk/pubs/download/brexit02.pdf.

Edwards, S. (1998). Openness, productivity and growth: What do we really know? *Economic Journal, 108*(447), 383–398.

Eichengreen, B., & Boltho, A. (2008). *The economic impact of European Integration* (CEPR Discussion Paper No. 6820). London: CEPR. Available via: http://eml.berkeley.edu/~eichengr/econ_impact_euro_integ.pdf.

Eicher, T. S., Henn, C., & Papageorgiou, C. (2012). Trade creation and diversion revisited: Accounting for model uncertainty and natural trading partner effects. *Journal of Applied Econometrics, 27*(2), 296–321.

Emerson, M., Aujean, M., Catinat, M., Goybet, P., & Jacquemin, A. (1988). *The Economics of 1992.* Oxford: Oxford University Press. Available via: http://ec.europa.eu/economy_finance/publications/publication7412_en.pdf.

Estevadeordal, A., & Taylor, A. M. (2008). *Is the Washington consensus dead? Growth, openness, and the great liberalization, 1970s–2000s* (NBER Working Paper No. 14264). Available via: http://www.nber.org/papers/w14264.pdf.

Europe Economics. (2013). *Optimal integration in the single market: A synoptic review.* London: Department of Business Innovation and Skills. Available via: https://www.gov.uk/government/uploads/system/uploads/attachment_data/file/224579/bis-13-1058-europe-economics-optimal-integration-in-the-single-market-a-synoptic-review.pdf.

European Commission (EC). (2013). *Transatlantic trade and investment partnership: The economic analysis explained.* Bruselles: European Commission. Available via: http://trade.ec.europa.eu/doclib/docs/2013/september/tradoc_151787.pdf.

European Commission (EC). (1996). *Economic evaluation of the internal market* (European EconomyReports and Studies, No. 4). Luxembourg: Office for Official Publications of the European Communities. Available via: http://ec.europa.eu/archives/economy_finance/publications/archives/pdf/publication7875_en.pdf.

EC (European Commission). (2007). *Treaty of Lisbon amending the treaty on European Union and the treaty establishing the European Community* [Lisbon Treaty]. Official Journal of the European Union, 50, C306. Luxembourg: Office for Official Publications of the European Communities. Available via: http://eur-lex.europa.eu/legal-content/EN/TXT/?uri=OJ:C:2007:306:TOC.

Fetherston, M., Moore, B., & Rhodes, J. (1979). EEC membership and UK trade in manufactures. *Cambridge Journal of Economics, 3*(4), 399–407.

Feyrer, J. (2009). *Trade and income-exploiting time series in geography, technical report* (NBER Working Paper No. 14910). Available via: http://www.nber.org/papers/w14910.

Frankel, J. A., & Romer, D. (1999). Does trade cause growth? *American Economic Review, 89*(3), 379–399.

Gasiorek, M., Smith, A., & Venables, A. J. (2002). The accession of the UK to the EC: A welfare analysis. *Journal of Common Market Studies, 40*(3), 425–447.

Harrison, G., Rutherford, T., & Tarr, D. (1994). *Product standards, imperfect competition, and completion of the market in the European Union* (World Bank Policy Research Working Paper No. 1293). Available via: https://www.gtap.agecon.purdue.edu/resources/download/3524.pdf.

HM Treasury. (2005). *EU membership and trade.* Available via: https://www.gov.uk/government/uploads/system/uploads/attachment_data/file/220968/foi_eumembership_trade.pdf.

HM Government (HMG). (1970). *White paper, Britain and the European Communities: An economic assessment* (Cmnd 4289). London: HMSO.

HM Government (HMG). (2013). *Review of the balance of competences between the United Kingdom and the European Union—The single market.* London: The Stationary Office. Available via: https://www.gov.uk/government/uploads/system/uploads/attachment_data/file/227069/2901084_SingleMarket_acc.pdf.

HM Government (HMG). (2016). *The best of both Worlds: The United Kingdom's special status in a reformed European Union,* The Stationary Office, London. Available via: https://www.gov.uk/government/uploads/system/uploads/attachment_data/file/502291/54284_EU_Series_No1_Web_Accessible.pdf.

Ilzkovitz, F., Dierx, A., Kovacs, V., & Sousa, N. (2007). *Steps towards a deeper economic integration: The internal market in the 21st Century—A contribution to the single market review* (European Economy—Economic Papers No. 271). Brussels: European Commission. Available via: http://ec.europa.eu/economy_finance/publications/publication784_en.pdf.

IMF. (2016). *IMF direction of trade statistics 2016.* Washington, DC: IMF. Available via: www.data.imf.org.

Irwin, G. (2015). *Brexit: The impact on the UK and the EU.* London: Global Counsel. Available via: http://www.global-counsel.co.uk/system/files/publications/Global_Counsel_Impact_of_Brexit_June_2015.pdf.

Maddison, A. (2008). The west and the rest in the world economy: 1000–2030. *World Economy, 9*(4), 75–100.

Magee, C. S. (2008). New measures of trade creation and trade diversion. *Journal of International Economics, 75*(2), 349–362.

McCallum, J. (1995). National borders matter: Canada–US regional trade patterns. *American Economic Review, 85*(3), 615–662.

McCombie, J., & Thirwall, A. P. (1994). *Economic growth and the balance of payment constraint.* London: Macmillan.

Miller, V. (ed.). (2016). *Exiting the EU: Impact in key UK policy areas* (House of Commons Library Briefing Paper No. HC 07213). Available via: http://researchbriefings.parliament.uk/ResearchBriefing/Summary/CBP-7213#fullreport.

Miller, M., & Spencer, J. (1977). The Static economic effects of the UK joining the EEC: A general equilibrium approach. *Review of Economic Studies, 44*(1), 71–93.

Minford, P., Mahambare, V., & Nowell, E. (2005). *Should Britain leave the EU? An economic analysis of a troubled relationship.* Cheltenham: IEA and Edward Elgar.

Minford, P., Gupta, S., Le, V. P. M., Mahambare, V., & Xu, Y. (2015). *Should Britain leave the EU? An economic analysis of a troubled relationship* (2nd ed.). IEA and Edward Elgar, Cheltenham.

Monteagudo, J., Rutkowski, A., & Lorenzani, D. (2012). *The economic impact of the services directive—A first assessment following implementation* (Economic Paper No. 456). European Commission, European Economy—DG Economic and Financial Affairs. Available via: http://ec.europa.eu/economy_finance/publications/economic_paper/2012/pdf/ecp_456_en.pdf.

Monti, M., & Buchan, D. (1996). *The single market and tomorrow's Europe—A progress report from the European Commission.* Office of the Official Publications of the European Communities, Luxembourg and Kogan Page, London. Available via: http://aei.pitt.edu/42345/1/A5494.pdf.

Myrdal, G. (1957). *Economic theory and underdeveloped regions.* London: Duckworth.

OECD. (2016a). *The economic consequences of Brexit: A taxing decision* (OECD Economic Policy Paper No. 16). Available via: http://www.oecd.org/eco/The-Economic-consequences-of-Brexit-27-april-2016.pdf.

OECD. (2016b). *Trade statistics: G20 International Trade G20 (MEI).* Last updated 5 November 2016. Available via: http://stats.oecd.org/.

Office for National Statistics (ONS). (2015). *Pink book—Geographical breakdown of the current account.* London: The Stationary Office. Available via: http://webarchive.nationalarchives.gov.uk/20160105160709/   http://www.ons.gov.uk/ons/publications/re-reference-tables.html?edition=tcm%3A77-382775.

Ottaviano, G. I. P., Pessoa, J. P., Sampson, T., & Van Reenen, J. (2014a). *Brexit of Fixit? The trade and welfare effects of leaving the European Union.* LSE: Centre for Economic Performance 016. Available via: https://ideas.repec.org/p/cep/ceppap/016.html.

Ottaviano, G., Pessoa, J. P., & Sampson, T. (2014b). The costs and benefits of leaving the EU. CEP mimeo. Available via: http://cep.lse.ac.uk/pubs/download/pa016_tech.pdf.

Pain, N., & Young, G. (2004). The macroeconomic impact of UK withdrawal from the EU. *Economic Modelling, 21*: 387–408. Available via: http://www.niesr.ac.uk/sites/default/files/publications/1-s2.0-S0264999302000688-main.pdf.

Portes, J. (2013). Commentary: The economic implications for the UK of leaving the European Union. *National Institute Economic Review, 266*, F4–9. Available via: http://www.niesr.ac.uk/sites/default/files/commentary.pdf.

PricewaterhouseCoopers LLP (PwC). (2016). *Leaving the EU: Implications for the UK economy*. London: PricewaterhouseCoopers LLP. Available via: http://news.cbi.org.uk/news/leaving-eu-would-cause-a-serious-shock-to-uk-economy-new-pwc-analysis/leaving-the-eu-implications-for-the-uk-economy/.

Rodriguez, F., & Rodrik, D. (2000). Trade policy and economic growth: A sceptic's guide to the cross-national evidence. *NBER Macroeconomics Annual, 15*, 261–325.

Rodrik, D. (2006). Goodbye Washington consensus, Hello Washington confusion? *Journal of Economic Literature, 44*(4), 973–987.

Roeger, W., & Sekkat, K. (2002). Macroeconomic effects of the single market program after 10 Years, background paper of the European Commission, Brussels, II- A- 1/W D(2002).

Sapir, A. (1992). Regional integration in Europe. *Economic Journal, 102*(514), 1491–1506.

Singh, K. (2000). *Taming global financial flows: Challenges and alternatives in the era of financial globalisation*. London: Zed Books.

Springford, J., & Tilford, S. (2014). *The great British trade-off: The impact of leaving the EU on the UK's trade and investment*. London: Centre for European Reform. Available via: http://www.cer.org.uk/publications/archive/policy-brief/2014/great-british-trade-impact-leaving-eu-uks-trade-and-investmen.

Straathof, S., Linders, G.-J., Lejour, A., & Mohlmann, J. (2008). *The internal market and the Dutch economy: Implications for trade and economic growth* (CPG Netherlands Document No. 168). Available via: http://www.cpb.nl/sites/default/files/publicaties/download/internal-market-and-dutch-economy-implications-trade-and-economic-growth.pdf.

TFEU (Treaty on the Functioning of the European Union). (2007). Consolidated version of the treaty on the functioning of the European

Union. *Official Journal of the European Union* (26.10.2012). Vol. C 326, 47–390. Available via: http://eur-lex.europa.eu/legal-content/EN/TXT/ PDF/?uri=CELEX:12012E/TXT&from=EN.

Thompson, G., & Harari, D. (2013). *The economic impact of EU membership on the UK* (House of Commons Library Briefing Paper SN/EP/6730). Available via: http://researchbriefings.parliament.uk/ResearchBriefing/ Summary/SN06730#fullreport.

United Nations Conference on Trade and Development (UNCTAD). (2013). *Non-Tariff measures to trade*. Geneva: United Nations. Available via: http:// unctad.org/en/PublicationsLibrary/ditctab20121_en.pdf.

Viner, J. (1950). *The customs union issue* (2014 ed.). Oxford: Oxford University Press.

Wall, S. (2012). *The official history of Britain and the European community—Vol 2*. London: Routledge.

Webb, D., Keep, M., & Wilton, M. (2015). *In brief: UK-EU economic relations* (House of Commons Library Briefing Paper (HC 06091)). London: The Stationary Office. Available via: http://researchbriefings.parliament.uk/ ResearchBriefing/Summary/SN06091.

Williamson, J. (2004). The strange history of the Washington consensus. *Journal of Post Keynesian Economics, 27*(2), 195–206.

Winters, L. A. (1985). Separability and the modelling of international economic integration—UK exports to five industrial countries. *European Economic Review, 27*(3), 335–353.

World Bank. (2015). *MFN (Most Favourite Nation) tariff rate 1988–2014*. Available via: http://data.worldbank.org/indicator/TM.TAX.MRCH. WM.AR.ZS?locations=EU.

World Data Bank. (2016a). Tariff rate series. World Development Indicators.

World Bank. (2016b). *Trade as percent of GDP Report*. Available via: http:// databank.worldbank.org/data/reports.aspx?source=2&series=NE.TRD. GNFS.ZS&country=GBR.

World Trade Organisation (WTO). (2013). *Factors shaping the future of world trade* (World Trade Report 2013). Geneva: World Trade Organisation. Available via: https://www.wto.org/english/res_e/booksp_e/world_trade_ report13_e.pdf.

World Trade Organisation (WTO). (2015). *World Tariff Profiles 2015*. Geneva: WTO. Available via: https://www.wto.org/english/res_e/booksp_e/tariff_ profiles15_e.pdf.

4

Foreign Direct Investment (FDI)

The inflow of Foreign Direct Investment (FDI) is typically associated with a variety of economic benefits, ranging from increased productivity to enhanced innovation and technological development. The UK has been relatively successful in attracting inward flows of FDI, and consequently it has been one of the areas where it is suggested that Brexit may have a negative impact. Thus, it is important to assess the veracity of predictions made by the various studies which have examined this question, to test whether these provide a firm evidence base for UK policy makers with the responsibility to manage the transition towards independence from the EU.

Definition—What Is FDI?

Foreign Direct Investment (FDI)[1] may be defined as the acquisition by firms, governments or individuals, in one (source) country, of assets in another (host) nation, for the purpose of controlling the production, distribution and/or other productive activities. It is the aspect of control of the productive process which distinguishes FDI from the more

© The Author(s) 2017
P.B. Whyman and A.I. Petrescu, *The Economics of Brexit*,
DOI 10.1007/978-3-319-58283-2_4

passive international portfolio investment—i.e. where firms, governments or individuals purchase securities, including shares and bonds, in another country. Whereas portfolio investment is typically undertaken to spread risk by diversifying holdings in multiple securities, and where investors do not typically seek to influence the management of the organisation, FDI involves the concentration of investment specifically in order to control production. It is not a short term investment, but rather seeks to acquire a long term controlling interest (IMF 2013). This has been defined by the IMF (2013) as exceeding 10% of equity ownership, whereas for the OECD (2008: 17), it relates to where the direct investor owning at least 10% of the voting power of the direct investment organisation.

The international business literature proposes that firms tend to consider FDI once they have developed certain competitive advantages that they feel they can more effectively exploit by engaging in a strategic location of production abroad. Hence, rather than export goods and services, they may choose to maintain direct control over the process in order to minimise transaction costs and/or to retain control over technological and other elements of the production process together with organisation knowledge (Morgan 1997). Assuming rational action, firms must be responding to, firstly, incentives to locate production abroad, rather than export from their existing home base, and secondly, a separate set of incentives to internalise the production process. The latter may centre upon the perceived risk inherent within the principal-agent problem. This occurs when the owner (or principle) has to reply upon an agent to fulfil objectives established by the principal, and this has the potential to lead to sub-optimal solutions, due to differences in self-interest. Resolution of the principle-agent problem may require costly solutions, involving the provision of additional incentives for the agent or otherwise intensive monitoring of their activities. Risks may include the threat of theft of technological knowledge, or, less dramatically, the provision of greater opportunities for the diffusion of technological knowledge and hence erosion of competitive advantage, together with possible loss of reputation and goodwill due to the operations of low quality franchise operations.

FDI can take a number of forms:

1. Greenfield investment—this is where a foreign-based company establishes a new enterprise, as a subsidiary
2. Mergers and Acquisitions (M&A)—i.e. when an existing firm is taken-over by a foreign owner
3. Acquisition of share capital in an existing subsidiary, joint venture or through purchasing a sizeable stake in an existing firm sufficient to ensure a lasting management involvement
4. Acquisition of loan capital, such as corporate bonds, which provides a similar involvement in the management of the enterprise as (3)
5. Lending to an existing subsidiary
6. Unremitted profit being re-invested in the host economy rather than being remitted to the home parent company.

Magnitude of FDI

The UK has been consistently effective in attracting inward flows of investment. According to the latest figures, the UK attracted a record number of foreign investment projects,[2] although that does not

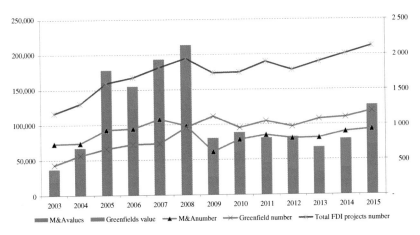

Fig. 4.1   Value and number of FDI projects in the UK, 2003–2015, at current prices (US$m). *Source* UNCTAD (2016b)

Panel A. Over the period 1970 -1990.

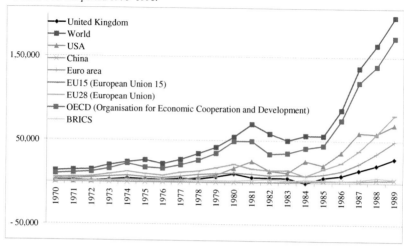

Panel B. Over the period 1990-2014.

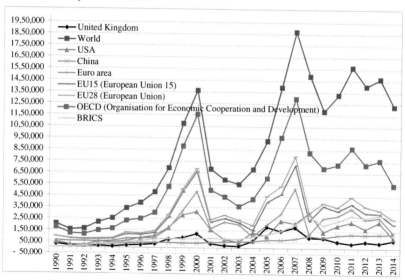

Fig. 4.2 UK inward FDI flows, comparison across world and selected countries, in million US Dollars. *Source* UNCTAD (2016b). *Notes* Measured in million US Dollars at 2014 prices and 2014 exchange rates. Panel A and Panel B have a different scale on the vertical axis, in order to allow for an easier comparison

necessarily equate to a record magnitude of inward FDI flows, as can be seen from Fig. 4.1. The high point for the value of FDI flows was actually in 2008, immediately prior to the global financial crisis.

As illustrated in Fig. 4.2, the UK has remained fairly consistently the largest recipient of inward FDI within the EU (UKTI 2015). It is possible that one reason for this has been the success of the UK in attracting the European headquarters of firms based outside the EU (HMG 2013: 39), although government Ministers prefer to emphasise the supportive economic environment created for business activities within the UK (UKTI 2015).

Placing these achievements into a broader global context, UK attractiveness for inward FDI flows compares rather well with many of the leading individual economies, albeit only ever attracting a small fraction of overall global FDI flows (see Fig. 4.2). In 2015, the UK was ranked as the twelfth largest recipient of inward FDI flows, receiving inward investment of around £26.7 billion, which is a significant net boost to the national economy. However, UK investment levels were significantly lower than the three largest recipients of global FDI for that year, namely the USA, China and Hong Kong (UNCTAD 2016a: 5).

There is, however, considerable volatility in recorded levels of global inward FDI flows, which obscures the relative ranking of individual nations (see Fig. 4.3). For example, in 2015, the UK received £34.7 billion and was the seventh largest FDI recipient, whilst in 2014 and 2013, the equivalent figures were £48 billion and £32 billion, and being ranked fourth and ninth largest recipient, respectively (UNCTAD 2015a: 71).

One reason for recorded volatility derives from the impact that a small number of very large investments or disinvestments can make upon one year's figures. A second concerns the large shifts in recorded FDI arising from intracompany loans—i.e. where a parent company, located in a home economy, can advance a load to a subsidiary located in a separate host economy, or vice versa (UNCTAD 2015a: 73). These loans may be designed to facilitate strategic investment activity, or to benefit from differentials in national interest rates, or to evade national regulation and/or taxation through a form of transfer pricing (see for example, UNCTAD 2015a: 190–197). Consequently, it is perhaps better to view FDI flows

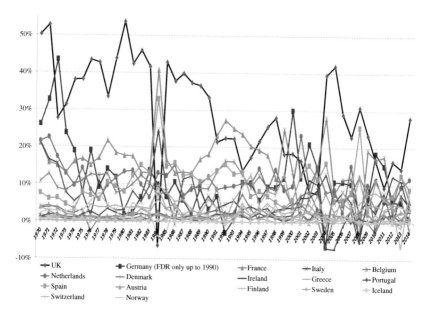

Fig. 4.3 Proportion of inward EU FDI (% of total EU inward investment flows), 1970–2014. *Source* UNCTAD (2016b). *Notes* A country's share of EU FDI is calculated as a percentage out of the total EU inward FDI for the respective year. Shares of inward FDI are shown for all countries, however: the UK, Denmark and Ireland joined the EU in 1973, Greece in 1981, Portugal and Spain in 1986, while Austria, Finland and Sweden joined in 1995. Three non-EU member states are also shown, for comparative purposes, namely Iceland, Switzerland and Norway

over a period of time rather than concentrate too heavily upon 1 year's figures. When viewed on that basis, over the past two decades, the UK has been consistently one of the largest recipients of inward FDI amongst advanced economies, and received the largest share amongst EU economies (Driffield et al. 2013: 9–10; Bank of England 2015: 4). One set of estimates suggests that, over the past decade, it has ranked fourth in the world, behind the USA, China and India, hosting around 19% of new FDI projects located in Europe, compared to France with 14.7% and Germany with 12.7% (EY 2015: 11).

When comparing the frequency of inward FDI flowing into the UK with global FDI flows, however, the achievement is slightly less impressive, as UK historical rates of inward FDI have conformed quite closely

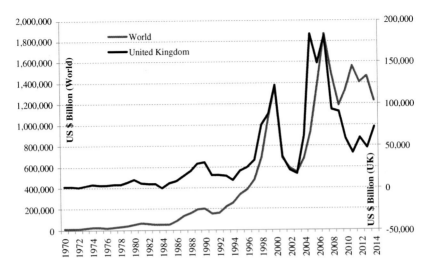

Fig. 4.4 Comparison of the flows of inward FDI into the UK and World, 1970–2014). *Source* UNCTAD (2016b)

to overall global patterns. This is illustrated in Fig. 4.4, where global FDI is represented by a different scale to UK inward investment on the plural y-axes. Accordingly, this diagram indicates that the rise in inward UK flows have occurred according to a similar trend as the expansion of global flows, albeit according to a different magnitude. Thus, whilst the UK is particularly attractive as a host for FDI investment within Europe, it is largely performing in accordance with, rather than superseding, world trends.

Moreover, as highlighted in Fig. 4.2, there is evidence that developing economies, and Europe in particular, may be experiencing a gradual decline in their share of global inward FDI flows, as emerging and developing economies absorb an increasing proportion of total international investment (Driffield et al. 2013: 8; UNCTAD 2015a: 30). The period of most pronounced decline in the share of inward investment going to developed economies coincided with the 2008 financial crisis, and it is therefore quite possible that this reflects a temporary phenomenon rather than a permanent shift in the attractiveness of developed economies as the location for inward investors. Indeed, according to the very latest data, there was a sharp recovery recorded in the flows of FDI destined for Europe and America in 2015 (UNCTAD 2016a: 4). Thus, without the benefit of a few more years of data, it is problematic to correctly forecast the future development of FDI flows into the developed nations, including the UK.

Discussion of inward FDI should not, however, detract from the fact that the UK is a net outward investor, with a larger external than internal stock of FDI. In 2015, for example, UNCTAD (2016a: 200) records that the UK held around £1025.4 billion of outward FDI stock whereas inward investor stock in the UK accounted for £971.6 billion—a 5.5% surplus of outward over inward investment stock. Indeed, the UK remains the third largest source of outward FDI behind the USA and Germany. Outward investment may benefit the UK if it leads to the strengthening of UK firms, through facilitating technology transfer and/or economies of scale resulting from enhanced market opportunities, and it should lead to future benefits for the balance of payments as profits made overseas are partially repatriated to the home company. However, these advantages are longer term than the short run loss of investment and reduction in demand in the home economy arising from the outflow of this investment capital.

It should additionally be noted that these values of FDI stock are significantly less significant than recorded levels of portfolio investment, which are between ten and 15 times larger (HMG 2013: 39).

Origin of FDI

The EU is the source for approximately 46% of the stock of inward FDI for the UK (Bank of England 2015: 91). This represents a significant shift since 2001 (see Fig. 4.5), when almost half of inward investment originated in the Americas, and with only a third of the total from the EU (Driffield et al. 2013: 9–10, 56–7). The peak level of EU investment flows into the UK occurred in 2009 (Irwin 2015: 12). The EU's share of UK outward FDI is a little smaller, at around 43%, but this is still a higher proportion of the total than the USA and

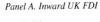

Panel A. Inward UK FDI

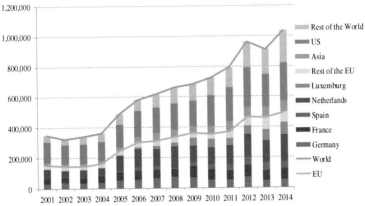

Panel B. Outward UK FDI

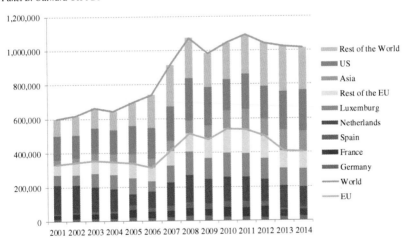

Fig. 4.5 The Stock of inward and outward UK FDI, by selected geographical areas and country, 2001–2014. *Source* ONS (2017)

Asia combined. Again, this represents a similar shift from the 1990s, when the USA would have represented around half of the total (Bank of England 2015: 91).

Composition of FDI

Whilst the popular conception of FDI may revolve around the construction of a Japanese car plant on a 'greenfield' site, somewhere in the North East or the Midlands, the reality is that the vast majority of inward FDI into the UK involves mergers and acquisitions (M&A)—i.e. the take-over of an existing British company (Driffield et al. 2013: 11). This is illustrated in Fig. 4.6. Relatively liberal UK laws concerning corporate ownership and the take-over of domestic companies have facilitated these purchases (Milne 2004: 21–22).

The overwhelming majority of FDI occurs in the service sector, rather than in manufacturing, and this share has been increasing in recent years (see Fig. 4.7). Thus, in 2014, fully 71% of inward FDI stock was located in the service sector, whilst manufacturing accounted for 19% and the primary sector, which comprises mainly of mining and energy extraction industries, the remaining 10%. Global figures for inward FDI indicate that investment tends to be focused upon services, as they received approximately 63% of all inward FDI in 2012, compared to 26% for manufacturing and 10% in the primary sector

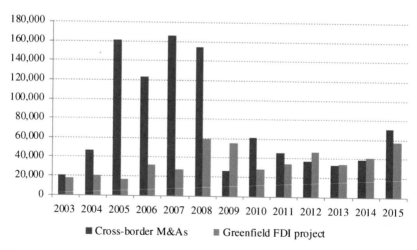

Fig. 4.6 The value of cross-border Mergers and Acquisitions (M&As) compared to greenfield FDI projects in the UK, 2003–2015 (US$m). *Source* UNCTAD (2016a) annex tables

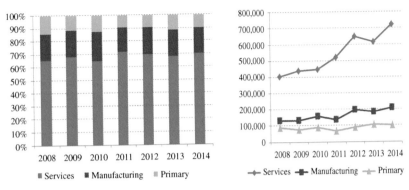

Fig. 4.7 Net inward FDI stock in the UK by sector, 2008–2014 (% and £m). *Source* Authors' compilation of data, based on ONS (2014a) and ONS (2010): 79. *Notes* All values are in 2011 prices (values of prices in 2011)

(UNCTAD 2015a: 12). UK figures therefore follow this general trend, albeit that the dominance of the service sector in UK inward FDI is disproportionately greater than the global position.

The composition of FDI matters for two main reasons. The first relates to whether or not inward investment has a significant impact upon the UK economy. It is easy to conceive that 'greenfield' investment is likely to have a net positive effect upon employment and output, because this is adding an element of production of goods or services that did not previously exist, unless, of course, it displaces existing production carried out by UK firms who may have to reduce output as a result of the new competition. Yet, even here, the expectation would be that there should be efficiency gains as a result of the FDI.

The situation is less clear cut with inward FDI that involves a foreign take-over of an existing UK-owned firm. Whilst it is certainly positive in balance of payments terms, that finance flows into the UK economy to pay the existing shareholders for their selling their shares to the new owners, it is not certain that this money will be utilised to invest in other UK enterprises. Indeed, it could be alternatively invested in non-productive assets, such as paintings, or less productive assets such as real estate, or alternatively transferred to holdings in other nations either via outward FDI or portfolio investment. For the business itself, the transfer of ownership may bring in new techniques, technology and/or expand operations, thereby generating additional output and employment opportunities, or it may not. Indeed, it is perfectly possible that the new owners may wish to run down UK operations of their new acquisition, in order to reduce competition for their existing operations. Consequently, the net effect of inward FDI needs to be assessed on a case by case basis, rather than be assumed to be inevitably positive.

The second reason why the composition of FDI is important when seeking to ascertain its potential impact upon the UK economy, relates to the diverse ability of businesses, working in different sectors, to deliver the increased dynamism that may be found in theory textbooks. For example, it may prove easier for manufacturing than in many areas of the service sector, for FDI to introduce newer forms of technology, innovation and deliver skills spillovers to the UK economy, with consequent impact upon productivity and an improvement in the balance of payments.

Determinants of FDI

The ability to attract inward flows of FDI depends upon many different factors, including:

1. The size and growth of the host market—current and future demand conditions signal inward investors (Pain and Lansbury 1997; Driffield and Munday 2000).
2. Access to resources or strategic assets, such as technology or production methods protected by legal patent, to which the TNC wishes to gain access (Dunning 1988).
3. The degree of openness (Pain and Lansbury 1997; Driffield et al. 2013: 27).
4. Economic stability (HMG 2013: 40).
5. The strength of commercial law, contract enforcement (including intellectual property) and the predictability of the business climate (UNCTAD 2015a: 177).
6. Distance and transportation costs (Egger and Pfaffermayr 2004).

7. Infrastructure (Fredriksson et al. 2003).
8. Corporate tax rates (Hines 1996).
9. The cost of factors of production (UNCTAD 2015a: 177). This can be affected by access to low cost capital, whilst relative unit costs may be influenced by government policy, as the maintenance of a buoyant level of aggregate demand is associated with lower unit costs (Arestis and Mariscal 1997, 2000).
10. Labour skill levels and labour market flexibility (Haaland and Wooton 2007; HM Treasury 2003).
11. The quality of institutions (Wren and Jones 2012).
12. Exchange rates (Froot and Stein 1991).
13. Agglomeration (clustering) (Driffield et al. 2013: 36; Driffield and Munday 2000).
14. English language ability (HMG 2013: 40).

The relative significance of the various factors is difficult to establish, and may change over time. These individual factors can be grouped together to highlight three main motivations underlying FDI, namely (UNCTAD 2015a: 177):

1. *Resource-seeking investments*—Inward investment of this type is often concerned with gaining access to raw materials or different types of technology, in order to facilitate production. These firms tend to be relatively capital intensive and therefore they can be sensitive to policy or cost changes which may impact upon their long term returns.
2. *Market-seeking investments*—Inward investors within this category are more concerned with finding new markets for their products than with inputs to their productive processes. Thus, they are primarily concerned with market *demand* and less concerned with supply factors. The fact that the UK is the fifth largest economy in the world is of particular significance for inward investors, however there will be a proportion of TNCs who operate within the UK as a 'export platform' to the SIM (HMG 2013: 40) and who may consider the relocation of certain activities elsewhere within the EU.
3. *Efficiency-seeking investments*—This group of inward investors are more concerned with the cost and efficiency of their inputs (i.e.

capital, labour and raw materials) and the costs inherent in maintaining their supply chains, rather than the demand for their products. They are, therefore, sensitive to the differential costs of factors of production and the impact of economic policy decisions upon their business model, including taxation but also regulations impacting upon trading costs. In the latest available Global Competitiveness Index, produced by the World Economic Forum, the UK ranks ninth out of 144 nations.[3] Moreover, since Brexit, the devaluation of sterling will have further enhanced the competitive position of the UK for this group of international investors.

The significance of the different motivations may help to explain why, for example, TNCs state concern over the cost of labour within different nations, yet the majority of FDI stock is invested in high wage and relatively high tax developed economies (Weiss 1998: 186).

EU Membership

The significance of current EU membership, and the future impact upon FDI arising from the different models of trade relationship that the UK negotiates with the EU upon its withdrawal, derives from how more limited access to the SIM may impact upon inward flows of FDI. Those studies which have examined the issue have typically found that EU membership has coincided with an increase in inward FDI over and above the levels that might have been expected given the increase in international investment flows over time (Barrell and Pain 1998; Deutsche Bank 2013: 10). Furthermore, it has been suggested that the advent of the SIM played a significant role in making EU nations more attractive to international investors, and hence diverted FDI towards EU member states (Baldwin et al. 1996).

It is difficult, however, to isolate the impact of one variable out of so many, over a 40 year time period, and it has proven even more difficult to establish the means by which any theoretical benefit might be translated to the UK real economy (Rodrik 2008; Miller 2016: 27). For example, Ramasamy and Yeung (2010) suggest that, rather than EU membership being a decisive factor, it is rather the degree of openness of a nation which determines inward FDI flows. Yet, very few studies have sought to disentangle these two possible variables.

Moreover, whilst advocates for greater regional economic integration argued that inward flows of FDI into the UK would be damaged by reluctance to join the single currency (e.g. Begg et al. 2003: 5, 28), this turned out not to be the case, suggesting that it is uncertainty that is more of a problem than closer economic integration with the EU per se (Driffield et al. 2013: 44). This might suggest, therefore, that, once the UK government has established a clear new relationship with the EU post-Brexit, previous advantages will reassert themselves and inward flows of FDI may not be deterred.

Impact of FDI upon the UK Economy

Theoretical Effects

Foreign Direct Investment (FDI) is associated with the import of capital and the introduction of new technology (Barrell and Pain 1997; Driffield and Taylor 2006; Pain and Wakelin 1998). Together with the introduction of innovative forms of work organisation (Bloom et al. 2012b), and competitive effects (Bank of England 2015: 38), this may thereby potentially improve aggregate productivity and allocative efficiency, whilst facilitating the rising skill level of the workforce through the provision of high-skill employment opportunities (Dunning 1988; De Mello 1999; Harris and Robinson 2002). Technological and productivity spillovers may produce beneficial externalities for domestic producers (Borensztein et al. 1998; Aitken and Harrison 1999; Driffeld and Munday 2000). Furthermore, inward investment may generate an expansion in employment opportunities (Dunning 1993) and additionally provide an important source of government revenues (UNCTAD 2015a: 184).

The significance of FDI for labour productivity can be inferred from studies which have highlighted the fact that exporting firms have significantly higher productivity levels than firms servicing the domestic market, whilst TNCs are found to have significantly higher levels of productivity than domestic owned firms (Griffith et al. 2004; Helpman et al. 2004; Keller and Yeaple 2009). This finding appears to hold for the UK (Haskel et al. 2002). Furthermore, the Treasury concluded that a 1% increase in the stock of inward investment is associated with a 0.04% increase in the level of technology, with subsequent productivity effects (HM Treasury 2016: 182).

This benign view of FDI, and the apparent technological and productivity advantages arising from export-orientated firms, is challenged on the basis that these advantages are merely selection effects—i.e. that more efficient firms tend to seek to capitalise on their existing advantages through exporting to reach a larger market, rather than the process of exporting subsequently bestows these advantages. As a result, public policy designed to attract inward FDI and enhance exporting will have only a weak impact upon aggregate productivity and technological capacity within the economy (Rodrik 2004: 30). Indeed, whilst the economic theory suggests a positive relationship between FDI and various measures of improved performance, at firm and economy level, very few of these studies are able to substantiate these assumptions and/or the direction of any causality (Görg and Greenaway 2004; Driffield et al. 2013: 25).

Net effects are, however, often difficult to identify (Driffield et al. 2013: 25). Certain studies may suggest that FDI leads to rising investment in the domestic manufacturing sector (Driffield and Hughes 2003), producing capital deepening effects as domestic producers upgrade their own capital stock (De Mello 1999). However, other research concludes that domestic firms react to increased competition generated by FDI by reducing output and investment, at least in the short term (Buffie 1993; Aitken and Harrison 1999), and thus FDI replaces rather than supplements domestic capital formation (Hejazi and Pauly 2003).

The net impact of FDI will depend upon long-term repatriation of profits to the home economy and the fact that initial inward capital transfer may be offset by a reluctance to permit inter-subsidiary competition. In addition, FDI may attract employment away from existing producers, thus causing a loss of employment in the domestic sector (Driffield and Taylor 2000; Driffield et al. 2013: 15–16). It may also involve 'reverse spillovers'—i.e. when inward investment occurs in order to secure access to technology otherwise unavailable to the home company (Driffield and Love 2003). Deadweight effects arise from a reduction in competition arising from the takeover of an existing producer, whether inadvertently or as a strategic intent to displace local producers in order to increase potential monopoly profits (Hymer 1960; Cowling and Sugden 1987). Indeed, the Preface to the most recent UCTAD (2016) report on this topic may hint at this problem when it noted that substantial recorded increases in FDI flows in recent years have not led to an equivalent increase in productive capacity.

FDI can, therefore, be a compliment or substitute for international trade (Grossman and Helpman 1994: 39; USITC 2000: 4–19). The traditional Heckscher-Ohlin-Samuelson approach treats FDI and trade as substitutes, given that the international mobility of factors of production may substitute for international trade, as production occurs locally in the host economy rather than in the home economy and being exported to the other nation (Dunning 1988; Liu et al. 2001). However, this need not be the case. For example, whilst market-seeking FDI might substitute localised production for previous export activity, efficiency-seeking FDI may complement trade (Gray 1988). WTO (2013: 84) analysis indicates a modest positive association between the foreign content of exports and the level of gross manufacturing exports, although this apparent relationship does not prove causality. In other words, it does not prove whether a rising share of foreign owned exports leads to increased export activity in the host economy, or whether this form of FDI is attracted by this superior export track record. Hence, the question of whether FDI and trade are compliments and substitutes depends which of these motivations for FDI predominate.

Notwithstanding these reservations, the attraction of inward flows of FDI has become an important policy objective for national governments and regional development agencies (Young et al. 1994; Wren and Taylor 1999). Under the correct conditions, FDI may have the potential to improve the competitive position of both home and host economies, and can enhance local economic development. However, this is not automatic and it depends upon the policy framework within which FDI operates (OECD 2008: 14). Indeed, advocates of unilateral free trade suggest that this would make reliance upon spillovers from FDI unnecessary, as the economic structure of the UK economy would shift towards its underlying competitive advantages a natural consequence of having to compete at world prices (Minford et al. 2005: 14–15).

FDI and the UK Economy

The UK is disproportionately reliant upon the continuing flow of inward FDI (see Fig. 4.8). In part, this is a consequence of the small size and scope of its manufacturing sector. Proposals to re-balance the UK economy would, if realised, facilitate an expansion of UK manufacturing and, as a result, would reduce the over-dependence upon FDI. Brexit could facilitate this process (see Chap. 8). However, in the short term, until these effects are realised, the magnitude of FDI flows and persistence of spillover effects will remain particularly important for the UK economy.

The approximately 45,000 foreign affiliates operating within the UK economy represent less than 2% of the total number of firms, yet they

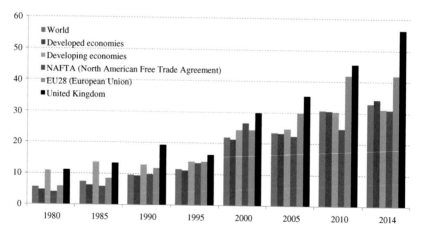

Fig. 4.8 FDI stocks as percentage of gross domestic product for the UK and Selected Global Regions, 1980–2014. *Source* UNCTAD (2016b)

account for around 13% of the UK employment and a little over a third of total output (Driffield et al. 2013: 5, 12). In the manufacturing sector, foreign owned firms are even more pronounced, accounting for around 42% of manufacturing investment and 38% of manufacturing output (Driffield et al. 2013: 64–65). Thus, despite the difficulty experienced by economic studies in measuring the impact of possible positive spillovers upon national economies, there is limited evidence to suggest that this may provide a modest benefit to the UK (Haskel et al. 2002; Aghion et al. 2009).

One area in which FDI is particularly important for the UK economy concerns research and development (R&D) expenditure, where foreign owned firms undertook slightly over half of the UK's total R&D spend in the three most recent years where data is available (see Fig. 4.9). The dominance of foreign owned firms is even more pronounced in the motor vehicle industry, where they accounted for approximately 80% of all R&D expenditure between 2001 and 2010; the equivalent share of R&D expenditures exceeded 40% of the UK total in the consumer electronics, machinery and equipment, optical and precision instruments, computer programming, food products,

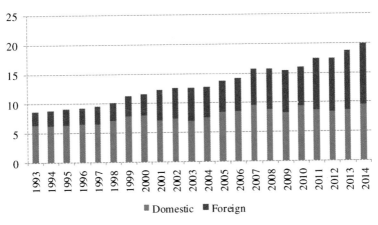

Fig. 4.9 Expenditure in R&D performed in UK business by foreign and domestic firms in current prices (£bn), 1993–2014. *Source* The authors, based on ONS (2014b)

beverages and tobacco, and finally the chemical sector, (Driffield et al. 2013: 64).

This is important for three reasons. Firstly, R&D investment provides a boost to current aggregate demand whilst providing a simultaneous potential enlargement to future productive capacity. Secondly, R&D investment is a primary means for delivering innovation and/or technological change. Both of which will have a potential impact upon economic growth. Thirdly, this disproportionate reliance upon foreign owned firms to deliver crucial innovation and technological advance demonstrates both the significance that FDI plays in driving the efficiency of the UK economy, but also the relative weakness of domestic firms and the consequent fragility of the UK economy due to its continued reliance upon firms with fewer natural anchors to the UK economy.

Paradoxically, therefore, Brexit can provide both a threat to UK prosperity, if it results in the UK being a less attractive destination for these foreign owned firms, with the result of a medium term decline in R&D and hence reducing future growth potential. However, it may also enable UK public policy to seek to reinvigorate UK manufacturing industry through an active industrial policy, which, if successful, would raise the share of R&D undertaken by domestic firms and boost future growth potential. It is the balance of these two forces which may, in part, determine the net impact of Brexit upon the UK economy in the medium and longer term.

The Impact of Brexit

There is relatively scant direct evidence pertaining to the measurable impact of EU membership upon FDI, and even less which disaggregates predicted effects for each individual member states (Ebell and Warren 2016: 125). Indeed, many of the economic studies, produced to evaluate the potential impact arising from Brexit, have either used estimates made in earlier studies, or else they have bundled FDI flows in with trade effects (Emmerson et al. 2016; 32–34; PwC 2016: 55). Or they have excluded it altogether (Dhingra et al. 2016: 9). Despite this lack of a strong evidential base, however, membership of the EU, and through this full access to the SIM, has been one factor generally considered to be one attractor for inward investors to consider the UK as a favourable location (Barrell and Pain 1998). Many suggest that this will be one of the most significant costs associated with withdrawal from the EU (Fairbairn and Newton-Smith 2016: 18). This may occur via a reduction in positive spillovers that may result, leading to lower productivity growth (Pain and Young 2004; PwC 2016: 31–32), although other studies identify broader effects upon jobs, output and UK GDP.

One way in which economic studies have sought to estimate the likely impact of EU membership upon FDI, and indeed upon the GDP of member states more generally, has been to use 'gravity modelling'. This method seeks to isolate the impact arising from different trade relationships by controlling the effects of other explanatory variables, such as distance, historic ties, together with the size of the nations concerned in both GDP and population. It is well known that transport costs rise with distance, and therefore nations with a close proximity will tend to trade more than with others more geographically distant, whilst larger and wealthier countries will tend to buy more goods and services. Thus, failing to control for these effects will give a misleading impression as to whether joining a block of nations, such as the EU, has a significant impact upon trade and inward investment flows.

Using this method, various estimates have been generated for the impact of EU membership upon FDI flows. Brenton et al. (1999) found only indeterminate effects, for most of the nations in their model, whilst Straathof et al. (2008: 70) found that EU membership increased inward investment into the Netherlands by approximately 18%, compared to 17% for the rest of the EU (25). Bruno et al. (2016: 9) produced a range of estimated positive EU membership effects upon inward flows of investment into the UK, ranging from 14 to 38%, depending upon the particular statistical techniques used in the calculation. The OECD (2016: 31), drawing its gravity estimates from previous studies by Fournier et al. (2015: 10) and others, utilises multiple estimates for predicted decline in FDI in its various models; these range from 10 to 45% of inward FDI flows.

The NIESR produced a range of forecasts depending upon the type of post-Brexit trade relationships formed between the UK and the

EU. They ranged from 9.7% should the UK join the EEA, 17.1% if pursuing the Swiss model of negotiating bilateral FTAs, and 23.7% if replying upon WTO trade rules (Ebell and Warren 2016: 127). HM Treasury (2016: 131) sought to produce similar estimates, but unfortunately, their model didn't work very well, and they resorted to the rather dubious assumption that inward investment will change in direct proportion to any trade effects arising from Brexit (HM Treasury 2016: 130, 174–175, 185). This latter decision was taken even though it is well appreciated that FDI can be a substitute for international trade, rather than necessarily being a compliment, as firms take the decision that it might make financial sense to establish productive facilities abroad rather than continue to export goods made in the home nation (Gray 1988). They additionally, added an initial element, by estimating that a fall in FDI would cause a subsequent fall in productivity, such that after 15 years, productivity would be between 2 and 2.8% lower under EEA membership, between 3 and 6% under bilateral FTAs and between 3.7 and 7.7% under the WTO option. A summary of these forecasts are included in Table 4.1.

It is, however, easy to over-emphasise the consequences which arise from these predictions (Capital Economics 2016: 27). Firstly because, as this chapter has indicated, there are many inter-related determinants of FDI. Moreover, sunk costs and agglomeration effects are likely to deter existing foreign-owned production from relocating out of the UK. It is more likely that, if the UK did become less attractive for a proportion of international investors, they would respond by slowing the rate of new investment into the UK rather than relocating all existing facilities (Pain and Young 2004: 393). This still has real effects, but these will be experienced more gradually and it would not, therefore, represent as sudden a shock as might be anticipated. Moreover, this would lead research studies to over-estimate likely FDI effects arising out of Brexit, if they simply base future predictions upon past experience (e.g. Bruno et al. 2016: 8), without adjusting for inertia and/or sunk cost effects.

A second reason why the small group of studies that do exist have produced such widely differing estimates of the probable impact of Brexit upon FDI relates to whether their data included all inward investment into the EU, from anywhere in the world, or was more

Table 4.1 Summary of key gravity estimates, FDI and Brexit

	Gravity results (%)	Brexit impact (%)		
		Optimistic (EEA)	Central (Bilateral, FTA)	Pessimistic (WTO)
HM Treasury (2016)		−10	−15/−20	−18/−26
Fournier et al. (2015)	17–22 (OECD wide)			
OECD (2016)		−10	−30	−45
Straathof et al. (2008)	17			
Bruno et al. (2016)	14/33/38 (av. 28)	−12	−25	−28
Ebbell and Warren (2016) [NIESR]		−9.7	−17.1	−23.7

narrowly focused upon intra-EU investment flows. Straathof et al. (2008: 55) produced two estimates; one relating to intra-EU flows, which suggested a 25% impact of EU membership on trade, but for inward investment from the rest of the world, the effect was a more modest 11–13%. Bruno et al. (2016) includes all inward investment entering EU member states from anywhere in the world, and produces a range of effects ranging from 13 to 32% depending upon statistical methods adopted. Thus, from this narrow range of studies, it is difficult to make definitive statements. Yet, what evidence does exist would seem to suggest that those studies focusing upon intra-EU effects are likely to produce larger estimates of EU membership effects, and thereby generate larger predicted negative impact arising from Brexit, than other studies which include inward investment from outside the EU. This would seem reasonable, since it is likely to assume that investors operating within the EU would be more likely to view Brexit with concern, as this may bring a change to their internal marketplace, compared to investors from the US or Asia, where the EU SIM is only one factor amongst many to consider when determining favourable investment locations.

Thirdly, all of the economic studies have been undertaken according to the simplifying maxim, *ceteris paribus* (all relevant factors remaining constant), and therefore they do not take into consideration any policy changes which may mitigate any negative effects. Similarly, they assume away any impact upon the perceptions of international investors which may derive from those changes which are likely to arise as a result of Brexit. These factors may include the creation of a more attractive regulatory framework for international investors, or the more active management of the exchange rate to enhance the competitive position of those firms exporting from the UK, or, indeed, alternative trade relationships which may be formed over time with the rest of the world. It would be wrong to criticise such studies for failing to include all possible future permutations in their calculations, or else models would get very complex and a simple narrative would be lost. Nevertheless, this fact should lead to a degree of caution in the interpretation of the meaning of the results. The fact that a study might conclude that Brexit may lead to a fall in FDI *if nothing else changes*, is not the same as a firm prediction that FDI flows *will* inevitably fall; rather it is a warning that national policymakers have to take these factors into account when they formulate policy responses to ensure that this predicted eventually does not occur.

Fourthly, the various studies tend to develop panel data by aggregating evidence drawn over a number of years. However, this obscures whether there may be differential FDI effects over time. For example, it might be a reasonable assumption to anticipate that a nation will reap its largest effects during the initial period of EU membership but, unless other factors change (such as deeper integration through membership of the single currency, for example), this boost to FDI flows may gradually diminish as EU membership becomes established. Indeed, this possibility appears to be supported by the Bank of England (2015: 23), who note that the earlier years of EU membership were more strongly associated with attracting FDI into the UK, whereas evidence for subsequent time periods is more difficult to isolate from other effects. Similar conclusions are reached by Campos et al. (2014: 16), thus suggesting that a positive initial impact derived from joining the EU may have diminished over time.

Finally, it is worth noting that similar concerns have been raised in relation to the debate about whether the UK should join the single European currency, where it was suggested that failure to participate would be likely to reduce inward FDI into the UK (Begg et al. 2003: 5). Yet, the opposite has been the case, with large increases in FDI inward flows despite the UK adopting an increasingly firm position against joining the Euro.

This criticism of the economics literature can, itself, be over-done. Indeed, Portes (2013: F7) makes a convincing argument that the increased level of uncertainty surrounding Brexit would be likely to have a negative impact upon inward FDI flows into the UK. However, the magnitude and duration of any potential fall in FDI is more questionable. It would seem to depend upon those factors assumed away in the economic studies—i.e. the impact of related policy interventions upon stabilising the expectations of international investors and boosting UK growth prospects, alongside the nature of the trade relationships the UK is able to negotiate with the EU and the rest of the world (Mansfield 2014: 43; Capital Economics 2016: 3, 27).

Attitude Surveys—International Investors

Predictions made by econometric modelling are one source of evidence, but another derives from surveying actual or potential international investors to gauge their perceptions and interpret their future investment intentions resulting from changed circumstances. The Ernst and Young 'attractiveness survey' (EY 2015: 7–8), utilised evidence drawn from 406 inward investor respondents, indicated that 54% of respondents stated that it would have no impact upon their future investment intentions, 19% suggested that investment may be delayed during a period of uncertainty, whilst a further 12% predicted that investment would be reduced, against 9% that claimed it would be increased (see Fig. 4.10). This would indicate that there might be a net fall in the number of FDI investments of net 3% (i.e. 12% reductions minus 9% increased investment), with around 19% of investors responding to uncertainty by delaying their future investments.

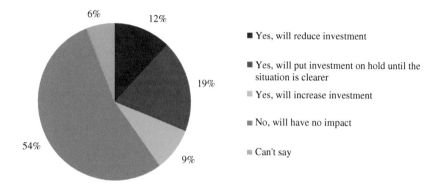

6%   12%

19%

54%

9%

■ Yes, will reduce investment

■ Yes, will put investment on hold until the situation is clearer

■ Yes, will increase investment

■ No, will have no impact

■ Can't say

Fig. 4.10 Perception of Brexit impact on investment plans in answer to the survey question: 'Does the possibility of the UK leaving the EU after 2017 have any impact on your investment plans between now and the end of 2017?' *Source* Based on EY (2015: 7)

Disaggregating these overall figures by global region indicates that, whilst 72% of North American and 66% of Asian respondents considered that a lower degree of integration into the EU would *improve* the attractiveness of the UK as a place to invest, this figure was only 38% for respondents from Western Europe (EY 2013: 35). This finding would suggest that, were the UK to withdraw from EU membership, this may reduce the attractors for European investors, yet this may be partly or wholly compensated by an increased attraction for investors from North American and Asia.

The EY (2015: 9) survey additionally invited investors to comment upon whether 'Brexit', combined with continued access to the EU SIM, would make the UK more or less attractive as an FDI destination. This question is a little imprecise, because, when considering all of the various models of trade relationship the UK may negotiate with the EU during the withdrawal process, *all* options would involve some form of access to the SIM, albeit that the *degree* of access varies considerably. Moreover, perhaps surprisingly, when asked to assess the importance of different potential attractors for FDI, access to the EU SIM ranked only sixth on the list (EY 2015: 29). Nevertheless, just under half of those surveyed believed that the change would make no significant difference to the attractiveness of the UK as an investment location, whilst 22% of investors believed that the UK would become a more attractive destination and 31% considered that it would become less attractive.

Despite this stated viewpoint, however, the same survey indicates that 54% of those surveyed expected the UK's attractiveness to *increase* over the next 3 years, with 39% anticipating that it will remain the same and only 5% expecting a slight or significant decrease (EY 2015: 28). These expressed opinions are almost identical to the previous year, when the referendum bill was passed by Parliament, with the exception that those surveyed anticipating a decline in UK attractiveness has declined in number. Thus, whilst the EY survey indicates a degree of nervousness amongst international investors about the UK's withdrawal from EU membership, it would appear that other factors combine to outweigh any potential negative impression. This conclusion is in line with the economic theory which highlights a multiplicity of determinants of inward flows of FDI, rather than one factor, such as access to the SIM, predominating across all investors and companies operating in all market types.

This survey has one primary weakness, in that it focuses upon the number of FDI projects but not their *value*. This weakens the usefulness of the survey because, from this data, it is impossible to ascertain whether the smaller group who are more attracted to the UK post-Brexit are likely to invest more or less than the slightly larger group who view Brexit with greater concern.

A second source of survey data can be drawn from the work of IPSOS MORI in 2013, whose respondents encompassed CEOs, chairmen, CIOs, board members, directors and partners of 101 companies based in the UK. This survey does not seek to discover the perceptions and investment plans of *potential* inward investors, but rather the attitudes of those who are already embedded within the UK economy. The results suggest that perhaps 10% of current inward investors would seriously investigate relocating at least some of their operations out of the UK as a result of Brexit, with a further 27% less certain but who might re-consider the location of their facilities, whereas, for the majority, UK withdrawal from the EU would have little impact (Punhani and Hill 2016: 10) (see Fig. 4.11). Relocation does not, therefore, seem a realistic prospect for the almost two thirds of inward investors who are

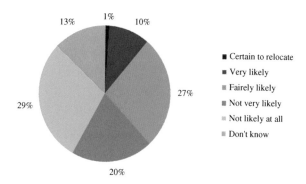

Fig. 4.11 Perception of Brexit impact on single market access and relocation decisions in answer to the survey question: 'In a scenario where the UK left the single market, how likely is it that your firm would relocate at least some of its headcount from the UK to a location within the single market?' *Source* Based on Punhani and Hill (2016: 11)

already operating in the UK. However, the fact that 10% of respondents state their willingness to consider relocating some of their production facilities elsewhere, should encourage the UK government to provide a range of incentives to lessen the concerns of this group of inward investors. This might be through ensuring a competitive currency of a level to nullify any increase in costs arising from possible tariff costs, or through better designing national regulation to better meet the needs of producers, or the use of industrial policy to enhance the efficiency of UK-located activities (see Chap. 8 for further discussion).

UNCTAD survey data has the advantage of a much larger sample size than the Ernst and Young or IPSOS MORI surveys, and its results indicate that the national market remains the most important determinant of FDI for both the manufacturing and service sectors (UNCTAD 2009: 18). Similarly, even during a period when potential investors were fully aware of the possible withdrawal of the UK from the EU, international investors still viewed the UK as the third most promising host economy for FDI in 2016 and the fourth in 2017 (UNCTAD 2015a: 26).

Using a slightly different approach, a YouGov survey, carried out for the CBI, found that 42% of the 415 CBI members surveyed felt that

Brexit would have a slight or significant detrimental impact upon the ability of UK firms to attract inward international investment from within the EU and 32% from outside the EU. For inward FDI as a whole, 75% of respondents believed that this would decline, with just over half of these predicting it would do so by a significant amount.[4] This particular study is interesting for the insight that it provides into business (and particularly big business) opinion in the UK, but it is not as useful as the Ernst and Young or UNCTAD surveys, given that the latter were questioning international investors—i.e. the people who are likely to be undertaking the FDI themselves—rather than business-people within the UK, many of who have no connection with inward investment and therefore could claim no particular insight into likely future developments.

The various examples of survey evidence provide useful data on investor perceptions and future intentions. However, they do not quantify potential impact, and nor should an expressed attitude be treated as necessarily equivalent to that firm actually changing its behaviour. Nevertheless, where data concerning future behaviour is by definition limited, survey evidence may be one of the best, albeit imperfect and imprecise, guides to future behaviour that is available.

Policy Response

The appropriate policy response to managing inward flows of FDI, following Brexit, depends upon the assessment of the impact upon the UK economy. In the short term, the balance of payments gain derived from the inflow of overseas capital is certainly an advantage, particularly if trade flows to the EU are likely to be affected by whatever relationship the UK negotiates with the EU. However, in the medium and longer term, the reliance of the UK upon the continued attraction of inward flows of FDI is problematic, both because this highlights the weakness and imbalances which persist in the UK economy, but also because the spillovers which economic theory would suggest arise from inward investment are difficult to substantiate in practice. Consequently, UK policymakers may wish to consider a two pronged approach, namely to:

1. Seek to reassure international investors in the short term, since the economy is currently over-reliant upon their contribution to certain sectors of the economy and mitigating a very large balance of trade deficit through inward flows of capital.
2. Utilise a package of measures, including an industrial strategy, to seek to rebalance the UK economy in the medium term, through facilitating the expansion of the manufacturing sector, and thereby reducing the current over-reliance upon FDI to drive R&D and raise productivity through perhaps elusive technological spillovers.

Short term options to enhance the attractiveness of the UK as a FDI location, certainly relative to the rest of the EU, could include lowering the cost for inward investors, through reducing regulatory costs and/or taxation (Irwin 2015: 13). This approach need not be a 'race to the bottom', with the UK seeking to undercut EU standards, since cost cutting can equally be achieved through a deregulation and liberalisation agenda, or through the realisation of economies of scale through underpinning production by aggregate demand management and thereby reducing unit costs. Either approach should prove attractive to efficiency-seeking inward investors.

For market-seeking investors, however, the main determinants are the wealth and growth rate of the national economy, together with access to other international markets. Given that most FDI flowing into the UK is in services, and this sector tends to be more focused upon the national market rather than international exporting possibilities, then a macroeconomic strategy aimed at ensuring continued good levels of economic growth in the UK economy should reassure a large proportion of inward investors. The Bank of England's recent stimulus package will assist in this regard, but the Chancellor of the Exchequer needs to compliment this initiative with fiscal measures designed to boost growth and reduce uncertainty. For a significant minority, however, the resolution of the withdrawal negotiations with the EU, and the particular model for future trade relationships selected, will have a significant bearing upon whether these investors are reassured or will gradually disinvest from the UK economy.

Conclusions

There is a clear and consistent consensus amongst economists, business-people and policy makers that FDI provides positive benefits for the UK economy, whether through technological and productivity spillovers in the microeconomy, or compensating for the very large trade deficit in terms of UK balance of payments. Indeed, the UK is probably more reliant upon the continuation of FDI flows, at least in the short term, than most similarly sized economies. Thus, a number of those studies, produced during the recent European referendum, sought to measure the likely impact of Brexit upon FDI flows. The conclusions appeared clear cut—i.e. that withdrawal from the EU would result in a substantial drop in FDI, with consequent negative impact upon productivity and growth.

The problem with this consensus, as has been demonstrated in this chapter, is that it is based on only a small number of academic studies and opinion surveys, each of which has methodological weaknesses. Moreover, the range of forecasted impacts is quite wide, and is due to different assumptions and data selection involved in the design of the individual studies. Surveys appear to suggest only a modest drop in inward investment following Brexit, whereas gravity models forecast a much larger potential decline, albeit with individual predictions being very heavily dependent upon data selection and the resolution of future trading arrangements. Yet, this matters because policy makers need to have an accurate diagnosis about the health of the UK economy and potential future threats to its development, and thus the confusion about whether FDI is likely to drop by a manageable 10%, or a more difficult 30%, is quite important.

What all of the different methods agree upon, however, is that, without any corrective action being undertaken, there is likely to be a drop in inward investment, at least in the short-run. The qualification in this statement is important, because policy interventions can mitigate any such effects, should they be sufficient to safeguard the future growth prospects of the UK economy and/or compensate for any increased costs arising from future trading relationships. Thus, the recent measures announced by the Bank of England, and the depreciation in the value of sterling, will both have contributed towards improving the confidence of inward investors and hence lessened any negative impact.

Notes

1. For a good over-view of the theory and evidence pertaining to FDI, see Moosa (2002).
2. http://www.bbc.co.uk/news/business-37216175.
3. http://reports.weforum.org/global-competitiveness-report-2014-2015/rankings/.
4. http://news.cbi.org.uk/news/8-out-of-10-firms-say-uk-must-stay-in-eu/yougov-cbi-eu-business-poll/.

References

Aghion, P., Blundell, R., Griffith, R., Howitt, P., & Prantl, S. (2009). The effects of entry on incumbent innovation and productivity. *Review of Economics and Statistics, 91*(1), 20–32.

Aitken, B. J., & Harrison, A. E. (1999). Do domestic firms benefit from direct foreign investment? Evidence from Venezuela. *American Economic Review, 89*(3), 605–618.

Arestis, P., & Mariscal, I. (1997). Conflict, effort and capital stock in UK wage determination. *Empirica, 24*(3), 179–193.

Arestis, P., & Mariscal, I. (2000). Capital stock, unemployment and wages in the UK and Germany. *Scottish Journal of Political Economy, 47*(5), 487–503.

Baldwin, R.E., Forslid, R., & Haaland, J.I. (1996). 'Investment creation and diversion in Europe'. *World Economy, 19*, 635–659.

Bank of England. (2015). *EU Membership and the Bank of England*. London: Bank of England. Available via: http://www.bankofengland.co.uk/publications/Documents/speeches/2015/euboe211015.pdf.

Barrell, R., & Pain, N. (1997). Foreign direct investment, technological change and economic growth within Europe. *Economic Journal, 107*(445), 1770–1786.

Barrell, R., & Pain, N. (1998). Real exchange rates, agglomerations, and irreversibilities: Macroeconomic policy and FDI in EMU. *Oxford Review of Economic Policy, 14*(3), 152–167.

Begg, D., Blanchard, O., Coyle, D., Eichengreen, B., Frankel, J., Giavazzi, F., Portes, R., Seabright, P., Venables, A., Winters, L. A., & Wyplotz, C. (2003). *The consequences of saying no: An independent report into the economic consequences of the UK saying no to the Euro.* London: Britain in Europe. Available via: http://faculty.london.edu/rportes/research/BeggCommissionReport.pdf.

Bloom, N., Genakos, C., Sadun, R., & Van, R. J. (2012a). Management practices across firms and countries. *Academy Of Management Perspectives, 26*(1), 12–33.

Bloom, N., Sadun, R., & Van Reenen, J. (2012b). Americans do I.T. better: US multinationals and the productivity miracle. *American Economic Review, 102*(1), 167–201.

Borensztein, E., DeGregorio, J., & Lee, J.-W. (1998). How does foreign direct investment affect economic growth? *Journal of International Economics, 45,* 115–135.

Brenton, P., Di Mauro, F., & Lücke, M. (1999). Economic integration and FDI: An empirical analysis of foreign investment in the EU and in Central and Eastern Europe. *Empirica, 26*(2), 95–121.

Bruno, R., Campos, N., & Estrin, S. (2016). *Gravitating towards Europe: An econometric analysis of the FDI effects of EU membership*, mimeo. London School of Economics. Available via: http://cep.lse.ac.uk/pubs/download/brexit03_technical_paper.pdf.

Buffie, E. (1993). Direct foreign investment. *Crowding Out, and Underemployment on the Dualistic Economy, Oxford Economic Papers, 45,* 639–667.

Campos, N. F., Coricelli, F., & Moretti, L. (2014). *Economic growth from political integration: Estimating the benefits from membership in the European Union using the synthetic counterfactuals method* (IZA Discussion Paper Series 8162). Bonn. Available via: http://anon-ftp.iza.org/dp8162.pdf.

Capital Economics. (2016). *The economics impact of 'Brexit': A paper discussing the United Kingdom' relationship with Europe and the impact of 'Brexit' on the British economy.* Oxford: Woodford Investment Management LLP. Available via: https://woodfordfunds.com/economic-impact-brexit-report/.

Cowling, K., & Sugden, R. (1987). *Transnational monopoly capitalism.* London: Wheatsheaf Books.

De Mello, L. R. (1999). Foreign direct investment-led growth: Evidence from time series and panel data. *Oxford Economic Papers, 51*, 133–151.

Deutsche Bank. (2013). *The single European market—20 years on.* Frankfurt: Deutsche Bank. Available via: https://www.dbresearch.com/PROD/DBR_INTERNET_EN-PROD/PROD0000000000322897/The+Single+Europe an+Market+20+years+on%3A+Achievements,+unfulfilled+expectations+%26+further+potential.pdf.

Dhingra, S., Ottaviano, G., Sampson, T., & Van Reenen, J. (2016). *The consequences of Brexit for UK trade and living standards*, Centre for Economic Performance (CEP) and London School of Economics and Political Science (LSE). Available via: http://cep.lse.ac.uk/pubs/download/brexit02.pdf.

Driffield, N. L., & Hughes, D. R. (2003). Foreign and domestic investment: Complements or substitutes? *Regional Studies, 37*(3), 277–288.

Driffield, N. L., & Love, J. H. (2003). FDI, technology sourcing and reverse spillovers. *The Manchester School, 71*(6), 659–672.

Driffield, N. L., & Munday, M. C. (2000). Industrial performance, agglomeration,and foreign manufacturing investment in the UK. *Journal of International Business Studies, 31*(1), 21–37.

Driffield, N. L., & Taylor, K. (2000). FDI and the Labour Market: A review of the evidence and policy implications. *Oxford Review of Economic Policy, 16*(3), 90–103.

Driffield, N. L., & Taylor, K. (2006). Domestic wage determination: Regional spillovers and inward investment. *Spatial Economic Analysis, 1*(2), 187–205.

Driffield, N., Love, J., Lancheros, S., & Temouri, Y. (2013). *How attractive is the UK for future manufacturing Foreign direct investment?* London: Foresight-Department of Business, Innovation and Science. Available via: https://www.gov.uk/government/uploads/system/uploads/attachment_data/file/277171/ep7-foreign-direct-investment-trends-manufacturing.pdf.

Dunning, J. H. (1988). The eclectic paradigm of international production. *Journal of International Business Studies, 19*(1), 1–29.

Dunning, J. H. (1993). *Multinational enterprises and the global economy.* Harrow: Addison-Wesley.

Ebell, M., & Warren, J. (2016). The long-term economic impact of leaving the EU. *National Institute Economic Review, 236*, 121–138.

Egger, P., & Pfaffermayr, M. (2004). Distance, trade and FDI: A Hausman-Taylor SUR approach. *Journal of Applied Econometrics, 19*, 227–246.

Emmerson, C., Johnson, P., Mitchell, I., & Phillips, D. (2016). *Brexit and the UK's public finances* (IFS Report 116). Institute for Fiscal Studies, London. Available via: http://www.ifs.org.uk/uploads/publications/comms/r116.pdf.

Ernst and Young (EY). (2013). *EY's attractiveness survey—UK 2013*. London: Ernst and Young. Available via: http://www.ey.com/Publication/vwLU-Assets/Ernst-and-Youngs-attractiveness-survey-UK-2013-No-room-for-complacency/$FILE/EY_UK_Attractiveness_2013.pdf.

Ernst and Young (EY). (2015). *EY's attractiveness survey—UK 2015*. London: Ernst and Young. Available via: http://www.ey.com/Publication/vwLUAssets/The_UK_Attractivness_Survey_2015_-_full_report/$FILE/1595088_UKAS_report_2015_FINALWEB.pdf.

Fairbairn, C., & Newton-Smith, R. (2016). *Brexit—The business view*, Lecture at London Business School, Monday 21st March. Available via: http://news.cbi.org.uk/business-issues/uk-and-the-european-union/eu-business-facts/brexit-the-business-view-pdf/.

Fournier, J.-M., Domps, A., Gorin, Y., Guillet, X., & Morchoisne, D. (2015). *Implicit regulatory barriers in the EU single market: New empirical evidence from gravity models* (OECD Economics Department Working Papers No. 1181). Available via: http://dx.doi.org/10.1787/5js7xj0xckf6-en.

Fredriksson, P. G., List, J. A., & Millimet, D. L. (2003). Bureaucratic corruption environmental policy and inbound US FDI: Theory and evidence. *Journal of Public Economics, 87*, 1407–1430.

Froot, K., & Stein, J. (1991). Exchange rates and foreign direct investment: An imperfect capital markets approach. *Quarterly Journal of Economics, 196*, 1191–1218.

Görg, H., & Greenaway, D. (2004). Much ado about nothing? Do domestic firms really benefit from foreign direct investment? *World Bank Research Observer, 19*, 171–198.

Gray, H. P. (1998). International trade and foreign direct investment: The interface. In J. H. Dunning (Ed.), *Globalization trade and foreign direct investment* (pp. 19–27). Oxford: Elservier.

Griffith, R., Redding, S., & Simpson, H. (2004). Foreign ownership and productivity: New evidence from the service sector and the R&D lab. *Oxford Review of Economic Policy, 20*(3), 440–456.

Grossman, G. M., & Helpman, E. (1994). Endogenous innovation in the theory of growth. *Journal of Economic Perspectives, 8*(1), 23–44. Available via: https://www.researchgate.net/profile/Elhanan_Helpman/publication/4722290_Endogenous_Innovation_in_the_Theory_of_Growth/links/56adf60e08ae19a38515eda3.pdf.

Haaland, J. I., & Wooton, I. (2007). Domestic labour markets and foreign direct investment. *Review of International Economics, 15*(3), 462–480.

Harris, R., & Robinson, C. (2002). The effect of foreign acquisitions on total factor productivity: Plant-level evidence from UK manufacturing, 1987–1992. *Review of Economics and Statistics, 84*(3), 562–568.

Haskel, J. E., Pereira, S. C., & Slaughter, M. J. (2002). *Does inward foreign direct investment boost the productivity of domestic firms?* (NBER Working Paper No. 8724). Available via: http://www.nber.org/papers/w8724.pdf.

Hejazi, W., & Pauly, P. (2003). Motivations for FDI and domestic capital formation. *Journal of International Business Studies, 34*, 282–289.

Helpman, E., Melitz, M. J., & Yeaple, S. R. (2004). Export versus FDI with heterogeneous firms. *American Economic Review, 94*, 300–316.

HM Treasury. (2003). *The green book: Appraisal and evaluation in central government.* London: The Stationary Office. Available via: https://www.gov.uk/government/uploads/system/uploads/attachment_data/file/220541/green_book_complete.pdf.

HM Treasury. (2016). *HM treasury analysis: The long term economic impact of EU membership and the alternatives.* London: Cm 9250, The Stationary Office. Available via: https://www.gov.uk/government/uploads/system/uploads/attachment_data/file/517415/treasury_analysis_economic_impact_of_eu_membership_web.pdf.

Hines, J. R. (1996). Altered states: Taxes and the location of foreign direct investment in America. *American Economic Review, 86*(5), 1076–94.

HM Government (HMG). (2013). *Review of the balance of competences between the United Kingdom and the European union—The Single Market.* London: The Stationary Office. Available via: https://www.gov.uk/government/uploads/system/uploads/attachment_data/file/227069/2901084_SingleMarket_acc.pdf.

Hymer, S. (1960). *The international operations of national firms; A study of direct foreign investment.* Cambridge Massachusetts: MIT Press.

IMF. (2013). *Balance of payments manual* (6th ed.). Washington DC: IMF. Available via: https://www.imf.org/external/np/sta/bop/BOPman.pdf.

Irwin, G. (2015). *Brexit: The impact on the UK and the EU.* London: Global Counsel. Available via: http://www.global-counsel.co.uk/system/files/publications/Global_Counsel_Impact_of_Brexit_June_2015.pdf.

Keller, W., & Yeaple, S. (2009). Multinational enterprises, international trade, and productivity growth: Firm-level evidence from the united states. *The Review of Economics and Statistics, 91*(4), 821–831.

Liu, X., Wang, C., & Wei, Y. (2001). Causal links between foreign direct investment and trade in China. *China Economic Review, 12*, 190–202.

Mansfield, I. (2014). *A blueprint for Britain: Openness not isolation*. London: Institute for Economic Affairs. Available via: http://www.iea.org.uk/sites/default/files/publications/files/Brexit%20Entry%20170_final_bio_web.pdf.

Miller, V. (ed.). (2016). *Exiting the EU: Impact in key UK policy areas* (House of Commons Library Briefing Paper No. HC 07213). Available via: http://researchbriefings.parliament.uk/ResearchBriefing/Summary/CBP-7213#fullreport.

Milne, I. (2004). *A cost too far? An Analysis of the net economic costs and benefits for the UK of EU membership*, Civitas. London. Available via: http://www.civitas.org.uk/pdf/cs37.pdf.

Minford, P., Mahambare, V., & Nowell, E. (2005). *Should Britain leave the EU? An economic analysis of a troubled relationship*. Cheltenham: IEA and Edward Elgar.

Moosa, I. A. (2002). *Foreign direct investment: Theory, evidence and practice*. Basingstoke: Palgrave.

Morgan, K. (1997). The learning region: Institutions innovation and regional renewal. *Regional Studies, 31,* 491–503.

OECD. (2008). *OECD benchmark definition of foreign direct investment* (4th ed.). Paris: OECD. Available via: https://www.oecd.org/daf/inv/investment-statisticsandanalysis/40193734.pdf.

OECD. (2016). *The economic consequences of Brexit: A taxing decision* (OECD Economic Policy Paper No. 16). Available via: http://www.oecd.org/eco/The-Economic-consequences-of-Brexit-27-April-2016.pdf.

Office of National Statistics (ONS). (2010). *Business monitor MA4—Foreign direct investment involving UK companies*. Available via: https://www.google.co.uk/url?sa=t&rct=j&q=&esrc=s&source=web&cd=1&cad=rja&uact=8&ved=0ahUKEwj6ioqixOrRAhWbOsAKHUblDj8QFggjMAA&url=http%3A%2F%2Fwww.ons.gov.uk%2Fons%2Frel%2Ffdi%2Fforeign-direct-investment%2F2010-ma4%2Fbusiness-monitor-ma4-2010.pdf%3Fformat%3Dcontrast&usg=AFQjCNE9OZT7jOSmlOQ5i6p088I80bn9Vw.

Office of National Statistics (ONS). (2014a). *Foreign direct investment involving UK companies*. Inward tables. Dataset. Available via: https://www.ons.gov.uk/businessindustryandtrade/business/businessinnovation/datasets/foreigndirectinvestmentinvolvingukcompanies2013inwardtables.

Office of National Statistics (ONS). (2014b). *Business enterprise research and development*. London: ONS. Available via: https://www.ons.gov.uk/

economy/governmentpublicsectorandtaxes/researchanddevelopmentexpend-
iture/bulletins/businessenterpriseresearchanddevelopment/2014.

Office of National Statistics (ONS). (2017). National archives. Available via: http://webarchive.nationalarchives.gov.uk/20160105160709/http://www.ons.gov.uk/ons/publications/re-reference-tables.html?edition=tcm%3A77-392545.

Pain, N., & Lansbury, M. (1997, April). Regional economic integration and foreign direct investment: The case of German investment in Europe, *National Institute Economic Review, 160*, 87–99.

Pain, N., & Wakelin, K. (1998). Export performance and the role of foreign direct investment. *Manchester School* Supplement, *66*(S), 62–88.

Pain, N., & Young, G. (2004). The macroeconomic impact of UK withdrawal from the EU. *Economic Modelling, 21*, 387–408. Available via: http://www.niesr.ac.uk/sites/default/files/publications/1-s2.0-S0264999302000688-main.pdf.

Portes, J. (2013). Commentary: The economic implications for the UK of leaving the European union. *National Institute Economic Review*, No. 266, F4–9. Available via: http://www.niesr.ac.uk/sites/default/files/commentary.pdf.

PricewaterhouseCoopers LLP (PwC). (2016). *Leaving the EU: Implications for the UK economy.* London: PricewaterhouseCoopers LLP. Available via: http://news.cbi.org.uk/news/leaving-eu-would-cause-a-serious-shock-to-uk-economy-new-pwc-analysis/leaving-the-eu-implications-for-the-uk-economy/.

Punhani, S., & Hill, N. (Credit Suisse Report). (2016). *Brexit: Breaking up is never easy, or chea.* Zurich: Credit Suisse. Available via: https://doc.research-and-analytics.csfb.com/docView?language=ENG&format=PDF&document_id=806936650&source_id=emrna&serialid=lPu6YfMSDd9toXKa9EPxf5HiNBEoWX2fYou5bZ6jJhA%3D.

Ramasamy, B., & Yeung, M. (2010). The determinants of foreign direct investment in services. *The World Economy, 33*(4), 573–596.

Rodrik, D. (2004). *Industrial policy for the twenty-first century.* Available via: https://myweb.rollins.edu/tlairson/pek/rodrikindpolicy.pdf.

Rodrik, D. (2008). Industrial policy: Don't ask why, ask how. *Middle East Development Journal*, Demo Issue, 1–29. Available via: https://www.sss.ias.edu/files/pdfs/Rodrik/Research/Industrial-Policy-Dont-Ask-Why-Ask-How.pdf.

Straathof, S., Linders, G.-J., Lejour, A., & Mohlmann, J. (2008). *The internal market and the Dutch economy: Implications for trade and economic growth* (CPG Netherlands Document No. 168). Available via: http://www.cpb.nl/sites/default/files/publicaties/download/internal-market-and-dutch-economy-implications-trade-and-economic-growth.pdf.

United Kingdom Trade and Investment (UKTI). (2015, June 17). UK wins a record number of investment projects and maintains position as top investment destination in Europe. *UKTI Press Release.* Available via: https://www.gov.uk/government/news/uk-wins-a-record-number-of-investment-projects-and-maintains-position-as-top-investment-destination-in-europe.

United Nations Conference on Trade and Development (UNCTAD). (2009). *World investment prospects survey 2009–2011.* Geneva: United Nations. Available via: http://unctad.org/en/Docs/diaeia20098_en.pdf.

United Nations Conference on Trade and Development (UNCTAD). (2015). *World investment report 2015.* Geneva: United Nations. Available via: http://unctad.org/en/PublicationsLibrary/wir2015_en.pdf.

United Nations Conference on Trade and Development (UNCTAD). (2016a). *World investment report 2016.* Geneva: United Nations. Available via: http://unctad.org/en/PublicationsLibrary/wir2016_en.pdf.

United Nations Conference on Trade and Development (UNCTAD). (2016b). *Foreign direct investment: Inward flows, annual.* Available via: www.unctad.org/fdistatistics.

United States International Trade Commission (USITC). (2000). *The impact on the US economy of including the United Kingdom in a free trade agreement with the United States, Canada and Mexico* (Investigation No. 332–409). Washington DC: USITC.

Weiss, L. (1998). *The myth of the powerless state: Governing the economy in a global era.* Cambridge: Polity Press.

World Trade Organisation (WTO). (2013). *World trade report 2013: Factors shaping the future of world trade.* Geneva: World Trade Organisation. Available via: https://www.wto.org/english/res_e/booksp_e/world_trade_report13_e.pdf.

Wren, C., & Jones, J. (2012). FDI location across British regions and agglomerative forces: A Markov analysis. *Spatial Economic Analysis, 7*(2), 265–286.

Wren, C., & Taylor, J. (1999). Industrial restructuring and regional policy. *Oxford Economic Papers, 51,* 487–516.

Young, S., Hood, N., & Peters, E. (1994). Multinational enterprises and regional economic development. *Regional Studies, 28*(7), 657–677.

5

Regulation

One of the areas where EU membership has been criticised as impacting negatively upon the UK economy concerns EU imposed rules and directives. Regulation is introduced to solve a problem in the economy, either to curb behaviour or activity which is deemed to have negative consequences upon individuals or society in general, or to resolve an incident of market failure. It may prevent collusion, enhance competition, restrict damaging environmental consequences, limit the exposure of the real economy to excessive behaviour in the financial sector, provide a minimum standard of working environment for employees and/or protect consumers against sharp business practices and unsafe products. One of the more significant elements of EU-determined regulation relates to the set of common rules and standards established to facilitate trade within the SIM. The elimination of duplicate standards, previously required for exporters to multiple EU member nations, was expected to lower the costs of trade within the SIM and, indeed, around half of CBI members, when surveyed, state that they have directly benefited from this process (CBI 2013: 11). Regulation can, moreover, promote the formation of complex cross-border supply chains and thus

© The Author(s) 2017
P.B. Whyman and A.I. Petrescu, *The Economics of Brexit*,
DOI 10.1007/978-3-319-58283-2_5

be business-facilitating (McFadden and Tarrant 2015: 41, 60). Hence, BAE Systems has stated that EU regulation can deliver:

> ...substantial market benefits from the establishment of technical standards for new products driven by collaborative research; and to the extent that those standards are exported to other countries or contribute to wider international agreements, they can enhance industry competitiveness outside the EU. (HMG 2013a: 41–42)

Regulation is, in short, intended to produce benefits for the economy.

If effective, however, it will almost inevitably also impose costs upon those required to comply. Consequently, whilst welcoming the beneficial effects of stable and effective markets, businesses and other organisations are concerned about the regulatory burden inherent in any regulatory framework; particularly in relation to those rules that are regarded as unnecessary or badly designed to achieve their objectives (NAO 2001: 1). Not surprisingly, therefore, the Institute of Directors found that 60% of its members wanted to reduce unnecessary regulation as the top priority in any EU reform agenda.[1] Similarly, the CBI (2013: 7, 11, 18) reported that a majority (52%) of its members surveyed considered that, should the UK withdraw from the EU, then the overall regulatory burden on their organisations would be reduced. Moreover, there would appear to be some academic support for the perception that EU regulation was the source of the 'heaviest burdens on business'(HoC 2009: Ev76). Or, again, that the majority of the cumulative regulatory burden imposed upon UK businesses, when measured by value, originates in the EU (Ambler et al. 2010: 2).

During the referendum campaign, EU regulation was criticised on three main grounds, namely that:

1. An excessive proportion of UK laws and regulations arise due to EU-imposed decisions;
2. The burden of EU regulations is excessive because it impacts on those UK businesses, particularly SMEs, which do not sell into the SIM;
3. EU regulations are less efficient than national regulations and therefore they do not provide as much benefit to costs imposed.

This chapter will therefore seek to examine each of these claims in turn. Apart from clarifying the validity of the evidence debated in the recent referendum campaign, this is important because Brexit offers the opportunity to redesign a national regulatory framework for UK businesses. Thus, if it is established that national regulation has a greater proportional benefit for the UK economy than that generated by EU regulation, then this should be an area where the UK will materially gain from withdrawal from the EU.

What Proportion of UK Laws Derive from the EU?

There is considerable disagreement over the proportion of UK law derived from the EU. For example, one estimate contained within a written parliamentary answer, given by an undersecretary in the Ministry of Justice to the German Bundestag in April 2005, suggested that approximately 84% of all laws and regulations adopted or passed into German law, between 1998 and 2004, originated in the EU (Gaskell and Persson 2010: 37–38). At the other extreme, the then Minister of State for Europe, MacShane, claimed that only 9% of UK laws derived from the EU,[2] whilst the House of Commons Library calculated an average figure of 14.1%, between 1997 and 2009 (Miller 2010: 16–17). This latter period obviously omits the time period when EU regulations were more prevalent. Indeed, Fig. 5.1 indicates that the number of EU laws peaked at over 14,000 instruments in the early 1980s, with a second, lower peak recorded in the mid-1990s (Miller 2010: 12–13).

The discrepancy arises from divergent definitions of what constitutes EU law. If the estimates include only those laws established through EU directives, then the proportion of UK laws determined by the EU is correspondingly small. If, however, the calculations include all 'soft law' regulations and rules that compliment these legal regulations, then the proportion is much greater. Christiensen (2010: 12) calculates that, from the mid-1990s, soft law has exceeded the combined total

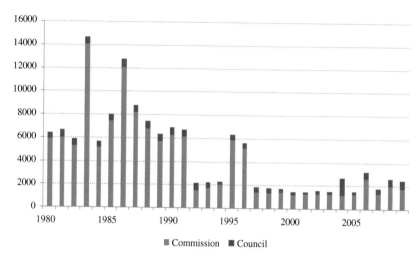

Fig. 5.1 EU Commission and Council legislation adopted by the UK, 1980–2009. *Source* Data taken from the 'Institutions and other Bodies' section of Commission Reports on the Activities of the European Union and from 2005 were provided directly by the European Commission Secretariat and collated by Miller (2010: 12)

number of new directives and EU regulations. Indeed, in the year 2000, Christiensen estimates that there were more than 2500 examples of new soft laws introduced by the EU, compared to around 800 regulations and around 100 directives. Accordingly, the House of Commons Library concludes that it is quite plausible to justify any estimate which lies between 15 and 50%, depending upon the methodology utilised (Miller 2010: 24).

Is There a Problem with EU Regulation?

In seeking to assess whether withdrawal from the EU will have any significant impact upon the regulatory burden imposed upon the national economy, the starting point is to assess whether the UK suffers from any obvious competitive disadvantage. Superficially, the answer would seem to be in the negative, as Fig. 5.2 indicates that the UK is considered to

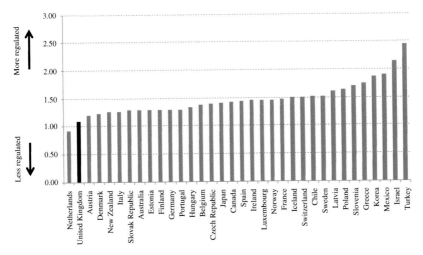

Fig. 5.2 Product market regulation index for selected countries, 2013. *Source* Compiled by the authors from data available at OECD Statistics (2013)

be one of the most lightly regulated of the OECD nations (Irwin 2015: 14; Springford 2016: 1). However, the fact that EU regulation has not prevented the UK from maintaining a relatively liberal approach up until this point does not preclude the possibility that it has prevented an even more advantageous position for the UK, and nor does it rule out the possibility that Brexit may facilitate the realisation of this more advantageous regulatory regime.

Most UK Businesses do not Export into the SIM

One reason why the burden of EU regulation is considered to be excessive arises from the fact that, as a full EU member, all UK firms and organisations are subject to the rules and regulations established to form the basis of the SIM (in addition to social and environmental standards), yet only a small minority of UK firms actually engage in international trade with other EU member nations. Most UK firms are wholly engaged in trading within the UK domestic market.

Operating beyond national borders incurs sunk costs, whether in terms of establishing a new client base, translation, search and regulatory costs (Anderson and van Woncoop 2004). As a result, only the larger and most productive firms tend to trade (Driver 2014: 14). This concentration of firms which engage in international trade is not particularly unusual in international context. Barely 4% of US firms export, including only around 18% of US manufacturing firms and, of these, only around 15% of the value of their output is actually exported (Bernard et al. 2007: 105, 108–109). Leading European nations have a similar experience, albeit that the proportion of output traded is closer to a quarter of the total (WTO 2013: 84–85). Indeed, the share of total export value accounted for by the largest exporters is significantly lower in the UK than in most leading developed nations, with the top 1% of exporters accounting for 80.9% of US exports, 59% in Germany, 48% in Belgium, 44% in France and 42% in the UK. When expanding the group to the top 10% of exporters, the difference narrows, as these firms account for 96.3% of US exports, 90% in Germany, 84% in both France and Belgium, together with 80% in the UK (WTO 2013: 87).

Calculating the proportion of firms that export is not altogether straightforward, however, because there are different ways of counting. For example, whilst there were 5.4 million private sector businesses recorded in 2015, there were only 2.45 million of these registered for VAT and/or PAYE, which is only 44% of the total number of UK firms, with the remainder being too small to qualify for paying VAT and who do not have any employees (BIS 2015: 1, 5; ONS 2015a). Thus, if the percentage calculation uses the figure for total number of firms in the UK, it will produce a result less than half the figure if the calculation uses only those firms registered for VAT.

The figures used by HMRC (2015: 1) suggest that, in 2014, there were approximately 143,000 businesses which exported goods to other EU member states, employing a total of 9.8 million people, with 210,000 businesses importing goods from other EU member states, employing 12.3 million. Unfortunately, there are no equivalent figures for services and therefore the estimate produced, of only 5% of UK businesses exporting goods to the EU, is too restrictive (BIS 2016:

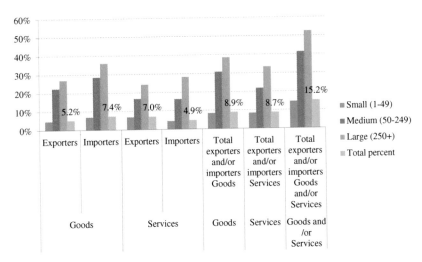

Fig. 5.3 The percentage of UK establishments engaging in exporting and/or importing goods and services to/from the rest of the world, by size of business, 2014. *Source* ONS (2015b)

7). If, as has been suggested, services account for around one quarter of trade with the EU by value, then a more accurate figure might be 6.25%.[3] Another complication is that the figures make it difficult to distinguish whether some firms both import and export, or whether these are distinctive activities. This matters, when calculating the number of firms that trade with the EU, because if they are distinct, the number will be around 350,000, whereas if firms both import and export, numbers could be only 210,000. Interestingly, the Department for Business Innovation and Skills (BIS) adopts the lower estimate. Finally, using a slightly different selection of data, the Office for National Statistics (ONS) have produced their own estimates, which are actually quite close to the HMRC figures. They assess that around 5.2% of UK firms export and 7.4% import goods, with the equivalent figures for services being 7 and 4.9% respectively, with the services sector being predominant amongst UK exporters (Figs. 5.3 and 5.4).[4] Using the earlier estimate that services account for around one quarter of trade with the EU, this would imply that around 5.7% of UK businesses export goods and services, and 6.8% import from the EU.

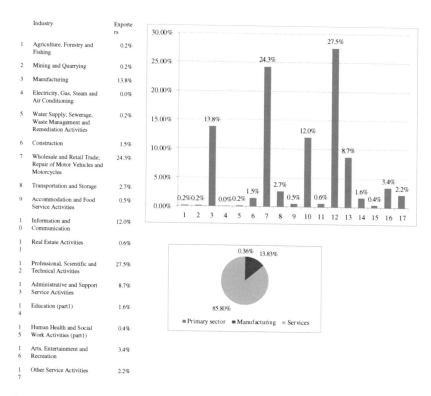

	Industry	Exporters
1	Agriculture, Forestry and Fishing	0.2%
2	Mining and Quarrying	0.2%
3	Manufacturing	13.8%
4	Electricity, Gas, Steam and Air Conditioning	0.0%
5	Water Supply; Sewerage, Waste Management and Remediation Activities	0.2%
6	Construction	1.5%
7	Wholesale and Retail Trade; Repair of Motor Vehicles and Motorcycles	24.3%
8	Transportation and Storage	2.7%
9	Accommodation and Food Service Activities	0.5%
10	Information and Communication	12.0%
11	Real Estate Activities	0.6%
12	Professional, Scientific and Technical Activities	27.5%
13	Administrative and Support Service Activities	8.7%
14	Education (part1)	1.6%
15	Human Health and Social Work Activities (part1)	0.4%
16	Arts, Entertainment and Recreation	3.4%
17	Other Service Activities	2.2%

Fig. 5.4 The distribution of UK exporters, by main industry and sector, 2014. *Source* ONS (2015b)

The evidence would therefore suggest that only a small fraction of UK firms engage in international trade with the EU, and those that do are disproportionately larger firms. Indeed, one estimate suggests that 59.1% of firms exporting to the EU in 2014 have 250 or more employees (Harris and Li 2007; HMRC 2015: 7). Yet, despite most of UK businesses operating within the domestic market, all of them have to abide by EU regulations that apply *as if* they were engaging in trade with other EU nations. This places an onerous burden upon Small and Medium Sized Enterprises (SMEs), which represent over 99% of all private sector businesses in the UK, employing 15.6 million people, representing 60% of all private sector employment, and with a combined annual turnover of £1.8 trillion, representing 47% of all private sector turnover (BIS 2015: 1). Indeed, the EU has recognised the significance of this issue and had proposed consultation about lightening the burden of regulations upon the smallest, micro businesses (HMG 2016: 20–21). Nevertheless, any resulting gain would only be felt in the medium term, and therefore, when calculating the impact of UK withdrawal from the EU, it is suggested that one benefit would be felt by the vast majority of SMEs who do not trade with the EU in having to bear the cost of SIM regulations (Business for Britain 2015: 122–123; Capital Economics 2016: 13).

This claim is, however, disputed on two grounds. The first notes that SMEs might not trade with EU nations directly, but their activity may be part of a process which does so indirectly, if they participate in the supply chains of larger enterprises, who themselves do trade with the EU. One estimate is that this would affect around 15% of SMEs (BIS 2016: 2). If this figure was added to the figure for direct exporters, it would indicate that perhaps as much as one quarter of UK firms were involved, either directly or indirectly, in trading with EU member states. Of course, this does not necessarily undermine the burden of regulation argument, because this would still leave three quarters of UK firms having to comply with regulations which had little direct or indirect relevance. Moreover, since the larger exporting companies would need to comply with SIM regulations in any case, there is an argument that, for most regulations, they could cover any administrative burden themselves rather than this being spread to all sections of their supply chains.

The second argument, however, is more interesting. It suggests that it would be 'unworkable' to exempt UK firms who do not export from having to comply with SIM rules and regulations, because they remain part of the SIM and thereby they compete with competitors from other EU nations in the UK domestic market (Springford 2016: 2). In essence, whilst the UK remains within the SIM, the argument is that exempting UK firms that do not export into the rest of the EU gives them an unfair competitive advantage against other EU firms who might seek business within the UK domestic market. According to this perspective, there are only two viable alternatives: to either continue to apply common rules across the SIM, which would apply to all UK firms while ever the UK remains a full participant in the SIM, or for the UK to withdraw from the SIM and pursue one of the other alternative trading relationships with the EU that are discussed in Chap. 9.

The Estimated Costs and Benefits of EU Regulations

There have been a number of calculations made concerning the cost of EU regulations. Congdon (2014: 5, 26–35), for example, estimated that it costs between 5.25 and 7% of UK GDP. He further disaggregated this regulatory burden into measures pertaining to climate change and renewable energy regulations of between 1.75 and 2.25% of UK GDP, social and employment regulation costing between 2.5 and 2.75% of UK GDP, financial regulation between 0.5 and 0.75% of UK GDP and the balance of regulatory costs of between 0.75 and 1.25% of UK GDP (Congdon 2014: 30). This analysis focuses rather narrowly upon the costs of regulation, rather than considering the associated benefits. Hence, whilst the effect of EU regulation such as the Temporary Agency Workers Directive imposes costs upon businesses who fall within its sphere of influence, through payment of higher wages, this has a positive macroeconomic effect in boosting demand which is likely to offset some of this cost to the economy, and yet is not included in Congdon's calculations (McFadden and Tarrant 2015: 41).

A second approach has involved use of the Regulatory Impact Assessments (RIAs) generated by the UK government, which attempt to measure the potential costs and benefits associated with individual national and EU-originated regulations.[5] These RIAs were introduced in the UK in 1998, and the intent is to identify both the direct costs and benefits of each example of regulation, together with the opportunity cost (or calculated risks) of not intervening (NAO 2001). The RIA assessment includes administrative costs for organisations and regulators, in maintaining and monitoring the regulatory framework, in addition to the practical impact arising from individuals and companies having to comply with the regulation through changing behaviour or introducing new training to ensure compliance with the new rules.

There are a number of weaknesses with the RIA approach, not the least of which being that not all regulations are subject to a RIA assessment. Indeed, figures from Ambler et al. (2010: 13, 22) would suggest that in only around 60% of regulations studied, and more particularly only 52% of EU regulations, identified costs for businesses, whilst the corresponding figures for benefits were less than in 40% of cases. Secondly, RIA assessments do not tend to assess wider economic impacts, which may derive from a more regulated business reducing its output as a result of health and safety measures in the case of asbestos manufacture, or energy intensive industries in the case of environmental regulation (Thompson and Harari 2013: 20). Moreover, in order to estimate future economic impacts, the RIA system discounts effects according to the usual rules employed by the civil service, which involves use of a discount rate (the Social Time Preference Rate), which is estimated at 3.5% per annum (HM Treasury 2003). This is a practice which Ambler et al. (2010: 18) regard as 'wholly unrealistic', because the discount rate is an inadequate means of estimating future impacts amidst uncertainty about regulatory impact. This is a reasonable criticism, yet there is a need to estimate the impact of regulations over time and therefore future projections have to be discounted to take account of opportunity costs.

Whatever the weaknesses with the approach, RIA data has been utilised by research teams working with the British Chambers of Commerce (BCC) and the 'think tank' *Open Europe* to estimate the cumulative costs and benefits of EU regulations. The BCC 'Burdens Barometer' estimated the cumulative cost of the major regulations, introduced in the UK between 1998 and 2010, to total £88.3bn, with 68.8% of this, representing £60.8bn, originating from the EU.[6] By contrast, *Open Europe* calculated the cumulative cost of regulation, introduced since 1998, to have cost the UK economy £176 billion over this 11 year period, with 71% of this total, amounting to £124 billion, having its origin in the EU (Gaskell and Persson 2010: 7). Part of the reason for this discrepancy in data concerns the number of cases analysed; the Open Europe study examined 1950 RIAs, whereas the BCC study analysed only the largest 144 RIAs.

A detailed examination of the RIAs indicates that there are a few regulations which have a disproportionate impact upon the overall cost burden for the UK economy. For example, *Open Europe* estimates that the most significant 100 EU regulations cost the UK economy £33.3 billion per annum.[7] Hence, the costliest 5% of EU regulations impose 26.9% of the estimated burden upon UK businesses. Moreover, the five costliest EU regulations were estimated to cost approximately £19 billion per year and representing more than 15% of the total cost imposed by EU-derived regulations. The report states these as:

1. The UK Renewable Energy Strategy—promotion of renewable energy, including biofuels, with a recurring cost of £4.7bn per annum.
2. The Capital Requirements Regulation and Directive (CRD IV)—strengthening the regulation of the banking sector, with an estimated recurring cost of £4.6bn per annum.
3. The Working Time Directive—limiting working hours and requiring annual leave of 5.6 weeks per year, with a recurring cost of £4.2bn per annum.
4. The EU Climate and Energy Package—establishing targets to meet greenhouse gas reduction, embodying the EU emissions trading system, with a recurring cost of £3.4bn per annum.
5. The Temporary Agency Workers Directive—guaranteeing equal pay and conditions for those working through employment agencies with employees working in businesses doing equivalent work, with a recurring cost of £2.1bn per annum.

When considering regulations by type, the *Open Europe* report indicates that EU employment legislation is the largest regulatory category, costing the UK economy £38.9 billion between 1998 and 2009, and accounting for 22% of total regulatory costs, followed by EU environmental regulation (18%), and with EU health and safety regulation and EU financial regulation both accounting for 5% of total regulatory costs for the UK economy (Gaskell and Persson 2010: 8).

The conclusion that EU regulations would appear particularly burdensome for the business community is tempered by two caviats. The first is that it is possible that a proportion of these costs derive from national government's 'gold plating' EU regulations as they translate Directives into national law, through adding additional requirements, and thereby increasing burdens upon firms, consumers and employees over and above the original intent of the EU regulation (HMG 2013). National governments have some discretion over how to translate Directives into UK law, although this is not the case with EU Regulations or Decisions, where they are imposed without the requirement for national legislation (Thompson and Harari 2013: 20). Gaskell and Persson (2010: 13–14) remain sceptical that this is a significant problem, even though their database does not allow for the type of cross-national comparative analysis which would be necessary to resolve the question. However, as can be noted from the work of Christiensen (2010: 12), the number of Directives represent only a very small proportion of the total volume of the totality of EU rules and regulations, and therefore it is likely that national government 'gold plating' is not likely to be more than of marginal significance.

The more important qualification is that this analysis, thus far, has focused upon the costs but not the benefits of regulation. Yet, the purpose of regulation is to achieve a positive net benefit for the economy as a whole, even if this does place a disproportionate burden upon the business community. Hence, when seeking to determine the relative merits of individual policy interventions, it is preferable to use the Hicks-Kaldor criteria that it should be considered to be successful if the net gains exceed net costs, such that, in principle, those who gained from the measure could fully compensate the losers (Layard and Glaister 1994: 6).

The BCC analysis rejects the inclusion of forecast benefits, preferring to focus more narrowly upon the burden of regulation for businesses. Indeed, it criticises the inclusion of benefits for other stakeholders in the analysis as being 'deeply flawed' and 'lack credibility' (Ambler et al. 2010: 2, 17). However, the *Open Europe* studies, by contrast, do include an estimation of potential benefits. Indeed, they note that the benefits that the RIAs ascribe to these same 100 EU regulations were estimated to be around £58.6 billion per year. This suggests that the benefits of these regulations *exceed* the costs, producing a benefit-to-cost ratio of

1.76. This would appear to contradict the claim that EU regulations are costly to the UK economy. This conclusion is uncertain, however, because 78.5% of these predicted benefits arise from only three EU regulations, and, moreover, *Open Europe* suggest that estimates of net benefits derived from one of these measures may be of questionable validity.[8] When testing the full range of 1950 regulations, *Open Europe* found that the benefit-to-cost ratio was 1.02 for the range of EU regulations examined (Gaskell and Persson 2010: 10). Thus, according to this evidence, EU regulations probably do little net harm to the UK economy, but neither are they a particular benefit.

Are National Regulations More Beneficial to the UK Economy?

The *Open Europe* analysis includes evidence pertaining to the efficiency of national vis-à-vis EU regulation; in that, it finds that UK-sourced regulations deliver a benefit-to-cost ratio of 2.35. In other words, whereas EU regulations have produced on average £1.02 worth of benefits for every £1 of costs imposed, UK regulations have delivered benefits of £2.35 (Gaskell and Persson 2010: 10). A similar estimate, produced by the Department for Business Innovation and Skills (BIS), calculated that the benefit-to-cost ratio for UK regulation introduced in the year 2008–2009, was 1.85, although this figure would increase to a value of around 4, if the disproportionate impact of one rather large piece of (pensions) legislation was removed from the calculation. Breaking the figures down further, BIS estimated that primary legislation produced a net benefit-to-cost ratio of 2.82 and secondary legislation 5.57.[9]

Given that BIS figures are based upon only those regulations introduced within 1 year, and that they only partially include recurring impacts derived from measures introduced in previous years (Gaskell and Persson 2010: 36), some discrepancy in the results is inevitable. Nevertheless, the BIS results do seem to reinforce the conclusions, reached by *Open Europe*, that national regulations are, on average, more effective in that they deliver greater net benefits than supranational regulations. Moreover, these conclusions have been repeated in a major UK government report (HMG 2013a: 41–42).

One plausible reason for this difference relates to the fact that EU regulations, by definition, have to apply across all member states, and therefore must be a one-size-fits-all solution to a perceived problem. Yet, this may be expected to be less capable of accounting for differences in individual circumstances pertaining within individual nations. Consequently, super-national regulations are more likely to create friction and be less effective in achieving the desired outcome than national alternatives designed with individual circumstances in mind. However, it may also be partly due to the particular areas where the UK government regulates, which may result in a disproportionate benefit relative to those in which EU regulation is dominant (Thompson and Harari 2013: 21). This would, however, be a little surprising, because of the claims made that the benefits arising from the SIM are particularly significant.

A second possible interpretation is that EU regulations may be concentrated in those areas where few net benefits may be delivered relative to other areas where national regulations predominate (Thompson and Harari 2013: 21). McFadden and Tarrant (2015: 41), for example, suggest that one reason behind the relatively disappointing net benefit arising from EU regulations is that a sizeable share of EU regulations, introduced between 1998 and 2009, were concerned with employment and environmental legislation, which may have given rise to relatively low economic returns. This is plausible, albeit that critics of EU regulation may equally argue that a proportion of this regulation was unnecessary and that, even if introduced to solve problems that impinge upon the UK economy, it may still be better solved at national rather than supra-national level. Consequently, whilst it is difficult to properly test this proposition before the UK completes Brexit, and nationally designed regulation supersedes current EU regulations, it would nevertheless appear that there is sufficient prima facie evidence to conclude that there does appear to be a measurable difference in the effectiveness of national vis-à-vis EU regulation. Thus, following Brexit, the ability to custom the UK's regulatory framework to the specific and identifiable needs of its economy might be anticipated to generate a net beneficial impact.

Regulation After Brexit

Outside of the EU, the UK will have greater flexibility to devise and operate its own tailor-made regulatory framework. There should be some advantages to be realised from developing rules to best fit the needs of the national economy, rather than adapting EU requirements which have been devised for application across a large and diverse set of member states. Indeed, the scant evidence that does exist would indicate that, on average, national regulations deliver a far superior benefit-to-cost advantage. Thus, even were the UK to continue to regulate the same industries as within EU membership, the simple act of doing so more smartly and with greater focus upon the specific needs of the economy or industry should deliver real economic benefit.

Estimates of this impact vary, according to assumptions made about the feasibility of deregulation. For example, Congdon (2014: 5) estimates that the regulatory burden imposed by the EU equates to 6% of UK GDP, whilst *Open Europe* calculations suggest that the 100 costliest EU regulations impose a burden equivalent to 7.1% of 2016 UK GDP.[10] According to these more significant estimates, there would be considerable scope to reduce any regulatory burden once independent from the EU. However, it is reasonable to assume that there may be significant political resistance to deregulating some social and environmental regulations, such as reducing the minimum number of days of annual leave set out in the Working time Directive, or watering-down climate change targets set out in EU renewable energy and climate change regulations (Capital Economics 2016: 3; PwC 2016: 23). As a result, the positive boost to the UK economy might prove to be 'surprisingly limited' (Springford (2016: 4, 7). Indeed, the Economists for Brexit (2016: 29) estimate is that savings made from reducing the regulatory burden might be equivalent to perhaps 2% of UK GDP, whilst another estimate, made by PwC (2016: 9), suggests that plausible reductions in regulatory costs may amount to a mere 0.3% of UK GDP by 2030. Moreover, the evidence gleaned from RIA estimates may indicate that benefits derived from EU regulations more or less cover their costs, and therefore, whilst businesses might benefit from a reduction of EU regulations following Brexit, this would be offset by losers amongst other stakeholders in the UK.

There is, however, a more significant finding that flows from the analysis of the RIA's, and that concerns the apparent superiority of national compared to supranational regulation. If, as the evidence generated by BIS and *Open Europe* suggests, UK regulation produces roughly 2.3 times more net benefits than EU regulations, then, *ceteris paribus*, the repatriation of regulatory control should generate a significant positive boost to the UK economy. Thus, even if the UK, following withdrawal, were to continue to regulate the UK economy in exactly the same areas as if still within the EU, but that these regulations were designed and implemented by the UK government rather than being designed for the benefit of all member states across Europe, then it might be anticipated that the result would be 2.3 times more beneficial than previously.

It is difficult to estimate the likely magnitude of this effect, given that it depends upon rather scant evidence produced by only a handful of studies. Moreover, it could be anticipated that not all former EU regulations could be so easily redesigned by national government. Environmental regulations, for example, may require greater commonality with former EU partners given that they deal explicitly with international spillovers. Nevertheless, to seek to illustrate the point, taking the *Open Europe* £124bn estimate of the cumulative cost of EU regulations over a decade to be a starting point, then, were it possible to redesign all former EU regulations on the same basis as national regulations, these estimates would indicate that the UK may benefit by up to a possible £285bn over the first decade after Brexit. To present this in today's values, these figures require discounting by 3% per year, which would result in an estimate of some £211bn of net benefit, which would be equivalent to 4.5% of current UK GDP. Thus, even without the UK taking advantage of the opportunity provided by Brexit to pursue a path of significant deregulation (Congdon 2014: 31), and even assuming that only a fraction of the total number of regulations could be effectively redesigned to provide this degree of positive impact to the UK economy, there is the plausible expectation that Brexit may deliver significant economic benefits in this area.

Any regulatory gains from Brexit will, additionally, depend upon the form of trade relationship that the UK negotiates with the EU during the withdrawal process. If, for example, the UK decides to remain a full participant in the SIM, through EEA membership, then former EU rules will continue to apply and there will be few regulatory gains. Indeed, an Open Europe assessment is that participation in the EEA would still leave the UK with around 94% of former regulatory costs, but without the ability to participate in the determination of the rules.[11] If the UK prefers to agree a Free Trade Agreement (FTA) with the EU, or indeed, if it prefers to reply on international trade governed by the World Trade Organisation (WTO) rules, then it is probable that EU regulations will only apply to those firms which choose to trade within the SIM. This will reduce the regulatory burden on the remaining 85-plus per cent of UK firms, but the downside of this arrangement is that the UK will have less input into the formation of EU regulations and therefore they may not prove so advantageous as previously experienced by those firms who trade with other EU nations (Portes 2013: F6).

Notes

1. 'IoD calls on all parties to accept need for EU reform', 28 September 2015, http://www.iod.com/influencing/press-office/press-releases/iod-calls-on-all-parties-to-accept-need-for-eu-reform.
2. http://www.publications.parliament.uk/pa/cm200405/cmhansrd/vo050322/text/50322w46.htm.
3. http://www.publications.parliament.uk/pa/cm201212/cmhansrd/cm120327/text/120327w0005.htm#1203281002290.
4. http://webarchive.nationalarchives.gov.uk/20160105160709/ http://www.ons.gov.uk/ons/rel/abs/annual-business-survey/exporters-and-importers-in-great-britain--2014/sty-exporters-and-importers.html.
5. A database of these IA's are available via: http://www.legislation.gov.uk/ukia. If you would like to read more about the origin, design

and application of RIAs, then you may wish to consider Dunlop and Radaelli (2016).

6. http://www.thamesvalleychamber.co.uk/uploads/Policy/BurdensBarometer2010.pdf.
7. http://openeurope.org.uk/intelligence/britain-and-the-eu/top-100-eu-rules-cost-britain-33-3bn/.
8. http://openeurope.org.uk/intelligence/britain-and-the-eu/top-100-eu-rules-cost-britain-33-3bn/.
9. http://www.publications.parliament.uk/pa/cm200809/cmhansrd/cm091021/wmstext/91021m0001.htm; https://www.theyworkforyou.com/wms/?id=2009-10-21c.55WS.1.
10. http://openeurope.org.uk/intelligence/britain-and-the-eu/top-100-eu-rules-cost-britain-33-3bn/.
11. http://www.theguardian.com/politics/2015/mar/16/eu-exit-norway-option-costs-thinktank.

References

Ambler, T., Chittenden, F., & Miccini, A. (2010). *Is regulation really good for us?* London: British Chambers of Commerce. Available via: http://www.britishchambers.org.uk/assets/downloads/policy_reports_2010/is_regulation_really_good_good_for_us.pdf.

Anderson, J. E., & van Wincoop, E. (2004). Trade costs. *Journal of Economic Literature, 42*(3), 691–751.

Bernard, A. B., Jensen, J. B., Redding, S. J., & Schott, P. K. (2007). Firms in international trade. *Journal of Economic Perspectives, 21*(3), 105–130.

Department for Business Innovation and Skills (BIS). (2015). *Business population estimates for the UK and regions 2015.* London: BIS. Available via: https://www.gov.uk/government/uploads/system/uploads/attachment_data/file/467443/bpe_2015_statistical_release.pdf#page=3.

Department for Business Innovation and Skills (BIS). (2016). *BIS estimate of the proportion of UK SMEs in the supply chain of exporters.* London: BIS. Available via: https://www.gov.uk/government/uploads/system/uploads/attachment_data/file/524847/bis-16-230-smes-supply-chains-exporters.pdf#page=7.

Business for Britain. (2015). *Change or go: How Britain would gain influence and prosper outside an unreformed EU.* London: Business for Britain. Available via: https://forbritain.org/cogwholebook.pdf.

Capital Economics. (2016). *The economics impact of 'Brexit': A paper discussing the United Kingdom' relationship with Europe and the impact of 'Brexit' on the British economy.* Oxford: Woodford Investment Management LLP. Available via: https://woodfordfunds.com/economic-impact-brexit-report/.

Confederation of British Industry (CBI). (2013). *Our global future: The business vision for a reformed EU.* London: CBI. Available via: http://www.cbi.org.uk/media/2451423/our_global_future.pdf#page=1&zoom=auto,-119,842.

Christiensen, J. G. (2010). EU legislation and national regulation: Uncertain steps towards a European public policy. *Public Administration, 88*(1), 3–17.

Congdon, T. (2014). *How much does the European Union cost Britain?* London: UKIP. Available via: http://www.timcongdon4ukip.com/docs/EU2014.pdf.

Driver, R. (2014). *Analysing the case for EU membership: How does the economic evidence stack up?* London: The City UK. Available via: https://www.thecityuk.com/research/analysing-the-case-for-eu-membership-does-the-economic-evidence-stack-up/.

Dunlop, C. A. & Radaelli, C. M. (eds.). (2016). *Handbook of regulatory impact assessment.* Cheltenham: Edward Elgar.

Economists for Brexit. (2016). *The Economy after Brexit.* London: Economists for Brexit. Available via: https://static1.squarespace.com/static/570a10a460b5e93378a26ac5/t/5722f8f6a3360ce7508c2acd/1461909779956/Economists+for+Brexit+-+The+Economy+after+Brexit.pdf.

Gaskell, S., & Persson, M. (2010). *Still out of control? Measuring eleven years of EU regulation* (2nd ed.). London: Open Europe. Available via: http://archive.openeurope.org.uk/Content/documents/Pdfs/stilloutofcontrol.pdf.

Harris, R., & Li, Q. C. (2007). *Firm level empirical study of the contribution of exporting to UK productivity growth* (Cm 7101). London: The Stationary Office. Available via: https://www.gov.uk/government/uploads/system/uploads/attachment_data/file/243285/7101.pdf.

HM Government (HMG). (2013a). *Review of the balance of competences between the United Kingdom and the European Union—The single market.* London: The Stationary Office. Available via: https://www.gov.uk/government/uploads/system/uploads/attachment_data/file/227069/2901084_SingleMarket_acc.pdf.

HMG. (2013b). *International education: Global growth and prosperity*. London: The Stationary Office. Available via: https://www.gov.uk/government/uploads/system/uploads/attachment_data/file/340600/bis-13-1081-international-education-global-growth-and-prosperity-revised.pdf.

HMG (HM Government). (2016). *The best of both Worlds: The United Kingdom's special status in a reformed European Union*, The Stationary Office, London. Available via: https://www.gov.uk/government/uploads/system/uploads/attachment_data/file/502291/54284_EU_Series_No1_Web_Accessible.pdf.

HM Treasury. (2003). *The Green book: Appraisal and evaluation in central government*. London: The Stationary Office. Available via: https://www.gov.uk/government/uploads/system/uploads/attachment_data/file/220541/green_book_complete.pdf.

HM Revenue and Customs (HMRC). (2015). *UK trade in goods statistics by business characteristics*. London: HMRC. Available via: https://www.gov.uk/government/uploads/system/uploads/attachment_data/file/476593/IDBR_OTS_2014.pdf.

House of Commons Regulatory Reform Committee (HoC). (2009). *Themes and trends in regulatory reform: Ninth report of Session 2008–09*, Vol. II, HC 329-II, London: The Stationary Office. Available via: http://www.publications.parliament.uk/pa/cm200809/cmselect/cmdereg/329/329ii.pdf.

Irwin, G. (2015). *Brexit: The impact on the UK and the EU*. London: Global Counsel. Available via: http://www.global-counsel.co.uk/system/files/publications/Global_Counsel_Impact_of_Brexit_June_2015.pdf.

Layard, R., & Glaister, S. (1994). Introduction. In R. Layard & S. Glaister (Eds.), *Cost-benefit analysis*. Cambridge: Cambridge University Press.

McFadden, P., & Tarrant, A. (2015). *What would 'Out' look like? Testing Eurosceptic alternatives to EU membership*. London: Policy Network. Available via: http://www.policy-network.net/publications/4995/What-would-out-look-like.

Miller, V. (2010). *How much legislation comes from Europe?* (House of Commons Library Research Paper No. HC10/62). Available via: http://researchbriefings.parliament.uk/ResearchBriefing/Summary/RP10-62.

NAO. (2001). *Better regulation: Making good use of regulatory impact assessments* (HC 329). London: The Stationary Office. Available via: https://www.nao.org.uk/wp-content/uploads/2001/11/0102329.pdf.

Office for National Statistics (ONS). (2015a). *Statistical bulletin: UK business: Activity, size and location—Business enterprises analysed by legal form, industry, region and employment size band*. London: The Stationary Office. Available via: https://www.ons.gov.uk/businessindustryandtrade/business/activitysizeandlocation/bulletins/ukbusinessactivitysizeandlocation/2015-10-06.

Office for National Statistics (ONS). (2015b). *Exporters and importers in Great Britain, 2014. Part of annual business survey, exporters and importers in Great Britain.* London: The Stationary Office. Available via: http://webarchive.nationalarchives.gov.uk/20160105160709/ http://www.ons.gov.uk/ons/rel/abs/annual-business-survey/exporters-and-importers-in-great-britain–2014/sty-exporters-and-importers.html.

Portes, J. (2013). Commentary: The economic implications for the UK of leaving the European Union. *National Institute Economic Review, 266,* F4–9. Available via: http://www.niesr.ac.uk/sites/default/files/commentary.pdf.

PricewaterhouseCoopers LLP (PwC). (2016). *Leaving the EU: Implications for the UK economy.* London: PricewaterhouseCoopers LLP. Available via: http://news.cbi.org.uk/news/leaving-eu-would-cause-a-serious-shock-to-uk-economy-new-pwc-analysis/leaving-the-eu-implications-for-the-uk-economy/.

Springford, J. (2016). *Brexit and EU regulation: A bonfire of the vanities.* London: Centre for European Reform. Available via: https://www.cer.org.uk/sites/default/files/pb_js_regulation_3feb16.pdf.

Thompson, G., & Harari, D. (2013). *The economic impact of EU membership on the UK* (House of Commons Library Briefing Paper SN/EP/6730). Available via: http://researchbriefings.parliament.uk/ResearchBriefing/Summary/SN06730#fullreport.

World Trade Organisation (WTO). (2013). *World trade report 2013: Factors shaping the future of world trade.* Geneva: World Trade Organisation. Available via: https://www.wto.org/english/res_e/booksp_e/world_trade_report13_e.pdf.

6

Migration

Introduction

Migration has proven to be a difficult issue for successive administrations (Streeck 2016; IMF 2016), at least partly because of the centrality of the EU's four fundamental freedoms, which includes the freedom of movement of people.[1] This principle is enshrined within Article 45 of the Treaty on the Functioning of the European Union (TFEU) and it proved to be impossible for former Prime Minister Cameron to significantly reform, in his negotiations with other EU members prior to the European referendum (Gill 2015; HMG 2016a). Without the ability to limit free movement of labour from the EU into the UK, the government's commitment to reduce annual net migration to the 'tens of thousands' was always going to be difficult, if not impossible to achieve. As a result, the Institute of Directors (IoD) suggests that the Brexit decision was partly a vote of no confidence in the government's ability to control migration (People Management 2016). Moreover, this issue is likely to be a point of contention in future Brexit talks with the EU, as continued free access to the Single Internal Market (SIM) is almost certainly going to require acceptance of the free movement of labour.

© The Author(s) 2017
P.B. Whyman and A.I. Petrescu, *The Economics of Brexit*,
DOI 10.1007/978-3-319-58283-2_6

Academic evidence on migration's economic impact can offer key answers to determining the weighing of considerations in the forthcoming negotiation process. The economic impact is not the only factor of relevance, since migration can have cultural and social effects too, such as potentially enriching a nation which is embracing diversity, while sometimes also creating unwelcome tensions and fragmentation. However, the economic argument is central. Does increasing migration place an unbearable strain upon public services, housing and infrastructure? Does immigrant labour displace existing residents in the UK labour market? Or does migration increase growth rates and pay more in taxes than drawn in benefits? Does migrant labour possess higher than average skill levels, in comparison with the existing labour force? This chapter will seek to evaluate the evidence pertaining the economic impact of migration.

The UK Labour Market—Brief Comparative Statistics

Definition

Economic migrants are people moving voluntarily from one country (country of origin) to a different country (country of destination) in search of better economic outcomes, such as wages, living standards and/or personal wellbeing. In this chapter, most of the discussion related to 'migration' is assumed to centre on economic migrants, to be distinguished from refugees (migrants moving involuntarily to a different country, trying to escape from adverse events such as famine, floods, earthquakes, or political unrest). Worldwide, the stock of migrants is composed predominantly of economic migrants, at 95% (IMF 2016).

There is a problem, however, when seeking to measure migration. For example, should migration figures amalgamate economic migrants and overseas university students, when the latter are only in the UK for a limited time and their ability to work during their studies is limited? Similarly, even the term 'resident' can prove difficult to define, thus making migration data less useful than otherwise desired (Migration Advisory Committee 2012: 46). Additionally, studies which have sought to examine the net cost or benefit to the UK, arising from migration, have produced differing results, at least partly due to how the economic effects were measured—and this comes down to the basics of difficulties in obtaining clear and usable statistics on migrants.

Population Density

The population density of a country is another factor to consider when examining the likely economic impact deriving from inward migration. For example, it may be anticipated that a nation with a lower population density might have fewer concerns than a higher density neighbour. Indeed, this may help to explain why Scotland has typically favoured continued inward migration from other EU member states[2] whilst England has been more anxious.

A high population density can lead to negative impact on housing, transportation, traffic congestion, the environment and many other factors. The demand in the UK for housing, and social housing in particular, has exceeded the supply of new properties to buy and rent for a number of years, with the consequence that purchase prices have risen faster than inflation, whilst concern has been expressed that borrowing multiples of salary may be reaching unaffordable levels.[3] Similarly, local authority waiting lists for public rented housing have remained high during recent decades.[4] Whilst there are multiple reasons for the relative shortfall in UK housing stock, including issues with the accessibility of finance and the failure of government policy in this area over a long period of time, it has been estimated that fully 36% of the increase in the number of households between 2008 and 2033 would be due to immigration (Migration Advisory Committee 2014). Hence, whilst not a primary cause of the UK's housing problems, inward migration may exacerbate its effects.

Between 1960 and 2000, the UK's population density grew rather gradually, from around 220 people per square kilometre to 240. However, since 2000, density has increased to a record high level of

270 in 2015 (WDI 2016). This highest rate of increase for UK statistics has occurred during the period of the recent two EU enlargements. In terms of international comparisons, some nations with a relatively high stock of migrant labour have low population densities (i.e. Canada and Australia), whereas others have a high population density but have lower levels of inward migration (i.e. Belgium, Netherlands and Malta). Switzerland, Luxembourg and Germany are broadly comparable to the UK, with high levels of both migrant stock and population density (Fig. 6.1).

Demographics and the Labour Force

Global statistics indicate that the world has experienced an unprecedented rate of demographic growth during the past five decades, albeit that this rate has begun to slow down to around half of the 3% or more annual growth level that had been witnessed up to the 1960s (Fig. 6.2). The UK bucks this trend, given that its decline has been arrested over the past decade, contrary to the global and EU trend, growing faster than the average in OECD countries and the EU.

There are a number of factors which can affect the growth of the labour force, including:

1. Fertility rates
2. Age-dependency ratios
3. Participation rates amongst the population—i.e. female participation in the workforce, the proportion of the population in education and training
4. Retirement support (pensions) and qualifying ages
5. Net migration

Fertility rates, measured as number of people born per woman, are perhaps the most obvious way for most nations to increase their labour force in the medium term. The observable trend is that poorer, mainly agricultural nations, with high levels of child mortality, will tend to have higher fertility rates, whereas rising income levels tend to reduce

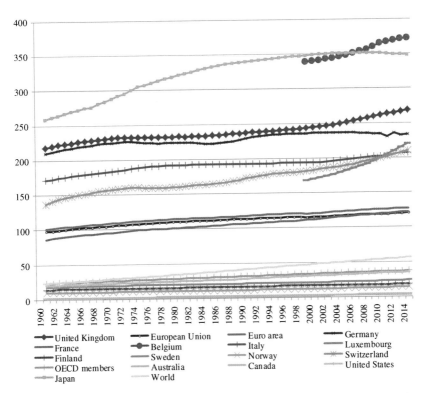

Fig. 6.1 Population density per square kilometre, 1960–2015. *Notes* The following are three countries are excluded from the Figure because their outlying high-density levels do not fit well on the scale shown: Malta (level of around 1000), Netherlands (levels increased from 400 to about 500) and India (levels tripled from 150 to 450). *Source* WDI (2016)

national fertility rates over time. Indeed, it is the decrease in worldwide fertility rates which can significantly explain why the world reached a turning point, marking the end of that exceptional period of demographic growth (World Bank Report 2015). Nevertheless, it is counterintuitive to note that the UK has experienced population growth despite its initially declining, and subsequently relatively stable fertility rates (Fig. 6.3).

The age composition of the labour force is important too, as this impacts upon three of the other factors pertaining to its expansion. A

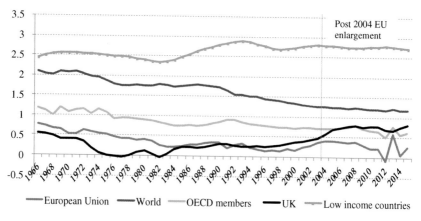

Fig. 6.2 Population growth per annum (%) *Source* World Data Bank (2016c)

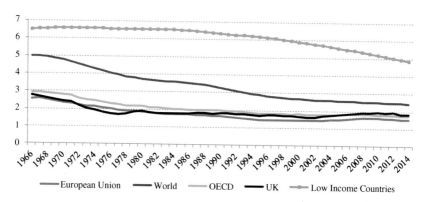

Fig. 6.3 Comparative view of the UK fertility rates, 1966–2015. *Source* World Data Bank (2016c)

higher proportion of older workers signifies a likely future reduction in the size of the labour force, and a larger share of those dependent upon the working population to support their retirement. This has the potential to create funding problems for public services, including pensions, healthcare and social care. A younger population, by contrast, will focus policy interventions upon education and training. Like other developed nations, the UK and EU have a growing age-dependency ratio issue that is likely to become more significant in the future (Fig. 6.4). The figures suggest that the British workforce is facing a relatively high dependency rate of 55% and it is currently set to need to sustain more dependents than at any previous point in the past 35 years.

To fund these societal needs, it is likely that either one or a combination of the following would occur: an increasing share of national growth be set aside for this purpose, taxation rise and/or the labour force be expanded to reduce the burden upon the working population. In terms of the latter option, this could be achieved through encouraging greater labour market participation from inactive groups, or delaying retirement (IMF 2016); both of these policy options have been adopted by successive UK administrations. However, for the purposes of this chapter, a net increase in migration could provide some assistance in this regard, both by expanding the labour force but additionally because migrant labour tends to be younger than the UK average and hence would slightly reduce the age composition of the UK population (IMF 2016; OECD 2017).

Net Migration

Net migration relates to the difference in the movement of people both into (immigration) and out of (emigration) a country. As can be seen in Fig. 6.5, annual net migration figures were the highest on record since the UK joined the EU, at 330,000 people in the latest full year where data is available (ONS 2016a).

In comparison with other EU(15) member states, UK net migration was not particularly high in the early years of its membership of the EU (see Figs. 6.5 and 6.6). However, this altered significantly with the 2004 EU enlargement. One reason for the large increase in migration from those nations joining the EU in 2004, is that the UK did not impose similar temporary restrictions upon the free movement of labour from these nations as virtually all other existing EU member states, and therefore the UK received a disproportionate share of such migrant labour during this period (see Fig. 6.6). Indeed, the inflow of EU nationals into the UK more than doubled after the 2004 EU enlargement (CBI 2016a), taking the total number of the migrant population within the UK from around 3.2 million in 1991 to over 7 million by 2011 (ONS

Panel A. Percent of population aged 0-14

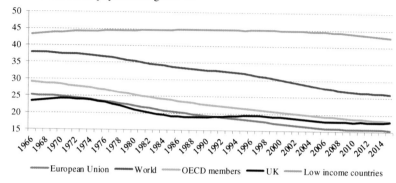

Panel B. Percent of population aged 65 and over

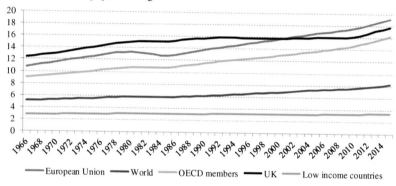

Panel C.Number of dependents per 100 people of working-age-the age-dependency ratio

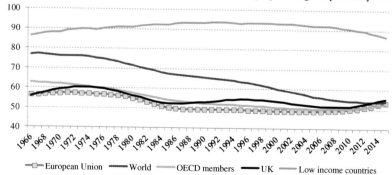

Fig. 6.4 Comparative demographics for the UK population, measured as % of total population. *Source* World Data Bank (2016c)

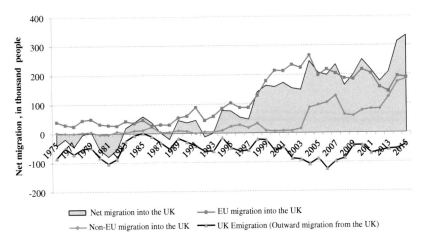

Fig. 6.5 Net international migration by citizenship, UK, 1975–2015. *Source* ONS (2016a)

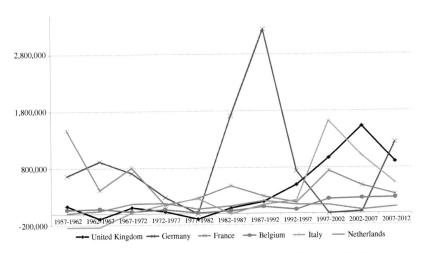

Fig. 6.6 Net migration cumulative for 5 year periods, selection of EU countries. *Note* The spike in Germany's migration statistics coincides with the reunification of Germany and a large number of East Germany citizens moving to West Germany. *Source* WDI (2016)

Panel A. EU countries with relatively positive net migration

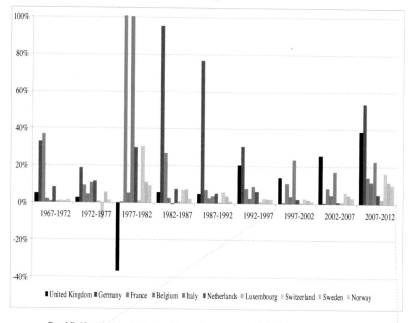

Panel B. Net migration for the ten EU member states which joined the EU in 2004 and 2007

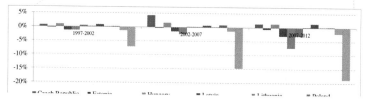

Fig. 6.7 Net migration per country, expressed as percentage of total EU net migration at 100%, selection of EU countries (Neither panel in this figure shows additive data. For instance in the period 1977–1982, in *Panel A*, France and Italy have each a level of net migration of nearly 100%, interpreted as equal to the total net migration within the EU. The numbers in Fig. 6.7 are not additive because EU net migration consists of the difference between immigrants into EU (going to any EU country) and emigrants from the EU, thus this statistic on EU net migration counts a different set of migrants than the French net migration (i.e. the difference between immigrants to France and emigrants from France). However, the assessment of these individual-country net migration flows, expressed in comparison to the total level of EU net migration, reveals the considerable size differences that net migration has across various EU counries)

2012). The UK's net total net migration level, between 2007 and 2012, equated to 0.9 million, which is a substantial figure and, indeed, it represents slightly less than 40% of the level of the net migration experienced by the whole of the EU area during this time period (see Fig. 6.7, Panel A). By 2016, it was reported that the number of people in work in the UK and who were born in other EU countries had risen to 6% of those employed (CBI 2016b:7).

Migrant Stock and Flow

Across the globe, only around 3.3% of the world population live in countries where they were not born, compared to 2.9% a quarter of a century earlier. Nevertheless, because of rising world population levels, the stock of migrants reached 250 million in 2015, experiencing a significant rise from 150 million in 1990 (IMF 2016). Comparing this with the picture depicted by Fig. 6.8, the increase in migration has centred upon the relatively high income developed nations, whose migrant stock has increased from 7.7 to 13.6% over this quarter of a century, while comparable figures for the EU as a whole indicate an increase from 5.7 to 10.7%.

In terms of the stock of migrant labour as a proportion of its total population, the UK has seen an increase too, from 6.4% in 1990 to 13.2% in 2015 (World Bank 2016a). This figure comprises both EU migrants and those born in non-EU countries; many of whom have family roots in Commonwealth countries (Eurostat 2011; ONS 2012). The figure remains low compared to nations such as Australia, Canada and the USA, which have migrant stock levels of around 28, 22 and 14% accordingly (see Fig. 6.8, Panel A). Still, the UK has become more likely in the past quarter of the century to figure among countries with the highest migration stock, relative to its neighbours in west Europe (see Fig. 6.8, Panel B).

▶ Note Panel A and Panel B have different scales, Panel B presenting a more detailed view of the period of time shown towards the end of Panel Panel A and with a different selection of countries. Source WDI (2016)

Panel A. Migrant stock as % of total population

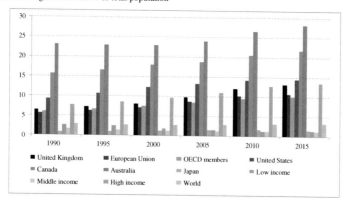

Panel B. Percentage point differences in migrant stocks (stocks measured as % of total population in respective country): difference between selected countries and the UK

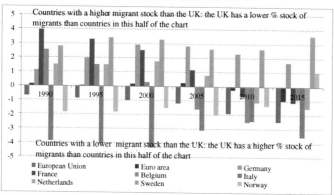

Note: The interpretation of the data in Panel B is, for example, that in 2015 Norway had an immigrant stock as percent of its own population which was higher by one percentage point than the respective figure in the UK.

Panel C. Migrant stock as % of total population

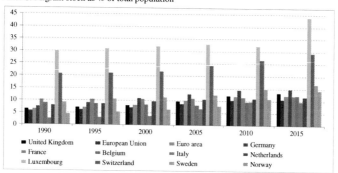

One point of note, for policy makers, considering the form of a post-Brexit trade relationship with the EU, concerns the fact that Switzerland has a much higher than average migrant share of its labour force (see Fig. 6.8 Panel C) and, since its bilateral arrangements with the EU involve its acceptance of the free movement of labour from other EU member states, this has caused a degree of tension (Booth et al. 2015: 73; Miller et al. 2016: 41).

Economic Theory and the Impact of Migration—A Brief Review

Motivations for Migration in Economic Theory

Economic theory has additionally sought to understand the motivations for labour mobility. One seminal theoretical contribution, made by Roy (1951), suggests that migrants could be categorised as 'positively selected' if they are among the most highly skilled in the country of origin (the country from which migrant leave), or 'negatively selected' if the migrants are relatively low-skilled in their country of origin. Inequality of economic outcomes in the country of origin, compared to the country of destination (the country to which migrants move), would be the main driving force of migration. Thus, economic models of migration can be conceptualised as being similar to ocean currents driven by temperature differences, in that migration is a movement between unequal areas in term of wages and, more generally, workers' desired economic outcomes.

Alternative explanations focus upon a range of *push and pull factors* which influence the relative attraction of potential work locations. Pull factors may include relatively high wages, but additionally work opportunities, employment and human rights, culture, climate and the familiarity of living and working in a country that shares certain

▶ **Fig. 6.8** Immigrant stock as percent of total population, comparative view of the UK and selected countries and country categories *Note* The interpretation of the data in Panel B is, for example, that in 2015 Norway had an immigrant stock as percent of its own population which was higher by one percentage point than the respective figure in the UK. *Source* WDI (2016)

characteristics with home. Push factors may include unemployment, low wages, discrimination, uncertainty, job insecurity, war, crime, political unrest and so forth.

In addition, *migrants' acceptance of risk* is suggested to have an impact upon migration flows and the attractiveness of potential host nations. For example, those more risk adverse may prefer a more egalitarian society, with a high level of social protection, whereas those who accept a greater degree of risk may prefer less equal economies, where success receives greater rewards. The potency of this effect should not be overstated, however, because EU member states such as the Slovak and Czech republics are more egalitarian societies than the EU norm, as measured by Gini coefficients, and yet the flow of migration is not from the UK and Germany to these nations (WDI 2016). Hence, whilst individual preferences related to risk aversion may be effective at the margin, it would appear that the decision to move is more related to potential future earnings. It is, however, possible that the provision of immediate and generous benefits can incentivise migration (Heitmüller 2002). It may also indicate why this became a focus for former Prime Minister Cameron in his renegotiation talks with the EU prior to the referendum. However, even here, given that the numbers of migrants in receipt of UK benefits are quite small, it is unlikely that this is a particularly powerful determinant of migration location (HoC 2015).

Applied in practice, the Roy model (Roy 1951), together with the push-and-pull model, can be very useful in helping to predict why people migrate towards economic areas with higher gross domestic product (GDP) per capita. Indeed, it can help to explain the predominantly East-West direction of the migration flows in the period post-2004 EU enlargement. There is a marked difference among, on one side, countries with a relatively high GDP per capita (e.g. GDP averages over the past decade being around US$40,000) including most of the western EU states, and, on the other side, countries which joined the EU after 2004. Except for Slovenia and Malta, none of the latter has had a GDP per capital averaging over the past decade higher than US$20,000(see Fig. 6.9). Statistics also reveal, at an international scale, a positive relationship between long-term real GDP per capita growth experienced by some countries—acting as a pull factor for migration—and

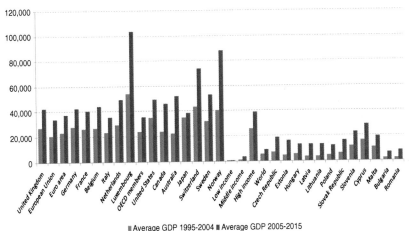

Fig. 6.9 Average GDP per capita in constant US$, selected countries, 1995–2015. *Source* World Bank (2016a)

an increase in the share of migrants expressed as percent of the total population in those countries (IMF 2016). This is in line with the UK experience of attracting a large flow of migrants from countries which have lower wages and GDP per capita, such as the more than 800,000 Polish migrants which alone represented by 2014 the single largest EU migrant population standing at nearly a third of the 2.9 million EU migrants (5% of the UK population) (ONS 2014).

Economic Impact of Migration in Theory

Economic theory has, as one of its key precepts, the notion that the free movement of labour is expected to bring economic benefits. Freedom in the supply and demand of labour allow workers and employers to meet in the labour market in order to negotiate, in the most simplistic economic analysis, two quintessential elements: the price of labour (the wage level), and the quantity of labour bought and sold (the number of workers, or the hours of work). Migration of labour, from one area to another, should result in a more efficient allocation of resources overall, as workers in an area with low wages move to another area with relative labour scarcity, and correspondingly higher wages, thereby causing a degree of equalisation of wage rates between the two areas.

The beneficiaries of labour mobility will, in this scenario, be the mobile (migrant) labour, who receives higher wages than previously paid in their home region, but also employers in the previously high wage area, since an increase in labour supply relative to the demand for labour will reduce the equilibrium wage that employers have to pay. However, it will prove disadvantageous for the existing workforce in the previously high wage area, who used to be employed at the previous (higher) wage rate. The introduction of a strong trade union or national minimum wage regulation could prevent wages from falling, but, unless the demand for labour rises alongside the increase in migrant labour, it may result in some unemployment for some of those who wish to work at this wage rate.

The neo-classical growth theory (discussed in more detail in Chap. 7) suggests that increasing the labour force will increase economic growth in the short term. This is based upon the assumption that all workers possess identical skills and abilities (homogenous labour), and hence adding more of this input to a process will result in greater output.

Moving away from this unrealistic textbook conception of a perfectly competitive economy, then the impact of migration will depend partly upon the relative skill level of migrants and the existing labour force. If migrant labour is more skilled than the existing workforce, then it has the potential to increase productivity and can reduce inflationary effects caused by labour supply bottlenecks in certain industries. However, it is now perfectly conceivable that a smaller net migration flow can actually increase economic growth if it is comprised of higher quality labour. In other words, the net growth impact depends upon the relative impacts of a smaller quantity of labour supply set against a higher quality of that labour.

Migration Seems to Have an Indeterminate Effect on Wages and Inequality

There are, however, further limitations with this predominantly neo-classical theory. There is, unfortunately, little consensus in the economics literature concerning the impact of migration on wages. For example, whilst one set of studies do not find significant changes in wages and employment for the existing workforce due to migration, others report low-skilled workers could suffer decreased wages following the arrival of a similarly low-skilled migrant flow (Aydemir and Borjas 2007; Borjas 2006). Indeed, a Bank of England report suggested that a 10% rise in the proportion of migrants working in a particular occupation may be associated with a decline in occupational wages rates of around 0.3%, albeit that unskilled or semi-skilled workers were likely to face a much higher fall in wages of around 2% (Nickell and Saleheen 2015: 18–24).

It has been suggested that increased competitive pressure, arising from migration, may result in a positive outcome in the long run, as low-skill UK workers would be incentivised to look for opportunities to upskill, train and improve their education (Peri 2014; IMF 2015). There is no convincing evidence on this point, however, and thus it remains unproven.

Overall, there is so far some common evidence to show that migration does not affect significantly the level of national wages (IMF 2015, Migration Advisory Committee 2014). Similarly, a number of studies on migration are summarised by the Migration Advisory Committee report (2012), based on a set of representative analyses attempting to examine the effects of migration. It shows that the impact of migrants on UK wages is relatively negligible, with small increases at the top of the wage distribution, while lowering wages at the bottom (Migration Advisory Committee 2012).

Moreover, as a further theoretical limitation, the theoretical prediction of migration acting as an equalising force between nations (such that wage rates converge around an international equilibrium) is either very long in gestation, or the equalising effect is so weak that it is overwhelmed by other economic forces. In reality, studies have found little evidence of wage or inflation convergence (Spiru 2010; Schnabl and Ziegler 2011), while in the UK there is some evidence that migration could have led to lower wages albeit with a small effect and only in relation to migrants arriving from the EU (Nickell and Saleheen 2015). Furthermore, a recent forecast warns that the UK is on the verge of experiencing the biggest rise in income inequality since the 1980s

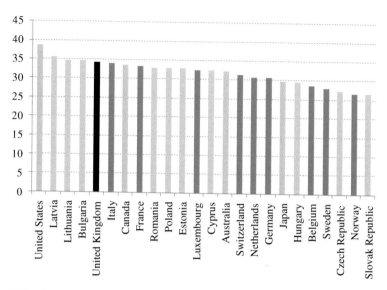

Fig. 6.10 Average Gini index, selected countries from the EU, outside the EU, and A10 countries, 2000–2014. *Note* the highest the Gini index, the higher the inequality. *Source* WDI (2016)

(Corlett and Clarke 2017). Despite being the world's fifth biggest economy (according to GDP) in 2015, and witnessing some of the largest disposable income growth rates of all developed countries even period immediately following the last recession, the UK suffers from high level of inequality (see Fig. 6.10), alongside a persistent gender pay gap, and a growing intra-country north-south divide (World Bank 2016b).

The impact of migration upon income distribution is indeterminate. Migrants moving from a low to a higher wage economy will reduce labour supply in their home nation and increase it in the host economy, such that, if it is assumed that all labour is homogenous, then there should be a movement towards greater equalisation of wages between the two nations. This might, in turn, encourage greater capital-labour substitution in the former home economy, given the now shortage of labour, which will potentially increase productivity, whereas the effect on the host economy may be the opposite. However, these effects are very long term and rather weak, given that the productivity, capitalisation, technological innovation and industrial structure of an economy are likely to have far greater impact upon future wage developments than the movement of labour between nations.

Acceptance of the fact that not all workers have the same skills, education and innate abilities means that these results may not, after all, predominate. For example, if migrant labour, attracted to the higher wage economy, possess above average levels of skills, then they should be able to enhance the productivity of the host nation, thus increasing the gap between former home and host nations (Atoyan et al. 2016). Remittances (monetary contributions sent home by migrants) may mitigate part of this effect, as these exceed 25% of GDP in certain impoverished nations, such as in Moldova or Nepal (IMF 2016). Similarly, the skill levels of migrant labour are likely to impact upon differentiated labour markets in which they gain employment, to the extent that an influx of very highly skilled engineers may reduce the existing engineering market premium for formerly scarce skills, or alternatively, an increase in low skilled warehouse or agricultural labour is likely to depress wages at the lower end of the income distribution spectrum.

Consequently, it is likely that the distributional consequences of migration, measured between and within nations, will depend upon the skill attributes of those engaged in migration. Moreover, this brief theoretical and application-based incursion into the foundations of how migration is understood, showcases some poignant insights into why it is important a country's migration policy be well-thought, and that macroeconomic forces leading to migration are given time to act for the benefit of those involved.

Migration Provides Access to Skilled Labour

One prominent feature of (particularly big) business opinion is that inward migration is beneficial by increasing the accessibility of high skilled labour and reducing related capacity bottlenecks (CBI 2016c). Paul Drechsler, Director of the Confederation of Business and Industry (CBI), has stated that restricting migration could seriously hurt the British economy (People Management 2016).[5] Similarly, a survey of

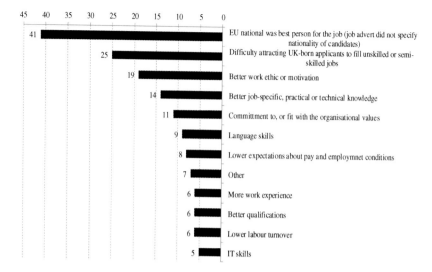

Fig. 6.11 Main reasons stated by UK migrant-employing organisations for hiring EU nationals. *Note* Of the 636 organisations surveyed in September 2016, 446 were in the private sector, 153 in the public sector and 37 in the voluntary sector (CIPD 2016b:14). *Source* CIPD (2016b: 14)

businesses employing 1.2 million people, equivalent to around 4.5% of the total British workforce, found that 64% of employers surveyed identified skills gaps as their main competitive threat and 58% expressed concern about continued access to skilled migrants to bridge this skills gap (CBI 2016a). Moreover, migrants are additionally rated very well by businesses in terms of their adaptability and work ethic (CIPD 2016a: 34–35; see also Fig. 6.11).

This positive attitude is reflected in the finding that the use of migrant labour is widespread, especially amongst larger UK businesses. A CIPD (2016b) survey, covering a representative sample of 62% of all UK migrant-employing organisations, reported that the largest concentrations of migrant labour could be found in the public sector, with 71% of organisations employing migrants. In the healthcare sector, the equivalent figure is 72%, whereas for larger firms employing over 250 people, the equivalent figure is 79%.

The fact that business organisations have identified migrant labour as one means of meeting skill shortages is not necessarily justification for continued EU migration. Such skilled labour could be drawn from elsewhere in the world, by relaxing restrictions placed upon inward migration from other nations as EU rules are tightened. Moreover, given that a proportion of current EU migrant labour is employed in relatively low skilled occupations,[6] there is no a priori reason why reducing numbers could not be focused upon these individuals and leave higher skilled workers unaffected. In addition, an alternative solution to current skills bottlenecks could involve UK businesses investing greater resources in training UK citizens to fulfil vacancies, rather than importing labour from abroad. It is plausible that one reason for business enthusiasm for continued access to migrant labour pools is the avoidance of this training expenditure, and accordingly this might be a consideration for policy makers as to whether it would benefit the nation to socialise such human capital investment. It might additionally be a point of consideration as to whether government should ensure an equitable distribution of the costs of such a programme through introducing a training levy for those businesses not already providing a certain level of skills enhancement training for their workforce.

One additional relevant issue to business and the workforce in the UK, which has been raised subsequent to the referendum decision, relates to the uncertainty faced by existing EU (but not UK) citizens living and working in the UK. It is understandable that the UK government has reserved this matter for inclusion in the forthcoming withdrawal negotiations with the EU, since similar rights of work and residency for UK citizens living elsewhere in the EU will also be affected and a common solution needs to be found for all concerned. Nevertheless, it does create uncertainty for all those involved and may deter future highly skilled migrants from living and working in the UK, to the potential detriment of the economy as a whole. It would, therefore, be sensible for this matter to be resolved at an early stage in the withdrawal negotiation process.

Migration May Lead to Higher Productivity

There is some evidence, from recent studies, that migration is positively associated with increased productivity (Alesina et al. 2015; Ortega and Peri 2014). Indeed, one such study estimates that a 1% increase in the share of migrants, as a proportion of a nation's total population, could lead, in the long term, to a 2% rise in GDP per capita (Jaumotte et al. 2016). The inference is that this apparent result is primarily associated with the inflow of highly skilled migrant labour. Interestingly, there has been an expansion of migration amongst this group across the OECD nations of over 70% between 2004 and 2014; comprising 31 million out of the 115 million immigrants, who make up approximately 10% of the total OECD population (OECD 2014a).

Another study indicates that a 1% increase in migrants as a share of all employees is associated with an increase of around 0.06% in labour productivity (Rolfe et al. 2013). Interestingly, this finding was irrespective of the skill mix between migrant and existing workers. This may suggest that at least part of this result may derive from either personal characteristics, such as divergence in work intensity, or it may alternatively relate to industry-related effects, whereby some (perhaps more capital-intensive) industries typically have a higher total factor productivity irrespective of the characteristics of their labour force.

Migration May Increase Flexibility

There is a paucity of research analysing the relationship between the utilisation of migrant workers and British firm-level performance. In fact, data have only recently begun to record the national composition of a workforce. The long-term labour market Workplace Employment Relations Surveys (WERS) dataset (BIS 2011), covering a representative sample of around 2600 workplaces in Britain in 2011, found that half of the workplaces responding (1123 workplaces) employed migrant workers, of which a fifth (208 workplaces) had a workforce where at least one-quarter of employees were migrants.

Academic literature using this dataset shows that UK businesses exhibit potential issues of concern with regard to the equal treatment of migrants in employment (Whyman and Petrescu 2014). For instance, workplaces with migrants were more likely to make use of casual work contracts, and, if migrants were from outside the EEA, then they were less likely to be employed in workplaces offering less training, but more likely to be part of organisations where pay levels are relatively low. According to the same study, migrant-employing firms were more flexible than their counterparts and, particularly in Europe, migrants are reported to contribute significantly to flexible labour markets (OECD 2014b; Whyman and Petrescu 2014). This degree of flexibility has the *potential* for increasing international competitiveness and enhancing the ability to meet variability in demand, particularly in niche markets.

These findings are similar to a 20-country study of OECD nations, conducted by Battisti et al. (2014), where migration was found to increase flexibility. Similarly, the CIPD (2016b) reported that UK firms were found to employ migrants due to their lower expectations about pay and employment conditions. Given that lower remuneration is a form of (cost) flexibility, then migration may enhance business flexibility, although this is not necessarily translated into more positive forms of (functional) flexibility, that are more likely to facilitate higher levels of productivity and economic growth (Appelbaum et al. 2000).

In general, workplace flexibility is perceived as a positive phenomenon in terms of business performance (CBI 2016c; Whyman and Baimbridge 2006; Whyman et al. 2015), although there is not always a mutual gain for employees from the whole range of flexibility initiatives (Whyman and Petrescu 2013). Indeed, 97% of those UK businesses surveyed, in 2016, reported that they saw flexible labour markets as essential to job creation (CBI 2016b). It was also suggested that flexibility assisted UK businesses to adjust their activities in response to recessionary pressures and thereby managing to remain competitive (CBI 2009).

Migration Appears to Have No Significant Impact on the Overall Unemployment Rate

A different consideration, relating to the impact of migrant labour, is whether it acts as a direct substitute for the existing UK labour force, thereby causing unemployment amongst such groups.

Employment and unemployment effects appear to provide mixed evidence, on this point, with one estimate suggesting that, between 1995 and 2010, for every 100 non-EU migrants who had been in the UK for less than five years and employed, 23 UK residents were displaced. However, when non-EU migrants had been living and working in the UK for in excess of five years, this displacement effect did not occur (Migration Advisory Committee 2012). The finding suggests that, whilst new migrants do appear to displace a (smaller) number of British workers, once they become more established in the UK labour force, any displacement effect ceases.

This could be due to a potential maturation of the job-matching process, as migrants gradually move into positions that better fit their skills and experience. Or, it could be that new market entrants tend to accept lower skill, lower wage jobs than more established migrants, and therefore they may tend to undercut and thereby displace British workers in those sectors of the economy where cost rather than skill considerations predominate. In any case, it would appear that such job displacement effects are temporary in nature, and seem to disappear once new migrants become a more permanent feature of the labour market.

The same study noted that further analysis would be useful to ascertain how these migrant-displacement relationships change during periods of rapid or stagnant economic growth, as the existence of any measurable displacement effects due to inward migration may be experienced more acutely during certain time periods than others—i.e. particularly during periods of economic stress.

In aggregate terms, it would appear that, despite the significant increase in migrant labour over the past decade and a half, the proportion of the total potential UK labour force in active employment is higher in 2015 than four decades previously (see Fig. 6.12).

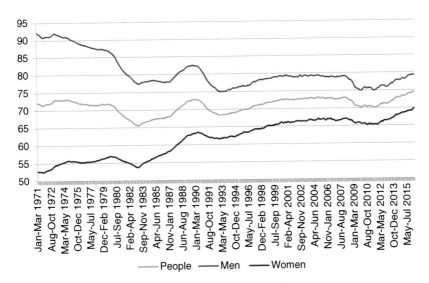

Fig. 6.12 UK employment rates, 1971–2015. *Source* ONS (2016)

Simultaneously, UK unemployment declined slightly between 2004 and 2014 (see Table 6.1). This is in line with analysis from the literature, which generally finds no link between migration and UK unemployment. For example, a study conducted by Dustmann et al. (2005) found that, between 1983 and 2000, there was little evidence of migrants contributing to overall unemployment rate rises in the UK, except for existing workers with intermediate qualifications.

A noticeable anomaly, in terms of unemployment statistics, is the increase in the proportion of UK residents with tertiary education who are unemployed, during the period of increased migration (OECD 2014a). This is not a solely UK phenomenon, given that most countries featured in Table 6.2 have experienced a similar effect. However, it does indicate either a potential over-supply of highly educated UK citizens, or, alternatively, that inward migration may have impacted disproportionately amongst this group. Clearly, there is a need for more research to properly understand this data and why UK business leaders continue to claim the existence of skills shortages at the same time

Table 6.1 Unemployment rate comparisons, UK versus a selection of EU and non-EU areas

	Average 1990–2003	Average 2004–2014	Change
Norway	4.3	3.4	-0.9
China	3.3	4.0	0.7
Switzerland	3.4	4.1	0.7
India	3.1	4.2	1.1
Japan	4.1	4.2	0.1
Netherlands	4.5	4.6	0.0
Luxembourg	2.8	5.0	2.2
Austria	4.7	5.1	0.4
Australia	7.6	5.2	-2.4
Middle income	4.8	5.6	0.9
Denmark	5.6	5.8	0.2
World	5.4	6.2	0.9
United Kingdom	**6.6**	**6.4**	**-0.2**
Malta	7.0	6.6	-0.4
Czech Republic	6.2	6.7	0.5
USA	5.1	6.8	1.7
Romania	6.9	6.9	0.0
Canada	8.4	7.1	-1.3
Slovenia	6.9	7.1	0.2
OECD members	6.9	7.1	0.2
High income	7.2	7.2	0.0
Sweden	7.6	7.5	-0.1
Germany	8.8	7.7	-1.1
Cyprus	3.3	7.7	4.5
Belgium	8.4	7.9	-0.5
Finland	13.1	8.1	-5.0
Italy	10.9	8.7	-2.2
Hungary	7.9	8.8	0.9
France	11.0	9.0	-2.0
European Union	9.9	9.1	-0.8
Estonia	10.6	9.3	-1.3
Ireland	7.9	9.4	1.6
Euro area	10.4	9.6	-0.7
Turkey	8.0	9.8	1.8
Bulgaria	15.8	9.9	-5.9
Portugal	5.5	10.5	5.0
Lithuania	15.0	10.7	-4.3
Arab World	12.2	11.0	-1.2
Poland	14.7	11.3	-3.4
Latvia	14.6	12.1	-2.5
Croatia	13.0	12.8	-0.3
Slovak Republic	15.2	13.7	-1.6

(continued)

Table 6.1 (continued)

	Average 1990–2003	Average 2004–2014	Change
Greece	10.3	14.9	4.6
Spain	17.0	16.6	-0.4

Source WDI (2016)

Notes Countries and areas outside the EU are highlighted in grey; post-2004 EU members are highlighted in green. A negative number in the 'Change' column shows an improvement, in that the unemployment rate has decreased in 2004–2014 compared to the previous period. For instance, the UK rate of unemployment decreased on average, with the change being in the order of 0.2 percentage points

as official statistics show a potential pool of highly educated labour remains untapped.

Migrants Could Ease the Demographic Burden and Have a Positive Financial Footprint

Internationally, and in the case of the UK too, there is evidence that migration could help ease the demographic burden of an aging workforce (IMF 2016), while also continue to help fill in the skill gaps highlighted by business and/or by the national health system. Migration studies have highlighted across the world that migrants tend to be of working-age, accounting to a very substantial 70% increase in European labour markets over the period 2004–2014, as well as contribute to human capital development and technological progress in the countries where they arrive (OECD 2014b).

Overall, studies have also shown that migrants typically contribute more in taxes and social contributions than they take out in benefits (OECD 2014b). One prominent study estimated that migrants arriving in the UK from EEA countries may have contributed a net £24 billion to government revenues, between 2001 and 2011, whilst the fact that migrant labour arrived having undertaken education and training may have saved the public sector a further £18 billion (Dustmann and Frattini 2014: F629). A later study finds similar favourable results, albeit that it calculated the fiscal benefit to be smaller, at less than 1%

Table 6.2 Unemployed with tertiary education, as percent of total unemployed

	Average 1990–2003	Average 2004–2014	Change
Czech Republic	3.7	6.3	2.7
Malta	2.7	6.6	3.8
Slovak Republic	3.0	6.9	3.9
Hungary	3.7	8.6	4.9
Romania	4.0	9.5	5.5
Italy	6.1	11.1	5.0
Austria	5.0	11.2	6.2
Bulgaria	9.2	11.3	2.2
Germany	12.7	11.8	-0.9
Poland	4.5	12.2	7.7
Croatia	9.8	12.2	2.4
Portugal	6.2	12.6	6.4
Latvia	9.2	13.2	4.0
Slovenia	6.3	15.3	9.0
Lithuania	17.2	15.3	-1.9
European Union	10.6	15.4	4.8
Turkey	7.6	15.5	7.8
Euro area	12.2	16.3	4.0
United Kingdom	**11.6**	**17.8**	**6.2**
Sweden	12.9	17.9	4.9
Australia	17.5	18.3	0.7
Finland	11.8	18.8	7.0
Netherlands	15.2	18.8	3.6
France	14.8	19.7	4.8
Belgium	13.7	20.2	6.5
OECD members	19.9	20.5	0.6
Norway	20.3	20.5	0.2
Estonia	17.1	20.6	3.5
Switzerland	15.8	20.6	4.9
Ireland	10.4	20.7	10.2
Spain	17.2	20.8	3.6
Greece	12.8	20.9	8.1
Denmark	16.6	21.6	5.0
Luxembourg	12.3	25.6	13.3
USA	**42.2**	**30.1**	-12.1
Japan	23.8	**31.5**	7.7
Cyprus	23.0	**31.5**	8.6
Canada	29.4	**33.2**	3.8

Source WDI (2016)

Table 6.3 A brief review of five studies analysing the fiscal impact of UK migration

Study	Reported magnitude of fiscal impact
Rowthorn (2008)	+£0.6bn
Rowthorn (2014)	-£0.3bn
Migration Watch (2006)	-£5bn (-0.3% UK GDP)
Gott and Johnston (2002)	+£2.5bn (+0.15% UK GDP)
Sriskandarajah et al. (2005)	-£0.4bn to +£1.9bn

Source Authors' compilation
Note all studies show EEA migrants have a higher impact than non-EEA migrants

GDP (Vargas-Silva 2015). Yet, other studies have typically produced a mixed set of results (see Table 6.3).

Part of the differences between the studies derives from how economic impacts are measured. Some studies, for example, focus exclusively upon taxation (benefit) and benefits (cost), yet this is a deficient method of analysis, in that it does not cover many other benefits of migration, that are harder to monetise, such as productivity or innovation contribution. The literature also excludes, for the most part, migration costs such as with housing, congestion increases or lower wages for low-skilled workers.[7] Finally, it may be that a different migration system, focusing upon more highly skilled labour, may produce a better return from migration, if not least since it can rationally be expected that highly skilled migrants would earn higher wages, thus be in the position to pay higher taxes.

Migration Could Help with Economic Growth

A significant study of 22 OECD countries, between 1986 and 2006, found immigration to be positively associated with economic growth; the causality being related to the human capital contribution that migrants bring to the country of destination (Boubtane et al. 2014). According to this study, the net effect is rather small, even in those countries with selective migration policies, perhaps boosting annual productivity growth in OECD nations by an average of three tenths of one per cent for every 50% increase in net migration (Boubtane et al. 2014:19). Importantly, the contribution of migrants to an economy is linked to how swiftly they integrate into the labour market (IMF 2016).

Social and economic policies for migrant integration would, therefore, play a key part in allowing a country to benefit from this ever growing resource.

The key determinant, identified in this study, is in migration raising the skill level within the workforce and thereby having a positive impact upon productivity and ultimately economic growth. However, it must be noted that a similar effect could, of course, be achieved through greater human capital investment in the existing UK workforce or through attracting non-EU skilled labour into the UK. This topic is covered in more detail in Chap. 7.

Difficulties in, and Critique of Cost—Benefit Migration Analysis in Academic Literature

Analysing migration patterns is one of the hardest labour market research tasks. The difficulty crucially stems from uncertainty concerning whether intended population movements do actually materialise, whether the initially intended migration destinations vary during the period of migration, and how quickly (or not) migrants return to their country of origin. Integration challenges stem from a low ability of migration research to predict what is, essentially, a hard to observe and hard to measure complex set of decisions taken by a diverse set of individuals on the one hand, and labour demand on the other, which itself constitutes an evolving landscape of industry in the UK. For example, in migration studies it has remained a challenge to predict the size or skill composition of migrants, or, indeed, propensity of migrants to return to the country of origin. It is difficult to ascertain the extent to which migrants are a cost or a benefit in terms of their pecuniary as well as non-pecuniary impact on the respective country's resources e.g. counting in the social or cultural impact is, intuitively, a difficult task. Consequently, the impact of migration is notoriously hard to predict.

Migration effects may differ according to the extent to which migrants and the existing workforce have (dis)similar skills, experience, and according to the length of time in a research study (Borjas 2003).

A good illustration of this point is the case of a well-known contribution to the literature: the controversial study of a labour market supply shock caused by the arrival in Miami (USA), almost overnight on the twentieth of April 1980, of about 125,000 migrants from Cuba. The initial influential analysis by Card (1990) seemed to show only marginal short run effects, contrary to expected theory that assumed such a shock would lower wages, as a sudden increase in labour supply relative to demand would be anticipated to reduce equilibrium wages. However, after more than 30 years of research, a new study by Borjas (2016), reappraising the evidence of the infamous Miami labour influx, suggests that too little time was given initially to the assessment. Instead, the new study identified a wage drop of between 10 to 30% that was concentrated amongst the lower-educated in Miami. This drop was due to a quintessentially important feature which the previous analysis had not paid enough attention to, namely the high *substitutability* (ease of replacement) of low-educated Miami workers by the Cuban migrant wave composed of at least 60% high-school dropouts.

On this point, theoretical assumptions sometimes may appear to limit the application of said theory and lead to very different outcomes, due to the large number of complex intervening factors that could sway the research outcomes. For instance, there is a need to ascertain to what extent migrants would be similar and hence potential substitutes for existing British workers, and to what extent they are dis-similar and therefore complimentary. The more distinct the new migrants from the existing labour force, in terms of personal characteristics such as education, skills, and linguistic ability, the lower the possibility of a lasting market shock (Peri 2014). In providing distinct skill sets, migrants may help to fill existing skill shortages and thereby enhance the performance of UK companies which, in turn, could generate more employment opportunities through the multiplier effect.

On the other hand, if migrants are potential substitutes for existing British workers, then direct competition, particularly amongst low skilled workers, may have a depressive effect upon wages of this segment of the existing labour force, of perhaps 3–4% in response to a 10% increase in the wage of migrants (Borjas 2003, 2016). It is possible, even in this circumstance, that this may deliver economic benefits to the UK economy, if existing workers displaced by new entrants retrain and/or are pushed into newer, more highly skilled sectors (Aiyar et al. 2016). However, if this up-skilling effect does not occur, then migration will lead to certain deadweight effects.

Another main impediment in assessing the outcomes of migration is the estimating the ability of migrants to fill in skill shortages. Skills have been usually hard to observe, and as a result, are often proxied by measuring education levels, even though the two concepts are not identical. Other studies may infer skill levels by assuming that wage levels reflect skills or productivity. This is even less precise. Still, it is useful to note that, increasingly, migrants arriving in advanced economies are generally highly educated, classified as having an education level above high school or equivalent (IMF 2016). Internationally, by 2010, highly educated migrants represented 6% of the population across advanced economies, three times as much as in the 1990s; medium-level educated workers also increased their share to 5% in 2010 from 2% in 1990s, while low-level educated migrant flows remained rather stable around 5% across these two decades (IMF 2016). Thus, there is evidence that the composition of migrants has shifted slowly towards more highly educated individuals, and away from less educated and low paid workers. Nevertheless, these figures still suggest that almost two thirds of the migrant stock, within advanced economies, work in medium or low skilled occupations. Furthermore, a report from the Bank of England indicates that inward migration from both EU and non-EU countries has become increasingly skewed towards low skilled occupations, which suggests that the current migration selection system is not sufficiently robust and selective if it is intended to fill skill shortages and enhance business performance (Nickell and Saleheen 2015: 10–12).

A further issue is directly related to the difficulty in ascertaining the benefit and costs of migration. This is an additional, even more pernicious, element of ambiguity plaguing migration studies. It is due to a gap in comprehensive migration research, whereby the quintessential challenge to overcome is the extent to which migration studies can be designed to measure, account for, and weight up accurately the purported benefits and costs ensuing from migrants arriving in a particular country of residence. It is a complex task to try to assess in more depth the impact of migration, such as via cost–benefit analyses, and the extant literature has not yet engaged fully with the ways in which migration can be examined better. For the most part, the fiscal benefits arising from migration are reduced to those taxes paid by the migrant workers, since this can be easily measured, whilst the costs are juxtaposed against benefits claimed by the migrant workers or their families. Yet, these are but two of the various channels through which migration influences an economy (Dustmann and Frattini 2010).

Ever more complex, new theoretical and empirical models of migration are needed in order to capture better the increasing variety of ways in which migrants may impact on the economy. For instance, current migration models are rather too narrowly focused on tracking ways in which migration influences wages and thereby taxes or benefits. They predict that there will be no change in a country's wage levels if migrants are similar to natives in their skill levels, and that migrants could influence the economy if migrants have a different demand for benefits or welfare services than the existing workforce (Dustmann and Frattini 2010). However, other ways in which migrants influence an economy are less observable or less quantifiable, yet important to study. These could include migration influences via innovation or the exposure to new ideas that migrants may bring into a workplace or a community, via technological transfers and/or via modifying the structure of the industry.

There have been significant changes in ways migration is analysed, and more change may be beneficial (Battisti et al. 2014). Models of migration usually had been of a canonical nature, whereby neo-classical assumptions held that migrants arrive in a closed, rigid economy which varies little to absorb the migrant wave. In contrast, in more modern models of migration, more flexibility is allowed, such as by having firms open new positions and creating new market opportunities that are more advantageous to the respective influx of skill migrants, whilst they additionally allow for both the existing workforce and migrant workers changing jobs, such that displacement might not imply unemployment but simply reflect movement within a dynamic labour market. A model of analysing migration, proposed by Battisti et al. (2014), goes beyond the complementary and substitutability analysis, by taking into account wage bargaining, job-search labour market frictions and fiscal redistribution. It is found that, among the OECD countries studies, migration has a higher positive impact in countries with fewer skilled existing workers, higher unemployment and rather inflexible labour markets. Thus, the conclusion is that migration has a significant role in helping the economy move towards higher employment rates, the gains from this outweighing the welfare costs, with both high-skill and low-end workers benefiting and median total gains from migrations being 1.19 and 1.0% respectively (ibid.). This finding is different than in studies which don't take job search friction into account. It also showcases the importance of migration policy being aligned and individually designed in the interest of the respective country.

Finally, as mentioned in this chapter elsewhere, a main drawback to furthering this broader migration cost–benefit analysis remains data availability, with particular need for recent data to help bring to light the ways current migration flows change the economic landscape of a country. The call for a more profound conceptual base for migration studies comes on the backdrop of some outdated assumptions in studies, such as there being 'permanence' in migration, whereas modern migration patterns exhibit a more prominent trend of return or short-term migration (Dustmann and Frattini 2010; Dustman and Weiss 2007). The main critique of the existing literature is that studies need to carry out careful assessments that are comprehensive, inclusive of total welfare effects of migration. However, too few studies carry out cost–benefit analyses, and the extant literature mainly focuses on too few aspects when trying to analyse the complex set of relationships between migration and economic outlook (Dustmann and Frattini 2010).

Conclusion

Labour market issues have provided a key focus for the July 2016 referendum debate, whether based on the prominence given to the perceived burden of migration, or the discussions concerning whether migrant labour from the EU resulted in a net benefit to the UK economy. The migration discussion is firmly rooted in the free movement of labour as one of the four 'freedoms', established within the Treaty of Rome. It is therefore a fundamental element of EU membership, currently needing to be strategically negotiated as part of the eventual chosen path for Britain exiting the EU by early summer 2019.

This chapter has evaluated the available evidence via main UK labour market statistics, extended back in time to the point when the UK joined the EU in 1970s. It has reviewed the evidence that UK net migration led to UK population (and density) growth, which would not have otherwise occurred if dependent upon fertility rates and a higher age-dependency ratio.

The evidence appears to suggest that the large inflow of migrant workers from the EU did not lead to a dramatic rise in overall unemployment, as the buoyant UK economy absorbed this influx with relatively few negative consequences, although the wages (and maybe sometimes the jobs) of unskilled existing workers may have been adversely affected. There is, additionally, some evidence that migration increases the flexibility of UK firms and this may have a positive effect upon performance. It may additionally ease any longer term welfare dependency concerns. However, the range of existing studies have found it difficult to isolate the full range of economic costs and benefits associated with migration, preferring to measure the differences between wages, taxes paid and benefits claimed. Yet, this is only a small part of the broader impact that may derive from migration.

One factor that does appear to be significant, concerns the ability for high skilled migrants to have positive effects upon the economy, whether by filling skills shortages for UK businesses or through enhancing flexibility and/or productivity. Nevertheless, even here, the evidence on their ability to contribute is mixed, since the proportion of highly skilled migrants is rising, across advanced economies, but unemployment of people with tertiary education remains substantially elevated in some countries including the UK. The co-existence of skill shortages and highly skilled unemployment are labour market phenomena needing further attention from policy makers. For instance, skill shortages may continue to be filled by migration from EU member states - which could be easier due to geographical proximity to the UK - while the UK could also encourage highly skilled migrants from elsewhere in the world, or alternatively increase human capital investment in its existing labour force.

Overall, it would appear that the (limited) evidence suggests that migration from the EU has had only a marginal economic impact upon the UK economy as a whole, albeit that it has had a small but measurable negative effect upon the wages of many unskilled workers. Findings from theory and its application point to the need to ensure that migration policy is fine-tuned to the needs of the British economy so that migrants' skills and labour market contribution overall are best utilised.

For more precise results, this chapter, in line with many of the migration studies it has mentioned, issues a call for further, more comprehensive research, into examining the net economic impact of exiting the EU membership with regard to migration, and, crucially, determining what would be the best migration policies to negotiate and implement hereafter.

Notes

1. For further information on the movement of EU nationals, see http://ec.europa.eu/social/main.jsp?catId=457.
2. https://www.theyworkforyou.com/sp/?id=2016-12-13.6.0.
3. https://www.ft.com/content/ef06b7fc-fd13-11e3-8ca9-00144feab7de.
4. https://www.gov.uk/government/uploads/system/uploads/attachment_data/file/493559/Local_Authority_Housing_Statistics__England__year_ending_March_2015.pdf.
5. As of December 14th, 2016, the Confederation of Business and Industry, which is the main body representing British employers, has voiced concern about the concept of a net migration target, advising that it needed to be abandoned and focus shifted on the right skill composition of migrants (BBC News 2016).
6. Migrants accounted for 16% of low skilled jobs in the UK in 2015, which more than doubled from 7% of low-skilled jobs in 1997, whereas the total number of workers (migrants and non-migrants) in the UK in low-skilled jobs had remained similar in 2015–1997, at about 13.4 million jobs; natives were employed in 84% of low-skilled jobs, as opposed to 93% in 1997 (Migration Advisory Committee 2014). Low-skilled

jobs are defined by the Office of National Statistics in accordance to the Standard Occupational Classification (SOC).

7. Lower wage levels post-migration are likely to lead to a fall in capital-labour substitution by employers, because cheaper labour (cheaper relative to capital) means firms opt for fewer uses of capital and technology and utilise instead more labour-intensive production processes. This could have pernicious effects for the economy, such as lower rates of technological progress.

References

Aiyar, S., Barkbu, B., Batini, N., Berger, H., Detragiache, E., Dizioli, A, et al. (2016). *The refugee surge in Europe: Economic challenges*. IMF Staff Discussion Note 16/02. Washington, DC: International Monetary Fund.

Alesina, A., Harnoss, J., & Hillel Rapoport, H. (2015). *Birthplace diversity and economic prosperity* (NBER Working Paper 18699). Cambridge, MA: National Bureau of Economic Research.

Appelbaum, E., Bailey, T., & Berg, P. (2000). *Manufacturing advantage: Why high performance work systems pay off*. Ithaca, NY: Cornell University Press.

Atoyan, R., Christiansen, L., Dizioli, A., Ebeke, C., Ilahi, N., Ilyina, A, et al. (2016). *Emigration and its economic impact on Eastern Europe*. IMF Staff Discussion Note 16/07. Washington: International Monetary Fund.

Aydemir, A., & Borjas, G. J. (2007). Cross-country variation in the impact of international migration: Canada Mexico, and the United States. *Journal of the European Economic Association, 5*(4), 663–708.

Battisti, M., Felbermayr, G., Peri, G., & Poutvaara, P. (2014, May). *Immigration, search, and redistribution: A quantitative assessment of native welfare* (NBER Working Paper No. 20131).

BBC News. (2016, December 14). Abandon net migration target, says CBI. Available via: http://www.bbc.co.uk/news/business-38305194. Accessed December 22, 2016

BIS (Department for Business Innovation and Skills). (2011). *The workplace employment relations survey (WERS)*. Available Via: http://www.wers2011.info/welcome/4587719945.

Booth, S., Howarth, C., Persson, M., Ruparel, R., & Swidlicki, P. (2015). *What if...? The Consequences, challenges and opportunities facing Britain outside EU*, Open Europe Report 03/2015. London. http://openeurope.org.uk/intelligence/britain-and-the-eu/what-if-there-were-a-brexit/.

Borjas, G. J. (2003). The demand curve is downward sloping: Re-examining the impact of immigration on the labor market. *The Quarterly Journal of Economics, 118*(4), 1335–1374.

Borjas, G. J. (2006). Native internal migration and the labor market impact of immigration. *Journal of Human Resources, 41*(2), 221–258.

Borjas, G. J. (2016). *The wage impact of the marielitos: Additional evidence* (NBER Working Paper No. 21850). Cambridge, MA: National Bureau of Economic Research.

Boubtane, E., Dumont, J. C., & Rault, C. (2014). *Immigration and economic growth in the OECD countries,* 1986–2006 (IZA Discussion Paper No. 8681).

Card, D. (1990). The impact of the mariel boatlift on the miami labor market. *Industrial and Labor Relations Review , 43*(2): 245–257.

CBI (Confederation of British Industry). (2009, June). *Employment trends 2009: Work patterns in the recession.* Report. London.

CBI (Confederation of British Industry). (2016a). *Leaving the EU: Implications for the UK economy,* PwC Report. Available via: http://www.cbi.org.uk/news/leaving-eu-would-cause-a-serious-shock-to-uk-economy-new-pwc-analysis/leaving-the-eu-implications-for-the-uk-economy/. Accessed April 30, 2016.

CBI (Confederation of British Industry). (2016b). *Making a success of Brexit: A whole-economy view of the UK-EU negotiations.* Available Via: http://www.cbi.org.uk/index.cfm/_api/render/file/?method=inline&fileID=65517601–5815-40CD-8C5BB94597795312. Accessed December 22, 2016.

CBI (Confederation of British Industry). (2016c). *People and partnership: CBI/Pertemps network group employment trends survey.* Available via: http://www.cbi.org.uk/cbi-prod/assets/File/pdf/ETS_report_proof_X.pdf.

CIPD (Chartered Institute of Personnel and Development). (2016a, September). *Attitudes to employability and talent.* Available Via: https://www.cipd.co.uk/Images/attitudes-to-employability-and-talent_2016_tcm18–14261.pdf. Accessed October 23, 2016.

CIPD (Chartered Institute of Personnel and Development). (2016b). *Labour market outlook: Autumn 2016.* Available via: https://www.cipd.co.uk/knowledge/work/trends/labour-market-outlookLast. Accessed November 24, 2016.

Corlett, A., & Clarke, S. (2017 February). *Living Standards 2017. The past, present and possible future of UK incomes.* Report. The Resolution Foundation. http://www.resolutionfoundation.org/publications/living-standards-2017-the-past-present-and-possible-future-of-uk-incomes/. Accessed February 01, 2017.

Dustmann, C., Fabbri F., & Preston, I. (2005). *The impact of immigration on the UK labour market*. Centre for Research and Analysis of Migration (CReAM) (*CReAM discussion paper* No. 0501). London: University College.

Dustmann, C., & Weiss, Y. (2007). Return migration: Theory and empirical evidence for the UK. *British Journal of Industrial Relations, 45*(2), 236–256.

Dustmann, C., & Frattini, T. (2010, September). Can a framework for the economic cost-benefit analysis of various immigration policies be developed to inform decision making and, if so, what data are required? Report prepared for the Migration Advisory Committee. Available via http://www.ucl.ac.uk/~uctpb21/reports/Cost&Benefits_veryfinal.pdf.

Dustmann, C., & Frattini, T. (2014). The fiscal effects of immigration to the UK, *Economic Journal, 124*(580), F953-F643.

Eurostat. (2011). *Labor force survey*. Brussels: The European Commission.

Gill, J. (2015). *The UK and the EU: Reform, renegotiation, withdrawal? A reading list* (House of Commons Library Briefing Paper No. HC07229). Available via: http://researchbriefings.parliament.uk/ResearchBriefing/Summary/CBP-7220#fullreport.

Gott, C., & Johnston, K. (2002), *The migrant population in the UK: Fiscal effects* (Development and Statistics Directorate Occasional Paper 77). London: Home Office, Available via: http://citeseerx.ist.psu.edu/viewdoc/download?doi=10.1.1.551.7697&rep=rep1&type=pdf.

Heitmüller, A. (2002). *Unemployment benefits, risk aversion, and migration incentives* (IZA Discussion Paper No. 610).

HMG (HM Government). (2016a). *The best of both Worlds: The United Kingdom's special status in a reformed European Union*, The Stationary Office, London. Available via: https://www.gov.uk/government/uploads/system/uploads/attachment_data/file/502291/54284_EU_Series_No1_Web_Accessible.pdf.

HoC (House of Commons Library). (2015). People from Abroad: What Benefits can they Claim? (House of Commons Library Briefing Paper No. 06847). London. Available via: http://researchbriefings.parliament.uk/ResearchBriefing/Summary/SN06847#fullreport.

IMF. (2015). *World economic outlook: Adjusting to lower commodity prices*. Washington, DC: IMF. Available via: http://www.imf.org/external/pubs/ft/weo/2015/02/pdf/text.pdf.

IMF. (2016). *United Kingdom: IMF Country Report*. No. 16/169. Washington, DC: IMF, Available via: https://www.imf.org/external/pubs/ft/scr/2016/cr16169.pdf.

Jaumotte, F., Koloskova, K., & Saxena, S. C. (2016). *Impact of migration on income levels in advanced economies, Spillover Note 8*. Washington: International Monetary Fund.

Migration Advisory Committee. (2012). *Analysis of the impacts of migration*, Migration Advisory Committee, London. Available via: https://www.gov.uk/government/uploads/system/uploads/attachment_data/file/257235/analysis-of-the-impacts.pdf.

Migration Advisory Committee. (2014). *Migrants in low-skilled work*, Migration Advisory Committee, London. Available via: https://www.gov.uk/government/uploads/system/uploads/attachment_data/file/333083/MAC-Migrants_in_low-skilled_work__Full_report_2014.pdf.

MigrationWatch UK. (2006). *The fiscal contribution of migrants* (Economic Briefing Papers 12). London: MigrationWatch UK, Available via: https://www.migrationwatchuk.org/briefing-paper/12.

Miller, V. (ed.). (2016). *Exiting the EU: Impact in key UK policy areas*. (House of Commons Library Briefing Paper No. HC 07213). Available via: http://researchbriefings.parliament.uk/ResearchBriefing/Summary/CBP-7213#fullreport.

Miller, V., Lang, A.., Smith, B., Webb, D., Harari, D., Keep, M, et al. (2016). Exiting the EU: UK reform proposals, legal impact and alternatives to membership (House of Commons Library Briefing Paper No. HC 07214). Available via http://researchbriefings.parliament.uk/ResearchBriefing/Summary/CBP-7214#fullreport.

Nickell, S. J., & Salaheen, J. (2015). *The impact of immigration on occupational wages: Evidence from Britain* (Bank of England Staff Working Paper No. 574). Available via: http://www.bankofengland.co.uk/research/Documents/workingpapers/2015/swp574.pdf.

OECD (Organisation for Economic Co-operation and Development). (2014a). *International Migration Outlook 2014*. Paris: OECD.

OECD (Organisation for Economic Co-operation and Development). (2014b). *Migration policy debates*. Paris: OECD.

OECD (Organisation for Economic Co-operation and Development). (2017). *OECD Factbook 2015–2016 - Economic, environmental and social statistics*. Paris: OECD. Available via: http://dx.doi.org/10.1787/factbook-2015-en. Accessed 12 January 2017.

ONS (Office for National Statistics). (2012, December). *International migrants in england and wales 2011*. London, UK.

ONS (Office of National Statistics). (2014). *Population of the United Kingdom by Country of Birth and Nationality*. Available via: https://www.ons.gov.uk/peoplepopulationandcommunity/populationandmigration/internationalmigration/datasets/populationoftheunitedkingdombycountryofbirthandnationality.

ONS (Office of National Statistics). (2016a, December). *Migration statistics quarterly report*, Figure 2. Available via: https://www.ons.gov.uk/peoplepopulationandcommunity/populationandmigration/internationalmigration/bulletins/migrationstatisticsquarterlyreport/dec2016. Accessed December 16, 2016.

ONS (Office of National Statistics) UK National Accounts. (2016). *Gross domestic product, chained volume measures: Seasonally adjusted*. Available via: https://www.ons.gov.uk/economy/grossdomesticproductgdp/timeseries/abmi/bb.

Ortega, F. & Peri, G. (2014). Openness and income: The role of trade and migration, *Journal of International Economics, 92*(2): 231–251.

Peri, G. (2014). Do immigrant workers depress the wages of native workers? (*IZA World of Labor, 42*).

People Management. (2016, October). CBI directors says 'drastic clampdown' on migrant workers must be scrapped, *People Management*. Available via http://www2.cipd.co.uk/pm/peoplemanagement/b/weblog/archive/2016/10/14/cbi-director-says-drastic-clampdown-on-migrant-workers-must-be-scrapped.aspx. Accessed October 29, 2016.

Rolfe, H., Rienzo, C., Lalani, M., & Portes, J. (2013). *Migration and productivity: Employer's practice, public attitudes and statistical evidence*. London: National Institute of Economic and Social Research. Available via: http://www.niesr.ac.uk/sites/default/files/publications/Migration%20productivity%20final.pdf.

Rowthorn, R. E. (2008). The fiscal impact of immigration on the advanced economies. *Oxford Review of Economic Policy, 24*, 560–580.

Rowthorn, R. E. (2014). *Large-scale immigration: Its economic and demographic consequences for the UK*. Civitas. Available via: http://www.civitas.org.uk/reports_articles/large-scale-immigration-its-economic-and-demographic-consequences-for-the-uk/.

Roy, A. D. (1951). Some thoughts on the distribution of earnings. *Oxford Economic Papers, 3*(2), 135–146.

Schnabl, G., & Ziegler, C. (2011). Exchange rate and wage policies in Central and Eastern Europe. *Journal of Policy Modelling, 33*(3), 347–360.

Spiru, A. (2010). Inflation convergence in the new EU member states from Central and Easter Euorpe. In R. Matousek (Ed.), *Money, banking and financial markets in central and Eastern Europe—20 Years of Transition* (pp. 197–228). Basingstoke: Palgrave.

Sriskandarajah, D., Cooley, L., & Reed, H. (2005). *Paying Their Way: The fiscal contribution of immigrants in the UK*. London: Institute for Public Policy. Available via:http://www.ippr.org/files/images/media/files/publication/2011/05/Paying%20Their%20Way_1352.pdf?noredirect=1.

Streeck, W. (2016). *Exploding Europe: Germany, the refugees and the British vote to leave.* (Sheffield Political Economy Research Institute (SPERI) Occasional Paper No. 31). Available via: http://speri.dept.shef.ac.uk/wp-content/uploads/2016/09/SPERI-Paper-31-Wolfgang-Streeck-Exploding-Europe.pdf.

Vargas-Silva, C. (2015). *The fiscal impact of immigration in the UK*. Oxford Migration Observatory, Oxford: Briefing Paper.

WDI (World Development Indicators). (2016). *World development indicators.* World Data Bank. Available via: http://databank.worldbank.org/data/reports.aspx?source=world-development-indicators. Accessed August 18, 2016.

Whyman, P. B., & Baimbridge, M. J. (2006). *Labour market flexibility and foreign direct investment* (Employment Relations Occasional Paper URN 06/1797). London: Department of Trade and Industry.

Whyman, P. B., & Petrescu, A. (2013). Partnership, flexible workplace practices and the realisation of mutual gains: Evidence from the British WERS 2004 dataset. *International Journal of Human Resource Management, 25*(6), 829–851.

Whyman, P. B., & Petrescu, A. I. (2014). Workforce nationality composition and workplace flexibility in Britain. *International Journal of Manpower, 35*(6), 776–797.

Whyman, P. B., Bainbridge, M. J., Buraimo, B. A., & Petrescu, A. I. (2015). Workplace flexibility practices and corporate performance. *British Journal of Management, 26*(3), 347–364.

World Bank. (2016a). *Trade as percent of GDP report*. Available via: http://databank.worldbank.org/data/reports.aspx?source=2&series=NE.TRD.GNFS.ZS&country=GBR.

World Bank. (2016b). *Gross capital formation report*. Available via: http://databank.worldbank.org/data/reports.aspx?source=2&series=NE.GDI.TOTL.ZS&country=#.

World Bank. (2016c). *World Development Indicators*. Available via: http://databank.worldbank.org/data/reports.aspx?source=2&series=NY.GDP.PCAP.CD&country=#.

World Bank Report. (2015). *Part II: Demographic change: Disparities, divergences and drivers.*

7

Economic Growth and Productivity

One of the primary motivations for the UK joining the EU was to reverse what was widely perceived at the time to be the UK's relative economic decline.[1] Whilst UK growth rates were actually quite reasonable over the early post war period, certainly when compared to more recent achievements, they were dwarfed by rates of expansion recorded by the six founder members of the EU who, between 1950 and 1973, expanded at 'unprecedented rates' (Eichengreen 2007). The UK enjoyed a 28% advantage in GDP per capita in 1950, compared to the original six members of the EU. Yet when the Treaty of Rome was signed in 1957, the gap had narrowed to 15%, and 10% by 1961, which was when the UK first began openly discussing the option of joining the EU. By the time the UK actually joined the EU, in 1973, its GDP per capita was 7% smaller than the EU(6) average.[2] Given the EU's superior economic growth, over this period, it is easy to understand the attraction for UK political leaders in perceiving EU membership, and the advantages for trade arising from its associated common market, as a means of arresting the UK's economic disadvantage (Congdon 2013: 44).

Yet, the belief that European integration was in some measure the catalyst behind this relative economic advance of the founder members of the EU, and moreover, the suggestion that subsequent UK

© The Author(s) 2017
P.B. Whyman and A.I. Petrescu, *The Economics of Brexit*,
DOI 10.1007/978-3-319-58283-2_7

accession to the EU would have a simultaneously positive impact upon its national economy, were always problematic. Economic theory is split over how (or even whether) economic integration may have any kind of temporary or permanent stimulus to economic growth rates. Moreover, the various studies undertaken to test this hypothesis have failed to produce the clear and unambiguous set of results that adherents would have anticipated. Nevertheless, predicted productivity and growth effects featured prominently in many of the studies seeking to estimate the potential economic impact of Brexit. Thus, this chapter seeks to draw these threads of theory and evidence together, to try to evaluate the likely growth effect arising from Brexit.

Economic Theories of Growth

The idea that economic integration is capable of improving the efficiency of an economy dates back at least as far as Adam Smith, who famously stated that 'the division of labour is limited by the extent of the market' (Smith 1776: 26). There are, broadly speaking, three main economic models which have been developed in the attempt to try to understand the determinants of economic growth. These are: (i) Keynesian, (ii) neo-classical (Solow) and (iii) endogenous growth models. Keynesian models will be dealt with in more detail later in this chapter, since they focus upon demand determinants of economic growth and are not normally used by those seeking to investigate whether economic integration impacts upon growth rates. Neo-classical and endogenous growth models, by contrast, focus upon supply-determinants of growth.

The Solow (1956) model adopts standard neo-classical assumptions of perfect competition and continuous market clearing, such that supply will create its own demand and the economy will tend towards full employment. Within this set of assumptions, economic growth is determined by a combination of the quantity of labour (labour supply) and capital, together with the rate of technological progress. Capital, it turn, is determined by demand and supply in the neo-classical market for money, via the market interest rate, and hence domestic savings will determine domestic investment in a closed economy. In an open economy, capital inflow, through the attraction of short term financial capital or longer term FDI, can have a further effect. Given diminishing returns to investment in physical capital, long term growth rates will be primarily determined by technological change, which is assumed to be exogenous, or independent of economic behaviour including economic policy intervention. Thus, the neo-classical model maintains that free factor movement promotes a convergence of income levels between nations, whilst economic integration cannot have a lasting effect upon growth rates. It can only have a minor effect through creating more stable economic conditions and thereby encouraging savings, therein lowering the cost of capital and facilitating further investment. Or, alternatively, it could encourage growth through the removal of restrictions upon the free flow of labour, thereby potentially increasing the labour supply and hence economic growth. Or, again, through the encouragement of FDI flows, thereby increasing the supply of capital. These quantity effects would, however, raise the level of income over the short term, but unless rates of migration or FDI flows continued to increase exponentially, they would not secure a permanent increase in economic growth rates over the longer term.

The problem with the neo-classical growth model is that it does not satisfactorily explain the differences in growth between different nations. The 'residual' for neo-classical growth models is often very high, implying that perhaps up to half of the recorded differences in growth rates between countries are not being successfully accounted for by this approach. Accordingly, a new endogenous growth model was developed, which allowed for heterogeneous capital and labour, whilst firms were assumed to be able to influence technological change through their own investment and strategic planning (Romer 1990). This new theory allows for the possibility of increasing returns to scale and firms having an incentive to invest in new technology and innovate in their production, to reap higher (excess) profits. Furthermore, economic integration can encourage greater competition, across a larger market area, and thereby promote greater efficiency (Baldwin 1989). In this conception, economic integration can have further impacts upon economic growth if increasing the size of the marketplace enables firms to increase production and benefit from greater economies of scale, thereby lowering the costs of production, increasing productivity and hence GDP. Higher profits provide the incentives for further investment and R&D, and this in turn should stimulate further growth. Economic integration may therefore, according to the endogenous growth model, have *permanent* not simply temporary effects upon economic growth rates if it is capable of accelerating technological innovation (Rivera-Batiz and Romer 1991; Cuaresma et al. 2008: 643–644).

Openness and Economic Growth

The insights provided by the neoclassical and endogenous growth theories have subsequently led to a broader association being established between the degree of 'openness' of an economy and economic growth. Openness, in this context, relates to the ease of movement of goods, services, labour and capital across borders (Bank of England 2015: 16). It is thought to assist nations in adopting the latest technologies, which can, in turn, increase the efficiency of their economies, thereby shifting them towards the global productivity frontier (Bank of England 2015: 33). This denotes the state of best practice available at any one period of time. One consequence might be, as suggested by the governor of the Bank of England that the UK economy may be able to grow more rapidly without generating inflation.[3]

Openness may change the incentives for firms to innovate and invest in new technology, as openness may increase competition and import penetration (Bloom et al. 2011), whilst simultaneously increasing potential returns that could be achieved through successful exporting into a more accessible overseas market (Rivera-Batiz and Romer 1991; Melitz and Trefler 2012). Furthermore, the inward flow of FDI, as was discussed in Chap. 4, may have positive productivity effects (Aghion et al. 2009).

There is a well-established literature which has sought to establish whether openness results in higher economic growth rates (Edwards 1998; Frankel and Romer 1999). A variety of studies have concluded that openness can increase growth rates due to a rise in investment and technology diffusion (Wacziarg 2001), and greater R&D (Bloom et al.

2011), whilst there is reasonable evidence that reducing trade barriers raises investment as a share of GDP and thereby *may* stimulate technological change (Barro 1991). However, initial positive findings were criticised on the basis that these studies suffered from missing variable bias—i.e. when factors, lying outside the model, have a measurable influence upon the results (Rodriguez and Rodrik 2000; Irwin and Terviö 2002). For example, Rodrik et al. (2004) found that institutional factors were a much larger influence upon economic growth rates than openness. In addition, whilst it can be readily established that wealthier nations tend to engage in a higher proportion of international trade than poorer nations, this is insufficient to establish the degree of causality (Feyrer 2009: 2). In other words, does higher trade lead to higher national income, or is the cause the other way around?

One study sought to get around this problem by introducing the idea that distance, in trade terms, is not fixed over time, as reductions in transportation costs (particularly air transport) alters the impact of physical distance between countries over time (Feyrer 2009: 3). For example, the cost of air freight declined by more than 92%, from around $3.87 per ton-kilometre in 1955 to under $0.30 in 2004, when expressed in constant currency (Hummels 2007: 137–138). Consequently, whist spatial distance remains the same, the ability to trade over distance becomes more cost effective, thereby facilitating a large expansion of trade over longer distances and reducing the advantages inherent in trade between close neighbours. The result of this study was to suggest that trade does appear to have a significant effect on income, such that variations in trade patterns can explain around 17% of the differences in growth rates across those nations included in the analysis, between 1960 and 1995 (Feyrer 2009: 23).

Competition and Productivity

A second aspect of the proposed openness effect occurs through the impact of greater competition, with subsequent influence upon productivity and growth. Competitive pressures are thought to facilitate productivity through disciplining firms to become more efficient or else they lose market share, and through pressuring firms into innovation which can lead to increased efficiency (Pilat 1996: 108–109, 129; CMA 2015: 2). As less efficient firms decline, resources are released and, if certain assumptions hold, are reallocated to the more efficient firms, thereby raising average productivity (Melitz and Redding 2012). Openness amplifies this process as a larger market is likely to enhance competition, certainly in the short run, whilst simultaneously broadening the scope for increased economies of scale (Melitz and Ottoviano 2008: 307–312; CBI 2013: 60). It may also improve the quality of supply chains (CBI 2013: 10). Consequently, were Brexit to result in the UK being excluded from participation in the SIM, concerns have been raised that productivity effects would be weakened (Portes 2013: F6).

There are, however, two problems with this rather straightforward view of the positive relationship between competition and productivity growth. The first is that the neo-classical growth model is founded upon the assumptions inherent within neo-classical economics. The two most prominent of these include: (i) perfect competition, where the marketplace is comprised of many small producers and consumers, each too small to influence the market price and with all but essential levels of profitability competed away in the long run; and, (ii) Say's Law, which holds that the economy tends towards full employment of all resources, as supply creates its own demand. The operation of these two assumptions enables the neo-classical model to deliver the positive productivity predictions, as perfect competition ensures the continuation of competitive pressures which forces firms to become more efficient, whilst Say's Law ensures that any resources released from an inefficient firm leaving the market will be automatically taken up and used by more efficient remaining and new entrant firms. Under these conditions, the Solow growth model holds that competitive pressures drive the expansion of the capital stock which, in turn, is a key determinant of economic growth in the short to medium term.

If these simplifying assumptions do not reflect real world reality, however, then the link between competition and growth is problematic. For example, given that firms invest in new technology when they see an opportunity to earn profits (Grossman and Helpman 1994: 27), intensive competition can both reduce the incentive to invest by lowering future profit expectations whilst also retarding the ability to do so through retained profits (Romer 1986; Aghion and Howitt 1992). Indeed, the neo-classical assumption of perfect competition makes the reduction in future profitability an inevitable feature of its model of growth. Thus, where domestic firms find it more difficult to compete, greater openness may cause a decline in domestic investment and hence slower rates of growth (Feenstra 1990; Grossman and Helpman 1994). This is not to dismiss the possibility that openness can have an impact on growth, but rather that it does not necessarily occur through greater competition.

The endogenous theory of economic growth, by contrast, holds that innovation and technological advance are more significant determinants of economic growth than the level of capital stock per se (Grossman and Helpman 1994: 24). It acknowledges that individual sectors are typically characterised by imperfect competition, where it is possible for producers to retain larger (excess) profits beyond the short run, as competition is not sufficiently intense to compete this away. As a result, these firms may respond to the greater market opportunities open to them through greater openness by innovating or investing in new technology, because they have the profit incentive and retained earnings to fund such investment (Aghion et al. 2005). In this way, it is possible for openness to impact on growth when competition effects are in fact sufficiently weak to facilitate the investment in technological development, but sufficiently strong to provide a necessary degree of market discipline to prevent inertia.

The problem in seeking to weigh the relative merits of these economic theories is that the evidence is imprecise and difficult to evaluate (Pilat 1996: 122, 130). There is a certain degree of evidence to support the idea that high rates of product market competition, characterised by high entry and exit rates into a given market, may promote market discipline and productivity growth (Nickell 1996; Disney et al. 2003; Tang and Wang 2005), encourage the adoption of new technology (Baily and Gersbach 1995), better management practices (Bloom and van Reenan 2010; Bloom et al. 2012) and innovation (Griffiths et al. 2010). However, other theorists found negative associations between product market deregulation and innovation (Griffith and Harrison 2004; Cincera and Galgau 2005), and between import penetration and productivity levels (Pilat 1996: 124). This suggests that it may not be openness per se that is important, but rather the ability of domestic producers to be in a position to take advantage of any new market opportunities through investing in new technology, innovating and hence enhancing their productivity and competitive advantage. Interestingly, Aghion et al. (2005, 2009) identified a possible inverted-U shape relationship between competition and innovation in the UK, inferring that, when competition is limited, an increase will result in increased innovation and productivity growth, whereas beyond a certain point, further increases in competition may damage these positive effects. Perhaps this is why there is only weak evidence that EU membership has had any noticeable impact upon productivity growth in member states (EC 1996: 180).

Openness in the UK and EU

If economic integration has an economic impact, then there should be overwhelming evidence to be gleaned from the experience of the EU, given that the EU has recorded faster increases in trade openness than other OECD nations (Bank of England 2015: 89). Indeed, it has been described as 'the most far reaching and successful integration project in history' (Badinger and Breuss 2011: 285). Perhaps surprisingly, given the importance of this issue, there have been relatively few studies which have sought to test this question (Badinger 2005: 51). Some of these have used the synthetic counterfactuals method, which is where a control group of other countries is chosen to reflect the characteristics of the chosen country(ies) prior to the intervention under investigation, which in this case would be accession to the EU. Estimation of the effect is made by comparing the subsequent behaviour of the target nation with this control group (Campos et al. 2014: 9). The strength and weakness of these studies is therefore quite obviously the closeness of fit of this control group. Other studies have utilised econometric techniques, whether using cross sectional or panel data. The issue for this group of studies is the sensitivity of their models to either the sample composition (i.e. the number of countries included and over which time period), and/or the robustness of the model to the inclusion or exclusion of different variables (Sapir 2011: 1213).

There are a number of studies that conclude that European integration has facilitated a temporary period of faster economic growth due to the reduction of trade barriers encouraging investment (Baldwin and Seghezza 1996). Estimates range from EU member state GDP being an average 5% higher than would otherwise have been the case, through to a maximum of 20% (Boltho and Eichengreen 2008; Badinger 2005). Henrekson et al. (1997: 1539), in contrast, concludes that European integration led to a *permanent effect* on the growth rate of between from 0.6 to 1.3% per annum. This study is particularly interesting because it found similar results for EFTA nations as for EU member states, which might point towards a general benefit arising from the reduction of trade barriers more generally, but not a specific EU effect per se. This conclusion of a permanent increase in economic growth rates is disputed by Eichengreen and Bolitho (2008: 24–26), who consider it to be unlikely. Nevertheless, they do accept that integration probably did provide a positive economic impact, as trade creation proved to be larger than trade diversion for most of the founder member states (Bayoumi and Eighengreen 1997; Eichengreen 2007). Moreover, whilst economies of scale would no doubt have been secured irrespective of the creation of the common market, this additional trade integration is likely to have provided some additional impetus.

By contrast, there have been a number of studies which have found no evidence that European integration has had any measurable impact upon growth rates, either temporary or permanent (Landau 1995; Vanhoudt 1999). Indeed, much of the observed increase in traded goods may be derived from a catching-up effect, whereby poorer nations benefit far more from accession to the EU than would a more developed economy, such as the UK (Cuaresma et al. 2008: 650–652).

The attempt to calculate the impact of EU membership on the degree of trade openness in the UK is, however, fraught with difficulties. It relies on a counter factual—i.e. what might have happened had the UK not joined the EU. Moreover, for the UK, which previously had well established, relatively low-tariff trading relationships with Commonwealth and North American countries, joining the EU was not a wholly trade-enhancing process, due to the trade diverting impact of the common external tariff.

In addition, many of the studies, upon which the openness hypothesis is based, have been called into question due to problems with missing variable bias (Rodriguez and Rodrik 2000; Rodrik et al. 2004). It is difficult to isolate the effects of European integration from other macroeconomic developments. For example, during the period when the customs union was being formed, all European economies were expanding rapidly. Whilst trade barriers were being dismantled within the EU common market, they were also being reduced across the globe through GATT and subsequently WTO multilateral trade agreements. Thus, it is difficult to identify precise causality. This is why this type of model suffers from missing variable bias and the robustness of its conclusions depending upon the selection of which countries to include in the analysis, over which time periods and the precise selection (or omission) of particular variables within the model (Cuaresma et al. 2008: 644–645). Hence, the majority of these papers concede that their results are fragile and not completely robust (Badinger 2005: 50; Henrekson et al. 1997: 1551; Boltho and Eichengreen 2008: 13).

There are additional elements which further complicate the interpretation of this evidence. For example, in order to simplify the analysis, studies tend to assume that nations have identical endowments and technologies in order to more easily isolate scale effects that may arise from economic integration. But they clearly do not. Hence, allowing a more realistic assumption of significant differences in endowments and technologies between nations implies that economic integration can result in resources shifting between different sectors and countries, potentially reducing growth rates in some member states even if it rises in others (Rivera-Batiz and Romer 1991: 550).

A further challenge is that the various studies show that any openness effect is not constant over time (Eichengreen 2007). Benefits for the UK, for example, would appear to have slowed considerably in more recent years, whilst for Ireland, they accelerated (Campos et al. 2014: 16). This has an obvious implication for any inclusion of a dynamic (openness)

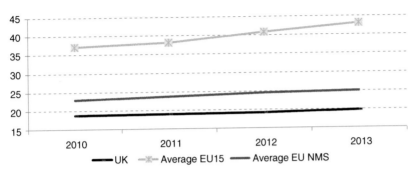

Fig. 7.1 Trade openness (trade as % GDP), 2010–2013. *Source* OECD National Accounts, (2016a)

effect in an analysis of Brexit, because the leading studies have assumed both that: (a) the past trends in European integration will continue much as they have done previously, despite data indicating that positive trade impetus may being slowly exhausted; (b) that the UK benefits at a similar rate to other EU member states; and (c) that this remains constant when predicted into the future.

One final complication concerning the interpretation of the evidence relating to the impact of European integration upon the UK's economy arises because its trade openness to the EU is lower than comparable intra-EU trade shares for other member states (see Fig. 7.1). This is partly a consequence of the UK being a relatively large economy, when compared to most EU member states, and it is an observable fact that larger economies tend to be in a position to supply most of their own needs internally, without resorting to international trade. Smaller states tend to have a greater propensity for trade. Japan and the USA, for example, have trade openness of around 6% and 7% respectively (OECD 2016a). It is also partly due to the UK having a more global trade orientation rather than focusing more upon regional (European) markets. As a result, even were it to be categorically proven that a deepening integration has benefitted the average EU member states, it is likely that the UK will benefit less from any economic integration effect than other EU nations.

Evidence from the UK—Did Joining the EU Reverse the UK's Relative Decline?

The UK joined the EU, at least in part, to reverse a perceived relative economic decline, in particular, compared to the original founders of the EU. In one sense, this has been successful, given that UK GNI per capita started lower than all but Italy of the EU(6) countries in 1973, but was recorded as being slightly above France in 2015.[4] However, the 4 decades of membership did not significantly reverse economic weakness identified by those advocating accession. Indeed, the UK actually experienced a reduction in realised growth during the period of EU membership (see Fig. 7.2), where the pre-membership (black) growth trend suggests an average annual growth rate of around 3.3%, whereas the (green) growth trend during the 4 decades of EU membership is a less impressive 2.6%. This is not to infer that there is necessarily a causal link between the two events, but rather that whatever growth dividends anticipated by advocates of EU accession did not materialise.

A second piece of evidence concerns the relative growth rate of the EU economy compared to the rest of the world. If the EU were growing more rapidly than the global average, then even if the UK failed to reverse its earlier decline relative to other EU member states, the UK could still have benefitted from its accession—as a slower moving boat on a fast moving tide. Unfortunately for the UK, this was not the case, as the EU as a whole became a slow growth area during the period of UK membership, with a particularly noticeable deterioration in relative growth performance occurring towards the end of the 1980s (see Fig. 7.3). It has been plausibly suggested that economic tightening, accompanying the creation of the EU single currency, together with the subsequent institutional fragility of the Eurozone, have proven to be part of the reason for this poor economic performance (Zarotiadis and Gkagka 2013). However, this period also coincided with the SIM being established, and thus it would appear that, whatever benefits this may have delivered to the EU economy, they were not sufficient to sufficiently offset any negative effects arising from the single currency's overall macroeconomic framework in order to accelerate EU growth rates. The CBI

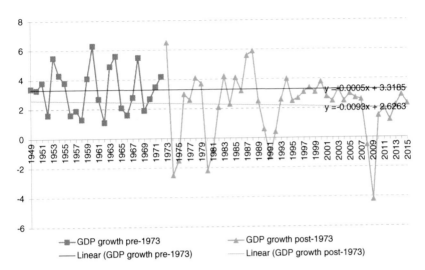

Fig. 7.2 UK GDP Growth Rates, 1949–2015 (Chained Volume Measure, with trendlines). *Source* Author calculations from ONS data

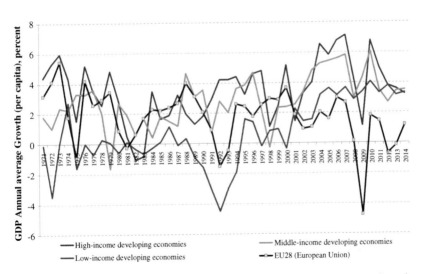

Fig. 7.3 Faster growth experienced by developing economies compared to the European Union, GDP annual average growth rate per capita. *Source* Authors' compilation of data from UNCTAD (2015b)

(2013: 110–111) shares this analysis, despite the irony that 2 decades previously, it had itself advocated UK participation in both the ERM and subsequently the single currency (CBI 1989; Eglene 2010: 92).

None of this evidence implies that EU membership has been responsible for the decline in UK economic growth during these 4 decades. There have been a number of far more potent shocks that the UK economy has experienced over this time period, including the multiple OPEC oil shocks in the 1970s, the disastrous monetarist experiment in the 1980s, the ERM crisis in 1990 and the financial crisis in 2008. Indeed, it is still possible for advocates of EU membership to argue that UK growth rates would have been even worse had the UK not been a member of the EU over this time period. Nevertheless, what this evidence indicates is that EU membership, whether positive or negative, was insufficiently significant to raise UK growth rates by more than whatever factors depressed growth trends. If it did have any positive effects, EU membership must have only a small impact upon economic growth, and hence Brexit should not prove overtly costly in terms of UK growth rates when measured over the medium term. If, alternatively, EU membership had a negative impact upon UK growth rates, then Brexit should be able to raise UK growth rates over time, by releasing the economy from the constraints imposed by EU membership.

It is, of course, possible that EU membership may be associated with a rise in UK productivity, but that, due to the economy producing at less than capacity, this is not reflected in growth figures. However, evidence from the Bank of England (2015: 48) indicates that UK output per person has remained pretty consistently around 25% lower than that achieved by the USA, and below that achieved by the EU(6) countries. A more useful measure of productivity, namely output per hour worked, takes account of the fact that working hours have fallen more rapidly in EU(6) than in the UK or US economies. Using this superior measure, UK output per hour worked increased from around 60% of the USA level in 1960, towards 80% of US levels by the start of the 2008 financial crisis, albeit falling back a towards 75% in the last few years. EU(6) productivity rose towards parity with US levels, before falling back towards 90% over the past decade.

This evidence leads to three conclusions. The first is that the UK has had a persistent productivity problem, when compared to the USA and even the EU(6) nations. This is most likely due to the failure of the UK economy to facilitate comparable rates of productive investment over a long time period. The second conclusion is that membership of the EU was not sufficient to significantly alter this performance. Output per person remained stubbornly unchanged across the whole of this half-century period, whilst output per hour worked did increase gradually, but more slowly than comparable EU(6) nations and certainly more slowly than that achieved by Japan. Thus, the third conclusion is that the anticipated productivity effect arising from UK accession to the EU either did not materialise or else any positive effect was overwhelmed by other macroeconomic phenomena. Essentially, if EU membership helped at all, the effect was fairly weak and a superior result could have been achieved by focusing upon other, more proven means of raising productivity. These include increasing the quantity of productive investment in the UK, enhancing education and skills training of the labour force and utilising macroeconomic tools alongside an active industrial policy to reinvigorate UK manufacturing industry, where higher productivity growth is more easily achieved than in the service sector.

The Impact of Brexit on Openness and Productivity

Certain commentators have registered their anxiety that Brexit may lead to a reduction in openness and, should this occur, this would have negative consequences for productivity, innovation and growth (CBI 2013: 60; Bank of England 2015: 32; BertelsmannStifung 2015: 4). However, there is no reason why Brexit will inevitably lead to a reduction in openness. In the very short term, the UK remains a member of the EU, pending the successful completion of withdrawal negotiations, and therefore there should be little effect. Future trading relationships with the EU could range from EEA membership, which would result in little change from the status quo, through possible customs union and FTAs, or else to trade based upon WTO rules. These different options are discussed, in more detail, in Chap. 9; however, for the purposes of this discussion, all involve a different degree of trade openness with the EU. The WTO option, for example, would involve the most independent relationship with the EU, and under this option trade would be likely to be subject to tariff barriers, which would reduce openness between the UK and the SIM.

Yet it would be a mistake to focus rather narrowly upon this relationship alone. Approximately 55% of UK exports are destined for sale outside of the SIM (Webb et al. 2015: 4). Moreover, the relatively slow growth of the EU would suggest that this proportion will only grow in the future. Therefore, it is perhaps the trade relationship that the UK negotiates with the rest of the world that will determine the future openness of the economy. There are certainly no a priori reasons why Brexit will inevitably lead to the UK becoming a more insular, inward-looking country.

A second issue relates to the inadequacy of the academic evidence which seeks to establish whether a link in fact exists between openness and productivity. There have been a number of studies which have examined this issue, but no clear consensus has emerged about whether increased competition will enhance or inhibit innovation and technological advance. Nor whether this tenuous association depends upon more significant factors (Englander and Gurney 1994), which may include investments in human and physical capital, improvements in infrastructure, together with a supportive institutional and macroeconomic environment.

For the UK in particular, there would appear to be an obvious disconnect between the nations being one of the leading global nations in academic research and innovation (HMG 2013a: 32–33; World Economic Forum, 2016: 359), yet is simultaneously consistently a below-average funder of higher education and R&D as a proportion of GDP amongst OECD nations (ONS 2015a: 10–12; OECD 2015: 96–97) (see Figs. 7.4 and 7.5). Whilst the factors determining productivity are difficult to isolate, it might be considered that this discrepancy between quality and funding of research and development in the UK, may be a more immediate and significant factor than openness when

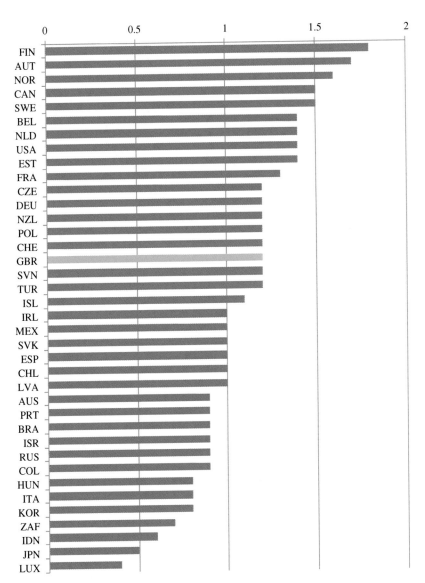

Fig. 7.4 Public spending on tertiary education as percent of GDP, various countries, 2012. *Source* OECD (2016c)

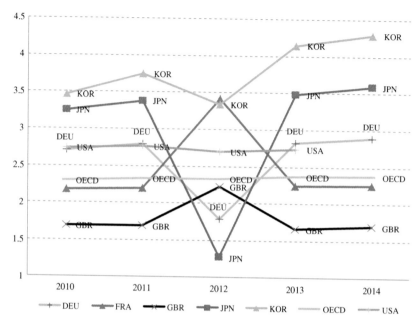

Fig. 7.5 Gross domestic spending on Research and Development, various countries, 2010–2014. *Source* OECD (2016b)

not all the parameters relating to future trading relationships are currently known.

Thirdly, there are two opposing consequences which are likely to arise from the degree of openness of the economy. The first is that increased openness may increase the dynamism of the UK economy, through the effects of increased competition or by reducing economic volatility as economic actors can diversify risks across countries and thereby insure against domestic and overseas shocks (Bank of England 2015: 3). However, the converse position is that openness results in the UK economy being more exposed to real and financial shocks from abroad. This contagion may increase the risk of the UK importing economic instability (Bank of England 2015: 11).

One final consideration relates to the fact that, even were European integration proven to have had a significant and lasting positive impact upon economic growth in the past, there is no evidence to suggest that this relationship will necessarily hold in the future (Badinger 2005: 74). It is entirely possible that any economic effects may have been exhausted, and that, since the degree of openness for most EU member states is already well in excess of 50% of national GDP, there would seem less scope for achieving a similar boost to growth in the future. Yet this complication is typically assumed away, by the most recent batch of studies examining the potential impact of Brexit.

Balance of Payments Constrained Growth

The standard economic argument for international economic integration is based upon the notion of comparative advantage, first developed by Ricardo (1817). This holds that trade is unambiguously to the advantage of all trade partners, because it allows specialisation which, in turn, facilitates economies of scale and lower costs for consumers (Thirwall 2011: 7). Thus, the balance of trade does not matter, and hence the argument that leaving the EU might improve the trade position of the UK is unimportant (Portes 2013: F9).

The problem with this idea is that it depends upon two primary assumptions. The first is that the terms of trade (i.e. or the relative prices of exports and imports), are primarily determined by trade flows, and consequently that the market should be self-correcting, through the appreciation of the currencies of nations with a trade surplus and/or depreciation of currencies for countries with a trade deficit. In reality, however, this is no longer the case, as financial speculative flows are substantially larger than trade-related flows in international currency markets (Singh 2000: 16). Without this automatic correcting mechanism, national currencies can under- or over-shoot and trade imbalances can persist into the long run.

The second assumption is the standard neo-classical foundation that supply creates its own demand (Say's Law) and therefore the economy remains constantly at or very close to full employment (Perraton 2014: 2). Accordingly, if trade balances automatically correct through market-determined changes in the exchange rate, and full employment is continuously maintained through supply-determined market forces, then economic growth will be determined by the supply of factors of production (capital and labour) and changes in productivity. Nevertheless, to the extent that these assumptions do not accurately describe the real world, outside of economic textbooks, and markets do not automatically self-correct, then large and persistent trade imbalances will have damaging economic consequences (Keynes 1973).

By contrast, Keynesian theory asserts that it is demand that drives the economy, to which supply adapts. Thus, aggregate demand promotes circular and cumulative causation (Myrdal 1957), as output growth induces further investment, technical progress and innovation, thereby facilitating economies of scale and hence generating enhanced productivity growth (McCombie and Thirwall 1997: 19; Thirwall 1997: 379–380; Perraton 2014: 3–4). One variant of this approach has become known as the constrained growth model, and was developed by Thirwall (1979), itself being an extension of the earlier Harrod super trade multipier (McCombie and Thirlwall 1994; Perraton 2003: 2). In essence, it is argued that the growth rate of a country is fundamentally influenced by the growth of its exports, and that demand can influence growth through its influence upon output, capacity, technological adaptation and productivity (Thirwall 2011: 4–5).

This virtuous circle can be disrupted, however, by constraints imposed by persistent trade imbalances. For example, should a country suffer a persistent trade deficit, as demand expands but before the short term capacity constraint is reached, then demand will be curtailed unless the nation offsets this trade gap through either overseas borrowing or attracting an inflow of capital. However, these are likely to be relatively short term options, as the former will creates obligations for future interest payments and eventual repayment. If the growth rate of the domestic economy exceeds the rate of interest on this foreign borrowing, then the ratio of debt liabilities to domestic income will not rise and the situation is sustainable for a time. However, eventually either growth will fall below this level or debt levels will create nervousness and cause investors to increase the risk premium and thereby raise the interest rate. In either case, if corrective measures not taken, the country would be in a debt trap situation (Arestis and Sawyer 1998: 185; Thirwall 2011: 15). Alternatively, inward investment could be attracted to offset any trade deficit on the balance of payments, but this would require the raising of domestic interest rates in order to attract inward flows of capital to finance the deficit, thereby deflating the economy and lowering economic activity. Thus, in either case, persistent trade deficits are likely to have a constraining effect upon national economic development and may well offset any real income gains arising from trade (Thirwall 2011: 8).

If a nation is unable to continue to finance the trade deficit, then demand will be curtailed, causing capacity to remain idle, investment to be postponed or cancelled, technological progress decelerated and product development slowed, thereby leading to less desirable exports for global consumers and further exacerbating trade difficulties. By contrast, a nation with a balance of payments surplus will be able to expand demand up to short term capacity. A virtuous circle might be formed, as the pressure of demand causes greater future investment, technological and product development, thereby increasing potential future capacity and the desirability of export products (Thirwall 1979: 429–431).

This theory links aggregate demand and the characteristics of goods produced, and, through this to the responsiveness of demand (elasticity) for UK exports and imports. The so-called Thirwall's Law, which is derived from this approach, suggests that long run national growth rates are determined by the ratio of the responsiveness of the growth of UK exports given an increase in global living standards (income elasticity of demand) relative to the equivalent income elasticity of demand for imports multiplied by world income growth (Arestis and Sawyer 1998). If UK exports are less attractive than the global average, and have a low-income elasticity, then the UK will be constrained to grow more slowly than the global average. If, alternatively, income elasticity is higher than the global norm, then growth can exceed the global growth rate (Thirwall 1979: 437–438). Creating favourable conditions for favourable product development through demand management is a necessary but not sufficient part of this process. However, an active industrial policy could make a further contribution (see Chap. 8 for further discussion).

The fact that individual nations will bear the brunt of any economic difficulties caused by trade imbalances does not, however, imply that other nations, whether in balance or running a surplus, will not also experience slower growth. If deficit nations grow more slowly because of their trade imbalances, they will be unable to purchase as many exports from the surplus nations, thereby unnecessarily limiting their growth rates. This global growth constraint is worsened if surplus nations seek to maintain their positive trade balances in the face of deficit nations seeking to restore their own trade balance, since this will cause yet further stagnation, as nations engage in competitive deflation. Keynes noted this unintended economic consequence when considering the design of an appropriate economic architecture for the period following the ending of the Second World War. His proposals for an International Clearing Union were sadly rejected in favour of the Bretton Woods system. Nevertheless, the principle of seeking to secure symmetrical trade adjustment remains an important insight (Thirwall 2011: 36–37; Whyman 2015).

UK Balance of Trade and Brexit

The insight provided by the constrained growth theory indicates how the UK's present very large trade deficit with the EU (see Table 7.1) can have a significant impact upon the growth potential of the economy. Moreover, as noted in Chap. 3, this trade deficit has been an almost permanent feature for the UK over the past 4 decades since accession

Table 7.1   UK Current Account Balance with Trade Blocs, 2015

Regional trade bloc	Current account balance (£m)
European Union (EU)	−89,468
European Economic Area (EEA)	−92,261
European Free Trade Association (EFTA)	−1220
North American Free Trade Agreement (NAFTA)	28,664
Mercosur	1976
ASEAN Free Trade Area (AFTA)	3255
Commonwealth (India, Canada, South Africa, Australia)	−2707

Source ONS (2015b)

to the EU, and has worsened considerably since the formation of the SIM. As evidenced in Chap. 4, the UK has deferred dramatic economic adjustment to reduce this deficit through its attraction of high levels of inward investment during the last 2 decades. However, this has meant that large sections of formerly UK-owned industrial and service sectors have been sold to foreign owners, with the result that future production and location decisions taken by these firms might be less influenced by national considerations. Moreover, it is questionable how much longer the UK's trade deficits can be offset in this way, particularly if FDI flows are temporarily reduced as a result of the uncertainty caused by Brexit, whilst future overseas borrowing may prove problematic for a government already struggling to reduce its debt incurred as a result of the 2008 financial crisis. Consequently, it is likely that the post-Brexit economic strategy will need to include a series of measures designed to reduce the current negative trade imbalance, lest it constrain the UK's future growth potential.

Interestingly, whilst Brexit may prove to be the catalyst for government having to address this fundamental economic imbalance, it may also facilitate its solution. For example, a more competitive exchange rate has the potential to have a positive impact upon UK economic growth rates through promoting exports. Simultaneously, an active industrial strategy can facilitate the expansion of those sections of the UK economy with the greatest growth potential, whist encouraging the development of new product ranges, some of whom may indeed increase the income elasticity of UK exports in the future. The combination of these measures should reduce growth constraints upon the UK economy significantly.

Conclusion

The evidence, as it currently stands, is not sufficiently robust to allow a definitive conclusion as to the likely impact of openness upon productivity and economic growth. Nevertheless, there is sufficient information for policy makers to consider when framing policy. For example, whilst competition is often viewed as always and in all cases having beneficial effects, the evidence reviewed in this chapter would suggest that this should be qualified by the ability of domestic (UK) firms to be in a position to respond positively to increased opportunities arising from increased openness. If domestic firms are disproportionately damaged by intensified competition, they may not be in a position to respond in the way the textbooks imagine, by investing in future capacity and new technology. Thus, to ensure that openness produces a positive result for the UK economy, policy makers may need to consider combining openness with an active industrial strategy to ensure that UK firms are in the best position to take advantage of any new opportunities as they arise.

The constrained growth model, furthermore, highlights the importance of the composition of trade between imports and exports, not simply its total volume, in terms of its impact upon aggregate demand and thereby upon investment, R&D, innovation and technological advance. The principle of cumulative causation implies that, once a competitive advantage had been established, and favourable macroeconomic conditions maintained, this should lead to a dynamic cycle whereby success begets success. However, the opposite is also true. In a situation whereby the UK has run up a massive trade deficit, unless policy intervention can successfully change the parameters sufficiently, cumulative causation will reinforce this economic weakness and this may potentially overwhelm any positive economic benefits arising from favourable trade integration. This, for the UK policy makers, is of paramount interest when determining what economic policy framework should be introduced to support the UK economy through the Brexit transition and into the future as an independent nation. That consideration is the focus of the next chapter.

Notes

1. http://voxeu.org/article/britain-s-eu-membership-new-insight-economic-history.
2. http://voxeu.org/article/britain-s-eu-membership-new-insight-economic-history.

3. http://www.bankofengland.co.uk/publications/Documents/other/treas-urycommittee/other/governorletter070316.pdf.
4. http://data.worldbank.org/indicator/NY.GNP.PCAP. CD?end=2015&locations=EU-GB-BE-FR-DE-IT-LU-NL&start=1973.

References

Aghion, P., & Howitt, P. (1992). 'A Model of Growth through Creative Destruction'. *Econometrica, 60*: 323–351

Aghion, P., Bloom, N., Blundell, R., Griffith, R., & Howitt, P. (2005). Competition and innovation: An inverted U relationship. *Quarterly Journal of Economics, 120*(2), 701–728.

Aghion, P., Blundell, R., Griffith, R., Howitt, P., & Prantl, S. (2009). The effects of entry on incumbent innovation and productivity. *Review of Economics and Statistics, 91*(1), 20–32.

Arestis, P., & Sawyer, M. (1998). Keynesian economic policies for the New Millennium. *Economic Journal, 108*(446), 181–195.

Badinger, H. (2005). Growth effects of economic integration: Evidence from the EU member states. *Review of World Economics/ Weltwirtschaftliches Archiv, 141*(1), 50–78.

Badinger, H., & Breuss, F. (2011). The quantitative effects of European post-war economic integration. In M. Jovanovic (Ed.), *International handbook on the economics of integration* (pp. 285–315). Cheltenham: Edward Elgar.

Baily, M., & Gersbach, H. (1995). Efficiency in manufacturing and the need for global competition. *Brookings Papers on Economic Activity: Microeconomics*, 307–358.

Baldwin, R. E. (1989). *On the growth effects of 1992* (NBER Working Paper No. 3119). Cambridge, MA: NBER. Available via: http://www.nber.org/papers/w3119.pdf.

Baldwin, R. E., & Seghezza, E. (1996). *Testing for trade-induced investment-led growth* (NBER Working Paper No. 5416). Available via: http://www.nber.org/papers/w5416.

Bank of England. (2015). *EU membership and the bank of england*. London: Bank of England. Available via: http://www.bankofengland.co.uk/publications/Documents/speeches/2015/euboe211015.pdf.

Barro, R. (1991). Economic growth in a cross-section of countries. *Quarterly Journal of Economics, 106*(2), 407–443.

Bayoumi, T., & Eichengreen, B. (1997). Is regionalism simply a diversion? Evidence from the evolution of the EC and EFTA. In T. Ito & A. O. Krueger (Eds.), *Regionalism vs. multilateral arrangements*. Chicago: University of Chicago Press.

BertelsmannStifung. (2015). *Brexit—Potential economic consequences if the UK exits the EU*, Future Social Market Policy Brief 2015/05, Gütersloh. Available via: https://www.bertelsmann-stiftung.de/fileadmin/files/BSt/Publikationen/GrauePublikationen/Policy-Brief-Brexit-en_NW_05_2015.pdf.

Bloom, N., & van Reenen, J. (2010). Why do management practices differ across firms and countries (*Centre for Economic Performance Occasional paper* No. 26). Available via: http://cep.lse.ac.uk/pubs/download/occasional/op026.pdf.

Bloom, N., Draca, M., & van Reenen, J. (2011). *Trade induced technical change? The impact of Chinese imports on innovation, IT and productivity* (NBER Working Paper No. 16717). Available via: http://www.nber.org/papers/w16717.pdf.

Bloom, N., Sadun, R., & Van Reenen, J. (2012). Americans do I.T. better: US multinationals and the productivity miracle. *American Economic Review, 102*(1), 167–201.

Boltho, A. & Eichengreen, B. (2008). *The economic impact of European integration* (CEPR Discussion Paper No. 6820). Available via: http://eml.berkeley.edu/~eichengr/econ_impact_euro_integ.pdf

Campos, N. F., Coricelli, F., & Moretti, L. (2014). *Economic growth from political integration: Estimating the benefits from membership in the European Union using the synthetic counterfactuals method* (IZA Discussion Paper Series 8162). Bonn. Available via: http://anon-ftp.iza.org/dp8162.pdf.

Confederation of British Industry (CBI). (1989). *European Monetary Union: A business perspective*. London: CBI.

Confederation of British Industry (CBI). (2013). *Our Global Future: The Business Vision for a Reformed EU*, CBI, London. Available via: http://www.cbi.org.uk/media/2451423/our_global_future.pdf#page=1&zoom=auto,-119,842.

Cincera, M., & Galgau, O. (2005). *Impact of market entry and exit on EU productivity and growth performance* (European Economy—Economic Papers No. 222). Brussels: European Commission. Available via: http://ec.europa.eu/economy_finance/publications/publication712_en.pdf.

Competition and Markets Authority (CMA). (2015). *Productivity and Competition: A summary of the evidence*. London: CMA. Available via: https://www.gov.uk/government/uploads/system/uploads/attachment_data/file/443448/Productivity_and_competition_report.pdf.

Congdon, T. (2013). How should Britain engage with other countries? Liberal internationalism vs regional power blocs. In A. Hug (Ed.), *Renegotiation, reform and referendum: Does Britain have an EU future?* Foreign policy centre, (pp. 42–46). London. Available via: http://fpc.org.uk/fsblob/1616.pdf.

Cuaresma, J. C., Ritzberger-Grunwald, D., & Silgoner, M. A. (2008). Growth, convergence and EU membership. *Applied Economics, 40*(5), 643–656.

Disney, R., Haskel, J., & Heden, Y. (2003). Restructuring and productivity growth in UK manufacturing. *Economic Journal, 113*(489), 666–694.

European Commission (EC). (1996). Economic evaluation of the internal Market (European EconomyReports and Studies, No. 4). Luxembourg: Office for Official Publications of the European Communities. Available via: http://ec.europa.eu/archives/economy_finance/publications/archives/pdf/publication7875_en.pdf.

Edwards, S. (1998), Openness, productivity and growth: What do we really know? *Economic Journal, 108*(447), 383–398.

Eglene, O. (2010). *Banking on sterling: Britain's independence from the Euro Zone.* Lanham, Maryland: Lexington Books.

Eichengreen, B. (2007). *The European economy since 1945: Coordinated capitalism and beyond.* Princeton, NJ: Princeton University Press.

Eichengreen, B., & Boltho, A. (2008). *The economic impact of European integration* (CEPR Discussion Paper No. 6820). London: CEPR. Available via: http://eml.berkeley.edu/~eichengr/econ_impact_euro_integ.pdf.

Englander, S., & Gurney, A. (1994). Medium term determinants of OECD productivity. *OECD Economic Studies, 22*, 49–109.

Feyrer, J. (2009). *Trade and income-exploiting time series in geography, technical report* (NBER Working Paper No. 14910). Available via: http://www.nber.org/papers/w14910.

Feenstra, R. C. (1990). *Trade and Uneven Growth,* (NBER Working Paper No. 3276). Available via: http://www.nber.org/papers/w3276.pdf.

Frankel, J. A., & Romer, D. (1999). Does trade cause growth? *American Economic Review, 89*(3), 379–399.

Griffith, R., & Harrison, R. (2004). *The link between product market reform and macroeconomic performance* (European Economy—Economic Papers No. 209). Brussels: European Commission. Available via: http://ec.europa.eu/economy_finance/publications/publication652_en.pdf.

Griffith, R., Harrison, R., & Simpson, H. (2010). Product market reform and innovation in the EU. *Scandinavian Journal of Economics, 112*(2), 389–415.

Grossman, G. M., & Helpman, E. (1994). Endogenous innovation in the theory of growth. *Journal of Economic Perspectives, 8*(1), 23–44. Available via: https://www.researchgate.net/profile/Elhanan_Helpman/

publication/4722290_Endogenous_Innovation_in_the_Theory_of_Growth/links/56adf60e08ae19a38515eda3.pdf.

Henrekson, M., Torstensson, J., & Torstensson, R. (1997). Growth effects of European integration. *European Economic Review, 41,* 1537–1557.

HMG. (2013a). *International education: Global growth and prosperity.* London: The Stationary Office. Available via: https://www.gov.uk/government/uploads/system/uploads/attachment_data/file/340600/bis-13-1081-international-education-global-growth-and-prosperity-revised.pdf.

Hummels, D. (2007). Transportation costs and international trade in the second era of globalization. *Journal of Economic Perspectives, 21*(3), 131–154.

Irwin, D. A., & Terviö, M. (2002). Does trade raise income? Evidence from the twentieth century. *Journal of International Economics, 58*(1), 1–18.

Keynes, J. M. (1973). The General theory and After Part 1—Preparation. In D. Moggridge (Ed.), *The collected writings of John Maynard Keynes.* London: Macmillan.

Landau, D. (1995). The contribution of the European common market to the growth of its member countries: An empirical test. *Review of World Economics, 131,* 774–782.

McCombie, J., & Thirwall, A. P. (1994). *Economic growth and the balance of payment constraint.* London: Macmillan.

Melitz, M. J., & Ottoviano, G. (2008). Market size, trade, and productivity. *Review of Economic Studies, 75,* 295–316.

Melitz, M. J., & Redding, S. J. (2012). 'Heterogeneous Firms and Trade'. *NBER Working Paper 18652.* Available via: http://www.princeton.edu/~reddings/papers/NBERw18652.pdf.

Melitz, M. J., & Trefler, D. (2012). Gains from trade when firms matter. *Journal of Economic Perspectives, 26*(2), 91–118.

Myrdal, G. (1957). *Economic theory and underdeveloped regions.* London: Duckworth.

Nickell, S. J. (1996). Competition and corporate performance. *Journal of Political Economy, 104*(4), 724–746.

OECD. (2015). OECD science, technology and industry scoreboard 2015. Paris: OECD. Available via: http://www.oecd-ilibrary.org/docserver/download/9215031ec007.pdf?expires=1471615882&id=id&accname=guest&checksum=4640CCE028C15A592E684D0F5A075D73.

OECD. (2016a). *National accounts, 2016.* Dataset: World indicators of skills for employment. Paris: OECD. Available via: https://stats.oecd.org/Index.aspx?DataSetCode=WSDB.

OECD. (2016b). *Gross domestic spending on R&D (indicator).* Available via: https://data.oecd.org/rd/gross-domestic-spending-on-r-d.htm.

OECD. (2016c). *Public spending on education (indicator).* Available via: https://data.oecd.org/eduresource/public-spending-on-education.htm.

Office for National Statistics (ONS). (2015a). *UK gross domestic expenditure on research and development 2014.* London: The Stationary Office. Available via: http://www.ons.gov.uk/economy/governmentpublicsectorandtaxes/researchanddevelopmentexpenditure/bulletins/ukgrossdomesticexpenditureonresearchanddevelopment/2014.

Office for National Statistics (ONS). (2015b). *Pink book—Geographical breakdown of the current account.* London: The Stationary Office. Available via: http://webarchive.nationalarchives.gov.uk/20160105160709/ http://www.ons.gov.uk/ons/publications/re-reference-tables.html?edition=tcm%3A77-382775.

Perraton, J. (2003). Balance of payments constrained growth and developing countries: An examination of Thirwall's hypothesis. *International Review of Applied Economics, 17*(1), 1–22.

Perraton, J. (2014). Economic growth in open economies: Balance of payments constrained growth—And beyond? (*University of Sheffield Department of Economics Working Paper,* No. JP300514). Available via: https://www.postkeynesian.net/downloads/soas14/JP300514.pdf.

Pilat, D. (1996). Competition, productivity and efficiency. *OECD Economic Studies, 27,* 106–146. Available via: http://www.oecd.org/eco/reform/17985473.pdf.

Portes, J. (2013). Commentary: The economic implications for the UK of leaving the European Union. *National Institute Economic Review, 266,* F4–9. Available via: http://www.niesr.ac.uk/sites/default/files/commentary.pdf.

Ricardo, D. (1817). *The principles of political economy and taxation.* New York: Dover Publications.

Rivera-Batiz, L. A., & Romer, P. M. (1991). Economic integration and endogenous growth. *The Quarterly Journal of Economics, 106*(2), 531–556.

Rodriguez, F., & Rodrik, D. (2000). Trade policy and economic growth: A sceptic's guide to the cross-national evidence. *NBER Macroeconomics Annual, 15,* 261–325.

Rodrik, D., Subramanian, A., & Trebbi, F. (2004). 'Institutions Rule: The primacy of institutions over geography and integration in economic development', *Journal of Economic Growth, 9*(2), 131–165.

Romer, P. (1986). Increasing returns and long run growth. *Journal of Political Economy, 94*(5), 1002–1037.

Romer, P. M. (1990). Endogenous technological change. *Journal of Political Economy, 98,* S71–S102.

Sapir, A. (2011). European integration at the crossroads: A review essay on the 50th anniversary of Bela Balassa's theory of economic integration. *Journal of Economic Literature, 49*(4), 1200–1229.

Singh, K. (2000). *Taming global financial flows: Challenges and alternatives in the era of financial globalisation.* London: Zed Books.

Solow, R. M. (1956). A contribution to the theory of economic growth. *Quarterly Journal of Economics, 70*(1), 65–94.

Tang, J., & Wang, W. (2005). Product market competition, skill shortages and productivity: Evidence from Canadian manufacturing firms. *Journal of Productivity Analysis, 23*(3), 317–339.

Thirwall, A. P. (1979). The balance of payments constraint as an explanation of international growth rate differences. *Banca Nazionale del Lavoro Quarterly Review, 32*(128), 45–53. Available via: http://ojs.uniroma1.it/index.php/PSLQuarterlyReview/article/viewFile/9407/9302.

Thirwall, A. P. (1997). Reflections on the concept of balance of payments constrained growth. *Journal of Post Keynesian Economics, 19*(3), 377–385.

Thirwall, A. P. (2011). *Balance of payments constrained growth models: History and overview* (University of Kent School of Economics Discussion Papers, No. KDPE-1111). Available via: https://www.kent.ac.uk/economics/documents/research/papers/2011/1111.pdf.

United Nations Conference on Trade and Development (UNCTAD). (2015b). *Annual average growth rate, GDP.* Available via: http://unctadstat.unctad.org/wds/TableViewer/tableView.aspx.

Vanhoudt, P. (1999). Did the European unification induce economic growth? In search of scale effects and persistent changes. *Weltwirtschaftliches Archiv/Review of World Economics, 135*(2), 193–220.

Wacziarg, R. (2001). Measuring the dynamic gains from trade. *World Bank Economic Review, 15*(3), 393–429.

Webb, D., Keep, M., & Wilton, M. (2015). In *brief: UK-EU economic relations.* (House of Commons Library Briefing Paper (HC 06091)). London: The Stationary Office. Available via: http://researchbriefings.parliament.uk/ResearchBriefing/Summary/SN06091.

Whyman, P. B. (2015). Keynes and the international clearing union: A possible model for Eurozone reform. *Journal of Common Market Studies, 53*(2), 399–415.

World Economic Forum. (2016). *The global competitiveness report 2015–2016.* Geneva: World Economic Forum. Available via: http://www3.weforum.org/docs/gcr/2015-2016/Global_Competitiveness_Report_2015-2016.pdf.

Zarotiadis, G., and Gkagka, A. (2013). European Union: A diverging union? *Journal of Post Keynesian Economics, 35*(4), 537–565.

8

Economic Policy Considerations

One remarkable feature of most studies which have sought to fore-cast the economic impact of Bresit, is that they have consistently ignored the role of macroeconomic policy in affecting the outcome. Presumably, this was to simplify the analysis, yet it was always going to be unrealistic. Indeed, almost immediately after the referendum result was announced, the Bank of England presented a significant stimulus package, whilst a new Chancellor of the Exchequer, Philip Hammond, announced a partial relaxing of the former tight fiscal stance. These measures contributed to the UK economy producing a very respectful economic performance, in the first full quarter after the referendum result, with a provisional growth rate of 0.5%[1]; thus confounding previous predictions, contained in many of the reports examined in this book, of a vote for Brexit causing an immediate recession.

It is certainly too early to draw conclusions from one or two sets of favourable economic data, and indeed, Article 50 has yet to be triggered and the negotiation period begin, yet, two conclusions can be drawn. Firstly, despite the undoubted potential for damage arising from the type of uncertainty unleashed in the immediate aftermath of the referendum result—not helped by the public utterances made by the former Prime Minister and Chancellor during and after the referendum

P.B. Whyman and A.I. Petrescu, *The Economics of Brexit*,
DOI 10.1007/978-3-319-58283-2_8

campaign—the swift action by policy makers restored confidence and prevented unnecessary economic damage. This leads directly on to the second conclusion, namely that the decision to omit the impact of macroeconomic policy from all of the major studies undertaken to examine the likely impact of Brexit most probably skewed their forecasts downwards. This matters, not simply because policy makers and business leaders have relied, in part, upon the accuracy of these studies to set their respective future strategies, but also because these studies have been interpreted as predicting likely outcomes from Brexit, rather than the more accurate interpretation which is that they were forecasts of *what might happen if no other actions were taken*. Failure to properly consider policy actions in these studies sadly undermined their accuracy and hence weakened their utility.

This chapter seeks to rectify this apparent reluctance to include economic policy in consideration of the economic impact of Brexit.

Macroeconomic Policy

Uncertainty

One of the negative consequences predicted to result from the Brexit result concerned the uncertainty generated for all economic actors (HMG 2016: 21). To some extent, this was likely to occur surrounding the referendum in any event, case, as each and every general election results in uncertainty as to the likely result and the subsequent consequences for either continuation or a shift in economic strategy (Credit Suisse 2016: 6; Punhani and Hill 2016: 5). Yet, the uncertainty relating to Brexit is of a different magnitude, since it concerns the commitment of the UK to remaking a fundamental economic relationship that had formed a key part of the UK economy for more than 4 decades. The range of forecasts, outlined in Chap. 1, reinforced the significance of this vote for many economic actors, and it is not therefore surprising that the uncertainty concerning the result of a tight referendum vote would be likely to have an economic impact, as firms defer investment decisions and/or hiring plans until the Brexit negotiations have been clarified (Punhani and Hill 2016: 3, 7).

Attempting to change the terms of the UK's relationship with the EU will inevitably create risks (CBI 2013: 132). Of course, the same would have been true when the CBI first advocated that the UK joined the then Common Market in the 1970s, and would have been equally true when the CBI lobbied for the UK joining the ERM and EMU in the 1990s. Thus, whilst any evaluation of the costs and benefits of a significant change in economic relations with other EU member states should consider the potential impact arising from uncertainty about the outcome; the fact that any change will inevitably involve a degree of uncertainty is not in and of itself a good justification for inaction. Moreover, risks emanating from Brexit have to be placed against risks which would occur if the UK remained within the EU. For example, it is not certain that the status quo position for the UK is tenable in the medium term, as Eurozone economies seek to strengthen the EU's economic governance to develop a more supportive infrastructure necessary to sustain the single European (Armstrong and Portes 2016: 6). Furthermore, risks of further economic contagion, arising from the continued fragility of the Eurozone, is equally concerning for other commentators (Business for Britain 2015: 30).

The Article 50 procedure is scheduled to last for two years, once triggered; before Easter 2017 on the current timetable. Yet, the full process of not only establishing a new trading relationship with the EU, but additionally restructuring the UK economy and negotiating future trade agreements with the rest of the world, will take longer than this to complete (Irwin 2015: 28). This will extent the period of uncertainty and there exists the potential for the twists and turns of negotiations to damage business confidence at any point throughout this process (McFadden and Tarrant 2015: 60). Indeed, it has been suggested that the EU may deliberately exacerbate this level of uncertainty, thus raising the direct economic costs of Brexit for the UK, in order to discourage disintegrative political forces elsewhere in Europe, even should this impart short term economic damage upon other EU member states (Irwin 2015: 29).

The most obvious manifestation of uncertainty occurs in the financial markets, where the value of stocks and currencies are reassessed against new evidence arising from any significant event, and their prices adjusted accordingly. There could be a higher risk premia charged in credit and equity markets (PwC 2016: 6, 8). The perceived underlying value of company stocks may shift, due to Brexit, based partly upon forecasts for how this will impact upon the domestic market and trade flows with Europe, but also on how individual companies may respond to shifts in their external environment. In the immediate aftermath of the referendum result, UK stock market valuation fell sharply, although this immediate paper loss was recovered within a few weeks, and stock market indexes are currently above their equivalent valuations prior to the referendum vote.

The price of currency exchange will partly reflect the future expectations of trade, given that exports represent a demand for sterling (as foreign purchasers generally have to settle their accounts with sterling), and imports a demand for other currencies, so that a worsening of the trade balance would imply a fall in the value of sterling and an improvement a rise, *ceteris paribus*. In reality, however, the vast bulk of currency trading is not based upon trade but involves one form or another of speculation. This explains the 'rollercoaster ride' that sterling took immediately preceding and following the referendum result, as speculators took contrary positions.[2] Overall, there was an expectation that sterling would depreciate, following a referendum vote to withdraw from the EU (Ebell and Warren 2016; Fairbairn and Newton-Smith 2016: 16; OECD 2016: 12), and, indeed, this has occurred. It is quite likely that the current rate has over-shot a more probable medium term sustainable rate. Nevertheless, the international competitive stimulus that this gives to UK exporters is likely to offset certain negative consequences arising from Brexit (Armstrong and Portes 2016: 5).

There are likely to be short term increases in the rate of inflation which occur due to the depreciation in the exchange rate, although given the very low current rates of inflation, these effects are not likely to be particularly significant, given that they will only persist for the year in which the depreciation occurs (Baker et al. 2016: 115). Finally, increased volatility of the exchange rate can have a detrimental effect upon the cost of trade and trade volumes. However, this is only really manifested if the volatility persists for a significant period of time, as companies typically hedge against the effects of currency variability in the short term (Pilbeam 2016). Indeed, the economics literature is fairly dismissive of the idea that exchange rate volatility has more than a negligible impact upon growth over the medium or longer term (Eichengreen and Bolitho 2008: 27).

One problem, with some of the analyses undertaken to predict the economic impact of Brexit, is that uncertainty has been modelled as though it is equivalent to risk. For example, a number of the economic studies have predicted that Brexit is likely to reduce trade with the EU and will lower business export earnings, which will, in turn, increase the cost of capital and temporarily increase the risk premium paid for borrowing funds for investment (Baker et al. 2016: 109; PwC 2016: 6, 22). It is this higher risk premia that is then utilised as a proxy for uncertainty, to produce estimates that UK GDP will grow more slowly over the medium term as a result of Brexit, albeit that these negative effects would cease to have an effect thereafter. However, there is a key difference between uncertainty and risk. Uncertainty embodies both 'risk', where uncertainty of outcomes can be represented by a known probability distribution, and more general 'uncertainty', when the probability distribution itself is unknown. Risk management, therefore, seeks to quantify risk wherever possible but realising that, however perceptive economic theory and accurate the predictions made by resulting economic models, knowledge remains incomplete in an ever-changing economy. Thus, policymakers have to resort to judgement about the probable results of actions, costs and benefits associated with various possible outcomes resulting from different policy options (Greenspan 2003).

The economics literature indicates that there is likely to be a negative impact upon business investment arising from increased uncertainty (Leahy and Whited 1996). Investment may be delayed or deferred (Bloom 2009; Bloom et al. 2014), particularly where firms have large existing fixed investment (sunk costs) (Pindyck 1988). To the extent that advocates of Brexit are successful in demonstrating potential gains arising from the Brexit process—perhaps through interest expressed by non-EU nations in negotiating future trade agreements with the UK or through utilising the greater policy flexibility post-withdrawal to rejuvenate UK manufacturing industry—this might, to some extent at least, offset other negative expectations (PwC 2016: 6).

There is also a potential impact upon the ability of the UK government to borrow as cheaply on international markets, as international investors might be less likely to wish to hold gilts, whilst ratings agencies could downgrade the value of UK government securities (Baker et al. 2016: 111). This problem is not as acute for the UK as for many national governments, since its gilt market is disproportionately domestic, with international investors only holding around one quarter of the total issue. Moreover, most government bonds are of longer than average duration, meaning that any short term problems would take a number of years before their impact became problematic. If uncertainty persisted into the medium term, the cost of debt financing, for businesses and governments alike, might rise (Baker et al. 2016: 114).

Investment

The 1971 White Paper, which sought to explain or justify the UK's decision to apply for membership of the EU (then EEC), raised the possibility that free access for UK exporters to the larger marketplace, comprising all EU member states, would be likely to lead to an increase in investment, production and increased efficiency through the realisation of economies of scale (HMG 1971: 11, 13–14). Unfortunately, this anticipated acceleration in UK productive investment did not occur. Instead, as can be seen in Fig. 8.1, following accession to the EU, UK gross capital formation has steadily declined, from around 25% in 1973, to 17.3% in 2015. Thus, the UK invests less, as a share of its national income today, than it did when it joined the EU 4 decades previously (Business for Britain 2015: 722–723). Given the evidence, presented in the previous chapter, that investment is one of the key determinants of economic growth and productivity, this long term failure inherent within the UK economy will have significantly limited its growth potential. Moreover, this under-performance is even more manifest when comparing the UK

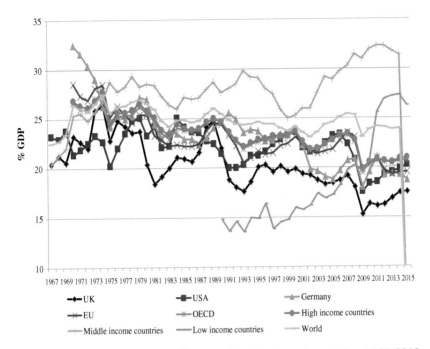

Fig. 8.1 Gross capital formation[24] as % of GDP, selected countries, 1967–2016. *Source* World Bank (2016)

record on investment with other nations. For example, one comparison, based on 2013 figures from the *CIA World Factbook*, ranked the UK only 140 out of 153 countries in terms of its share of GDP devoted to gross fixed investment.[3]

This dismal investment record has occurred despite a sharp increase in inequality levels within the UK. As national income has shifted from wages to capital, orthodox economic theory would have anticipated that productive investment would have been facilitated. Yet, the evidence suggests that lowering taxes upon entrepreneurs and capital holdings has not worked for the UK. Indeed, the latest research indicates that rising inequality has *depressed*, rather than boosted, economic growth (Chang 2010; OECD 2014).

None of this is to suggest that EU membership per se was to blame for this fall in investment, as, indeed, this had multiple causes.

Nevertheless, it does demonstrate that the anticipation of the gains to be made by joining the EU have not materialised in the way that their advocates expected.

Employment Impact from Brexit

One of the most dramatic claims, made both before and during the European referendum, concerned the suggestion, made by the former Deputy Prime Minister, Nick Clegg, that Brexit would 'jeopardise up to three million jobs in this country' (cited in Portes 2013: F8–9). A similar point was made by the then Chief Secretary to the Treasury, Danny Alexander, in 2014, when he stated that 3.3 million British jobs were connected, directly and indirectly, to the export of goods and services to the European Union. Whilst Angela Eagle, a minister of state in the previous Labour government, estimated this figure to be 3.5 million (cited in Webb et al. 2015: 9). Furthermore, the Treasury report, produced during the 2016 referendum campaign, reiterated the claim that a significant proportion of total employment—specifically 3.3 million jobs out of a total 33.8 million for the UK as a whole—is related to exports to the EU (HMT 2016a: 65).

The problem with these statements is not so much the veracity of the fact that a share of total employment in the UK is maintained due to the level of activity in the UK economy, some of which derives from exports made to the rest of the world, including other EU countries. However, the inference is that, should the UK withdraw from the EU, all of the activity related to trade with the EU would cease, and therefore in excess of 3 million people would lose their jobs. This is, of course, 'totally implausible, and certainly not based on evidence' (Portes 2013: F8–9). Even those theorists predicting the worst outcomes from Brexit, forecast that the vast majority of trade between the UK and the EU will continue much as before, even should tariffs be imposed. Thus, to allude to the possibility that all such trade would be imperilled is unwarranted. Indeed, the Treasury itself, in a statement made to the campaigning organisation *Open Europe*, clarified the position that the figures cited by Alexander and Eagle were 'not an estimate of the impact of EU membership on employment' (Webb et al. 2015: 9).

Other studies have accepted this point. Capital Economics (2016: 18) dismissed such claims as 'wild overstatement', whilst Pain and Young (2004: 406) concluded that there was no reason to suppose that unemployment would rise significantly were the UK to withdraw from the EU. PwC (2016: 3) suggested that any such employment effects would be perhaps a tenth of the more publicised claims; adding perhaps 1–2% on to unemployment rates in the short term, but having no significant longer term effects beyond this temporary shock. Yet, even should these negative impacts occur, there is no automatic reason as to why they should result in employment losses, rather than reductions in real wages or price changes, if the economy is sufficiently flexible to adjust through price rather than quantity effects. Moreover, as discussed in the earlier chapters, even those predictions of trade reductions with the EU tend to over-estimate net effects for the UK economy, by ignoring the mitigating effects created by a more competitive rate of sterling, cost reductions from replacing supra-national with national regulation, the introduction of active economic policy interventions and the possible expansion of trade elsewhere in the world if the European market became a more difficult marketplace for UK exporters.

The conclusion is, therefore, that it is difficult to calculate a specifically employment-related 'Brexit' effect that is identifiably distinct from more general macroeconomic factors.

Designing Economic Policy for an Independent UK

Short Run—Dealing with Uncertainty

On 4th August 2016, shortly after the European referendum result and the resignation of the former Prime Minister (Cameron), the Bank of England sought to diffuse any short term uncertainty by introducing a series of measures to bolster confidence and facilitate adjustments in the UK economy. These measures included[4]:

1. A reduction in the bank rate from 0.5 to 0.25%.
2. The introduction of a new Term Funding Scheme (TFS), designed to ensure that the reduction in the bank rate fed through to the borrowing rates faced by households and firms.
3. A new extension of quantitative easing (QE), involving the purchase of £10 billion worth of UK corporate bonds and a further £60 billion expansion of the asset purchase scheme for UK government bonds. This takes the total stock of these asset purchases to £435 billion.

The objective of this package was to provide a small stimulative effect, but perhaps more importantly it would signal the financial markets and other economic actors that the Bank of England was ready to take whatever action it perceived to be necessary to stabilise the economy. Monetary stimulus would occur partly through the reduction in the interest rate, although given rates were already at historically low levels, this is unlikely to achieve much of a monetary boost. The QE measures are intended to increase the price of government bonds, which are typically described as 'gilt edged' securities, often foreshortened to 'gilts'. This reduces their yields, which is intended to lower the cost of financing public borrowing, whilst simultaneously incentivising investors to switch towards riskier assets which provide greater returns, but which should also provide the finance required to facilitate private sector productive investment. The problem with QE is that it operates indirectly, and therefore much of its stimulus can be absorbed by the financial sector, if channelled through banks desperate to rebuild their balance sheets. However, *The Economist* publication remains convinced that the QE programme is having the desired effect.[5]

There are other economic policy measures that could be taken to reinforce this package. For example, the government could consider introducing a fiscal inventive to boost productive investment, such as a tax allowance or support for R&D. Particularly if this incentive were to be time limited, so that qualifying investment would have to take place within the next few years, this could encourage firms to bring forward investment rather than defer decision-making. In addition, the macroeconomic stance of the government is particularly important in creating the parameters within which firms make investment decisions. If the economy is growing at or above trend, firms are more likely to invest as they believe they can sell their products. Indeed, it is the expectations held by business people of future profitability that predominantly determines present investment, whilst realised profits largely finance this new investment (Kalecki 1971; Arestis 1989: 614). Hence, if macroeconomic policy focuses upon promoting growth, it is more likely that investment will be forthcoming as business people will lose out if they fail to invest in new products, processes and technology, in order to take advantage of favourable market conditions. This latter policy stance is particularly important for that proportion of investment which is not financed through borrowing from financial institutions or through equity markets, but rather financed through retained earnings.

Medium Term—Economic Regeneration

There are three elements to a medium term redesign of economic policy, namely:

1. Macroeconomic management capable of facilitating economic regeneration, promoting economic growth and full employment.
2. Competitive exchange rate management to offset any increase in trade costs with the EU, whilst facilitating a long term objective of eliminating the current very large trade deficit and restoring trade balance.
3. Utilising the UK's independent status to negotiate future trade agreements both with the EU but, perhaps more importantly in the long run, a range of nations and/or trade blocs in the rest of the world whose rapid growth rates indicate their increasing importance in the marketplaces for UK goods and services in the future.

The rejuvenation and rebalancing of the UK economy will involve an active industrial strategy, but this will, in turn, depend upon government ensuring the maintenance of a sufficiently attractive economy in which economic activity is encouraged to take place. Unfortunately, this is where there is a weakness in much of the analysis that has been undertaken by supporters of Brexit, because they tend to base their recommendations upon neo-classical foundations, thereby assuming that the economy will automatically tend towards the full employment of all resources, together with an optimistic reading of the efficient market hypothesis developed at the University of Chicago. On this basis, microeconomic interventions (such as deregulation) or fiscal incentives (such as cutting business taxation) are viewed as providing a sufficient set of incentives to economic actors to reinforce market solutions capable of achieving these goals. This is despite the fact that this approach has been tried repeatedly, over the past few decades, and it has not worked.

The alternative is to acknowledge that businesses produce and invest because they think they can sell their goods or services, rather than because labour or capital have become a little less expensive then international competitors, and therefore it is *demand* that drives the economy, not supply. Hence, it is the task of government to manage the level of aggregate demand in the economy, to ensure that there is a sufficient level to facilitate the full employment of resources, encourage business investment and ensure a decent level of economic growth. Aggregate demand impacts directly upon the real economy because it influences, and in turn is influenced by, the rate of investment, which changes the stock of capital and thereby affects productive capacity and employment (Rowthorn 1995, 1999; Alexiou and Pitelis 2003: 628). Moreover, a larger capital stock will permit a higher level of aggregate demand, and hence both higher output and employment, without resulting in an increase in inflation.

This approach emphasises the importance of public investment in infrastructure, because of the impact this has upon the efficiency and productivity of UK firms, thereby increasing their international competitiveness. It additionally 'crowds in' private investment, as firms in the private sector pick up these contracts and expand their operations, thereby increasing their ability and desire to employ more workers and invest greater sums in new machinery and new technology (Aschauer

1990). The importance of infrastructural spending has not been lost upon the new Chancellor of the Exchequer, in his most recent Autumn Statement (HMT 2016b). However, there is not yet a firm relationship that has been established at the heart of economic policy that identifies the crucial role of aggregate demand as the driver of the economy. Instead, infrastructural spending is viewed rather in isolation, as a stand-alone economic instrument rather than as an integrated overall economic approach. This needs to change if the UK is to create the high growth macroeconomic framework within which firms wish to expand, entrepreneurs wish to invest and consumers to continue to spend. In short, macroeconomic policy requires a Keynesian foundation to be truly effective.

Secondly, over the medium term, the depreciation of sterling is likely to boost UK exports whilst reducing the level of imports and/or encouraging import substitution, thereby providing a secondary boost to domestic producers. The economics literature indicates that periods of competitive (or undervalued) exchange rates can have significant positive effects upon those industrial sectors that have significant growth potential (Rodrik 2008). Indeed, there is evidence that exchange rate undervaluation lay behind the rapid increase in the growth rates of European economies up until the 1970s, whereas subsequent revaluation and a tighter macroeconomic stance has slowed this pace of development (Perraton 2014: 12). Thus, exchange rate management would appear to be an effective macroeconomic management tool. Data for 2009, drawn from OECD-WTO TiVA datasets, suggest that UK exports are price elastic, which indicates that a change in price will have a proportionately greater impact upon the quantity of that good or service demanded. In this instance, the estimate was made that a 10% change in the price of UK export prices would likely lead to a change in exports volumes of between 15 and 25% (Driver 2014: 7).

Given that the UK will remain a full member of the SIM for the next two years, even were Article 50 to be triggered no later than Easter 2017 as is currently proposed, a more competitive exchange rate should facilitate a necessary reduction in the UK's currently very large current account deficit. Indeed, the Bank of England expects that it could be sufficient for this to halve over the next three years.[6] If, at the end of the withdrawal transition period, the UK had negotiated a FTA with the EU, then the maintenance of a competitive exchange rate should continue to further erode the UK trade deficit with the rest of the continent, albeit at a slowing rate over time as higher import prices cause a gradual deterioration in the boost provided by an initial currency depreciation. If, however, the UK reverts to trading on the basis of WTO rules, then the maintenance of a competitive currency is even more important, as it could offset, fully or partially, any increase in the costs of exporting due to the re-erection of trade barriers with the EU. Even though, as was discussed elsewhere in this volume, the costs associated with these barriers are much lower today than they were still in the 1970s when the UK joined the EU, they could have a negative effect upon UK exports if not offset via the exchange rate.

Thirdly and finally, Brexit provides the UK with the *opportunity* to explore alternative trade relationships with EU member states but, more importantly in the long run, also faster growing nations elsewhere in the world. The UK will be free to negotiate its own preferential trade deals with whomever it chooses. This could be with former close trading partners in the Commonwealth and would most likely also embrace the establishment of closer economic ties with the USA. Indeed, it is plausible that President Trump might be a more receptive partner than the previous US administration. It is likely that the UK will seek to establish a series of FTAs with some or all of these nations, in the immediate period following the formal withdrawal from the EU. These preferential trade agreements are likely to boost non-EU trade and offset any negative consequences pertaining to trade with the EU, in full or in part. Moreover, the net benefit derived from non-EU trade surpluses is likely to rise over time, as faster growth rates outside Europe lead to higher demand for UK products; the precise relationship depending upon the elasticity of the goods and services exported.

The greater flexibility of manoeuvre, however, is subject to the application of multilateral trade rules, policed by the World Trade Organisation (WTO). This limits discrimination[7] which might otherwise occur in matters of international trade. For example, it prevents non-tariff barriers from imposing different technical standards upon imported and domestic goods, and also ensuring that every WTO member offers 'Most Favoured Nation' (MFN) treatment to the goods, services and intellectual capital of all other WTO members. Moreover, the WTO does not allow tariffs to be raised for a particular category of good or service, once introduced, without its consent.[8]

The WTO additionally limits the use of public subsidies which would otherwise be perceived as creating an unfair advantage for the exporting nation, except in certain circumstances.[9] These exceptions include cases where they promote regional regeneration, the restructuring of certain industrial sectors particularly responding to changes in trade and economic policies such as presumably the impact of Brexit, encouraging research and development especially in high tech industries, assisting the development of infant industries, introducing local preference in public procurement and when avoiding environmental problems (Rubini 2004: 152). All of these exceptions to the WTO rules would, therefore, be available to an independent UK, seeking to rebalance its economy through promoting manufacturing industry, and ensuring that economic growth spread more evenly across the whole nation, as often described by the use of the phrase promoting the 'Northern Powerhouse'. Thus, within the WTO rules, an independent UK may have considerably greater flexibility in terms of rejuvenating its manufacturing sector, which will have the added benefits of raising productivity and potentially growth rates, whilst reducing its large trade deficit (Business for Britain 2015: 141–142).

Microeconomic Policy

The macroeconomic policy framework to be set by the UK government following Brexit will be of considerable importance in determining the ultimate success or failure of the decision, taken by the British electorate, for the country to pursue independent economic development. However, microeconomic policy will be no less significant in dealing with challenges that Brexit will entail for specific sectors of the economy. Given that the UK economy has a very large trade deficit, particularly with our EU neighbours, and the economy relies too heavily upon finance and the professional services rather than manufacturing industry to restore trading balance, then industrial policy can play an important role in restoring greater balance to the economy. Noting the conclusion reached by Rodrik (2006: 986), that 'more selective, and more carefully targeted policy initiatives … can have very powerful effects on igniting economic growth in the short run', this chapter, therefore, explores the potential arising from policy interventions in these areas.

Industrial Policy

Industrial policy is intended to resolve market imperfections and thereby enhance the efficiency of the productive sector (Greenwald and Stiglitz 2012). That, however, is a very broad statement, and it can encompass both interventions designed to promote greater competitive pressures within a sector or national economy, or to promote the development of a firm or sector identified as having long term growth potential. It may, equally, focus upon seeking to solve macroeconomic problems, such as the UK's currently excessive trade deficit, through the promotion and expansion of the UK's manufacturing sector.

There are two types of industrial policy. 'Vertical' or selective industrial policy seeks to combine planning support for industry, with state investment, and infrastructural projects. Policy interventions are targeted at specific firms or sectors, to enhance their efficiency and ultimately secure international competitive advantage. Hence, this has often been characterised by critics as governments attempting to 'pick winners', or to create 'national champions' (Cohen 1977). By contrast, 'horizontal' industrial policies are more general and passive in nature, focusing upon reducing constraints to the operation of market forces and the creation of a low tax, low regulation business environment. Horizontal policy could additionally include investment in education and infrastructure, as this benefits the economy in general, and does not focus upon specific sectors.

There are, of course, difficulties in maintaining this distinction between vertical and horizontal forms of industrial policy, as any intervention will inevitably disproportionately benefit one firm or industry. Thus, a decision to expand technical education may form part of a horizontal skills policy, it will be of more benefit for engineering and IT firms than for agriculture or large parts of the service sector. Similarly, the decision to extend the railway network in the north of England, through the so-called Northern Powerhouse programme, will disproportionately benefit those industrial clusters which are spatially connected to this new infrastructure. Moreover, there is a further weakness with the horizontal approach, in that, because this disproportionate benefit occurs as a by-product of the intervention, rather than through its specific design, it becomes more difficult to monitor the effectiveness of the measure(s) and to prevent 'leakages', thereby potentially reducing the effectiveness of the intervention (Chang 2009: 13–15).

Formulations of industrial policy as either conforming to vertical or horizontal approaches have difficulty in devising satisfactory policy interventions seeking to enhance business networks and thereby realise the agglomeration effects arising from clusters of specialised firms, operating within a given locality. The expectation is that networks will generate positive spillovers, whether through the creation of a labour force specialising in the skills and knowledge required by the sector in question, or through innovation that emerges through a combination of collaboration and competition (Chinitz 1961; Porter 1998: 78). Consequently, the creation of networks is occasionally considered to be a third type of industrial strategy.

The most notable examples of vertical industrial policy encompass the strategies adopted by Japan, South Korea, Taiwan, Singapore and, more recently, China (Chang 2009: 2–4).[10] However, the list of nations adopting what would now be regarded as vertical forms of industrial policy could also include the USA, since the state financed between half and two-thirds of national R&D expenditure between the 1950s and 1980s, principally in the fields of defence-aerospace and healthcare, and it is in many of these areas where the US subsequently established a technological lead (Chang 2009: 7–8). Indeed, Mazzucato (2013) outlines, in detail, how publically funded research provided the foundation for many of the most prominent recent examples of product innovation, including pharmaceuticals, renewable energy and personal electronics such as the iPod, iPad and battery technology. Moreover, the UK was only the first amongst multiple nations (including Germany) which pursued what would now be described as an infant industry programme, where the development of selected industries were protected by high tariffs, before the UK accepted the principle of free trade which allowed these now mature industries to realise their competitive advantage (Chang 2009: 10).

The economics literature has not, unfortunately, produced a clear consensus upon the effectiveness of different modes of industrial policy. There have, for example, been a number of studies which have concluded that vertical policy fails to deliver its intended increase in productivity (Krueger and Tuncer 1982; Lee 1996). Yet, they typically suffer from problems of omitted variable bias and difficulties in interpretation of causality. For example, if a study records a negative association between intervention and industrial performance, does this indicate that industrial strategy has had negative effects upon the industry or alternatively that the problems of the industry were so intractable that a more sizeable state intervention was necessitated to try and solve deep-set problems? Moreover, other econometric studies indicate that total factor productivity is higher in those nations which adopt an import-substitution form of industrial policy rather than a market-orientated alternative although, again, it is difficult to assign causality (Bosworth and Collins 2003). Hence, there is no persuasive body of evidence which can point conclusively to whether industrial policy produces superior or inferior economic outcomes (Rodrik 2006: 9–10). Nevertheless, there has been a significant increase of interest in a more active industrial policy proving indispensable to national economic development (Lin and Monga 2010).

Industrial policy intervention has one significant weakness, which needs to be acknowledged, namely the potential for regulatory capture by business interests. Indeed, there is sufficient evidence to suggest that, where initiatives become entrenched in the medium or long term, they deteriorate in effectiveness and can run the risk of corruption or capture by industrial interests to secure economic rents (Rodrik 2004: 1, 17).

This does not, however, negate the potential for industrial policy intervention, but rather it highlights the importance of designing an end point, at which point the intervention will be withdrawn, alongside the proper monitoring and policing of the various industrial policy measures. Democratic accountability and transparency could help to prevent the abuse of policy intervention measures.

Industrial Policy Within the EU

The EU initially pursued a vertical form of industrial policy, seeking to develop a set of European businesses capable of competing with US TNCs. However, during the past 2 decades, policy has shifted towards a horizontal approach. Indeed, to illustrate the extensiveness of this shift in approach, the former European Commissioner in charge of competition policy, Neelie Kroes, argued that concerns over retaining national control over what are regarded to be 'strategic assets' is 'outdated – the language and the mindset are those of yesterday's people, not of these who have the guts to look forward with ambitious realism'; a viewpoint dismissed as 'contrary to the spirit and the letter of the laws underpinning the European Union' (Kroes 2006: 3). Vertical industrial policy was, furthermore, rejected by Kroes (2006: 4, 6) on the grounds that it would result in decreasing competitiveness, whilst state aid was decried as crowding out private sector investment.

The advent of the SIM further reinforced this shift in approach, as the SIM held that national promotion of domestic industry was discriminatory and therefore not consistent with competition rules. Vertical industrial policy would, by definition, give preference to, or advantage for, domestic products vis-à-vis those produced elsewhere in the EU (Kennedy 2011: 47–48; Barnard 2016: 82–84). One area in which EU rules therefore constrain the operation of industrial policy is in the setting of national standards to products, which encompasses the implementation of various 'buy national' campaigns. Indeed, the European Commission has prevented previous attempts to run 'buy British', 'buy Irish' and even 'buy local' campaigns, because these were deemed to be discriminatory. From the perspective of those who view the SIM as a means of creating a single integrated European economy, these rules would appear perfectly reasonable, as they prohibit what is regarded as unfair competition.

Yet, its operation does result in a number of strange consequences. For example, the prevention of 'buy local' campaigns prevents governments from seeking to reduce the number of food miles generated by global food companies and supermarket chains, and prevents in particular public bodies creating a guaranteed market for local food producers which may reduce food waste and have beneficial environmental and regional development outcomes. Similarly, these rules have prevented national governments from requiring products that portray themselves as souvenirs of a given nation from having to contain an indication of their country of origin. Thus, consumers purchasing an item to remind them of a specific country, are to have no information provided to guide them in their choice except by the manufacturers' voluntary participation in labelling their products (Barnard 2016: 84). Furthermore, in the field of renewable energy, the European Court ruled against national or regional rules requiring electricity suppliers to purchase specific quantities of renewable energy from their local region, on the grounds that this discriminated against energy produced elsewhere in the EU (Barnard 2016: 83). However, the result of this ruling frustrates the establishment of local energy generation, which many experts suggest can be produced at lower levels of energy lost through transmission grids, with resultant cost and emissions advantages (Armstrong 2015).[11]

A second area where SIM rules inhibits vertical industrial policy intervention concerns public procurement. In order to ensure free competition across the SIM, public authorities are required to make tender details widely available across the EU and may not discriminate against any firm because it is registered or located in a different EU country.[12] The intention is to create a 'level playing field' for firms across the EU to bid for tenders that, in aggregate, approximate to 14% of EU GDP per annum.[13] However, public procurement could alternatively be used to establish a core market for local producers, to meet developmental or environmental objectives. It could, for example, introduce a preference for local produce to reduce food miles and raise nutritional food provision for public services (i.e. hospitals, schools, retirement homes, prisons), or to help to establish a market for local renewable energy. Similarly, it could facilitate the expansion of the UK engineering industry by ensuring that local producers receive part of the increased demand arising from the Northern Powerhouse public investment intended to renew transportation links in the North of England. In the absence of the greater industrial policy flexibility which will arise post-Brexit, comments from Sir Andrew Cook, Chairperson of William Cook Rail (a large engineering employer in South and West Yorkshire), would suggest that this opportunity is currently being squandered.[14]

A third area where the EU restricts industrial policy relates to its rules relating to state aid. This may be defined as where public assistance is provided on a selective basis to a firm or group of firms either directly by public authorities or via an instrument over which the state has significant control (BIS 2015: 4–5). This would include not only subsidies and tax credits funded through the national budget, but also assistance from regional or local government, public guarantees, state holdings of all or part of a company, the provision of goods and/or services on preferential terms, and funding provided via quasi public bodies such as the National Lottery.[15] If this assistance has any effect, it will strengthen the firm or firms targetted by the measure, and will therefore be deemed as distorting competition and fall foul of EU SIM competition laws.

There are exceptions to this rule, of course, relating to the provision of very small amounts of assistance (i.e. less than €200,000 over 3 years) and what fall under the category of 'General Block Excemption Regulation' (GBER), which include the following:

- Regional aid.
- Assistance provided to SMEs in the form of investment aid, operating aid and SMEs ' access to finance.
- Environmental protection.
- Research and development and innovation.
- Training aid.
- Recruitment and employment aid for disadvantaged workers and workers with disabilities.
- Rebuilding after natural disasters.
- Social aid for transport for residents for remote regions.

- Broadband infrastructures.
- Culture and heritage conservation.
- Sport and multifunctional recreational infrastructures.
- Local infrastructure.
- Rescue and restructuring aid for firms in difficulty.[16]

Each of these categories has its own rules and ceilings placed upon the maximum amount of permitted state aid (BIS 2015: 9). Moreover, these exemptions only apply when assistance is provided to any and all eligible firms from across the EU, irrespective of their nationality of ownership, where their headquarters are located and even, perhaps surprisingly, whether they have any current operations within the country offering the aid. It is, however, permissible to restrict assistance to those firms that have some form of operations within the national boundary of the government offering the assistance at the time that the assistance is provided (EC 2016: point 7).

It is a fair criticism to note that the UK has chosen not to utilise its flexibility within these exemptions to operate a more active form of industrial policy (e.g. see Fig. 8.2), and hence the limited forms of industrial policy that are permitted by the EU could have been pursued

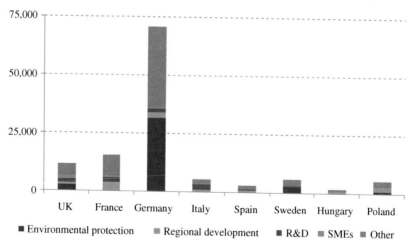

Fig. 8.2 Non-crisis aid expenditures by main objectives (€m at 2014 values), selected countries, 2014. *Source* Eurostat (2016)

more vigorously. Nevertheless, the desire to pursue deeper European integration, through the realisation of the SIM and moves towards a single European economy, necessarily limits the potential for the full range of options available to a more active form of industrial policy. Instead, the EU has placed greater emphasis upon regional (EU-wide) competitiveness, utilising measures to encourage the development of small and medium sized enterprises (SMEs) and the knowledge economy (Bartlett 2014: 4–5). This was latterly extended, through provisions established in the Lisbon Treaty, to provide elements of sector-specific support (EC 2010; Uvalik 2014: 2–3). The stated goal was to support the growth of the EU's industrial sector to approximately one fifth of EU GDP by 2020 (Pellegrin et al. 2015: 10).

The Potential for Industrial Policy Following Brexit

Brexit offers the potential to operate a more active industrial policy unhindered by SIM competition and state aid rules. Rodrik (2008) suggests that the ideal form of industrial policy would be one that combines vertical and horizontal elements, namely where the government identifies specific sectors with high growth potential and provides targeted support to aid their development, whilst simultaneously creating a broader framework conducive to industrial development more generally. The former could include tax credits, subsidies or directed credit. Investment could be directed through a state investment bank, of the type prominent in countries such as Japan, South Korea, Canada, Germany and China, charged with supporting infant industries with recognised future growth capacity. The case for a state investment bank is made persuasively in an IPPR report (Dolphin and Nash 2012).

Given their provision of lower cost credit and financial services to businesses not adequately served by the private sector financial institutions, state investment banks have the ability to support capital development more generally and potentially enhance countercyclical macroeconomic policy in the process (Mazzucato and Penna 2014: 4–5). The current state-owned British Business Bank could develop into fulfilling this more strategic role, possibly along the lines of the German

Kreditanstalt für Wiederaufbau (KfW), which both fulfils the role of a national state investment bank whilst simultaneously provides funding to regional state investment banks in Germany.[17] Interestingly, a proposal has already been developed, along these lines, by the Shadow Chancellor McDonnell.[18]

Active industrial policy could additionally include the re-institution of a public interest test for takeovers, thereby preventing the foreign takeover of strategic industries. A variant of this approach could involve the state acquiring a 'golden share' in certain sectors to prevent outcomes that might prove undesirable to the economy as a whole, such as the relocation of the headquarters, or research and development functions, offshore.

Public procurement could be utilised as an active policy tool to facilitate the development and growth of selective UK industries. As previously mentioned, this could include the creation of a market for local food produce or locally generated renewable energy. Whilst the UK would still be bound by WTO rules (Irwin 2015: 16),[19] requiring open and transparent conditions for competition to be included in all public procurement procedures, the difference is that these only apply to those procurement activities that form part of the nation's coverage schedules.[20] At present, the UK is included as a part of the EU, and it is their rules that apply. However, upon withdrawal from the EU, the UK government would have the opportunity to redesign its public procurement procedures to better meet the needs of economic development objectives, if it so chose.

To ensure that this active industrial policy is sustainable, it is important to ensure that public and private stakeholders have a 'symbiotic' rather than 'parasitic' relationship (Mazzucato 2013: 30). Too often state support for innovation in the private sector combines the socialisation of risk with the privatisation of gains, which is precisely the flawed balance of costs and benefits that underpinned the irrational exuberance and excessive risk taking by the financial institutions, thus precipitating the 2008 global financial crisis (Mazzucato 2013: 34, 203). A true partnership requires a means of sharing both the costs and the benefits derived from the initial public investment. This could involve the state taking a stake in the enterprise, thereby receiving a share of the rewards arising from the development of products drawing upon this publically funded invention or innovation.

There are a number of criticisms which are likely to be levied at the introduction of a more active industrial policy. Firstly, there is the suggestion that state investment 'crowds out' private investment. This is based upon the neo-classical theory of the market for money, whereby there is a finite amount of funds available, at the prevailing equilibrium rate of interest, to be borrowed to invest in productive activities as well as less productive forms of assets. If this theoretical construct is accepted as a proxy for reality, then, if the economy is operating at full employment, any public sector borrowing to invest in UK businesses will either increase demand relative to the supply of funds, thereby increasing the interest rate paid by all borrowers and thereby making investment less profitable, or else it will substitute public for private borrowing. In either case, the result would be less beneficial than adherents of industrial policy would claim. If the further assumption is added that private investment is always superior to public investment, then it would be unlikely that state investment will produce beneficial effects that would exceed these predicted costs.

The problem with this criticism is that the theory on which it is founded is fundamentally flawed. Whereas money markets might have once resembled the neoclassical characterisation in the early days of capitalism, the reality in the twenty first century is that most investment occurs through a combination of retained earnings and bank credit (Kalecki 1971). There is not a finite amount of credit but, rather banks can create money based (sometimes rather loosely) upon their deposits and other assets. Consequently, there is no a priori reason for crowding out to necessarily occur. Moreover, to do so, neo-classical theory requires the economy to be operating at full capacity, so there are not underutilised or unused assets that could be seamlessly employed. The theory achieves this through the simplifying assumption of 'Say's Law', which holds that supply creates its own demand, which, in turn, implies that the economy will always be automatically self-correcting towards the full employment of all resources. There can, under this assumption, never be a situation where demand deficiency persists, and both capital and workers remain idle. Yet, any cursory perusal of economic history will demonstrate the fragility of this assumption. The economy is often away from its equilibrium position for long periods of time. Indeed, so much so that many have suggested that the concept of equilibrium itself is a theoretical abstraction from reality. However, the pertinent point for this discussion is that crowding out does not occur if the economy is operating at less than full employment. Indeed, in circumstances of less than full employment, public investment can often 'crowd *in*' further private sector investment. Moreover, since an essential part of the intention of industrial policy is to actively shape markets, to enhance their future productive potential, then crowding out arguments are less tenable (Mazzucato and Penna 2014: 27).

A second criticism is that, by operating selective measures favouring one firm or industry over another, industrial policy weakens competition policy (Irwin 2015: 17). However, if the free operation of market forces has not been sufficient to deliver the UK sufficient industrial capacity, with future high growth potential, sufficient to eliminate its current large trade deficit, then there would appear to be an a priori justification for considering this type of intervention.

A third criticism is that industrial policy does not work because the state is incapable of 'picking winners'. Presumably, those who advocate this position also hold that venture capital funds, and the financial markets more generally, are presupposed to have a monopoly of insight into future market conditions and the growth potential of each and every individual firm and productive sector (Baldwin 1969). This viewpoint is largely based upon a vague understanding of the 'efficient market hypothesis' (Farma 1970). Contrary to popular belief, this theory does not state that markets are always and everywhere efficient and do not exhibit excessive volatility, but rather that even if they should do so, predictions of future movements in securities prices are a random walk and hence, on average, no investor can make consistently greater returns than another. Yet, the rather limited scope of the original theory has been taken by policy makers and those economists who perhaps should read the original texts, to imply market superiority.

Yet, there are plenty of examples that can be given where state assistance has assisted in the development of international competitive industries, whether car production in Japan or steel in South Korea, because the state had the long term vision often lacking in financial markets more focused upon short term gains (Chang 2002).[21]

Moreover, the fact that industrial policy may occasionally fail in its choice of investments does not undermine the need for the state to undertake this role if the private sector is unable or unwilling to nurture these developments. Venture capitalists often fail in their investment selections, but they are judged not on individual interventions, but rather upon the balance of their entire portfolio. State investments should be similarly assessed on the same basis, so the inevitable losses sustained in certain businesses are likely to be more than offset by the successes in other ventures (Mazzucato and Penna 2014: 23–24). As Rodrik (2004: 25) aptly summarises the position; if governments make no mistakes when operating an active industrial policy, it implies that they are not trying sufficiently hard.

As a good starting point, to identify sectors with good productive growth potential, Chang suggests that one strategy would be to focus upon those emergent sectors, such as alternative energy and those developing applications from new materials, on the basis that there are fewer established firms dominating these markets.[22] In terms of renewable energy, one obvious field in which successful innovation could generate large returns, would concern battery technology, both for personal electrical devices but perhaps more significantly for electric cars and to be able to successfully store renewable energy power generation. Research is currently examining the potential for lithium-air batteries, which are hypothetically far more efficient than the current ion batteries in contemporary usage, together with sodium-ion and redox flow batteries, which, should technical issues be satisfactorily resolved, be scaled up to facilitate renewable energy from providing a greater share of UK energy needs, even when the wind is not blowing or the sun shining.[23]

A second example might be to focus upon applications of new materials such as graphene, which was discovered at the University of Manchester and for which two academics won the 2010 Nobel Prize in Physics. Graphene is a crystalline form of carbon, in which a single layer of carbon atoms are arranged in a regular hexagonal pattern. It is the thinnest known material yet discovered, yet is also the strongest; indeed, it is estimated to be 100 times stronger than steel. Despite being crystalline in structure, it is quite elastic and has the best thermal conductivity of any material. As a consequence, the range of potential applications to which this substance can be put signifies the potential gains for those organisations that are able to establish themselves as first-movers in these markets. Yet, despite graphene being discovered in Manchester, the UK has filed less than 1% of graphene-related patents (IPO 2015: 7). China, by contrast, has 29% of patents, whilst fully 47% have been filed in China; the difference presumably relating to non-Chinese companies deciding to file patents in China as this is where they propose developing the related product range(s) (IPO 2015: 7–9). This is not simply a reflection of the relative sizes of individual nations, since South Korea has registered almost as many graphene-related patents as their larger neighbour, with 25% of the global total. The response by the UK government, to establish a £235 million advanced manufacturing research centre at the University of Manchester, is a welcome but rather belated recognition of the significance of this sector (HMT 2014: 50).

A second strategic approach that a more active industrial strategy could pursue is to identify those types of technologies which have scale or agglomeration economies, and which are unlikely to receive sufficient long term investment in the absence of public intervention. There are a number of reasons why this may be the case. It may be that certain industries are capital intensive and thereby requiring a substantial initial fixed-cost outlay before economies of scale can be realised (e.g. the national grid, telecommunications networks or the railways). Or alternatively it might be that the financial markets perceive that investments are too risky or too long term to realise reasonable shorter term profits (e.g. aerospace in the 1970s). A third category concerns technologically advanced or innovative industries. The problem for investors is that innovation is fundamentally uncertain, and hence it is problematic to accurately predict the probability of success. Hence, innovation requires the type of patient, long-term finance that state investment banks or other forms of public investment are perhaps more capable of providing, alongside a supportive policy environment designed to support high-tech and high growth business development. Industrial policy could, therefore, provide assistance for these activities but it would do so less by identifying specific industries to receive public support, but rather the specific types of technological innovation to promote (Rodrik 2004: 14). This is the framework that some have characterised as an 'entrepreneurial state' (Mazzucato and Penna 2014: 23).

Alongside the provision of funding for dynamic industries or areas of technological innovation, industrial policy has the potential to create a supportive business environment within which these firms can operate. Given that innovation can be constrained by the lack of demand for the resulting products or activities, particularly where large initial investments are required to realise the innovative gains, businesses are likely to remain cautious or slow to innovate unless they are confident about future market conditions (Rodrik 2004: 4, 12–13). Expectations about future profitability is the motivation behind future investment, whilst realised past profits largely finance such investment (Keynes 1936: 135–141; Kalecki 1971). Moreover, historical evidence would suggest that investment tends to be concentrated where capital productivity is growing the fastest (Baumol et al. 1989). Thus, if industrial policy can contribute towards stimulating industrial expansion and enhancing total factor productivity, it should enhance broader economic policy objectives. There are clear synergies between macroeconomic and industrial policy; the former can create a supportive structure within which the latter can better operate, whilst the latter can stimulate industrial expansion and thereby support macroeconomic goals.

One area where Rodrik (2004: 30) does not suggest focusing industrial policy is, perhaps surprisingly, the attempt to influence the locational decisions of TNCs and thereby attract FDI. His reasoning is quite clear: that there is insufficient evidence to justify the belief that FDI results in significant productive externalities and that associations between higher productivity and exporting firms are the result of selection effects (i.e. that successful and efficient firms tend to export rather than exporting causing their productivity advantage). Hence, directing public funds to subsidise the activities of TNCs would be an inefficient use of resources and do little to enhance productive capacity.

Industrial policy would be particularly important for the UK to deal with the consequences of Brexit. Irrespective of the final form of trade agreement negotiated with the EU following withdrawal, there will be a degree of industrial restructuring which will inevitably follow. This could involve some repositioning of European supply chains, and whilst certain industries are likely to expand due to a more competitive exchange rate and global sales opportunities, other industries may contract as a result of their reliance upon European trade in protected sectors. Industrial policy can help to ease this transition, through provision of information, the financing of infrastructure improvement and compensation for externalities (Lin and Monga 2010). Indeed, Rodrik (2004: 15) notes that industrial restructuring rarely occurs in the absence of government involvement and assistance.

Industrial policy could provide a means of assisting those sectors, such as vehicle manufacture, which are likely to face a tariff rate of perhaps 8.5% if a FTA could not be negotiated with the EU and future trade relied upon WTO 'most favoured nation' rules. In Chapter Three it was noted that this may raise costs for the industry by around £1.4 billion and that, whilst the UK government could certainly afford to fully compensate the vehicle manufacturing industry for this increase in their costs, the fact that such a crude approach might breach WTO rules would suggest that any public assistance to the car industry would take a different form. For example, since the car industry undertakes considerable research and development (R&D), and WTO rules allow for state support for this activity to be provided up to three quarters of the total cost, this would appear to be an obvious means of achieving a 'double dividend' in terms of negating additional costs for a strategically important industry whilst simultaneously increasing investment and productivity in the process. Another permissible alternative would be to provide support upon the basis of developing disadvantaged areas of the country. However, this option is less likely to result in the positive growth and productivity effects of R&D support, and therefore is a less desirable form of policy intervention. Finally, a more general (horizontal) industrial policy intervention to promote export activities, perhaps through provision of advice and support in overseas markets (Chang 2009), would provide indirect assistance to the vehicle manufacturing industry, as it accounts for 9.5% of total UK exports. This latter measure would, additionally, be worthwhile for the UK economy as a whole, as it could help to ensure that UK companies could reap the maximum benefits arising from any future trade agreements to be negotiated between the UK and other nations.

Active Labour Market Policy

An active industrial policy would be enhanced if it were operated within a supportive macroeconomic framework, and alongside measures adopted to enhance human capital development. Active labour market policies can embody both demand and supply-side measures (see Table 8.1). The former reinforce counter-cyclical stabilisation by eliminating skills shortages and structural rigidities, whilst the latter ease market adjustment by achieving a higher employment level at a given rate of inflation and promote structural change by reducing structural rigidities, search and transaction costs (Layard et al. 1991). Examples of demand measures include public works schemes, employment subsidies to individual firms, control over the release of tax-exempt private investment funds and state purchases placed with firms and in localities where unemployment would otherwise increase. Supply-side measures, in contrast, focus upon skill enhancement and enabling individuals to adapt to changing needs of the labour market (DfEE 1997). These measures seek to ease the market adjustment process by achieving a higher employment level at a given rate of inflation whilst simultaneously accommodating structural change (Whyman 2006).

Policy interventions to promote education and skills formation, in order to close skills shortages and improve the functioning of the labour market, are useful policy instruments for government to utilise in any circumstances. However, these measures may become more important in the particular conditions likely to persist following Brexit, given the fact that many businesses have become perhaps overly dependent upon the importation of migrant labour to meet various labour force requirements. Should Brexit result in a reduction in the quantity of net

Table 8.1 Different types of labour market policies

Matching	Supply	Demand
Public employment services • Information • Job placement • Counselling	Subsidised geographical mobility Free labour market training Subsidised in-house labour training	Public relief work Recruitment wage subsidies Youth teams Sheltered employment

migration, labour market policy could provide one means of reducing the production constraints imposed by persistent skill shortages in specific sectors. Of course, Brexit may result in the adoption of an EEA-type agreement with the EU, which would involve acceptance of the free movement of labour, and therefore there would be no change to the current entry rules for EU citizens. Moreover, were the UK to decide to impose greater control over EU immigration following independence, the design of any work permit system that may be introduced is intended to allow sufficient migration in order to meet skills requirements for UK businesses. However, given that any system of immigration control is difficult to apply with flexibility, it is probable that active labour market policy would be a useful means of moderating any unintended effects of a new work permit system, whilst providing assistance to UK companies as they might seek to expand their internal training and/or apprenticeship schemes.

Conclusion

In contrast to the range of economic studies published before the European referendum, this chapter has sought to highlight the crucial importance of a more active economic policy stance in order to maximise the benefits, and minimise the costs, arising from Brexit. The maintenance of a high level of aggregate demand provides the platform for the economy to continue to expand, as businesses overcome the inevitable degree of uncertainty that will arise during the withdrawal process and continue to invest in new capacity and innovative technology. A competitive exchange rate will offset some or all of the additional export costs that may arise from trading with the EU, depending upon which model of relationship is ultimately negotiated. Industrial and labour market policy will become more essential post-Brexit, as the UK economy has the potential to rebuild its industrial base, if freed from some of the constraints imposed by SIM rules, and thereby start to address some of the fundamental weaknesses with the UK economy—i.e. low productivity and high trade deficit. The successful design and implementation of this more active role for economic policy will determine its success, and very possibly also the success or failure of Brexit itself. It is that important.

Notes

1. https://www.ons.gov.uk/economy/grossdomesticproductgdp/bulletins/grossdomesticproductpreliminaryestimate/julytosept2016.
2. http://www.cnbc.com/2016/06/23/currencies-on-brexit-rollercoaster-pound-gyrates-with-early-results-trickle-in.html;   http://www.bbc.co.uk/news/business-36515816.
3. http://www.indexmundi.com/g/r.aspx?v=142.
4. http://www.bankofengland.co.uk/publications/Documents/inflationreport/2016/irspnote040816.pdf; http://www.bankofengland.co.uk/publications/Pages/news/2016/008.aspx; http://www.bankofengland.co.uk/markets/Pages/apf/default.aspx.
5. http://www.economist.com/news/britain/21704762-how-misunderstanding-about-qe-led-lots-misleading-headlines-bank-englands-new.
6. http://www.bankofengland.co.uk/publications/Documents/inflationreport/2016/irspnote040816.pdf.
7. GATT 1947, Part I, Article I, incorporated into GATT 1994 as Annex 1A to the WTO Agreement 1994; GATT 1947, Part II, Article III, incorporated into GATT 1994 as Annex 1A to the WTO Agreement 1994.
8. Understanding on the Interpretation of Article II.1(b) of GATT 1994, incorporated into GATT 1994 as Annex 1A of the WTO Agreement 1994.
9. See the WTO Agreement on Subsidies and Countervailing Measures, incorporated into GATT 1994 as part of Annex 1A to the WTO Agreement 1994.
10. Industrial policy was additionally utilised by France, Finland, Norway and Austria during this period, whilst Italy (e.g. Emilia-Romagna) and Germany (e.g., Baden-Württemberg) also pursued regional industrial policy, creating "industrial districts" through directed credits, often through regional state banks, together with the provision of assistance with export marketing and assistance with R&D funding (Piore and Sabel 1984). All of these economies outperformed other large OECD economies between 1950 and 1987 (Chang 2009: 7–8).

11. See also UK government select committee conclusions, contained within http://www.publications.parliament.uk/pa/cm201314/cmselect/cmenergy/180/18006.htm.
12. http://europa.eu/youreurope/business/public-tenders/rules-procedures/index_en.htm.
13. https://ec.europa.eu/growth/single-market/public-procurement_en.
14. http://www.bbc.co.uk/iplayer/episode/b083gkjs/look-north-yorkshire-late-news-01122016.
15. http://ec.europa.eu/competition/state_aid/overview/index_en.html.
16. http://ec.europa.eu/competition/publications/cpb/2014/009_en.pdf.
17. https://www.dbresearch.com/PROD/DBR_INTERNET_EN-PROD/PROD0000000000380779.pdf.
18. https://www.theguardian.com/politics/2016/jul/18/labour-vows-to-set-up-national-investment-bank-to-mobilise-500bn.
19. https://www.wto.org/english/tratop_e/gproc_e/gproc_e.htm.
20. https://www.wto.org/english/tratop_e/gproc_e/gp_gpa_e.htm.
21. http://www.ibtimes.com/yes-government-can-pick-winners-ha-joon-chang-268043.
22. http://www.ibtimes.com/yes-government-can-pick-winners-ha-joon-chang-268043.
23. https://www.theguardian.com/business/2016/aug/20/do-we-even-need-hinkley-point-smart-usage-windpower-hi-tech-batteries?CMP=Share_iOSApp_Other.
24. As a technical note, according to the World Bank this is gross capital formation, not gross fixed capital formation; the difference being that Gross capital formation (formerly gross domestic investment) consists of outlays on additions to fixed assets (i.e. land improvements, plant, machinery and other equipment purchases, together with the improvement of physical infrastructure such as roads, railways, buildings, schools and hospitals), and the net change in inventories.

References

Alexiou, C., & Pitelis, C. (2003). On capital shortages and European unemployment: A panel data investigation. *Journal of Post Keynesian Economics, 25*(4), 613–631.

Arestis, P. (1989). On the Post-Keynesian challenge to neo-classical economics: A complete quantitative macro-model for the UK economy. *Journal of Post-Keynesian Economics, 11*(4): 611–629.

Armstrong, H. (2015). *Local energy in an age of austerity: Preserving the value of local and community energy.* London: NESTA. Available via: http://www.nesta.org.uk/sites/default/files/local_energy_in_an_age_of_austerity.pdf.

Armstrong, A., & Portes, J. (2016). Commentary: The economic consequences of leaving the EU. *National Institute Economic Review, 236,* 2–6.

Aschauer, D. (1990). *Public investment and private sector growth.* Washington DC: Economic Policy Institute.

Baker, J., Carreras, O., Ebell, M., Hurst, I., Kirby, S., Meaning, J., et al. (2016). The short-term economic impact of leaving the EU. *National Institute Economic Review, 236,* 108–120.

Baldwin, R. E. (1969). The case against infant-industry protection. *Journal of Political Economy, 77*(3), 295–305.

Barnard, C. (2016). *The substantive law of the EU: The four freedoms* (5th ed.). Oxford: Oxford University Press.

Bartlett, W. (2014). *Shut out? South east Europe and the EUs new industrial policy* (LSE Europe in Question (LEQS) Discussion Paper No. 84/2014). Available via: http://www.lse.ac.uk/europeanInstitute/LEQS%20Discussion%20Paper%20Series/LEQSPaper84.pdf.

Bloom, N. (2009). The impact of uncertainty shocks. *Econometrica, 77*(3), 623–685.

Bloom, N., Floetotto, M., Jaimovich, N., Saporta Eksten, I., & Terry, S. (2014). Really Uncertain Business Cycles, *US Census Bureau Center for Economic Studies,* No. CES-WP-14-18. Available via: https://www2.census.gov/ces/wp/2014/CES-WP-14-18.pdf.

Bosworth, B. P., & Collins, S. M. (2003). The empirics of growth: An update. *Brookings Papers on Economic Activity, 34*(2), 113–179.

Business for Britain. (2015). *Change or go: How Britain would gain influence and prosper outside an unreformed EU.* London: Business for Britain. Available via: https://forbritain.org/cogwholebook.pdf.

Capital Economics. (2016). *The economics impact of 'Brexit': A paper discussing the United Kingdom' relationship with Europe and the impact of 'Brexit' on the British economy.* Oxford: Woodford Investment Management LLP. Available via: https://woodfordfunds.com/economic-impact-brexit-report/.

Chang, H.-J. (2002). *Kicking away the ladder: Development strategy in historical perspective.* London: Anthem Press.

Chang, H.-J. (2009). Industrial policy: Can we go beyond an unproductive confrontation? Plenary Paper for Annual World Bank Conference on Development Economics, Seoul, South Korea, 22–24 June. Available via: http://siteresources.worldbank.org/INTABCDESK2009/Resources/Ha-Joon-Chang.pdf.

Chang, H.-J. (2010). *23 things they don't tell you about capitalism*. London: Allen Lane.

Chinitz, B. (1961). Contrasts in agglomeration: New York and Pittsburg. *American Economic Review: Papers and Proceedings, 51*, 279–289.

Cohen, S. (1977). *Modern capitalist planning: The French model* (2nd ed.). Berkeley: University of California Press.

Confederation of British Industry (CBI). (2013). *Our global future: The business vision for a reformed EU*. CBI, London. Available via: http://www.cbi.org.uk/media/2451423/our_global_future.pdf#page=1&zoom=auto,-119,842.

Department for Business Innovation and Skills (BIS). (2015). *State aid: The basics guide*. London: BIS. Available via: https://www.gov.uk/government/uploads/system/uploads/attachment_data/file/443686/BIS-15-417-state-aid-the-basics-guide.pdf.

Department for Education and Employment (DfEE). (1997). *Learning and working together for the future*. London: Department for Education and Employment.

Dolphin, T., & Nash, D. (2012). *Why we need a British investment bank*, London: Institute for Public Policy research (IPPR). Available via: http://www.ippr.org/files/images/media/files/publication/2012/09/investment-future-BIB_Sep2012_9635.pdf?noredirect=1.

Driver, R. (2014). *Analysing the case for EU membership: How does the economic evidence stack up?* London: The City UK. Available via: https://www.thecityuk.com/research/analysing-the-case-for-eu-membership-does-the-economic-evidence-stack-up/.

Ebell, M., & Warren, J. (2016). The long-term economic impact of leaving the EU. *National Institute Economic Review, 236*, 121–138.

European Commission (EC). (2010). *An integrated industrial policy for the globalisation era: Putting competitiveness and sustainability at centre stage*. COM(2010) 614, Commission of the European Communities, Brussels. Available via: http://eur-lex.europa.eu/legal-content/EN/TXT/?uri=celex:52010DC0614.

European Commission (EC). (2016). *General block exemption regulation (GBER): Frequently asked questions*. Brussels: Commission of the European

Communities. Available via: http://ec.europa.eu/competition/state_aid/legislation/practical_guide_gber_en.pdf.

Eichengreen, B., & Boltho, A. (2008). *The economic impact of European integration* (CEPR Discussion Paper No. 6820). London: CEPR. Available via: http://eml.berkeley.edu/~eichengr/econ_impact_euro_integ.pdf.

Eurostat. (2016). *Non-crisis aid statistics.* Available via: http://ec.europa.eu/competition/state_aid/scoreboard/index_en.html.

Fairbairn, C., & Newton-Smith, R. (2016). *Brexit—The business view.* Lecture at London Business School, Monday 21st March. Available via: http://news.cbi.org.uk/business-issues/uk-and-the-european-union/eu-business-facts/brexit-the-business-view-pdf/.

Farma, E. F. (1970). Efficient capital markets: A review of theory and empirical work. *Journal of Finance, 25,* 383–417.

Greenspan, A. (2003). Monetary policy under uncertainty'. presented as a *symposium sponsored by the Federal Reserve Bank of Kansas City.* Jackson Hole, Wyoming, 29 August. Available via: http://www.federalreserve.gov/boarddocs/Speeches/2003/20030829/default.htm.

Greenwald, B. C., & Stiglitz, J. E. (2012). Industrial policies, the creation of a learning society and economic development. In J. E. Stiglitz, J. Esteban, & J. L. Yifu (Eds.), *The industrial policy revolution I: The role of government beyond ideology* (pp. 43–71). London: Palgrave.

HM Treasury. (2014). *Autumn Statement 2014.* Cm 8961. London: The Stationary Office. Available via: https://www.gov.uk/government/uploads/system/uploads/attachment_data/file/382327/44695_Accessible.pdf.

HM Treasury. (2016a). *HM treasury analysis: The long term economic impact of EU membership and the alternatives.* Cm 9250. London: The Stationary Office. Available via: https://www.gov.uk/government/uploads/system/uploads/attachment_data/file/517415/treasury_analysis_economic_impact_of_eu_membership_web.pdf.

HM Treasury. (2016b). *Autumn statement 2016,* Cm 9362. London: The Stationary Office. Available via: https://www.gov.uk/government/uploads/system/uploads/attachment_data/file/571559/autumn_statement_2016_web.pdf.

HM Government (HMG). (1971). *The United Kingdom and the European communities—White Paper, Cmnd 4715.* London: HMSO.

HMG [HM Government]. (2016). The process for withdrawing from the European Union, Cm 9216, The Stationary Office, London. https://www.gov.

uk/government/uploads/system/uploads/attachment_data/file/504216/
The_process_for_withdrawing_from_the_EU_print_ready.pdf.

Intellectual Property Office (IPO). (2015). *Graphene: The worldwide patent landscape in 2015.* Newport: Intellectual property Office. Available via: https://www.gov.uk/government/uploads/system/uploads/attachment_data/file/470918/Graphene_-_the_worldwide_patent_landscape_in_2015.pdf.

Irwin, G. (2015). *Brexit: The impact on the UK and the EU.* London: Global Counsel. Available via: http://www.global-counsel.co.uk/system/files/publications/Global_Counsel_Impact_of_Brexit_June_2015.pdf.

Kalecki, M. (1971). *Selected essays on the dynamics of the capitalist economy 1933–1970.* Cambridge: Cambridge University Press.

Kennedy, T. P. (Ed.). (2011). *European law* (Vol. 5). Oxford: Oxford University Press.

Keynes, J. M. (1936). *The general theory of employment, interest and money.* London: Macmillan. 1973 edition.

Kroes, N. (2006). Industrial policy and competition law and policy. *Speech given at Fordham University School of Law, New York City*, 14th September 2006. Available via: http://europa.eu/rapid/press-release_SPEECH-06-499_en.htm?locale=en.

Krueger, A. O., & Tuncer, B. (1982). An empirical test of the infant industry argument. *American Economic Review, 72*(5), 1142–1152.

Layard, R., Nickell, S., & Jackman, R. (Eds.). (1991). *Unemployment: Macroeconomic performance and the labour market.* Oxford: Oxford University Press.

Leahy, J., & Whited, T. M. (1996). The effects of uncertainty on investment: Some stylized facts. *Journal of Money, Credit, and Banking, 28*(1), 64–83.

Lee, J.-W. (1996). Government interventions and economic growth. *Journal of Economic Growth, 1*(3), 391–414.

Lin, J. Y., & Monga, C. (2010). *Growth identification and facilitation: The role of the state in the dynamics of structural change* (The World Bank Policy Research Working Paper No. 5313). Available via: http://documents.worldbank.org/curated/en/438321468164948980/pdf/WPS5313.pdf.

Mazzucato, M. (2013). *The entrepreneurial state: Debunking public v's private sector myths.* London: Anthem Press. 2015 edition.

Mazzucato, M., & Penna, C. C. R. (2014). Beyond market failures: The market creating and shaping roles of state investment banks. *Science Policy Research Unit* (Working Paper No. SWPS 2014-21), University of

Sussex. Available via: https://www.sussex.ac.uk/webteam/gateway/file. php?name=2014-21-swps-mazzucato-and-penna.pdf&site=25.

McFadden, P., and Tarrant, A. (2015). *What would 'Out' look like? Testing eurosceptic alternatives to EU membership.* London: Policy Network. Available via: http://www.policy-network.net/publications/4995/What-would-out-look-like.

OECD. (2014). *Focus on inequality and growth.* Paris: OECD. Available via: https://www.oecd.org/social/Focus-Inequality-and-Growth-2014.pdf.

OECD. (2016). *The economic consequences of Brexit: A taxing decision* (OECD Economic Policy Paper, No. 16). Available via: http://www.oecd.org/eco/The-Economic-consequences-of-Brexit-27-april-2016.pdf.

Pain, N., & Young, G. (2004). The macroeconomic impact of UK withdrawal from the EU. *Economic Modelling, 21:* 387–408. Available via: http://www.niesr.ac.uk/sites/default/files/publications/1-s2.0-S0264999302000688-main.pdf.

Pellegrin, J., Giorgetti, M. L., Jensen, C., & Bolognini, A. (2015). *EU industrial policy: Assessment of recent developments and recommendations for future policies.* Director General for Internal Policies—European Parliament, Brussels, PE 536.320. Available via: http://www.europarl.europa.eu/RegData/etudes/STUD/2015/536320/IPOL_STU%282015%29536320_EN.pdf.

Perraton, J. (2014). Economic growth in open economies: Balance of payments constrained growth—and beyond? *University of Sheffield Department of Economics* (Working Paper, No. JP300514). Available via: https://www.postkeynesian.net/downloads/soas14/JP300514.pdf.

Pilbeam, K. (2016). *How Brexit fears are shaking the currency markets.* The Conversation, London. Available via: http://theconversation.com/how-brexit-fears-are-shaking-the-currency-markets-61057.

Pindyck, R. S. (1988). Irreversible investment, capacity choice, and the value of the firm. *The American Economic Review, 78*(5), 969–985.

Piore, M., & Sabel, C. (1984). *The second industrial divide.* New York: Basic Books.

Porter, M. (1998). Clusters and the new economics of competition. *Harvard Business Review*, November–December, *76*(6), 77–90.

Portes, J. (2013). Commentary: The economic implications for the UK of leaving the European Union. *National Institute Economic Review*, No. 266, F4-9. Available via: http://www.niesr.ac.uk/sites/default/files/commentary.pdf.

Punhani, S., & Hill, N. [Credit Suisse Report]. (2016). *Brexit: Breaking up is never easy, or cheap.* Zurich: Credit Suisse. Available via: https://doc. research-and-analytics.csfb.com/docView?language=ENG&format=PDF& document_id=806936650&source_id=emrna&serialid=lPu6YfMSDd9to XKa9EPxf5HiNBEoWX2fYou5bZ6jJhA%3D.

PricewaterhouseCoopers LLP (PwC). (2016). *Leaving the EU: Implications for the UK economy.* London: PricewaterhouseCoopers LLP. Available via: http://news.cbi.org.uk/news/leaving-eu-would-cause-a-serious-shock-to-uk-economy-new-pwc-analysis/leaving-the-eu-implications-for-the-uk-economy/.

Rodrik, D. (2004). *Industrial policy for the twenty-first century.* Available via: https://myweb.rollins.edu/tlairson/pek/rodrikindpolicy.pdf.

Rodrik, D. (2006). Goodbye Washington consensus, hello Washington confusion? *Journal of Economic Literature, 44*(4), 973–987.

Rodrik, D. (2008). Industrial policy: Don't ask why, ask how. *Middle East Development Journal,* (Demo Issue), 1–29. Available via: https://www.sss.ias. edu/files/pdfs/Rodrik/Research/Industrial-Policy-Dont-Ask-Why-Ask-How. pdf.

Rowthorn, R. E. (1995). Capital formation and unemployment. *Oxford Review of Economic Policy, 11*(1), 26–39.

Rowthorn, R. E. (1999). Unemployment, wage bargaining and capital-labour substitution. *Cambridge Journal of Economics, 23*(3), 413–425.

Rubini, L. (2004). The international context of EC state aid law and policy: The regulation of subsidies in the WTO. In A. Biondi, P. Eeckhout, & J. Flynn (Eds.), *The law of state aid in the European Union* (pp. 149–188). Oxford: Oxford University Press.

Uvalik, M. (2014). *The role of the state in economic growth: Industrial policy in Europe.* Columbia: Centre on Global Economic Governance. Available via: http://cgeg.sipa.columbia.edu/sites/default/files/cgeg/Paris%20 Brief%20-%20Milica%20Uvalic%20-%20Industrial%20Policy%20in%20 Europe_1.pdf.

Webb, D., Keep, M., & Wilton, M. (2015). *In brief: UK-EU economic relations* (House of Commons Library Briefing Paper (HC 06091)). London: The Stationary Office. Available via: http://researchbriefings.parliament.uk/ ResearchBriefing/Summary/SN06091.

Whyman, P. B. (2006). *'Third Way' Economics.* London: Palgrave.

World Bank. (2016). *Gross capital formation report.* Available via: http://data-bank.worldbank.org/data/reports.aspx?source=2&series=NE.GDI.TOTL. ZS&country.

9

Alternative Trading Models After Brexit

The analysis contained in the rest of the book is, in part, predicated upon the successful outcome of withdrawal negotiations with the EU, and the formation of new trading relationships both with the EU but just as importantly with the rest of the world. There are a range of options the UK negotiators could seek to pursue, in this regard, and this chapter seeks to outline their relative merits and drawbacks. Before turning to the examination of these various options, however, it is important to set this within the context of the process of withdrawal.

The Process of Withdrawal

Unilateral Withdrawal

It has been suggested that the UK could avoid the Article 50 process and unilaterally withdraw from the EU by simply repealing the 1972 European Communities Act and relying on the Vienna Convention on the Law of Treaties (Batten 2013). This states that no provision of an international treaty can override a fundamental aspect of national

© The Author(s) 2017
P.B. Whyman and A.I. Petrescu, *The Economics of Brexit*,
DOI 10.1007/978-3-319-58283-2_9

constitutional law Parliamentary sovereignty, and hence the right to self-determination are fundamental principles of international law. Thus, the argument goes, since Parliament limited its sovereign rights through passing the 1972 EEC Act, it retains the ability to take back these rights at any time through repealing this legislation.[1]

This position is challenged by a House of Lords report, which suggests that the introduction of Article 50 of the Treaty on European Union has taken preference over the Vienna Convention general provisions, and hence simply repealing the 1972 EEC Act no longer applied (HoL 2016: 4;Miller and Lang 2016: 7–8). Hence, according to this legal advice, Article 50 of the Treaty on European Union is 'the only lawful route available to withdraw from the EU' (HMG 2016: 7). Repealing the 1972 EEC Act, without first going through the Article 50 process would, according to this perspective, not remove all obligations under international law and would be likely to create a hostile environment in which the UK would undoubtedly find it difficult to negotiate new trading relationships (HMG 2016: 13). Thus, it would appear to be the rational approach to utilise the Article 50 procedure to secure a favourable path to withdrawal. Yet, even this conclusion is subject to a certain lack of clarity, as other legal opinion makes the case that the UK would have to repeal the 1972 EEC Act *before* it could trigger Article 50 (Miller and Lang 2016:13).

Article 50

The Treaty on European Union (TEU), as amended by the Lisbon Treaty, came into force on 1st December 2009, and it established for the first time the right to unilaterally withdraw from the EU according to its own constitutional arrangements (HoL 2016: 3). It is this procedure that the Prime Minister, Theresa May, has pledged to trigger by the end of March 2017, which infers that the UK will have withdrawn from the EU by late Spring 2019, unless additional time for negotiations is unanimously agreed between all member states.[2] The parliamentary process enabling this process is in the process of being ratified as this book goes to print.

The process is relatively straightforward. A member state wishing to withdraw notifies the European Council (in writing) of its intention and this triggers the Article 50 process, and at this point the EU Commission will engage in negotiating a withdrawal agreement (Booth et al. 2015: 14-15). This will determine the framework of its future relationship with the European Union and, once an agreement is reached, will require an enhanced majority vote (20 out of 27) in the Council of Ministers and a simple majority of the European Parliament before it can come into force (Baker et al. 2016: 108; HMG 2016: 9). The final withdrawal agreement would have to be ratified by an Act of Parliament, alongside the repeal of the European Communities Act 1972 which took the UK into the EU (Miller et al. 2016: 29).

The negotiation period must take a minimum of two years, although this time limit can be extended by the unanimous agreement of remaining member states. If this consensus was not forthcoming, the EU Treaty's would cease to apply to the withdrawing member state after this two year time period (Booth et al. 2015: 14). Many commentators have suggested that this two year timetable is optimistic, given previous experience of negotiating free trade agreements. Indeed, the OECD (2016: 17) notes that FTAs negotiated between the EU and Australia took 3 years to complete, whereas agreements with South Korea and Mexico took 4 and Canada a total of 5 years before final ratification. However, it is perhaps instructive to note that, the only country to withdraw from the EU thus far, Greenland,[3] negotiated its withdrawal (with Danish assistance) within two years (Miller and Lang 2016: 20, 26–27). Thus, the timetable is not wholly unrealistic, although the number of EU directives and regulations introduced over the thirty years since Greenland's withdrawal from the EU might suggest a more protracted process (Miller and Lang 2016: 20, 26–27).

The twin-track approach of seeking to negotiate withdrawal from the influence that EU legislation and rules have upon the UK economy, whilst simultaneously seeking to agree a future trade relationship with the EU, is potentially complex. However, one simplifying procedure, which would reduce the complexity of withdrawal negotiations, would be for the UK to begin by transposing EU regulations *en masse* to British law. Each of these measures could be subsequently reconsidered, over a longer time period, following the formal act of withdrawal, and individual regulations could be modified, repealed or retained as befits the national interest. It would appear, from comments made by the new UK administration, that this approach is being seriously considered.[4]

The issue of negotiating trade agreements between the UK and the EU might also be less onerous than deals made with third party countries, since the UK starts off from the position of having identical standards and regulations as all of the other EU member states. Agreement on the compatibility of standards, and maintenance of common regulations in specific areas, might, therefore, be more easily achieved between the UK and the EU than would be the case with nations starting from a less harmonised position.

Perhaps unsurprisingly, the Article 50 process is biased against the member state wishing to withdraw from the organisation, in that, despite remaining a full member of the EU until its formal withdrawal is complete, Article 50(4) prevents it from participating in discussions about the formulation of the withdrawal agreement in either the European Council or Council of Ministers (Miller et al. 2016: 24–25). It is presumed that it can do so on the other side of the negotiating table, but even this is not clear in the stated protocol. Moreover, once Article 50 is triggered, the EU can set the negotiating timetable, and can accelerate or delay the process within this two year time slot. Nevertheless, one factor which may help to reduce this power differential, and provide the UK with an additional bargaining card during the withdrawal negotiations, concerns suggestions that, unless the UK agreed to allow continued access to its market as under the current arrangements, the EU may have to compensate affected countries with which it has a trade agreement, as a result of the 'shrinking' of the market from what was originally agreed (Miller 2016: 24).

One positive decision has been that negotiations on future trade agreements can take place concurrently with withdrawal negotiations, rather than consecutively. This adds a further complication because, if the final agreement impacts upon policy areas reserved to individual member states, such as preferential access to the SIM or including foreign policy aspects, as recent FTAs negotiated by the EU have done, the process will be classified as a 'mixed agreement' and require additional ratification by every national parliament in the EU.[5]

It is probable that the withdrawal agreement will propose certain transitional arrangements to ensure that vested rights would continue for a time following the formal withdrawal from the EU, in order to prevent citizens of one nation from suddenly becoming illegal immigrants in another, or those arrested under the European Arrest Warrant demanding to be released (Miller et al. 2016: 49–52). The status of EU nationals living and working in the UK, and UK nationals living and working in the EU, will be a key aspect of the negotiation process. Similar issues may include reciprocal arrangements relating to EU nationals using the NHS, UK pensioners drawing UK pensions in EU member states alongside their access to health and social care in these countries (Booth et al. 2015: 16–17). In addition, it is probable that there will need to be transitory arrangements which phase in shifts from the CAP and CFP in order to prevent causing substantial disruption to industries which need longer time periods to re-orientate their activities. Whilst a machine plant may be able to retool their machinery in a day or two, agriculture has a longer time lag, since once a crop is planted, farmers are committed until harvest. Finally, the withdrawal agreement may consider whether the UK wishes to continue participation in certain EU schemes, for example, including student mobility (Erasmus) and research programmes (Horizon). In both cases, non-EU countries are currently participants in these programmes, via 'Associated' status.[6]

It is perhaps not surprising, since the Article 50 process has not yet been tested[7], that the withdrawal process has raised a number of difficult legal questions (HMG 2016:7). The first of these is whether the Sewel Convention would apply to legislation intended to facilitate the UK withdrawing from the EU, since this would arguably impact upon devolved powers, or whether this would fall into the category of matters reserved for the determination of the national UK government (Miller et al. 2016: 30–32). The recent Supreme Court ruling would suggest that this is not the case.[8] Another point of confusion is over whether an Article 50 notification, once given, can be withdrawn—in other words, if, before formal withdrawal from the EU has taken place, whether the UK could theoretically change its mind and remain a member (HoL

2016: 5; Miller and Lang 2016:15–16). It is clear, however, that once a member state has withdrawn, should it wish to re-join the EU, Article 50(5) states that it would have to re-apply as if it were a new applicant, with no concessions made due to its former membership (Miller et al. 2016: 26). This would seem to sound a cautionary note for those political parties, primarily the Liberal Democrats and the SNP, who have advocated campaigning for either the UK to seek future membership of the EU or, in the case of the SNP, to seek to retain EU membership for Scotland should it gain independence from the rest of the UK.

The only thing that seems certain from all of this is that, given the multiplicity of interpretations of the legal treaties, the process of withdrawal from the EU is likely to be a bonanza for specialists in international law.

Alternative Trade Arrangements

Participants in the referendum campaign, from both sides, stated their confidence that the UK could certainly survive and prosper outside of the EU.[9] However, the choices that the UK government make, in relation to their preferred model and the trade-offs they are willing to accept in withdrawal negotiations with the EU, will go some way to determine the degree to which Brexit will deliver modest or substantial future economic development opportunities.

One area where an independent UK may gain from withdrawal from the EU concerns its ability to negotiate future trade relationships with third parties. For EU member states, external trade agreements are co-ordinated at EU level through the Common Commercial Policy (CCP) (CEPR 2013: 11). Moreover, the EU represents all member states at the World Trade Organisation (WTO) and therefore, upon withdrawal, the UK would regain its seat, and therefore influence, within such international trade bodies (Milne 2004: 42–24; Miller 2016: 13). Indeed, the Change Britain organisation has reported that fourteen nations, including China, Brazil, India, Argentina and Australia, have publically stated their interest in negotiating a FTA with the UK once the Brexit process has been completed. Were these agreements successfully completed, this would represent a potential marketplace for UK exports of around £16.8 trillion[10], which is considerably larger than the GDP of the EU once the UK has withdrawn.

In contrast, it has been suggested that pooling technical expertise within the exclusive negotiating stance of the EU enhances the bargaining power of the combined negotiating unit, with the inference that the UK might find it more difficult to achieve as favourable deals if negotiating separately (Meunier 2005: 40; CEPR 2013: 21–23). Moreover, it has been suggested that the UK may have difficulty negotiating trade deals without the expertise developed by the EU. However, it has been noted that the UK has 1720 civil servants working on various elements of trade policy, and, moreover, there is an expectation that at least some of the experienced staff working for the EU on trade agreements were drawn from the UK and might therefore revert for conducting these tasks for the national government (Business for Britain 2015: 33).

Given the conflicting predictions, it is difficult to estimate the likely impact of the UK gaining more freedom in its ability to negotiate future trade agreements. The net effect would appear to depend upon whether flexibility of movement proves to be more decisive than any reduction in the bargaining power accruing to a larger economic grouping.

Potential Options for Managing Trade After Brexit

There have been various alternative trading models, advanced in the literature, which the UK may pursue as part of the withdrawal agreement with the EU and to forge new trade relationships with third parties. This chapter will briefly examine the main variants, which include:

1. Membership of the European Economic Area (the Norway model) or, alternatively, a variant of the EEA designated by advocates as 'SIM-lite'.
2. Negotiating a customs union with the EU (the Turkey model).
3. Bilateral agreements with the EU (the Swiss model).

Table 9.1 A Comparison between Full EU Membership and Five Potential Alternative Options for the UK

	EU membership	MODEL 1: EEA agreement (Norwegian option)	MODEL 2: Customs union (Turkish option)	MODEL 3: FTA-based approach (e.g. Canada, South Korea)	MODEL 4: Bilateral accords (Swiss option)	MODEL 5: WTO/MFN-based approach
Part 1						
Features	No customs costs 35 FTAs and more planned	Has to agree trade deals as part of EFTA 26 EFTA FTAs and more planned	No customs costs	Potential to agree sector-by-sector access to EU single market; Can agree other trade deals and set own import tariffs	Has to agree trade deals as part of EFTA 26 EFTA FTAs and more planned	Free from rules, can agree other trade deals, can set import tariffs, could cut import tariffs and customs checks
Obligations and issues	Common tariff on imports, free movement of people	Agriculture and fisheries face tariffs, customs costs, EU rules with no UK influence	Cannot make trade agreements, EU common tariff on imports; Adopt many EU rules	Customs costs on EU trade	Agriculture and fisheries face tariffs, customs costs, EU rules in sectors with access	Face EU external tariff as well as non-EU external tariffs
Tariffs	No	No or limited tariffs on goods; No access to 35 EU FTAs	No or limited tariffs on goods; No access to 35 EU/EFTA FTAs	No or limited tariffs on goods; No access to 35 EU/EFTA FTAs	No or limited tariffs on goods; No access to 35 EU FTAs	EU common external tariff and substantial non-tariff barriers

(continued)

Table 9.1 (continued)

	EU membership	MODEL 1: EEA agreement (Norwegian option)	MODEL 2: Customs union (Turkish option)	MODEL 3: FTA-based approach (e.g. Canada, South Korea)	MODEL 4: Bilateral accords (Swiss option)	MODEL 5: WTO/MFN-based approach
Full SIM access	Yes	Yes, near full access including financial services	No	No- FTA on goods but not on services	No- FTA on goods but not on services	No
Independent external trade policy	No and being part of Cap and Fisheries policy	No (but not part of CAP or Fisheries policy)	No	Yes	Yes	Yes
Charge tariff rate paid by EU suppliers on non-agricultural trade	Status quo (current situation as EU member)	No change from current situation	No change from current situation	Only if 'snapback' provision negotiated	No change from current situation	Yes, only up to binding levels specified in WTO accords
Free trade in on-agricultural goods	Status quo	No change from current situation	No change from current situation	No change from current situation	No change from current situation	No, tariffs allowed per WTO obligations
Exercise own agricultural trade policy and subsidies	Status quo	Depends on terms negotiated	Depends on terms negotiated	Depends on terms of FTA	Depends on terms negotiated	Yes, only up to binding levels specified in WTO accords
Rules of origin	Status quo	Would be introduced	No change from current situation	Would be introduced	No change from current situation	No change from current situation

(continued)

Table 9.1 (continued)

Part Two						
Freedom of movement of capital	Status quo	No change from current situation	Could be negotiated	Could be negotiated	No change from current situation	As per EU WTO obligations only
Freedom of movement of services	Status quo	No or little change from current situation	Would have to be negotiated	Would have to be negotiated	No or little change from current situation	As per EU WTO obligations only
Freedom of movement of people	Status quo	No or little change from current situation	Would have to be negotiated	Would have to be negotiated	No or little change from current situation	Only as prescribed in EU's WTO obligations
Independent immigration policy	No	No, due to movement of labour	Yes	Yes	Uncertain (Switzerland doesn't have freedom to restrict migration)	Yes
Influence over EU regulation	Yes, via voting	Engagement in construction of regulation but no voting rights	No	No	No	No
Regulatory sovereignty	No	No, regulation bust be consistent with EU norms or membership suspended	No, regulations must be consistent with EU norms or membership suspended	Yes, theoretically but regulations must be consistent with EU norms to access the SIM	Yes, theoretically but regulations must be consistent with EU norms to access the SIM	Yes

(continued)

Table 9.1 (continued)

Mutual recognition of regulations	Status quo	No or little change from current situation	Would have to be negotiated	Would have to be negotiated	No or little change from current situation	No
Must implement EU regulations	Status quo	No change from current situation	Not unless negotiated in CU	Not unless negotiated in FTA	No	No
Any financial contribution to the EU	Yes, full	Yes, but may be smaller	Not unless negotiated in CU	Not unless negotiated in FTA	Yes, but smaller	Yes, but may be smaller
Possible target of EU trade defence measures	Status quo	Yes	Yes, but could be negotiated	Yes, but could be negotiated	Yes	Yes
Benefit from any unilateral reforms	Status quo	Yes	Yes	Yes	Yes	Yes
Possible joint action with EU on third party protectionism	Status quo	Yes	Yes	Yes	Yes	Yes

(continued)

Table 9.1 (continued)

Part Three

Potential to negotiate further agreements with the EU	Status quo	Yes	Yes	Yes	Yes
Initiate own trade investigation against third party	Status quo	Yes	Yes	Yes	Yes
Initiate own FTA/CU negotiation with third party	Status quo	Yes	Yes	Yes	Yes
Change MFN applied tariff rates	Status quo	Yes, up to limits set down in WTO obligations	No	Yes, up to limits set down in WTO obligations	Yes, up to limits set down in WTO obligations
Define own, unimpeded negotiating mandate for FTA/CU	Status quo	Yes	No (common external tariff agreed with EU)	Yes	Yes
Conduct own negotiations for FTA/CU	Status quo	Yes	No	Yes	Yes

(continued)

Table 9.1 (continued)

Conclude negotiations of a FTA/CU	Status quo	No	Yes	Yes	Yes
Share with EU certain benefits of FTA/CU with third parties	Status quo	Yes if Third Party MFN clause in accords negotiated with the EU	Yes if Third Party MFN clause in accords negotiated with the EU	No	No

Notes EEA—European Economic Area; CU—Customs Union; SIM—Single Internal Market; CAP—Common Agricultural Policy; FTA—Free Trade Agreement; WTO—World Trade Organisation; MFN—Most Favourite Nation clause/agreement. Implications are commented (via check marks, question marks or crosses) from the perspective of attractiveness to UK policy

4. Concluding a FTA with the EU (the South Korean or South African model).
5. Reliance upon WTO rules for trade with the EU (the WTO or Greenland model).
6. Unilateral free trade (the Hong Kong model).

In addition, a number of alternative trade arrangements have been suggested, that an independent UK might wish to pursue, including forming closer ties with:

7. European Free Trade Association (EFTA).
8. The Commonwealth.
9. The Anglosphere or, as a variant, joining NAFTA.

When examining the various options for the UK's future trade relationships, it is important to be clear about the terminology. The 'single market', or more accurately the Single Internal Market (SIM), is more than an internal free trade area, where tariff free trade has been agreed for goods but not services. It is also more than a customs union, which is what the UK joined in 1973 and involves a FTA being extended by the imposition of a common external tariff, levied on non-members; it may, as in the case of the EU, additionally involve a common external trade policy. Instead, the EU SIM extends trade integration further, by adopting harmonisation of trade regulations and guaranteeing the freedom of movement of goods, services, capital and people. These 'four freedoms' form an integral part of the SIM and it would be difficult to negotiate a withdrawal agreement which sought to retain full access to the SIM without acceptance of this core element of the arrangement. Thus, when commentators discuss the option of the UK remaining within the SIM without the need for free movement of labour and possibly also free of EU trade regulation, it is difficult to reconcile how this would work. It is certainly possible to negotiate a new trade arrangement with the EU which delivers various degrees of free trade in some if not all sectors, and which does not involve the free movement of labour and/or capital, but this does not constitute full access to the SIM. This distinction can, perhaps, be better illustrated by examining each of the trading options available to the UK (see Table 9.1).

Option One: European Economic Area (EEA)— The Norwegian Model

The first option, for the UK to consider upon withdrawing from the EU, is to re-apply for membership of the European Free Trade Association (EFTA), where the UK was a founding member, and subsequently to use this conduit to apply for membership of the EEA. Established in 1992 and operational from 1994, the EEA extends the SIM. This includes acceptance of the free movement of trade, capital and people to EEA members, together with competition regulation, research and educational cooperation, consumer and environmental protection. EEA members are automatically part of the Schengen border-free travel area, which the UK, as full EU member, has refrained from joining, but as a non-member, acceding to the established EEA, there would be the expectation that it would do so unless an opt-out could be negotiated. The EEA does not, however, include participation in the CAP/CFP[11], or common foreign and security policy. Moreover, EFTA members of the EEA are not part of the EU customs union and are therefore free to operate their own external trade policy, subject to rules of origin regulations for exports into the EU (HoC 2013: 74).

This is the closest economic relationship that currently exists for countries outside of full EU membership, and comprises, alongside EU countries, Iceland, Liechtenstein and Norway. EFTA membership is a prerequisite for EEA participation and, as such, has to be ratified by all EU member states in addition to these three EFTA members (Miller et al. 2016: 39–40; Piris 2016: 7). Consequently, it is entirely plausible that any attempt made by the UK to join the EEA may be frustrated by a veto, either from an EU member state or, indeed, from an EFTA nation who prefers to preserve the current composition of the organisation and does not want the UK to re-join EFTA.

Securing full access to the SIM would minimise whatever loss of trade opportunities might arise with EU member states due to the UK's withdrawal. The CEPR (2013: 43), for example, argues that the economic benefits deriving from predictable access to the SIM may be an acceptable trade-off for the UK relinquishing policy independence across a

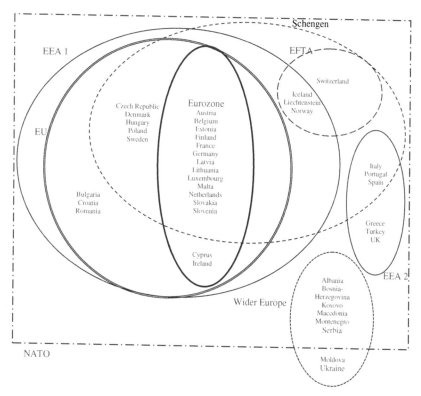

Fig. 9.1 An illustration of the highly complex variable geometry Europe and the potential for a new realignment between Eurozone-Core and SIM-lite-Periphery groupings. *Source* Authors drawing, based on Owen (2016: 2–3)

broad sphere. For the financial sector, it would be attractive since it would secure full 'passport' rights for UK financial firms to continue to operate within the EU and would arguably cause less economic disruption. Moreover, the EEA has been advanced as a potential interim step to eventual full withdrawal, thereby lessening the significant diplomatic burden that Brexit implies and the economic uncertainty created by the process of negotiation over post-membership relations with the EU.[12] Given that a majority of Members of Parliament supported the 'Remain' side in the UK European referendum campaign, and elements within both the Liberal Democrat and Labour parties have expressed their desire to retain as much access to EU markets as possible during the Brexit process, the EEA might prove to be a means of demonstrating acceptance of the referendum result whilst delivering the closest alternative to full EU membership.[13]

There are, however, three elements of the EEA package that would not be so welcome. The first is that, as already noted, the EEA presumes continued free movement of people across the EEA. Whilst there are undoubtedly many positive affects arising from this policy (see Chap. 6), the result of the UK referendum would seem to suggest that this would be contrary to the majority opinion of the UK population, who expressed a preference for more controlled immigration. Indeed, since participation in the Schengen area is currently part of its framework, acceptance of the EEA would represent an *extension* to the free movement of people that the UK has to date accepted.

A second issue concerns the inability of EEA nations to participate in all but the committee and other preparatory work underpinning the formation of those laws and regulations pertaining to the SIM and which impact directly upon their ability to trade. An EFTA Surveillance Authority[14] was established to monitor and enforce compliance with rules relevant to the EEA. As a result, public procurement has to be open to companies from all EEA signatories, telecommunications and transportation have to be liberalised, whilst all mergers in EEA nations are subject to the EU Commission. Since EFTA members often have higher safety standards than the EU norm, this requires them to be simplified, or accept lower technical standards, to ensure common rules apply throughout the SIM (USITC 2000: 2–17). Each EFTA state has a theoretical right of veto, in that they can refuse to accept new rules designed by the EU from coming into force in their territory. However this has never been exercised because it would prevent all EFTA nations from continuing to trade freely in the SIM.

This loss of influence in the setting of regulations would be problematic for the UK (McFadden and Tarrant 2015: 4, 65; Miller 2016: 22). To use the terminology of the CBI (2013: 16), the UK would move from being part of the process that determined standards for SIM trade to being a 'standards taker'. It would require the adoption of around two thirds of the EU's *acquis communautaire*, thus narrowing the freedom of movement that the UK would gain from withdrawal from the

EU (Miller et al. 2016: 40). It would leave in place 93 out of the 100 EU regulations identified by Open Europe to impose the greatest regulatory cost upon the UK.[15] Hence, the EEA option has been criticised as offering 'integration without representation' (Sejersted and Sverdrup 2012). The significance of this point is rejected by those who point to that fact that nations typically have little influence over an export market's regulations for most international trade (Minford, cited in HoC 2013: 76). Thus, the UK could be perceived as simply returning to a more 'normal' trading position. Nevertheless, it does imply a reduction in UK influence over regulations and technical specifications pertaining to the EU SIM. Whilst the EEA agreement, as currently constituted, might prove acceptable to small nations with limited opportunities to shape their economic environment, it would be unlikely to prove similarly attractive for a medium sized economy such as the UK (NOU 2012b).

The third drawback for choosing the EEA option concerns the financial contributions that EEA participants have to make to the EU for access to the SIM and/or in contribution towards the less developed EU member states. There are vastly different interpretations of this budgetary cost to Norway[16], and it is difficult to compare EU member states with EFTA countries participating in certain aspects of the EU through the EEA. Nevertheless, for the current budgetary period, 2014–2021, Norway is scheduled to contribute around €391 m directly for access to the SIM, €25 m to fund EU regional development, €447 m to facilitate participation in various EU programmes (including Erasmus and Horizon 2020) along with a further €6 m for participation in the Schengen scheme and other initiatives relating to justice and home affairs.[17] Norway's contribution to the EU therefore totals €869 m (£620 m) per annum, or around 0.76% of Norwegian GDP.[18] This makes Norway the tenth largest contributor to the EU despite it not being a member (NOU 2012a: 784; CBI 2013: 142).

This is a *gross* payment and, like the UK, Norway receives part of this money back again through payments from the various programmes in which it participates. This is very difficult to estimate for non-EU member states, and particularly so given that Norway participates in a number of programmes outside the framework of the EEA (Business for Britain 2015: 817). However, an estimate of net contributions being around half the gross figure might be reasonable[19], which would bring the plausible net contribution down to around 0.38% of Norwegian GDP. In addition, since EEA contributions are calculated according to GDP per capita, and Norway has a value more than twice that of the UK.[20] Hence, were the UK to participate in the EEA on similar conditions to Norway, the likely financial contribution that it might be expected to make to facilitate access to the SIM and participate in a wide range of EU programmes, would be in the region of 0.22% or £4.4bn per year. The estimate made by Business for Britain (2015: 817) is calculated slightly differently, and suggests that the UK might have a significantly smaller financial contribution to the EEA, or only around £850 m per annum. Whichever estimate proves to be the more accurate, the fact remains that the EEA would represent a considerable reduction relative to the current net UK contribution to the EU, even when taking into account the current rebate.

Advocates of the EEA might additionally wish to take account of the Norwegian government commissioned report examining their experience with the EEA agreement. This concluded that the freedom of movement of labour had reduced skill shortages whilst access to the EU SIM had provided a substantial benefit to Norwegian exporters (NOU 2012a, c). Free movement of labour is welcomed due to its contribution to facilitating growth in production and for those working in welfare services. However, there is concern over what the report terms 'social dumping'—i.e. where the influx of migrant labour undermines existing high quality working conditions, agreed at tripartite level between government, employers and the unions (NOU 2012a: Chap. 16; Norwegian Ministry of Foreign Affairs 2013: 37–39). Moreover, in terms of budgetary contributions, the report acknowledges that there has been reluctance to accept the large increases demanded of Norway, as part of the EEA agreement—i.e. rising from NOR125 m in 1992 to NOR2.8bn in 2010, representing a 2,240% increase (NOU 2012c: 17). Thus, for Norway, the EEA represents a political compromise and is, as such, a second best solution, given that it limits the policy independence of the state (NOU 2012c).

Given Norway's experience with the EEA, it would seem difficult for this option to reconcile the expressed opinion of the UK electorate, given during the recent referendum, in two vital respects. Firstly, the EEA agreement requires acceptance of rules and regulations determined by the EU, with only minor input from external EEA participants. This applies not only to those companies wishing to export into the EU SIM, where acceptance of other nations' standards is the norm, as long as these are not expressly developed as a means of trade protection (which would be against WTO rules), but would also include acceptance of EU decisions relating to social and employment regulations, environmental protection, competition policy and so forth. This would be difficult to reconcile with the referendum result indicating a preference for the UK to take back more control over its policy making. Secondly, the requirement to accept the 'four freedoms', as a prerequisite for full access to the SIM through the EEA, would appear to contradict the electoral opinion expressed during the UK referendum result. Indeed, it is worth noting that, as an EEA member, Norway has actually accepted more than twice the number of EU migrants per head of population than the UK (Booth et al. 2015: 53–54). Consequently, it would appear difficult for the UK to choose the 'Norway model' unless it were substantially revised.

Variable Geometry Europe

One variant of the EEA approach could be to create a new two-tiered option, sometimes described as 'SIM Lite', combining those EU member states and EFTA nations who would prefer to maintain membership of the SIM but with only a necessary level of minimal political integration (HoC 2013: 78–79; Booth et al. 2015: 64). This option might allow a new settlement, both for the UK but also establish a new form of looser membership for those nations wishing to restrict engagement with the EU to the economic sphere (see Fig. 9.1). This would, to a certain extent, simply recognise the emergence of a core Eurozone group, emerging within the EU, where participants had separate interests and were already holding separate meetings without the involvement of all EU member states. Nevertheless, previous suggestions to introduce a two-speed EU, including those made by former UK Prime Minister Major, have not proven to attract sufficient support across other EU member states.

It has been suggested that the closer integration, necessitated by the need to sustain the Eurozone, will inevitably transform the EU towards a 'variable geometry Europe' (Chopin 2013: 9). Indeed, whilst the EEA might not provide a solution for the UK as it currently stands, it would be possible to use this as the basis for a new realignment of the EU and EFTA members, with a core Eurozone intensifying economic and political integration, alongside an outer sphere of the EU more narrowly focused upon participation in the SIM (van Hulten 2011; Chopin 2016). However, despite previously favouring a solution of this type, Owen (2016: 2) now considers that the opportunity for such realignment has passed and may only return to the EU's agenda if the UK makes a success of its new independence from the EU.

Option Two: Customs Union—The Turkey Model

A second option, for the UK to consider, would be the formation of a customs union with the EU. This is the model that was adopted in 1996 between the EU and Turkey. In effect, this proposal would revert the trade relationship between the UK and the EU back to what existed when the UK joined the EU in 1973, until the advent of the SIM in 1992. It involves the combination of a free trade agreement (FTA), which enables tariff-free trade in goods between participants, supplemented by the adoption of the EU's common external tariff and trade policy (HoC 2013: 74; Miller et al. 2016: 37). It is the adoption of the common external tariff being imposed on all imports from countries not party to the customs union, and the adoption of a common trade policy whereby the EU continues to have sole control over the negotiation of trade agreements with third parties, which distinguishes a customs union from a FTA.

The reason for adopting a common external tariff is intended to solve a problem, encountered by FTAs, of tariff jumping. This occurs where signatories of a FTA levy different tariff rates, and therefore exporters in a country not party to the FTA agreement may seek to evade higher tariffs by exporting first to whichever member of the FTA has the lowest tariffs and, once their products are circulating within that country, re-exporting them (tariff free) to other parties to the agreement, thereby evading the higher part of prevailing national tariffs. FTAs seek to overcome this problem by imposing a 'rule of origin' regulation, whereby each exporter has to detail the proportion of the value of the product originating in the exporting nation, and levying full tariffs upon any good which does not exceed a stated minimum level. This solves the problem, but does so at an additional regulatory (administrative) cost for the exporting firms (Dinnie 2004; Fawcett 2015). As a result, customs unions are often claimed to be more credible than FTAs (Europe Economics 2013: 11), although it is a fact that there are considerably more FTAs in operation across the globe than customs unions (CEPR 2013: 16). Thus, there must be advantages to FTAs for the nations concerned that are not met by customs unions.

The adoption of a common trade policy is, in part, an extension to this rule, by preventing one of the customs union signatories from signing a separate trade deal with an external country, which allowed free or preferential access into that country and, from there, into the rest of the customs union area (Brenton and Manchin 2003). To prevent this, the customs union would either have to introduce 'rules of origin' regulation or agree a common trade policy, to close this alternative form of tariff jumping (CEPR 2013: 40–41).

The economic theory relating to customs unions typically begins with the work of Viner (1950), whose work demonstrated that, due to the common external tariff, customs unions could result in either trade creation or trade diversion. The former result led to production shifting from former high-cost domestic producers in the home economy to lower-cost external producers in a partner country, whilst trade diversion involves the shift from the lowest-cost producer in a nation not party to the customs union agreement to a higher-cost firm in a country within the union. Given the fact that Viner's work was founded upon the assumptions of neoclassical partial equilibrium theory, he viewed trade creation as an unequivocally positive result and trade diversion as negative. Later authors criticised this position, by demonstrating that, when consumption effects are considered, even trade diversion may increase both national and international welfare (Meade 1955; Lipsey 1957).[21] Similarly, if trade creation creates trade imbalances between nations, this can cause problems for the nation experiencing a persistent trade deficit. However, the standard theory tends to ignore the macroeconomic impact of preferential trade agreements (Mendes 1986). Yet, as discussed in Chap. 7, the net economic impact will depend upon the impact of trade agreements upon the balance of payments, which in turn impact upon economic growth.

The negotiation of a customs union with the EU would evade some of the problems noted with the EEA, in that it would not require the free movement of labour and it would limit the UK's exposure to European integration to the economic sphere, given that social, employment, energy, environmental and political aspects of the SIM would not be included in this package. It would also not require the UK to participate in the CAP, nor the CFP, and it would not include public procurement. Furthermore, Turkey has set a precedent since it participates in EU schemes such as Erasmus and is a net recipient of EU regional and transport funding.[22] Thus, should the UK wish to continue participation in such programmes, there should be no impediment to its so doing.

Nevertheless, there are a number of disadvantages with the 'Turkey model'. The first is that tariff free trade is confined to goods and not services. Given that the UK has a large trade deficit in goods with the EU, but a (smaller) trade surplus in services, this restriction is problematic. This potential weakness is limited at present by the fact that the SIM has never properly operated where services are concerned and, indeed, the inability of the UK to encourage further liberalisation in service provision across the EU may well derive from its competitive advantage in this area (Capital Economics 2016: 14). Hence, the UK will probably not be too badly affected by losing a theoretical advantage which has never been fully realised in any case. Nevertheless, it has been suggested that the SIM might be properly completed in the future (Ottaviano et al. 2014), and indeed potentially extended to encompass other nations through trade deals such as the (now stalled) Trade and

Trans-Atlantic Partnership (TTIP) with the USA. Were this to eventually be realised, the customs union option would indeed be a second best trade solution to full SIM access as guaranteed by the EEA.

A second concern focuses upon the fact that customs unions may reduce tariff barriers for goods, but they might not prevent non-tariff barriers (NTBs) (CBI 2013: 16). These can range from health and technical barriers on the one hand, which impose legal restrictions upon certain characteristics of goods or services, to administrative regulations which impose a delay or other costs upon trade, thereby reducing the volume traded.[23] Whilst the study of NTBs has been constrained by the weakness of data pertaining to non-tariff forms of trade restrictions, it is nevertheless the case that many economists specialising in international trade regard NTBs as imposing a higher cost than formal tariff forms of protectionism, albeit that their significance is being steadily reduced over time (De Sousa et al. 2012; UNCTAD 2013: 1, 14–15).

A third problem concerns the level of the common external tariff. In theory, the UK and EU would be required to reach an agreement over the level of this common tariff barrier, however, if this was not possible, it is most likely that the UK, like Turkey, would simply have to accept EU decisions on tariffs and trade deals in order to maintain free access to the EU market (CEPR 2013: 41). The practical consequence of this situation may not necessarily be significant compared to the status quo position, given that, as one full EU member amongst twenty-eight, the UK currently has little effective influence over the level of the common external tariff. However, this lack of control over factors impacting upon the UK's trade relationships with the rest of the world would be a disadvantage compared to the FTA alternative.

A fourth issue concerns financial contributions to the EU that may arise from participation in the customs union. As a net recipient of EU development support, this has not been an issue for Turkey, yet it is doubtful that the UK could participate in a customs union with the EU without being asked to make a financial contribution towards EU programmes. This would probably involve a sum somewhere between the Norway and Swiss models.

Finally, a customs union would most probably involve the acceptance of EU rules pertaining to competition, company take-over's and preclude certain forms of industrial policy. There is likely to be a divergence of opinions amongst economists on these points, regarding whether the continual imposition of EU rules on these matters represents an economic disadvantage or benefit. Nevertheless, they are included here as a potential problem with the 'Turkey model' because of the discussion, in the previous chapter, about the future potential for industrial policy if the UK chose to operate outside EU competition rules.

Interestingly, the CBI (2013: 12, 148) has expressed its concern that the 'Turkey model' would be 'the worst of the "half-way" alternatives, leaving the UK with very limited EU market access and zero influence over trade deals'. This strong expression of dissatisfaction is a little odd because, when the UK joined the 'Common Market' in 1975, a move strongly supported by the CBI, this was a customs union. Of course, the CBI may wish to argue that full EU membership is preferable to a reversion to a customs union trade agreement with the EU, because it does not embrace all of the elements of the SIM. Nevertheless, it is a little surprising that the organisation now rejects so firmly an approach it previously championed. Yet, it is still instructive that, when considering the best alternative model for the UK to pursue in its future trade relationship with the EU after Brexit, the CBI considers customs unions to be inferior to all other options.

Option Three: Bilateral Trade Agreements—The Swiss Model

The trade relationship agreed between the EU and Switzerland does not depend upon signing of a single, comprehensive FTA or formation of a customs union, but rather is the result of a number of twenty major, and 100 lesser, bilateral agreements. The bilateral approach provides the Swiss with greater flexibility than might be possible under the Norwegian or Turkey models, in that only those areas where mutual agreement can be forged are included in the series of treaty's (CBI 2013: 16). Thus, the Swiss bilateral agreements include public procurement and cooperation in research, but exclude participation in EU agricultural, energy, foreign, social and employment policies (Booth et al. 2015: 57).

The bilateral treaties provide tariff-free trade in goods but are rather more limited in terms of services. Here, the agreements do allow the provision of cross-border services for a period not exceeding a period of 90 days in a calendar year; a provision primarily introduced to allow limited access for employee or self-employed service providers to deliver occasional, short term activities across borders (Booth et al. 2015: 58). The agreements do not cover financial services, with the exception of the insurance industry and thus, without the inclusion of the 'EU passport' allowing financial firms to operate freely within the SIM, many Swiss banks have established subsidiaries within EU member states and must therefore satisfy the EU Commission that Swiss regulation is at least equivalent to that of the EU (Keep 2015: 12; Miller et al. 2016: 40–41). The composition of the bilateral treaties, therefore, have not proved to be sufficiently favourable to the Swiss who, like the UK under current arrangements, run a sizeable trade deficit with the EU. Indeed, they have found it difficult to extend basic trade in goods into areas where it has a comparative advantage (Booth et al. 2015: 46).

Switzerland does not have to accept the importation of legislation and regulations designed in the EU (the *acquis communautaire*), but only has to commit to *equivalent* legislation. Consequently, there is no uniformity in legislation. Given criticisms of the regulatory burden imposed on UK companies who do not trade with the EU, this might be viewed as a distinct advantage. Furthermore, the 'Swiss model' does not involve any transfer of decision-making to a supranational authority set up for the purpose of facilitating the trade agreement(s), and it is entitled to negotiate other trade deals with third parties and does not have to impose the EU's common external tariff (CEPR 2013: 45).

The bilateral agreements, however, do commit Switzerland to make a financial contribution to EU social and regional programmes in addition to those areas in which the bilateral agreements permit Swiss participation(Miller et al. 2016: 43). This includes participation in the research funding programme, Horizon 2020, albeit that this additional contribution is offset almost exactly through the ability of Swiss universities to win a similar level of research grants from the scheme

(Emmerson et al. 2016: 15). In the previous multi-year framework agreement, concluding in 2012, Switzerland contributed the equivalent of around £420 million per annum. If the UK adopted the Swiss model under the same conditions, given the fact that Swiss GDP per capita is approximately 1.5 times the UK rate, then UK contributions to the EU could fall to around £2.1 billion (Thompson and Harari 2013: 26–27).

The 'Swiss model' is also problematic for the UK in one other aspect, namely that the bilateral agreements stipulate that Switzerland accepts the free movement of labour from the EU (CBI 2013: 145). Indeed, partly as a result of its high GDP per capita and its geographical location towards the centre of the EU landmass, Switzerland has accepted a greater proportion of EU migrants per head of population than the UK. Thus, Booth et al. (2015: 59–60) note that, in 2013, fully 15.6% of the Swiss population had been born in an EU country, whereas the equivalent figure for the UK was 4.2%.

Tensions caused by the high level of inward migration contributed directly to a 2014 referendum decision for Switzerland to introduce quotas on EU migrants from 2017 and which, if introduced, would violate the free movement of labour clause in Switzerland's bilateral agreements with the EU. As a result, the EU has threatened to suspend the relevant trade deals if free movement is compromised and, because of a 'guillotine clause', this would cause all bilateral agreements to be suspended (Booth et al., 2015: 59–60). After two years of negotiations, it would appear that Switzerland decided to set aside what is supposed to be a binding referendum decision and impose only minor local job preferences, and thereby maintain its trading relationship with the EU.[24] Yet, this episode does expose the centrality within which the EU views the four freedoms as a core feature of its model of economic integration, which should be salutary for UK negotiators seeking to secure market access without simultaneously accepting the free movement of labour. Secondly, it raises a question as to the long term sustainability of the Swiss model, given the dissatisfaction of the Swiss electorate with the eventual resolution of the disagreement with the EU. Moreover, the EU has expressed its own dissatisfaction about the absence of the Swiss automatically adopting new EU legislation or regulation pertaining to areas covered by the bilateral agreements, claiming that the current approach creates 'legal uncertainty' (HoC 2013: 76–77). Thus, it may be possible that the EU would be very reluctant to concede an approach similar to the Swiss model to the UK (Booth et al. 2015: 73; Miller et al. 2016: 41).

Option Four: Free Trade Agreement (FTA)—The Canadian Model

Perhaps the most straightforward new trade arrangement that the UK may wish to negotiate with the EU concerns a free trade agreement (FTA). This is the most popular form of organised preferential trade agreement across the globe and a number of countries have negotiated a FTA with the EU, including South Africa, Mexico, South Korea and Canada. Given the enthusiasm with which the EU has begun embarking upon negotiating FTAs with individual countries and groups of nations, it would be slightly surprising if the EU were not interested in doing the same with the UK; a former member state and a large market for EU goods and services (Springford and Tilford 2014: 9).

It is not necessarily the ability to negotiate a FTA with the EU that might concern the UK negotiators, however, but rather whether the terms that can be negotiated would prove favourable to the UK economy. As the CBI (2013: 17) notes, the size or, more accurately, the economic weight and wealth of market of the country or trade organisation acting as negotiating partner in any FTA talks at least partially determines its bargaining power. In addition, it is also probable that the EU will not wish to reward Brexit by offering a favourable trade deal, for fear that this may encourage other countries considering their own loosening of ties with the organisation. It is, therefore, probable that the EU will hold, and wish to exercise, a stronger negotiating position than the UK in any such talks.

The fact that the EU has proven willing to negotiate trade agreements with nations such as Canada and South Korea, whose economies are much smaller than the UK's and whose trade with the EU, at 7.6% and 8.8% of total exports of goods and services respectively, are much smaller than current trade links with the UK, can be interpreted in two different ways (Booth et al. 2015: 72).It may indicate that, if the EU chooses to establish FTAs with economies much less significant to the future export success of its own producers, it may be considerably eager to negotiate a similar or better deal with a more substantive trading partner. However, it may equally suggest that the lesser impact of trade with Canada or South Korea, might make it easier for the EU to concede preferential trading conditions (Emmerson et al. 2016: 15–16). In either case, discussions may, involve the type of trade-off outlined by Miller (2016: 21), in order to achieve a mutually satisfactory balance between the degree of access granted to the SIM and UK freedom from budgetary contributions, social and employment regulation and/or product regulation.

The first issue that will determine the sustainability of the FTA relates to the breadth of its coverage. It would most likely secure tariff-free trade in goods but not necessarily services. Given the UK's particular competitive advantage in financial, educational and business services, it would be in the UK's interests to secure the maximum inclusion of services in any FTA, whereas the EU might be content to limit any agreement to goods, since this is where it has a large trade surplus. There should be scope for a mutually beneficial agreement, given the juxtaposition of the relative trade strengths, but it would require UK negotiators to be willing to accept potential trade according to WTO rules, to secure a favourable deal for the UK. It is worth noting, in this regard, that the FTA negotiated with Canada includes some agricultural goods and a significant proportion of services, although financial services are excluded (Emmerson et al. 2016: 15–16). This was achieved without the need for Canada to have to make a contribution to the EU budget, as some more recent commentators have suggested might be required in the case of the UK.[25]

A second negotiating issue would concern the status of those aspects which the EU has developed in support of its SIM, and which it might wish to impose on potential entrants to its markets. This may include competition policy, oversight of mergers and acquisitions, health and safety rules, labour market regulation, product standards and technical specifications for goods and services entering its market. One compromise might be to agree mutual oversight in some or all of these areas, however, even this concession would severely reduce the policy freedom of action arising out of Brexit for an independent UK. It would restrict the range of measures pertaining to employment, company law and could fatally weaken any attempt to rejuvenate UK industrial policy post-withdrawal. Issues pertaining to technical specifications are less problematic because, although sections of UK industry may bemoan the loss of influence upon the development of EU standards, it is nevertheless, the norm for exporters to have to comply with minimum standards set by the countries into which they wish to sell their produce.

Public procurement might form a third area for discussion. This is not necessarily straightforward. One strand of thought would suggest that UK producers may benefit from having the ability to bid for public contracts across the EU and, henceforth, the UK should seek to include public procurement as part of the FTA. However, there is a counter argument whereby the procurement processes of the UK public sector could be utilised, as part of a broader industrial strategy (as discussed in the previous chapter), to provide a demand base to encourage the development of the UK manufacturing sector. Public procurement could, for example, also be used as a means of encouraging small scale farmers to link more directly with sections of the public sector—i.e. schools, hospitals, elderly care facilities and/or prisons—where the sourcing of local foods could enhance the quality of meals but also reduce food miles, thereby providing environmental benefits. Initiatives along these lines have been previously blocked by the EU, not only in the UK but also in Ireland and Sweden, because they breached competition and public procurement rules (Barclay 2012).

If successfully negotiated, a FTA would have a number of advantages over the EEA since it is more narrowly focused upon the facilitation of international trade without having to accept additional elements of political and social integration (Milne 2004: 1). Similarly, a FTA has the advantage over a customs union that the UK would be free to determine the level of any tariffs it decided to levy and negotiate preferential trade agreements with other nations. However, FTAs do necessitate the introduction of 'rules of origin' regulations in order to prevent tariff-jumping, which would impose some additional administrative costs upon exporters alongside verification procedural costs on importers. This might prove particularly disruptive for those exporters who are part of time sensitive supply chains (CEPR 2013: 36; Miller 2016: 21). There have been a number of economic studies examining this issue, and found the costs of introducing this type of regulation to be within a range of 1–8% of the value of the goods, albeit that most results lie within the lower part of this range (Herin 1986; USITC 1996; Cadot et al. 2006; Manchin 2006; Brenton 2010; Abreu 2013: 19). Moreover, there are certain benefits derived from country of origin marking, including consumers using it as a proxy for the quality of goods and services (Hui and Zhou 2002). Country of origin labelling would, in addition, facilitate a 'buy British' campaign, of the type currently forbidden by EU rules but which would be available to policymakers post-Brexit. The evidence is that these campaigns, if designed correctly, can have a positive economic impact, both for UK exporters but also for domestic producers reducing import penetration (Chisik 2003; Dinnie 2008).

The flexibility associated with FTAs is constrained to the extent concerning how one agreement may impact upon another. For example, if 'third party MFN provisions' are to be included in a FTA, then any subsequent preferential trade agreement negotiated with one of the FTA partners would also apply to the other automatically (CEPR 2013: 37). This is a two-edged sword, because it could be used by the UK to ensure that it benefits from any more favourable trade agreements that the EU is able to negotiate with other nations, as a result of its greater bargaining position. Or else it could be used by the EU to ensure that the UK could not secure for itself a more favourable trade deal with a third party without the EU having access to the same favourable trade conditions. It might, therefore, be more difficult for the UK to gain a competitive advantage for its exporters over European rivals through negotiating FTAs with fast growing developing economies, if the EU insisted upon this type of clause in its FTA with the UK (CEPR 2013:47).

A FTA is also unlikely to involve any budgetary contribution to the EU, of the type required from other types of preferential trade

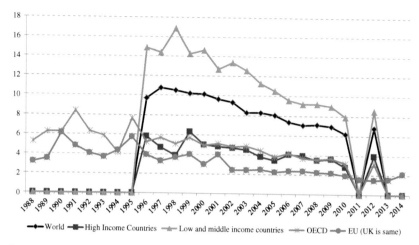

Fig. 9.2 Changing tariff barriers in the world and various regions, 1988–2014. *Source* Author's compilation of data sourced from the World Data Bank (2016)

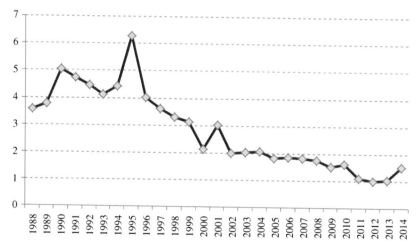

Fig. 9.3 EU average trade-weighted MFN tariff (%), 1988–2014. *Source* World Bank (2015)

deal (Emmerson et al. 2016: 15–16). It is also possible for FTAs to be expanded to include provisions on areas which usually lie outside of a standard trade agreement, such as the mobility of staff, FDI and other capital movements, intellectual property and so forth (CEPR 2013: 36–39). Whether the UK, having just decided to withdraw from a more comprehensive set of arrangements bundled together within EU membership, desires to move beyond a standard FTA is, however, another question.

Option Five: World Trade Organisation (WTO) 'Most Favoured Nation' (MFN)Model

The fifth alternative, available to the UK following withdrawal from the EU, would be to reject any kind of formal preferential trade arrangement with the EU, and instead revert to trading with all nations according to the rules set down by the World Trade Organisation (WTO). This is typically discussed in terms of the 'WTO model', although it was originally entitled the 'Greenland model' in the pioneering work of

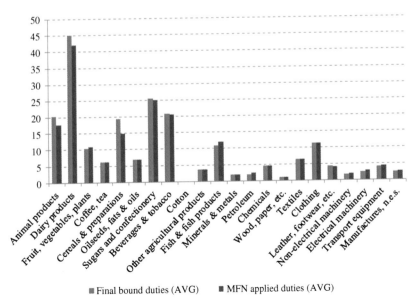

Fig. 9.4 Average EU final bound duties[43] and MFN applied tariffs. *Source* WTO (2016)

Burkitt et al. (1996). The successor of the former General Agreement on Tariffs and Trade (GATT), the WTO promotes the reduction in trade barriers through periodic multilateral trade agreements, which are binding on all nations who accept membership of the organisation. Already by 2005, the then WTO members represented 97% of global GDP, 96% of global trade and 91% of the world's population.[26] Given that WTO membership has grown to 164 member nations by the end of July 2016, these figures have risen to around 99% of global coverage.[27]

Whilst GATT agreements relate to trade in goods, GATS relate to trade in services, and it should be noted that multilateral progress towards free trade has advanced much further in the former than the latter. This is significant when considering trade between the EU and the UK, where the latter has a very large trade deficit in goods but a modest surplus in services, and reliance upon GATS provisions will not provide the same level of protection for future trade in services with the EU. However, for UK trade with most of the rest of the world, a good proportion of this is currently undertaken through reliance upon GATT and GATS agreements, and the UK has a trade surplus in both goods and services.

All preferential trade arrangements (PTAs) operate within the multilateral WTO rules and, although PTAs have expanded rapidly over the past three decades, they accounted for only around 35% of total world merchandisable trade as recently as 2008 (WTO 2011: 7). Thus, most world trade still occurs outside of formal trade agreements and depends upon what is termed the 'Most Favoured Nation' (MFN) rules. MFN tariffs are what countries commit to imposing on imports from other members of the WTO, unless the country is part of a preferential trade agreement. This is, in effect, the maximum tariff that can be charged to another WTO member. Thus, in the case of the UK withdrawing from the EU, the latter cannot impose higher tariffs on imports from the UK than it does on the same goods imported from another WTO member nation with whom the EU does not have a form of preferential trade agreement—i.e. a FTA or customs union (CEPR 2013: 35). Thus, for any reader who is concerned that the EU could discriminate against the UK in setting future trade terms more disadvantageous than for other non-EU members who it does not already include in some form of trade agreement, then WTO rules would prohibit this practice.

Reliance upon WTO rules will involve the imposition of tariffs upon some UK exports. Once, this would have imposed substantial costs upon UK exporters to Europe, and, indeed, the avoidance of such tariffs was a significant persuasive element in the UK deciding to join the EU over half a century ago. However, the work of the WTO has significantly reduced the level of tariffs applied throughout most of the world (see Fig. 9.2).

For the EU in particular, tariffs have declined to very low levels, particularly for non-agricultural goods. For example, according to WTO Figures[28], the 2013 average trade-weighted tariff for the EU (including the UK) was 3.6%; ranging from 2.3% for non-agricultural goods to 22.3% for agricultural produce. One reason for average trade-weighted tariffs on non-agricultural goods being so low is that around 26.5% of these products were traded duty free (i.e. without tariffs applied), whilst a further 37.5% received a tariff below 5% and, indeed, 91.1% of all non-agricultural goods received tariffs below 10%. For agricultural produce, the level of tariffs levied was significantly higher, although, even here, fully 31.7% of all products were traded tariff free. World Bank figures suggest that average trade-weighted EU MFN tariffs are even lower than the WTO estimates, at between 1–2% (see Fig. 9.3). These figures are comparable with other nations, exporting into the EU SIM. For example the USA and Switzerland, where trade-weighted tariffs applied to non-agricultural products were only 1.1% and 1.2% respectively, and agricultural products 2% for the USA to 23.7% for Switzerland.

This average, however, disguises the fact that the cost impact upon specific sectors of UK exporters can be more significant (see Fig. 9.4). Indeed, Booth et al. (2015: 27) note that around one third of UK exports to the EU are in sectors where the EU imposes relatively high tariffs.

These headline figures can be a little misleading, when commentators calculate a simple average of all tariff lines, because this does not take into account the relative importance, in terms of the value of goods sold. Accordingly, using UNCTAD figures to calculate trade-weighted

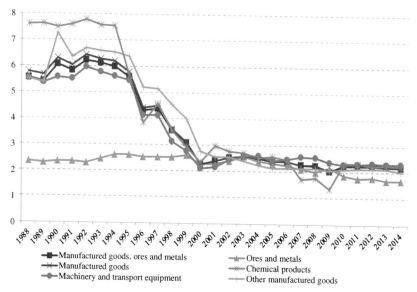

Fig. 9.5 EU average trade-weighted MFN tariffs (%), 1988–2014. *Source* UNCTAD (2016)

MFN tariffs for general categories of non-agricultural product ranges, indicates a general convergence around a rate of 2% (see Fig. 9.5).

The imposition of tariffs would be the largest disadvantage inherent within the 'WTO model'. When weighted according to the value of UK exports to the EU, these MFN tariffs may only impose an average cost upon UK exports of around 2–3%, which is a sum easily absorbed by UK exporters as it lies within the monthly fluctuations of a floating currency. However, since the tariff cost would fall disproportionately upon certain industries, such as car production, chemicals, tobacco, clothing, together with food and beverages, it might be advisable for the UK government to seek to use a proportion of budgetary savings arising from Brexit to compensate producers in these sectors. This might occur through a combination of research grants and training subsidies, aiming at enhancing the productivity of these industries whilst simultaneously compensating them for the rise in costs caused by tariffs.

In terms of advantages, the 'WTO model' offers the greatest degree of independence from the EU (Booth et al. 2015: 61–62;Minford 2016: 8). The UK would no longer have to implement EU-determined regulations and technical specifications for goods and services across the whole of the UK economy, but only that part which desired to export into the EU SIM. There would be no budgetary cost for trading along WTO lines, unless the UK sought access to specific EU programmes, such as Horizon 2020, for research collaboration, or Erasmus, to facilitate student mobility. The UK would have maximum freedom to negotiate its separate trade agreements with other countries and/or trade blocks, although the CBI (2013: 16) disputes the probable realisation of superior deals than membership of the EU or the EEA could secure. The UK could also resume its seat and vote at the WTO, rather than have to defer to the EU position, given its reserving trade policy to itself (Milne 2004: 42–45). In addition, one further advantage arising from the WTO model is the gain to the public purse arising from tariff revenues (CEPR 2013: 16).

Option Six: Unilateral Free Trade—The Hong Kong Model

Another alternative, available to the UK government following Brexit, is most closely associated with the work of Minford, from the University of Cardiff and the 'Economists for Brexit' (Minford et al. 2005; Economists for Brexit 2016). This suggests that, rather than the UK seeking to negotiate reciprocal trade relationships with the EU based on reciprocity, or levying equivalent tariffs upon the EU according to WTO MFN rules, the UK should instead adopt the 'Hong Kong model' of unilaterally eliminating all of its trade protection. One advantage would be that the UK would not need to seek concessions in bargaining with the EU over future trade agreements, whilst there is little need to renegotiate the EU's trade agreements with third parties as their impact on world prices is rather slight (Economists for Brexit 2016).

The rationale for this approach derives from the standard neoclassical theory of international trade, in that by removing tariffs, the UK would reduce the cost of imported goods for UK consumers and manufacturers who use inputs from abroad, and thereby reduce inflation, increase consumer welfare and improve the international competitiveness of UK exporters (Booth et al. 2015: 63). The competitive effect of cheaper import penetration into the UK market would, according to the theory, pressurise UK producers into increasing their efficiency.

One example might be in the area of agricultural goods, where the UK imports approximately £40 billion per year, three quarters of which derived from EU producers despite the fact that many of these items are sold above world prices due to the trade diversion caused by the EU's common external tariffs. If UK consumers were able to purchase similar goods at world prices, they would make significant savings and be able to use these funds to make other purchases, thereby providing a boost to the economy. There are a range of estimates which may substantiate this perspective, including Booth et al. (2015: 73) which cites an OECD estimate that EU agricultural tariffs may cost EU consumers around €10.7 billion per year, whilst Minford et al. (2015:116) suggests that the total cost of the CAP to the EU as a whole is around 0.9% of its GDP. Thus, eliminating the CET upon agricultural produce would have an immediate and positive impact upon the UK economy.

This would not, however, be the only effect, as the inflow of cheaper imported food would pressurise UK farms into either becoming more efficient or else many might be forced out of the market. Here, Booth et al. (2015: 73) cite evidence gleaned from New Zealand, when 15% of its farms became unviable when agricultural subsidies were withdrawn. Hence, one inevitable consequence of unilateral free trade would be to cause a structural shift in the UK economy. Inefficient producers, unable to produce at the new, lower world prices, would either increase productivity or they would cease to trade. Similarly, car firms establishing themselves in the UK in order to export into the SIM may wish to relocate a proportion of production elsewhere[29], whilst consumers would have the benefit of buying less expensive models from elsewhere in the world (Minford et al. 2015: 16–20). As a result, one of the more controversial aspects of the 'Hong Kong Model' would be the likely decline of that part of UK manufacturing industry which produces standardised products, which could be relocated to lower wage economies, although the authors of this approach suggest that services and 'hi-tech' manufacturing should be able to expand (Minford et al.

2015:73). Advocates of this model argue that workers and capital will be reallocated from less to more efficient producers, thereby increasing productivity and employment.

Those studies which have examined the potential for unilateral liberalisation, tend to produce positive effects. Ciuriac et al. (2015: 25–26), for example, suggests that this approach could provide a net benefit for the UK economy of perhaps 0.75% UK GDP by 2030. These conclusions are, however, dependent upon the theoretical underpinning of neoclassical theory. For example, it is assumed that factors of production are relatively homogenous and therefore easily interchangeable, whilst wages and prices are sufficiently flexible as to facilitate a relatively rapid movement from one equilibrium situation to another. Thus, the economy will remain at full employment for all of those who are willing to work at the prevailing market wage rate. Say's Law will prevail, in that supply will create its own demand, and therefore factors will move rapidly to new employment opportunities created by this new demand (Minford et al. 2015: 17).

Of course, this benign textbook model is highly questionable in the real world. The experience of the recent financial crisis should have demonstrated to all but the most enthusiastic adherents to economic orthodoxy, that disequilibrium can persist for more than a short transitional period. The economy can find itself in a demand deficient position, where individuals who want to work find it difficult to do so, and firms that cease to trade often results in capital scrapping rather than reallocation. Should structural reorganisation not occur rapidly, through price flexibility, it will likely do so through quantity effects, such as impacting upon output and/or employment. Supporters of this approach concede that there may be frictional unemployment, but do not accept the possibility (indeed, the probability) of more substantial medium term effects (Booth et al. 2015: 73–75).

The claim relating to raising productivity is also slightly suspect, because earlier structural change relied upon financial and business services replacing economic activity formerly undertaken by the manufacturing sector. Yet, the after-effects of the financial crisis and a reversal of the previous over-expansion of the banking sector means that it is less likely for high value added services to absorb a higher proportion of the labour force, should sections of manufacturing acclimatise to the unilateral trade model by downsizing. It is quite plausible that retail may absorb a proportion of this surplus labour, but replacing car production with an expansion of burger or coffee outlets would hardly contribute to an increase in productivity. Indeed, it is the conclusion reached in Chap. 8 of this book that the greater freedoms offered by Brexit should be utilised in order to strengthen not weaken the UK manufacturing sector. Consequently, it is the adjustment mechanism for the UK economy to absorb significant structural change, arising from the unilateral withdrawal of tariff protection, which is the largest single weakness with the 'Hong Kong model'.

Option Seven—EFTA

The option to re-join EFTA is typically discussed alongside a supplementary application for membership of the EEA. However, there is nothing to prevent the UK from eschewing the latter and instead participating in EFTA as one element in a post-EU strategy. EFTA is a much smaller entity than the EU, having only four member nations— i.e. Iceland, Liechtenstein, Norway and Switzerland—and representing a total GDP of €0.9bn.[30] UK membership should, therefore, be attractive to other EFTA members, who would otherwise lose tariff-free trade with the UK market. Set against this, the UK would become far the largest single member of EFTA and this would change the dynamic of the organisation, which some current members may find unsettling.

Whilst potentially attractive as part of any post-Brexit global trading realignment, EFTA membership in isolation is simply too small to replace any significant amount of lost trade with the EU should negotiations fail to agree some form of free trade agreement. Hence, whilst not necessarily agreeing with Piris (2016: 7–8) that, due to the advent of the EEA, EFTA has become 'an empty shell', it is certainly true that, as currently constituted, it is too small to represent more than part of any future trade strategy developed by the UK.

Option Eight—The Commonwealth

One potential trade relationship, arguably neglected during the UK's focus upon regional European trade, concerns the 54 nation Commonwealth.[31] These markets formed a significant proportion of UK trade prior to it joining the EU. However, membership of the EU customs union meant replacing favourable trade terms for Commonwealth countries, jointly described as the system of 'imperial preference', with the EUs Common External Tariff (CET). This raised the prices of goods traded between the UK and other Commonwealth nations, thereby encouraging trade displacement in favour of the EU internal market. At the time, this process was viewed as the UK turning its back upon the past and joining what was, at the time, a high growth group of European economies.

More recently, however, the EU has become a slow growth area, whereas the Commonwealth contains within it countries which have recorded strong periods of economic growth—i.e. India, Australia, Canada, New Zealand, Singapore and Malaysia. The Commonwealth economy comprises of 2.2 billion people, of which more than 60% are under the age of 30, living in 53 independent countries. It represents around 15% of global GDP, which is larger than the Eurozone and, largely due to the high growth rates recorded by India, is predicted to grow larger than the EU by the end of the decade.[32] Consequently, there is a good argument to be made for an independent UK to have a greater focus upon exploring potential trade opportunities within this group of nations, with which it has historic ties and pre-existing layers of cooperation. Indeed, former Foreign Secretary Hague highlighted the potential for increased trade relations with Commonwealth nations back in 2010.[33]

Critics note that there are already FTAs in place between the EU and 18 Commonwealth nations, with a further 14 awaiting ratification.[34] Consequently, the UK did not need to withdraw from EU membership to take advantage of this potential trade relationship. Indeed, the UK has recorded substantial increases in exports to Commonwealth nations in recent years, whilst still an EU member, thus indicating that there might be little more to gain from a reorientation of trade priorities as an independent nation.[35] *The Economist* magazine, for example, described the suggestion that the Commonwealth might prove a replacement for any lost trade with the EU following Brexit, as 'the ultimate Eurosceptic fantasy'.[36]

These are good points. Nevertheless, it would be churlish to fail to recognise the fact that membership of a regional trade bloc tends to cause exporters to focus upon regional trade opportunities, particularly when encouraged to do so by a common external tariff that makes the forging of complex supply chains a little more complex and expensive than would otherwise be the case. If withdrawal from the EU does not involve continued access to the SIM, UK exporters will have greater incentives to focus more on trade opportunities outside Europe, and Commonwealth nations, with shared history and cultural ties, would seem a good starting point. Indeed, there is an emerging body of research which suggests that cultural and historic ties, including trust between nations and commonality of language, are significant influences upon the development of international trade (Algan and Cahuc 2010; Guiso et al. 2009). Thus, it would make sense for the UK to look to use the leverage provided by cultural and historical linkages with Commonwealth nations to build closer trading relationships.

Option Eight—The Anglosphere

Another potential alternative would be to consider whether what has been termed an 'Anglosphere' might provide the basis for economic and political partnership for an independent UK (Bennett 2004). In a similar way to the Commonwealth option, these nations share a common language, operate according to common law, together with shared cultural and historical ties. Indeed, the research, referred to in relation to the Commonwealth option, would appear to be even more relevant for Anglosphere nations (Algan and Cahuc 2010; Guiso et al. 2009).

When considered as a bloc, the Anglosphere has more than one quarter of the world's GDP, and this advantage is amplified if considering GDP per capita measured according to purchasing power parity

(Kotkin and Parulekar 2011: 29–30). Moreover, Milne (2004: 30) suggests that, if the UK had been a member of what he terms an Anglo-Saxon-Celtic group of nations (namely the USA, Canada, Australia and New Zealand), its growth profile would have been higher than recorded as a member of the; in the process raising GDP by around 6% between 1993 and 2003. Given the difficulties in counterfactual comparison, it is difficult to assess the validity of this claim, except to refer back to the examination of economic growth (see Chap. 7), where UK accession to the EU did result in its growth rate declining slightly, over time, and the EU did shift from being a fast to slower growth economic bloc at around the same time.

It is, therefore, argued that Anglosphere nations—primarily the USA, Britain, Ireland, Canada, Australia and New Zealand—could develop closer cooperation around trade, scientific cooperation and security issues, without the need to develop the type of political integration favoured by the EU (Nesbitt 2001). Given these potential advantages, it is reported that a number of leading political figures, in the UK, Australia and Canada, have stated an interest in this concept (Miller et al. 2016: 46). Indeed, when comparing EU membership to the perceived advantages of the Anglosphere, Hannan, a Conservative MEP, argued that 'far from hitching our wagon to a powerful locomotive, we shackled ourselves to a corpse'.

Critics of this concept point to the fragility of the historical connections between the Anglosphere nations and that, whilst countries may share elements of culture, they do not necessarily have shared interests. Moreover, the idea itself is not new, being first proposed in imperial terms in 1911, but receiving only scant support at the time (Harries 2001). Nevertheless, like the Commonwealth option, the cultural and other ties between Anglosphere nations may facilitate closer trade arrangements and other forms of economic cooperation between sovereign nations. Both the new President of the USA and the New Zealand Prime Minister have expressed their interest in negotiating a free trade agreement with the UK shortly after the Brexit withdrawal process has been completed.[37]

Nafta

A perhaps more immediately practical option, considered by the US Senate Finance Committee, is whether an independent UK could join the North Atlantic Free Trade Agreement (NAFTA), which currently operates between the USA, Canada and Mexico. This option has been discussed by sections of the US Congress and the newly elected President of the USA, Trump, has registered his interest in pursuing a FTA with the UK, albeit not necessarily through the medium of NAFTA.

The US International Trade Commission (USITC) has even completed a report on the likely impact that UK participation in NAFTA may have upon the economies of all four nations. Conducted in 2000, but based upon trade data drawn from 1995, the report suggested that there would be significant trade effects, with UK exports to Canada rising by approximately 24% and the USA by 12.5%, with similar although smaller rises in imports from NAFTA nations, leading to an improvement in the UK's trade balance. This would not, however, be sufficient to compensate for a reduction of UK trade with the EU, albeit that imports into the UK would fall faster than exports, thereby further improving the UK's trade balance (USITC 2000: 4-13-14). The impact on FDI would likely reduce the output of US-owned manufacturing affiliates in the UK by 0.56%, which is a significantly smaller effect than many more recent predictions (USITC 2000: 4–19). Overall, in terms of macroeconomic effects, the report suggests that prices may decline slightly in the UK, whilst the modelling predicted insubstantial changes in national GDP, ranging from -0.02% for the UK to a zero change for the USA (USITC 2000: 4-16-17).

The USITC study is interesting partly because it was one of the first studies to seek to model the economic effect of UK withdrawal from the EU, and its prediction of an insubstantial impact on the UK economy of only −0.02% GDP is in sharp contrast to more recent studies. Moreover, even this result is likely to be more favourable to the UK if the exercise was repeated in 2016, because the share of UK exports taken by the EU is significantly lower now than it was in the mid-1990s. Similarly, the average trade weighted MFN tariff levied by the EU has fallen from a little over 6% in 1995 to around 1% today (Thompson and Harari 2013: 7). Hence, it would be reasonable to assume that the UK would lose less trade to the EU if the modelling was repeated with 2016 data, given the lower level of EU tariffs. Thus, whilst it is perilous to base current economic policy upon one study, conducted using data from two decades previously, the USITC predictions do provide a tantalising piece of evidence that UK withdrawal from the EU, and subsequent membership of NAFTA or alternatively a broader Anglosphere, might provide an interesting option for an independent UK. At the very least, it would be worth UK policymakers examining this option in more detail.

Trans-Pacific Partnership (TPP)

A variant of the above could include the UK considering an application to join the Trans-Pacific Partnership (TPP), currently being negotiated between the USA, Japan, Australia, Canada, New Zealand, Mexico, Singapore, Malaysia, Chile, Peru, Brunei and Vietnam.[38] Indeed, this has been suggested by the US Trade Representative Froman, who acted as former President Obama's principal advisor, negotiator and spokesperson on international trade and investment issues.[39] If realised, the TPP would be a substantial trade bloc. These nations already account for around 40% of global trade and have a combined population of around 800 million; were the UK to complete withdrawal from the EU and join the TPP, the trade bloc would have a population just short of twice as large as that of the EU.[40] Were the UK to join the TPP, it would be the third largest economy in the trade bloc.

The flaw in this proposal concerns the degree of opposition the TPP has provoked in the USA, including both candidates for the Presidency and US trade unions concerned about job losses and effects upon wages.[41] It has, furthermore, received criticism from progressive commentators, as it includes clauses which would appear to facilitate the penetration of national public services by trans-national corporations, which was one of the criticisms levied at the TTIP.[42] Moreover, since the TPP has already been finalised, the UK would have little influence over the development of the trade agreement, which might inadvertently disadvantage certain UK industries or national interests. Nevertheless, whilst the TPP may be in trouble in its current form, the revival of a different variant of the TPP could prove to be a fruitful option for an independent UK to pursue.

Evaluating the Alternative Trading Models

When seeking to evaluate the various options for the UK to consider, whilst reformulating its trading arrangements following Brexit, there are three key points to consider:

1. The short term balance of estimated economic impact deriving from each potential model
2. How the longer term predicted developments in the global economy may impact upon this calculus of costs and benefits
3. That there is a trade-off between achieving greater access to the EU SIM and achieving greater independence of action—particularly economic policy flexibility.

From the various reports discussed in Chap. 1 (and summarised in Table 1.8), there exists significant disagreement between forecasts of how the UK would fare under different trading arrangements, post-Brexit. 'Consensus' studies have suggested that closer trade agreements, either in the form of the EEA or the negotiation of a FTA, would cause less immediate disruption to trade flows and hence to the health of the UK economy. Yet, this view is certainly not universally held. Reports completed by Minford et al (2005), Minford (2016) and Booth et al. (2015) claim that greater economic flexibility would generate the most positive economic outcome. The lack of consensus, amongst these economic studies, is partly due to the assumptions on which they are based and the inclusiveness of their analyses. Moreover, few of these studies sought to examine the potential for trade expansion in the rest of the world; rather, focusing more narrowly upon the impact of UK-EU trade.

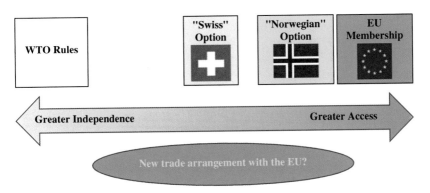

Fig. 9.6 Trade-offs between Policy Autonomy Independence and Access to EU Markets

Yet, the EU has become a slow growth area and as a result UK exports to the continent have begun to decline, signifying a shift away from regional to global trade orientation (Milne 2004; CBI 2013: 27; Business for Britain 2015: 30–2,697; ONS 2016).Whilst the EU SIM is likely to remain the largest single consumer of UK exports for the foreseeable future, its importance seems likely to decline over time. It is, of course, important to remain cautious about the accuracy of long range predictions, since it is not too long ago that commentators were making rather bold claims about the future dominance of the Japanese and BRIC economies—including Brazil and Russia. Nevertheless, it is likely that part of the post-Brexit strategy for the UK economy is for its exporters to re-orientate their activities to target faster growing sections of the global economy. Thus, whatever new trade relationship the UK negotiates with the EU, it has to be both compatible with policy intervention intended to enhance the efficiency and international competitiveness of UK businesses, and secondly, to facilitate the expansion of exports to the rest of the world. This may necessitate trading-off some access to EU markets for greater policy independence, if this is required to rebuild the UK industrial base (as illustrated in Fig. 9.6).

The result of the UK's withdrawal negotiations with the EU is unlikely to result in the off-the-peg adoption of one of the various trading models outlined in this chapter. Indeed, it is much more likely that the result would be a bespoke agreement, focused around the specific nature of UK-EU economic structures and trading patterns (CBI 2013: 152). Thus, whilst considerations of the alternative model so trade relationships are useful, in illustrating the type of advantages and disadvantages that may arise from different arrangements, they need not be as distinct as presented in this chapter. It would, for example, be perfectly possible to have a FTA which embodied some elements of the EEA, without having to accept the current version in operation with the three EFTA nations. Similarly, it is perfectly possible to create a hybrid FTA-light agreement, which combines free trade in certain areas but reliance upon WTO rules in other sectors.

Notes

1. See also http://gerardbattenmep.co.uk/wp-content/uploads/2016/07/Referendun-Victory-The-Road-to-freedom.pdf.
2. http://www.bbc.co.uk/news/uk-politics-37532364.
3. The only nation thus far to withdraw from the EU, namely Greenland in 1985, did so under quite different circumstances—i.e. subsequent to it gaining autonomy from Denmark, and following a referendum in which the population voted to withdraw from the EU in an uncannily similar result, and turnout, to the UK's own 2016 referendum (Miller et al., 2016:27). It did so under what is now Article 48 of the TEU, although this requires unanimous consent from other EU member states, which is not the legal justification upon which the UK would wish to reply (Miller and Lang, 2016: 7).
4. https://www.theguardian.com/politics/2016/oct/01/theresa-may-to-propose-great-repeal-bill-to-unwind-eu-laws.
5. FTAs negotiated by the EU Commission with external nations, including Colombia, Peru and most recently Canada, required ratification by national parliaments, as, indeed, will the TTIP negotiated with the USA, if this negotiation is satisfactorily completed. For further information, see European Commission Vice-President Maroš Šefčovič responding to national parliamentarians, via www.ec.europa.eu/transparency/regdoc/rep/3/2014/EN/3-2014-7557-EN-F1-1.pdf.
6. http://ec.europa.eu/programmes/erasmus-plus/sites/erasmusplus/files/files/resources/erasmus-plus-programme-guide_en.pdf,   pp.   22–24;

http://ec.europa.eu/research/participants/data/ref/h2020/grants_manual/hi/3cpart/h2020-hi-list-ac_en.pdf;   http://ec.europa.eu/research/participants/data/ref/h2020/wp/2014_2015/annexes/h2020-wp1415-annex-a-countries-rules_en.pdf.

7. Algeria seceded from France in 1962 to become an independent state outside the European Community. Greenland, an autonomous country within the state of Denmark, withdrew in 1985. These withdrawals took place before the Lisbon Treaty came into effect, and were therefore not conducted under Article 50. For Greenland, the issues were very limited, as the territory only sought Overseas Country and Territory status, rather than a full exit. Even so, withdrawal took three years: from a referendum decision in February 1982 to departure in February 1985.

8. http://www.telegraph.co.uk/news/2017/01/24/brexit-ruling-supreme-court-judgment-full/.

9. http://www.express.co.uk/news/politics/674392/project-fear-david-cameron-admits-britain-survive-eu-referendum-brexit-g7;   http://www.independent.co.uk/news/uk/politics/eu-referendum-britain-could-thrive-outside-europe-claims-david-cameron-a6726606.html; CBI (2013: 16).

10. http://www.telegraph.co.uk/news/2016/10/29/hard-brexit-could-help-secure-trade-deals-worth-double--eu-agree/.

11. Supplemental to the EEA agreement, Iceland has negotiated tariff free access to EU markets for its fishery exports by allowing limited access for EU fishing vessels in Icelandic territorial waters.

12. http://ukandeu.ac.uk/the-eea-a-safe-harbour-in-the-brexit-storm/.

13. http://www.policyreview.eu/can-the-uk-join-norway-in-the-eea/.

14. https://www.regjeringen.no/en/find-document/dep/UD/reports-to-the-storting/20002001/report_no-12_to_the_storting_2000-2001/7/id193725/.

15. http://openeurope.org.uk/intelligence/britain-and-the-eu/top-100-eu-rules-cost-britain-33-3bn/.

16. Thompson and Harari (2013:25); Dhingra et al. (2015:4); https://infacts.org/norwegians-pay-same-brits-eu-access/; Emmerson et al., (2016:2, 13–14); http://www.eureferendum.com/blogview.aspx?blogno=85515.

17. http://www.eu-norway.org/eu/Financial-contribution/.

18. http://www.ssb.no/en/nasjonalregnskap-og-konjunkturer/statistikker/knr/kvartal/2016-05-12?fane=tabell&sort=nummer&tabell=265699.

19. This is the estimate used by Emmerson et al. 2016: 13–14.

20. https://www.imf.org/external/pubs/ft/weo/2015/02/weodata/weorept.aspx?pr.x=21&pr.y=6&sy=2013&ey=2020&scsm=1&ssd=1&sort=country&ds=.&br=1&c=142%2C112&s=NGDPDPC&grp=0&a=.
21. For further reading on the economics of customs unions, and the work of Viner, you may wish to consider Baldwin and Wyplosz (2003), Chap. 5.
22. http://ec.europa.eu/enlargement/pdf/turkey/20160122-turkey-factograph.pdf.
23. A good overview of different types of NTBs is provided in.
24. https://www.theguardian.com/world/2016/sep/22/switzerland-votes-for-compromise-to-preserve-relations-with-eu.
25. https://www.theguardian.com/politics/2016/dec/01/brexit-secretary-suggests-uk-would-consider-paying-for-single-market-access.
26. https://www.wto.org/english/thewto_e/acc_e/cbt_course_e/c1s1p1_e.htm#fnt3.
27. https://www.wto.org/english/thewto_e/whatis_e/tif_e/org6_e.htm.
28. http://stat.wto.org/TariffProfile/WSDBTariffPFView.aspx?Language=E&Country=E28.
29. This position need not be exaggerated, as around two-thirds of car production in the UK is already destined for either the home or non-EU overseas markets. Moreover, Economists for Brexit (2016) acknowledge that support for specific industries may be available within their approach.
30. http://www.efta.int/statistics/efta-in-Figures.
31. Perhaps this should be more accurately 53 member nations, since Fiji is currently suspended.
32. http://www.telegraph.co.uk/news/newstopics/eureferendum/12193101/Brexit-will-allow-Britain-to-embrace-the-Commonwealth.html; http://www.worldeconomics.com/papers/Commonwealth_Growth_Monitor_0e53b963-bce5-4ba1-9cab-333cedaab048.paper.
33. *Britain's Foreign Policy in a Networked World*, Speech, Rt Hon William Hague, Thursday, 1 July 2010.
34. http://eulawanalysis.blogspot.co.uk/2015/11/the-eu-or-commonwealth-dilemma-for-uk.html.
35. http://blogs.lse.ac.uk/brexitvote/2015/12/10/the-commonwealth-and-the-eu-lets-do-trade-with-both/.
36. http://www.economist.com/blogs/bagehot/2011/10/britain-and-eu-3.

37. http://www.bbc.co.uk/news/uk-politics-38608716;   http://www.telegraph.co.uk/news/2017/01/27/congress-pushes-donald-trump-form-bilateral-trade-deal-uk/.
38. https://ustr.gov/tpp/.
39. http://www.express.co.uk/news/uk/687484/Obama-admin-Brexit-Britain-not-back-queue-trade-deal.
40. http://www.bbc.co.uk/news/business-32498715.
41. http://www.independent.co.uk/voices/ttip-american-ttp-trade-deal-bernie-sanders-hillary-clinton-donald-trump-barack-obama-looks-set-for-a7194336.html.
42. http://inthesetimes.com/article/18695/TPP_Free-Trade_Globalization_Obama.
43. When countries join the WTO, they make certain commitments as to the maximum tariff they will charge for each commodity line. These are then described as final bound tariffs. If the country charges tariffs above this level, they can be taken to WTO dispute settlement. Tariffs can be set below this level as long as this is non-discriminatory, unless via a preferential trade agreement (such as a FTA or customs union). For the UK, the MFN tariff rates will be the most relevant figure to consider.

References

Abreu, M. D. (2013). Preferential rules of origin in regional trade agreements, *World Trade Organisation Staff Working Paper* No ERSD-2013-05. https://www.wto.org/english/res_e/reser_e/ersd201305_e.pdf.

Algan, Y., & Cahus, P. (2010). Inherited trust and growth. *American Economic Review, 100*(5), 2060–2092.

Baker, J., Carreras, O., Ebell, M., Hurst, I., Kirby, S., Meaning, J., et al. (2016). The short-term economic impact of leaving the EU. *National Institute Economic Review, 236,* 108–120.

Baldwin, R., & Wyplosz, C. (2003). *The economics of european integration.* New York: McGraw-Hill.

Barclay, C. (2012). *Food miles.* House of Commons Library, No. SN/SC/4984. http://researchbriefings.parliament.uk/ResearchBriefing/Summary/SN04984.

Batten, G. (2013). *The Road to Freedom: How Britain can escape the EU.* Surbiton: Bretwalda Books.

Bennett, J. C. (2004). *The anglosphere challenge: Why the English-speaking nations will lead the way in the 21st century.* Lanham: Rowman and Littlefield.

Booth, S., Howarth, C., Persson, M., Ruparel, R., and Swidlicki, P. (2015). *What if...?: The Consequences, challenges and opportunities facing Britain outside EU.* Open Europe Report 03/2015, London. http://openeurope.org. uk/intelligence/britain-and-the-eu/what-if-there-were-a-brexit/.

Brenton, P. (2010). Preferential Rules of Origin. In J. P. Chauffour & J. C. Maur (Eds.), *Preferential trade agreement policies for development: A handbook* (pp. 161–178). Washington DC: World Bank.

Brenton, P., & Manchin, M. (2003). Making EU trade agreements work: The role of rules of origin. *The World Economy, 26*(5), 755–769.

Burkitt, B., Baimbridge, M., & Whyman, P. B. (1996). *Thereis an alternative: Britain and its relationship with the EU.* Oxford: CIB/Nelson and Pollard.

Business for Britain. (2015). *Change or Go: How Britain would gain influence and prosper outside an unreformed EU.* Business for Britain, London. https://forbritain.org/cogwholebook.pdf.

Cadot, O., Carrère, C., de Melo, J., & Tumurchudur, B. (2006). Product-Specific rules of origin in EU and US preferential trading arrangements: An assessment. *World Trade Review, 5*(2), 199–224.

Capital Economics. (2016). *The economics impact of 'Brexit': A paper discussing the United Kingdom' relationship with Europe and the impact of 'Brexit' on the British economy.* Woodford Investment Management LLP, Oxford. https://woodfordfunds.com/economic-impact-brexit-report/.

CBI [Confederation of British Industry]. (2013). *Our Global Future: The Business Vision for a Reformed EU.* CBI, London. http://www.cbi.org.uk/media/2451423/our_global_future.pdf#page=1&zoom=auto,-119,842.

CEPR. (2013). *Trade and Investment Balance of Competence Review.* Department for Business Innovation and Skills, London. https://www.gov.uk/government/uploads/system/uploads/attachment_data/file/271784/bis-14-512-trade-and-investment-balance-of-competence-review-project-report.pdf.

Chisik, R. (2003). Export industry policy and reputational comparative advantage. *Journal of International Economics, 59*(2), 423–451.

Chopin, T. (2013). Two Europe's. In Nevin, S. and Thillaye, R. (eds.), *Europe in Search of a New Settlement: EU-UK relations and the politics of integration.* Policy Network, London, 9-10. http://www.policy-network.net/publications_download.aspx?ID=8274.

Chopin, T. (2016). After the UK's EU Referendum: Redefining relations between the "two Europe's". *European Issues*, No. 399, Robert Schuman Foundation. http://www.robert-schuman.eu/en/doc/questions-d-europe/qe-399-en.pdf.

Ciuriak, D., Xiao, J., Ciuriak, N., Dadkhah, A., Lysenko, D., and Narayanan, G. B. (2015). *The trade-related impact of a UK Exit from the EU single market*. Research Report, April, Ciuriak Consulting, Ottawa. https://papers.ssrn.com/sol3/papers.cfm?abstract_id=2620718.

De Sousa, J., Mayer, T., and Zignago, S. (2012). Market access in global and regional trade. *Regional Science and Urban Economics, 42*(6): 1037–1052. http://econ.sciences-po.fr/sites/default/files/file/tmayer/MA_revisionRSUE_jul2012.pdf.

Dhingra, S., Ottaviano, G. I. P., & Sampson, T. (2015). *Should we stay or should we go? The economic consequences of leaving the EU*, Centre for Economic Performance, LSE. https://ideas.repec.org/e/pot15.html.

Dinnie, K. (2004). Country of origin 1965–2004: A literature review. *Journal of Customer Behaviour, 3*(2), 165–213.

Dinnie, K. (2008). *Nation branding: Concepts, issues, practice*. Abingdon: Routledge.

Economists for Brexit. (2016). *A vote for Brexit: What are the policies to follow and what are the economic prospects?* London: Economists for Brexit. Available via: http://www.economistsforbrexit.co.uk/a-vote-for-brexit.

Emmerson, C., Johnson, P., Mitchell, I., & Phillips, D. (2016). *Brexit and the UK's public finances* (IFS Report 116). Institute for Fiscal Studies, London. Available via: http://www.ifs.org.uk/uploads/publications/comms/r116.pdf.

Europe Economics. (2013). *Optimal integration in the single market: A synoptic review*. Department of Business Innovation and Skills, London. https://www.gov.uk/government/uploads/system/uploads/attachment_data/file/224579/bis-13-1058-europe-economics-optimal-integration-in-the-single-market-a-synoptic-review.pdf.

Fawcett, J. (2015). Origin Marking research – full report phases 1 and 2, Department for Business Innovation and Skills, London. https://www.gov.uk/government/uploads/system/uploads/attachment_data/file/408476/bis-15-94-compulsory-origin-marking-research-phase-1-and-2.pdf.

Guiso, L., Sapienza, P., & Zingales, L. (2009). Cultural biases in economic exchange? *The Quarterly Journal of Economics, 124*(3), 1095–1131.

Harries, O. (2001). The anglosphere illusion. *The National Interest*, Spring. http://www.prospectmagazine.co.uk/features/anglosphereillusions.

HMG [HM Government]. (2016). The process for withdrawing from the European Union, Cm 9216, The Stationary Office, London. https://www.gov.uk/government/uploads/system/uploads/attachment_data/file/504216/The_process_for_withdrawing_from_the_EU_print_ready.pdf.

HoC [House of Commons Foreign Affairs Committee]. (2013). *The Future of the European Union: UK government policy* – First Report of Session 2013–2014, Volume 1, HC-87-1, The Stationary Office, London. http://www.publications.parliament.uk/pa/cm201314/cmselect/cmfaff/87/87.pdf.

HoL [House of Lords European Union Committee]. (2016). *The process of withdrawing from the European Union.* House of Lords, London. http://www.publications.parliament.uk/pa/ld201516/ldselect/ldeucom/138/138.pdf.

Hui, M. K., & Zhou, L. (2002). Linking product evaluations and purchase intention for country-of-origin effects. *Journal of Global Marketing, 15*(3/4), 95–116.

Keep, M. (2015). EU Budget 2014–2020. *House of Commons Library Briefing Paper (HC 06455)*, The Stationary Office, London. http://researchbriefings.files.parliament.uk/documents/SN06455/SN06455.pdf.

Kotkin, J., and Parulekar, S. (2011). The anglosphere: We are not dead yet. In Kotkin, J. (ed.). *The new world order.* London: Legatum Institute. http://www.li.com/docs/default-source/surveys-of-entrepreneurs/new-world-order-2011_final.pdf, 28–38.

Lipsey, R. G. (1957). The theory of customs unions: Trade diversion and welfare. *Economica, 24*(93), 4–46.

Manchin, M. (2006). Preference utilisation and tariff reduction in EU imports from ACP countries. *The World Economy, 29*(9), 1243–1266.

McFadden, P., and Tarrant, A. (2015). *What would 'out' look like? Testing Eurosceptic alternatives to EU membership.* Policy Network, London. http://www.policy-network.net/publications/4995/What-would-out-look-like.

Meade, J. E. (1955). *The Theory of Customs Unions.* Amsterdam: North Holland.

Mendes, A. J. M. (1986). an alternative approach to customs union theory: A balance of payments framework to measure integration effects. *Journal of International Economic Integration, 1*(1), 43–58.

Meunier, S. (2005). *Trading voices: The European Union in international commercial relations.* Princeton, N.J.: Princeton University Press.

Miller, V. (ed.). (2016). Exiting the EU: Impact in key UK policy areas, *House of Commons Library Briefing Paper* No. HC 07213. http://researchbriefings.parliament.uk/ResearchBriefing/Summary/CBP-7213#fullreport.

Miller, V., and Lang, A. (2016). Brexit: How does the Article 50 process work? House of Commons Library Briefing Paper No. 7551. http://researchbriefings.parliament.uk/ResearchBriefing/Summary/CBP-7551#fullreport.

Miller, V., Lang, A., Smith, B., Webb, D., Harari, D., Keep, M., and Bowers, P. (2016). Exiting the EU: UK reform proposals, legal impact and alternatives to membership. *House of Commons Library Briefing Paper* No. HC 07214. http://researchbriefings.parliament.uk/ResearchBriefing/Summary/CBP-7214#fullreport.

Milne, I. (2004). *A cost too far? An Analysis of the net economic costs and benefits for the UK of EU membership*. Civitas, London. http://www.civitas.org.uk/pdf/cs37.pdf.

Minford, P., Mahambare, V., & Nowell, E. (2005). *Should Britain leave the EU? An economic analysis of a troubled relationship*. Cheltenham: IEA and Edward Elgar.

Minford, P., Gupta, S., Le, V. P. M., Mahambare, V., & Xu, Y. (2015). *Should Britain Leave the EU? An Economic Analysis of a Troubled Relationship – Second Edition*. Cheltenham: IEA and Edward Elgar.

Minford, P. (2016). *The treasury report on Brexit: A critique*. Economists for Brexit, London. http://static1.squarespace.com/static/570a10a460b5e93378a26ac5/t/5731a5a486db439545bf2eda/1462871465520/Economists+for+Brexit+-+The+Treasury+Report+on+Brexit+A+Critique.pdf.

Nesbit, J. C. (2001). *An anglosphere primer*. http://explorersfoundation.org/archive/anglosphere_primer.pdf.

Norwegian Ministry of Foreign Affairs. (2013). *The EEA agreement and Norway's other agreements with the EU*. Report to the Storting (Parliament) – White Paper Meld. St 5, Norwegian Ministry of Foreign Affairs, Oslo. Available at: https://www.regjeringen.no/contentassets/fc5aa7428fd-04f23af2a251d1c8c6710/en-gb/pdfs/stm201220130005000engpdfs.pdf.

NOU [Official Norwegian Report]. (2012a). *Utenfor og Innenfor: Norges avtaler med EU*. [Outside and Inside: Norway's agreement's with the EU], NOU 2012:2, Norwegian Ministry of Foreign Affairs, Oslo. https://www.regjeringen.no/contentassets/5d3982d042a2472eb1b20639cd8b2341/no/pdfs/nou201220120002000dddpdfs.pdf.

NOU [Official Norwegian Report]. (2012b). *Outside and Inside: Norway's agreements with the European Union – Other Parties' Views ion Norway's Agreements with the EU* - Chapter 13, NOU 2012:2, Norwegian Ministry of Foreign Affairs, Oslo. http://www.eu-norway.org/Global/SiteFolders/webeu/NOU2012_2_Chapter%2013.pdf.

NOU [Official Norwegian Report]. (2012c). *Outside and Inside: Norway's agreements with the European Union – The Way Forward –* Chapter 28, NOU 2012:2, Norwegian Ministry of Foreign Affairs, Oslo. http://www.eu-norway.org/Global/SiteFolders/webeu/NOU2012_2_Chapter_1.pdf.

OECD. (2016). The economic consequences of Brexit: A taxing decision, *OECD Economic Policy Paper*, No. 16. http://www.oecd.org/eco/The-Economic-consequences-of-Brexit-27-april-2016.pdf.

ONS [Office of National Statistics]. (2016). *UK's Top 10 Trading Partners.* http://visual.ons.gov.uk/uk-perspectives-2016-trade-with-the-eu-and-beyond/.

Ottaviano, G., Pessoa, J. P., and Sampson, T. (2014). The costs and benefits of leaving the EU. CEP mimeo. http://cep.lse.ac.uk/pubs/download/pa016_tech.pdf.

Owen, D. (2016). *Europe restructured: Vote to leave.* London: Methuen. http://www.lorddavidowen.co.uk/wp-content/uploads/2016/03/Europe-Restructured-160301.pdf.

Piris, J.-C. (2016). *If the UK Votes to Leave: The seven alternatives to EU membership.* London: Centre for European Reform. https://www.cer.org.uk/sites/default/files/pb_piris_brexit_12jan16.pdf.

Sejersted, F., and Sverdrup, U. (2012). Eurosceptics be warned - the 'half in, half out' EU integration model option is best left to Norway. *The Independent*, 5 October 2012. http://www.independent.co.uk/voices/comment/eurosceptics-be-warned-the-half-in-half-out-eu-integration-model-option-is-best-left-to-norway-8199849.html.

Springford, J., and Tilford, S. (2014). *The Great British Trade-Off: The impact of leaving the EU on the UK's trade and investment*, Centre for European Reform, London. http://www.cer.org.uk/publications/archive/policy-brief/2014/great-british-trade-impact-leaving-eu-uks-trade-and-investmen.

Thompson, G., and Harari, D. (2013). The Economic Impact of EU Membership on the UK. *House of Commons Library Briefing Paper* SN/EP/6730. http://researchbriefings.parliament.uk/ResearchBriefing/Summary/SN06730#fullreport.

UNCTAD [United Nations Conference on Trade and Development] (2013), *Non-Tariff measures to trade.* Geneva: United Nations. http://unctad.org/en/PublicationsLibrary/ditctab20121_en.pdf.

UNCTAD [United Nations Conference on Trade and Development]. (2016). *Most Favoured nation (MFN) tariff rates, weighted average - EU28 (European*

Union), 1988–2014. http://unctadstat.unctad.org/wds/TableViewer/tableView.aspx.

USITC [United States International Trade Commission]. (1996). *Country-of-origin marking: Review of laws, regulations and practices.* USITC, Washington DC. https://www.usitc.gov/publications/332/pub2975.pdf.

USITC [United States International Trade Commission]. (2000). *The Impact on the US Economy of Including the United Kingdom in a Free Trade Agreement with the United States, Canada and Mexico.* Investigation No. 332–409, USITC, Washington DC.

van Hulten, M. (2011). *To Get Out of this Crisis we need to Rebuild Europe from Scratch.* European Council on Foreign Relations. http://www.ecfr.eu/article/commentary_to_get_out_of_this_crisis_we_need_to_rebuild_europe_from_scratch.

Viner, J. (1950). *The Customs Union Issue.* Oxford University Press, Oxford, 2014 edition.

World Bank. (2015). *MFN (Most Favourite Nation) tariff rate 1988–2014.* http://data.worldbank.org/indicator/TM.TAX.MRCH.WM.AR.ZS?locations=EU.

World Data Bank. (2016). Tariff rate series. World Development Indicators.

WTO [World Trade Organisation]. (2011). *World Trade Report 2011: The WTO and preferential trade agreements – From coexistence to coherence.* World Trade Organisation, Geneva. https://www.wto.org/english/res_e/booksp_e/anrep_e/world_trade_report11_e.pdf.

WTO [World Trade Organisation]. (2016). *Tariffs and imports - Part A2.* http://stat.wto.org/TariffProfile/WSDBTariffPFView.aspx?Language=E&Country=E28.

Conclusion

This book has evaluated the existing evidence relating to the economic impact likely to arise from Brexit. It has noted the methodological flaws of many of the more prominent studies, and on which policy makers and other economic actors currently have to rely reaching the conclusion that the negative consequences they forecast are most likely exaggerated. Indeed, more recent studies, which have been completed just as this book is going to press, would seem to concur with this judgement (Gudgin et al 2017: 38–89).[1]

The existing economic studies are, however, important in that they highlight the areas that are disproportionately prone to negative consequences, such as in trade with the EU and in relation to investment being deferred or cancelled because of the uncertainty caused by the Brexit process. However, the importance of this work is not so much in its conclusions as to the magnitude of this impact, because most of these studies have ignored other relevant factors such as the potential to expand trade and investment with the rest of the (non-EU) world and they have assumed away the potential for government policy to ameliorate negative, and magnify positive, effects. Instead, it is that these studies, and hopefully this book, indicate to policy makers where they need to target their interventions, in order to reduce uncertainty through the stimulation of aggregate demand, aim to rebuild the UK's industrial base and increase the competitiveness of UK businesses, through an active industrial and labour market policy, to replace EU with national

© The Editor(s) (if applicable) and The Author(s) 2017
P.B. Whyman and A.I. Petrescu, *The Economics of Brexit*,
DOI 10.1007/978-3-319-58283-2

regulation more focused upon the needs of the domestic economy, and to maintain a competitive exchange rate to facilitate the Brexit process.

The choice of trading model, to establish once withdrawal from the EU has been completed, is an important part of this strategy, since it has the potential to either facilitate, or constrain, the structural change and policy flexibility that is required to make Brexit a success for the UK. There is a trade-off here, between greater access into the EU SIM and securing a necessary degree of policy flexibility. Any judgement about where this trade-off should occur will be, at least in part, determined by perceptions concerning the significance of economic problems facing the UK and the potential for economic policy intervention to provide a solution.

If, for example, an individual views the status quo position of the UK economy as essentially sound, and policy interventions having only weak effects, then they are more likely to advocate either continued EU membership or, as a second best alternative, they may consider participation in the EEA. For them, there is little to gain by more independent action and therefore continued market access is the overwhelming priority. For others, however, a judgement might be that the UK economy has a number of structural problems, not least the insufficient size of the manufacturing sector and the resultant weakness in productivity combined with the UK's very large trade deficit with the EU.

If they are of a neo-liberal persuasion, and agree that policy action has weak effects, then they may argue for complete liberalisation of the economy, along the lines of the Hong Kong model. Alternatively, if however they accept the evidence that active forms of economic policy can have significant impact upon the economy—and the reader needs look no further than the stabilisation achieved amidst the recent financial crisis or indeed the action of the Bank of England to reduce uncertainty immediately after the European referendum—then the trade-off might be to prioritise a trade relationship with the EU which is consistent with a necessary level of independence. The most obvious option here would be to seek to negotiate a FTA, including as greater portion of services as possible, since this is one area in which the UK has a competitive advantage. However, should this not prove to be possible, then it would be preferable for trade to revert to WTO rules rather than accept a form of trade agreement which unduly restricted the policy flexibility for the now independent UK.

Appendix

Authors' Estimations of Brexit Economic Impact

This book has sought to present and evaluate the available evidence required to assess Brexit's economic impact. However, it would not be fair for the authors to pass judgement upon other academic studies without us outlining our own interpretation of the evidence. Consequently, we intend to summarise our own assessment of the likely economic impact in this appendix. Please note, what follows is not the result of our own macroeconomic simulation modelling—that will be completed in a year's time, if our pending ESRC funding application is successful. Rather, this is our personal assessment of the evidence, as presented in this book. It depends upon the weight that we give to the perceived weaknesses in earlier studies, the degree to which we accept the theoretical work underpinning these same studies, and whether we believe that simplifying assumptions included in our own and other studies are justified or unfortunately bias the results. Nevertheless, however imprecise our own interpretations of the evidence, the resulting predictions do reflect what we consider to be Brexit's likely impact—i.e. relatively shallow short term costs, gradually being reduced as the economy adjusts to its independent status, and eventually net benefits assuming governments pursue the type of economic strategy that underpins our tentative predictions.

© The Editor(s) (if applicable) and The Author(s) 2017
P.B. Whyman and A.I. Petrescu, *The Economics of Brexit*,
DOI 10.1007/978-3-319-58283-2

Fiscal Savings: This item is quite straightforward. If the UK negotiates a FTA with the EU, or trades according to WTO rules, there should be an initial net annual saving of around 0.53% of UK GDP per annum. Given that the EU budget has grown over time, there is an expectation that UK contributions would have increased in future budgetary periods, had the UK remained a member of the EU, and therefore savings would be larger in the future.

Trade Effects: We consider the examples of gravity modelling, contained within most of the 'consensus' studies, to be inadequately calibrated to account for the use of historical data to predict future events, when the circumstances giving rise to previous outcomes no longer prevail. Specifically, the fact that the EU's CET was much higher in the past than at present will lead to an over-estimation of likely trade costs. As a result, we prefer to base out estimations upon the CEP-LSE study, which suggests that the static (short term) costs arising from reduced trade with the EU are likely to be in the range of 0.4% of UK GDP under a FTA. We think this is a reasonable estimate. We consider that their WTO predictions are over-estimated, due to their assumptions on NTBs, yet a presumption that trade with the EU could fall by the equivalent of perhaps 0.75% of UK GDP is plausible. Trade with the rest of the world is likely to gradually to rise thereafter, as exporters re-orientate their focus towards faster growing markets and as new preferential trade agreements may be signed with other countries such as the USA, Canada, New Zealand and Australia, all of whom having expressed a desire to begin trade negotiations once the withdrawal period has been completed. Consequently, we anticipate that negative trade effects will narrow over time, as increased trade with the rest of the world partly (or even wholly) offsets any decline with the EU.

Investment Effects: The evidence on potential future FDI flows is not particularly well developed, in our view. Those studies which used gravity modelling to estimate the effect of Brexit upon the inflow of FDI into the UK predicted rather large declines; ranging from 10% in the case of an EEA to almost half in the case of reliance upon WTO rules. Given the fact that most FDI entering the UK is in the service sector, and that a majority of this is orientated to primarily servicing the UK market and not being used as an export platform for sales into the wider

SIM, then it would seem to us that the more inflated estimates are most unlikely. Attitude Surveys, from existing and potential investors, indicate a much smaller effect upon FDI. Consequently, given the inadequate nature of the available evidence, our own estimate is rather tentative, namely anticipating a reduction of FDI flows of between 5 and 15%, depending upon the type of preferential trade agreement negotiated with the EU. Given that inward FDI flows in 2015 were approximately £26.7bn, this would imply a negative impact equating to between 0.28 and 0.84% of UK GDP. In the medium term, as the UK increases its trade with the rest of the world, the UK may become a more attractive host for FDI seeking to take advantages of the locational factors prevalent in the UK in order to export to these markets. This would reduce any short term negative FDI effect. Moreover, since a majority of FDI seeks to service the UK economy, the majority of future flows will be tied to its relative growth and prosperity. Hence, the ultimate success or failure of Brexit will determine the final shape of FDI flows.

Brexit is also likely to have a broader impact upon business investment, since this is a notoriously volatile component of national income, depending as it does upon what Keynes described as the 'animal spirits' of investors and business leaders. Businesses invest because they anticipate future profits, and draw a significant proportion of their funding from retained past profits. Consequently, it is the anticipation of having a sufficient level of demand in the target market(s) that drives investment. If businesses are uncertain about future events, they are more likely to hesitate and delay such investment which, since this is a key component of aggregate demand, will cause the economy to slow down unless one of the other major components (i.e. consumption, net government spending and net trade effects) increases by a level sufficient to offset this investment slowdown. Many of the 'consensus' studies modelled uncertainty as increases in risk premiums on the financing of investment, which is imprecise, as this assumes that investment is primarily drawn from financial markets and not retained earnings. Moreover, many of these studies had a seemingly inconsistent approach to the length of time that such uncertainty may prevail and, moreover, all of them ignored the potential impact of government policy in calming markets and reassuring investors. However, this is the key factor at play with respect to investment. If government adopts an active macro-economic policy stance, and ensures high levels of aggregate demand, the majority of businesses will continue to have positive expectations of future profitability and continue to invest in new capacity and new technology. Those firms that are disproportionately export-orientated will be reassured if the government commits to the maintenance of a competitive exchange rate, which will more than offset any negative trade effects arising from Brexit. Hence, *if* government pursues this type of economic policy stance, the authors conclude that investment effects, arising from uncertainty, will be minimal.

Dynamic effects: The authors are sceptical about the proposed linkage between the degree of openness of an economy and productivity. Put simply, we do not feel that this has been adequately proven. We do accept the economic benefits that may arise from securing economies of scale, and it would seem reasonable that larger markets may facilitate this process. But this effect may be similarly encouraged as a result of the attractions inherent in operating within a prosperous and growing domestic economy, and particularly if an attractive set of R&D incentives were introduced as part of an active industrial policy. Moreover, even if we were to accept the possibility that openness has a dynamic benefit, this does not necessarily equate to the fact that withdrawal from the EU will necessarily give rise to significant declines in the dynamism and hence efficiency of the UK economy. No-one is suggesting that the UK proposes to introduce protectionist barriers, behind which its industries are feather-bedded. Quite the contrary in fact, as the emphasis is upon exploring new trade relationships with the rest of the world. Hence, to the extent that openness determines dynamic effects, this will depend upon the eventual balance between any decline in trade with the EU and any increase in trade with the rest of the world. Given that this second part of the equation has not been adequately covered by the mainstream studies, we prefer to defer judgement upon dynamic effects unless or until sufficient evidence emerges.

Regulation effects: There have been some rather exaggerated predictions made concerning the likely magnitude of economic benefits which may derive from the UK replacing European with national forms of regulation. We consider it to be most unlikely that the UK would embark upon a wholesale de-regulation of its economy post-Brexit. Moreover, we do not accept the theoretical arguments that, based upon neo-liberal foundations, such a liberalisation would result in dramatically favourable economic effects. The economy does not behave in the way suggested by a second year textbook. Markets work more efficiently when properly regulated. However, this regulation is more efficiently designed and applied when controlled by government closer to the market(s) being regulated. Hence, there is every expectation that the replacement of supra-national EU regulation with more targeted national (UK) regulation, will have a positive economic effect. One estimate cited in this book suggests that this could benefit the UK economy by as much as 4.5% of its GDP, whereas another suggests that it could be as low as 0.3% of UK GDP. The difference between the two figures depends, in part, upon what proportion of regulations the different studies consider that it would be possible or desirable to replace. This, in turn, depends upon the future trade relationship that the UK agrees with the EU. If the UK joins the EEA, then there will be no significant regulatory savings, as SIM rules continue to apply. If the UK negotiates a FTA with the EU, then there will be scope to redesign regulations, since such agreements typically require 'equivalence' of regulations not their harmonisation. In the case of trading under WTO rules, UK exporters will have to abide by those regulations and rules applying to goods and services entering the SIM, in exactly the same way that they currently have to do in other markets such as the USA or China. However, the advantage for FTA and WTO options are that EU rules will only need apply to exporters and not the 94% of UK firms that never sell into the SIM, but currently have to abide by EU regulations. This will give rise to an economic benefit to the UK economy, which we cautiously estimate could be around 0.75% of UK GDP in the medium term.

Migration effects: The range of studies which have sought to estimate the net economic effect of migration into the UK have produced mixed results within a general range of either plus or minus 0.3% of UK GDP. However, this evidence remains rather weak, partly because these studies only encapsulated part of the likely economic impacts arising from net EU migration into the UK. In addition, a different set of studies have indicated that migration has a positive, albeit rather small, effect upon productivity levels. According to this result, halving current levels of net EU migration will *ceteris paribus* likely reduce UK productivity levels by perhaps 0.15% per annum. However, *if* any reduction in EU migration was concentrated amongst low skilled migrant labour, with a simultaneous increase in more highly skilled migrant labour from either EU or non-EU countries, then productivity levels within the UK economy should increase. The net result will therefore depend upon which of the two effects is predominant—quantity or quality (productivity) effects.

Economic policy: This is the factor that virtually all other studies tend to ignore, because it complicates an already complex analysis. Nevertheless, it is here that we consider Brexit has the *potential*, if correctly utilised, to realise its greatest benefit. In the short term, the maintenance of a competitive exchange rate should offset negative consequences arising from a forecast reduction in trade and FDI flows. This effect will gradually diminish over time, as higher import prices cause inflation to erode any competitive advantage. Independence from EU constraints will additionally allow the UK to introduce a more active industrial policy, aimed at regenerating its industrial base, and thereby contributing towards resolution of two of the UK's most intractable economic problems; namely its very large and persistent trade deficit, and its comparably low rates of productivity. SIM rules currently preclude some of the measures that a more active industrial policy might wish to utilise, and therefore Brexit offers the opportunity to introduce such initiatives. This would have more of a medium and long term

	Short Term	Medium Term	Long Term
Fiscal	+0.5	+0.6	+0.6
Trade	-0.4 to -0.8	-0.4 to -0.7	-0.3 to -0.5
FDI	-0.3 to -0.8	-0.2 to -0.5	-0.1 to -0.3
Investment	-0.5	0	+0.5
Regulation	+0.2	+0.6	+0.8
Migration (assuming a net reduction in EU migration combined with an increase in skilled migrant labour)	-0.2	0	+0.1
TOTAL (excluding economic policy effects)	*-1.5 to -0.6*	*0 to +0.6*	*+1.2 to +1.6*
Economic Policy	+0.3	+1	+2
TOTAL (including economic policy effects)	*-1.2 to -0.3*	*+0.9 to +1.6*	*+3.2 to +3.6*

NB: values subject to rounding

Fig. A.1 Summary of authors' predicted Brexit effects.

impact. The success of this approach would, of course, depend upon the intelligent design and efficient implementation of such policies. Brexit does not guarantee that this will occur; only that it provides the *potential* for this to occur. Nevertheless, if successful, this more active form of economic policy has the potential to overshadow all of the costs and benefits discussed elsewhere in this book. It could, indeed, be a game changer. Consequently, for the authors, it is this factor that, more than any other, will determine the ultimate success or failure of Brexit (Fig. A.1).

Note

1. http://researchbriefings.parliament.uk/ResearchBriefing/Summary/CBP-7893.

References

Algan, Y., & Cahuc, P. (2010). Inherited trust and growth. *American EconomicReview, 100*(5), 2060–2092.

Armstrong, A. (2016). EU Membership financial services and stability. *National Institute Economic Review, 236,* 31–38.

Armstrong, B. (2016). *Brexit—A great opportunity for Scottish fishing, Scottish fishermen's federation.* Available via: https://www.theguardian.com/politics/2016/sep/07/brexit-vote-great-relief-for-uk-fishing-.industry-lords.

Atkinson, P.E. (1997, April/May). New Zealand's Radical Reforms. *OECD Observer,* No. 205, 43–47. Available via: http://oecdobserver.org/news/fullstory.php/aid/2710/New_Zealand_s_Radical_Reforms.html.

Aydemir, A., & Borjas, G. J. (2007). Cross-country variation in the impact of international migration: Canada Mexico, and the United States. *Journal of the European Economic Association, 5*(4), 663–708.

Bank of England (2015, February). *One bank research agenda.* Bank of England Discussion Paper. Available via: http://www.bankofengland.co.uk/research/Documents/onebank/discussion.pdf.

Batten, G., & Stroilov, P. (2013). *The road to freedom: How Britain can leavethe European Union.* Surbiton: Bretwalda Books Ltd.

Bellamy-Foster, J., & Magdoff, F. (2009). *The Great Financial Crisis*. New York: Monthly Review Press.

Berden, K. G., Francois, J., Tamminen, S., Thelle, M., & Wymenga, P. (2009). *Non-tariff measures in EU-US trade and investment: An economic analysis*. Rotterdam: ECORYS. Available via: http://trade.ec.europa.eu/doclib/docs/2009/december/tradoc_145613.pdf.

Böwer, U., & Turrini, A. (2010). EU accession: A road to fast-track convergence? *Comparative Economic Studies, 52*(2), 181–205.

Bush, O., Knott, S. & Peacock, C. (2014). Why is the UK banking system so big and is that a problem? *Bank of England quarterly bulletin* Q4, 385–395. Available via: http://www.bankofengland.co.uk/publications/Documents/quarterlybulletin/2014/qb14q402.pdf.

Cabral, L., Poulton, C., Wiggins, S., & Zhang, L. (2006). *Reforming agricultural policy: Lessons from four countries*. Future agricultures Working Paper No. 2. Available via: http://www.future-agricultures.org/publications/research-and-analysis/915-reforming-agricultural-policy-lessons-from-four-countries/file.

Card, D. (1990). The impact of the Mariel Boatlift on the Miami labor market. *Industrial and Labor Relations Review, 43*, 245–257.

Carney, M. (2016, March 7). *Letter to Andrew Tyrie*. Available via: http://www.bankofengland.co.uk/publications/Documents/other/treasurycommittee/other/governorletter070316.pdf.

Cohen, S. (1977). *Modern capitalist planning: The French model* (2nd ed.). Berkeley: University of California Press.

Conlon, G., Ladher, R., & Halterbeck, M. (2017). *The determinants of international demand for UK higher education*. HEPI Report No. 91. London. Available via: http://www.hepi.ac.uk/wp-content/uploads/2017/01/Hepi-Report-91-Screen.pdf.

Department for Business Innovation and Skills (BIS). (2009). *The total benefit/cost ratio of new regulations 2008–2009*. London: BIS. Available via: http://data.parliament.uk/DepositedPapers/Files/DEP2009-2580/DEP2009-2580.pdf.

Department for Business Innovation and Skills (BIS). (2014). *The impact of the working time regulations in the uk labour market: A review of the evidence*. London: BIS. Available via: https://www.gov.uk/government/uploads/system/uploads/attachment_data/file/389676/bis-14-1287-the-impact-of-the-working-time-regulations-on-the-uk-labour-market-a-review-of-evidence.pdf.

Dietzenbacher, E., Los, B., Stehrer, R., Timmer, M., & de Vries, G. (2013). The construction of world input-output tables in the WIOD iroject. *Economic Systems Research, 25*(1), 71–98.

Economists for Brexit. (2016). *A vote for Brexit: What are the policies to follow and what are the economic prospects?* London: Economists for Brexit. Available via: http://www.economistsforbrexit.co.uk/a-vote-for-brexit.

Economic European Area (EEA) Agreement. (2011, November 15). *agreement on the European economic area updated.* Available via: http://secretariat. efta.int/~/media/Documents/legal-texts/eea/the-eea-agreement/Main%20 Text%20of%20the%20Agreement/EEAagreement.pdf. Accessed 05 June 2013.

Elliott, M. (2015, July 14). Greece makes further euro integration unavoidable—With big risks for the UK. *CityAM*. Available via: http://www. cityam.com/220062/greece-makes-further-euro-integration-unavoidable-big-risks-uk.

Emmerson, C., & Pope, T. (2016). Winter is coming: The outlook for thepublic finances in the 2016 Autumn Statement. IFS Briefing NoteBN188,Institute for Fiscal Studies, London. https://www.ifs.org.uk/ uploads/publications/bns/BN188.pdf.

Emmerson, C., Johnson, P., & Mitchell, I. (2016). *The EU single market: The value of membership versus access to the UK.* London: Institute for Fiscal Studies. Available via: http://www.ifs.org.uk/uploads/publications/comms/ R119%20-%20The%20EU%20Single%20market%20-%20Final.pdf.

European Commission (EC). (1992). *Treaty on European Union* [Maastricht Treaty]. Luxembourg: Office for Official Publications of the European Communities. Available via: http://europa.eu/eu-law/decision-making/trea-ties/pdf/treaty_on_european_union/treaty_on_european_union_en.pdf.

European Commission (EC). (1997). *Treaty of Amsterdam amending the treaty on European Union, the treaties establishing the European communities and certain related acts* [Amsterdam Treaty]. Luxembourg: Office for Official Publications of the European Communities. Available via: http://www.euro-parl.europa.eu/topics/treaty/pdf/amst-en.pdf.

European Commission (EC). (2011). *Financing the eu budget: report on the operation of the own resources system.* Commission Report on the operation of the own resources system, Staff Working Paper SEC(2011) 876 final/2. Available via: http://ec.europa.eu/budget/library/biblio/documents/fin_ fwk1420/proposal_council_own_resources__annex_en.pdf.

European Commission (EC). (2012). *Twenty years of the European single market: Together to new growth—main achievements.* Luxembourg: Office for Official Publications of the European Communities. Available via: http://ec.europa. eu/internal_market/publications/docs/20years/achievements-web_en.pdf.

European Communities. (2012). Consolidated versions of the treaty on European union and the treaty on the functioning of the European Union [Treaty on the Functioning of the European Union, TFEU], *Official Journal of the European Union*, Vol. 55, C326, Office for Official Publications of the European Communities, Luxembourg. Available via: http://eur-lex.europa.eu/legal-content/EN/TXT/?uri=OJ:C:2012:326:TOC.

Galati, G., and Moessner, R. (2011). *Macroprudential policy—A literature review*. (BIS [Bank of International Settlments] Working Papers No. 337). Available via: http://www.bis.org/publ/work337.pdf.

George, S. (1998). *An awkward partner: Britain in the European community*. Oxford: Oxford University Press.

Gnos, C., & Rochon, L.-P. (2005). What is next for the Washington consensus? *Journal of Post Keynesian Economics, 27*(2), 187–193.

Haldane, A. G. (2011, May 11–12). The Short Long, speech made at the 29th Société Universitaire Européene de Recherches Financières Colloquium: New Paradigms in Money and Finance? Brussels. Available via: http://www.bankofengland.co.uk/archive/Documents/historicpubs/speeches/2011/speech495.pdf.

Hall, K. (2013). A reformed European Union: The platform to realise our global future. In A. Hug (Ed.), *Renegotiation, reform and referendum: Does Britain have an EU future?* London: Foreign Policy Centre (pp. 17–19). Available via: http://fpc.org.uk/fsblob/1616.pdf.

Harris, D., & Rae, A. (2006). Agricultural policy reform and industry adjustment in Australia and New Zealand. In D. Blandford & B. Hill (Eds.), *Policy reform and adjustment in the agricultural sectors of developed countries* (pp. 83–104). Wallingford Oxfordshire: CAB International.

Head, K., Mayer, T., & Thoenig, M. (2014). Welfare and trade without pareto. *American Economic Review, 104*(5), 310–316.

HM Government (HMG). (2013). *Review of the balance of competences between the United Kingdom and the European Union—The single market*. London: The Stationary Office. Available via: https://www.gov.uk/government/uploads/system/uploads/attachment_data/file/227069/2901084_SingleMarket_acc.pdf.

HMG [HM Government]. (2016). The process for withdrawing from theEuropean Union, Cm 9216, The Stationary Office, London. https://www.gov.uk/government/uploads/system/uploads/attachment_data/file/504216/The_process_for_withdrawing_from_the_EU_print_ready.pdf.

House of Lords European Union Committee (HoL). (2016). *Revised transcript of evidence taken before The select committee on the European Union energy and environment sub-committee—Brexit fisheries*. London: House of Lords. Available via: http://data.parliament.uk/writtenevidence/committeeevidence.svc/evidencedocument/eu-energy-and-environment-subcommittee/brexit-fisheries/oral/37841.pdf.

Hug, A. (2013). Britain's precarious future. In A. Hug (Ed.), *Renegotiation, reform and referendum: Does Britain have an EU future?* 4–5. London: Foreign Policy Centre. Available via: http://fpc.org.uk/fsblob/1616.pdf.

Hutton, W. (1996). *The state we're in.* London: Vintage.

IMF. (2006). *Competition and firm productivity: Evidence from firm-level data* (IMF Working Paper WP/10/67). Available via: https://www.imf.org/external/pubs/ft/wp/2010/wp1067.pdf.

Johnson, B. (2016, February 22). There is only one way to get the change we want—Vote to leave the EU. *The telegraph.* Available via: http://www.telegraph.co.uk/opinion/2016/03/16/boris-johnson-exclusive-there-is-only-one-way-to-get-the-change/.

Johnson, R. W. M. (2000). *Reforming EU Farm Policy: Lessons from New Zealand* (IEA Occasional Papers No. 112). London: Institute of Economic Affairs. Available via: https://iea.org.uk/publications/research/reforming-eu-farm-policy-lessons-from-new-zealand.

Kelly, U. (2016). *Economic Impact on the UK of EU Research Funding to UK Universities.* Viewforth Consulting Ltd, produced for Universities UK. Available via: http://www.universitiesuk.ac.uk/policy-and-analysis/reports/Documents/2016/economic-impact-of-eu-research-funding-in-uk-universities.pdf.

Keynes, J. M. (1980). Activities 1940–1944: Shaping the post-war world—The clearing union. In D. Moggridge (Ed.), *The collected writings of John Maynard Keynes.* London: Macmillan.

Koske, I., Wanner, I., Bitetti, R., & Barbiero, O. (2015). *The 2013 update of the oecd's database on product market regulation: policy insights for oecd and non-oecd countries.* (OECD Economics Department Working Papers, No. 1200). Paris: OECD. Available via: http://dx.doi.org/10.1787/5js3f5d3n2vl-en.

Lebrecht, A. (2013). Fisheries. In J. Drew & M. Bond (Eds.), *The UK and Europe: Costs, benefits, options—The regents report 2013,* 129–138. London: Regents University London/Belmont Press. Available via: http://www.regents.ac.uk/files/regentsreport2013.pdf.

Lemos, S., & Portes, J. (2008). *New labour? The impact of migration from Central and Eastern European countries on the UK labour market* (IZA Discussion Paper No. 3756).

Lyddon, B. (2016). *The UK's liabilities to the financial mechanisms of the European Union.* London: The Bruges Group. Available via: http://www.brugesgroup.com/images/papers/ukliabilitiestotheeu.pdf.

Menon, A., & Salter, J.-P. (2016). Britain's influence in the EU. *National Institute Economic Review, 236,* 7–13.

Minsky, H. (1986). *Stabilising and unstable economy.* New Haven: Yale University Press.

Monks, J. (2013). Social and Employment Dimensions. In J. Drew & M. Bond (Eds.), *The UK and Europe: Costs, benefits, options—The regents report 2013* (pp. 156–163). London: Regents University London and Belmont Press.

Newlands, D. (2003). Competition and cooperation in industrial clusters: The implication for public policy. *European Planning Studies, 11*(5), 521–532.

National Institute of Economic and Social Research (NIESR). (2016, May 10). *The economic impact of leaving the EU*—Press release. Available via: http://www.niesr.ac.uk/sites/default/files/NIESR%20Brexit%20Press%20Release%20-%20May%2016%20fin.pdf.

Official Norwegian Report (NOU). (2012). *Outside and Inside: Norway's agreements with the European Union*—Chapter 1, NOU 2012: 2. Oslo: Norwegian Ministry of Foreign Affairs. Available via: http://www.eu-norway.org/Global/SiteFolders/webeu/NOU2012_2_Chapter_1.pdf.

O'Connor, A. (2005). *Trade, investment and competition in international banking.* Basingstoke: Palgrave.

OECD. (2013). *Product market regulation 2013.* Available via: http://stats.oecd.org/Index.aspx?DataSetCode=SNA_TABLE1.

OECD. (2014). *Is migration good for the economy?* Paris: OECD. Available via: https://www.oecd.org/migration/OECD%20Migration%20Policy%20Debates%20Numero%202.pdf.

Office of National Statistics (ONS). (2016). *Labour productivity.* April to June 2016. Release date: 6 October 2016.

Oxford Economics. (2009). *Regional economic performance: A migration perspective* (Department of Communities and Local Government Economics Paper No. 4). London: Department of Communities and Local Government.

People Management (2016, October). CBI directors says 'drastic clampdown' on migrant workers must be scrapped. *People Management.* Available via:http://www2.cipd.co.uk/pm/peoplemanagement/b/weblog/archive/2016/10/14/cbi-director-says-drastic-clampdown-on-migrant-workers-must-be-scrapped.aspx. Last accessed: 29 October 2016.

Piermartini, R., & Teh, R. (2005). *Demystifying modelling methods for trade policy* (WTO Discussion Paper No. 10). Switzerland: WTO. Available via: https://www.wto.org/english/res_e/booksp_e/discussion_papers10_e.pdf.

Polanyi, K. (1944). *The great transformation: The political and economic origins of our time* (2002nd ed.). Boston, Mass: Beacon Press.

Rotherham, L. (2009). *The price of fish: Costing the common fisheries policy.* London: Taxpayers Alliance. Available via: https://d3n8a8pro7vhmx.cloudfront.net/taxpayersalliance/pages/3647/attachments/original/1427450780/CFP.pdf?1427450780.

Royal Society. (2015). *UK research and the European Union: The role of the EU in funding UK research.* London: Royal Society. Available via: https://royalsociety.org/~/media/policy/projects/eu-uk-funding/uk-membership-of-eu.pdf.

Sirkeci, I. (2013). Population change and migration in Europe and the UK, in regents report. In J. Drew & M. Bond (Eds.), *The UK and Europe: Costs, benefits, options—The regents report 2013*, 16-26. London: Regents University London/Belmont Press. Available via: http://www.regents.ac.uk/files/regentsreport2013.pdf.

Smith, A. (1728). *An Enquiry into the Nature and Causes of the Wealth of Nations* (2008 ed.). Oxford: Oxford University Press.

Springford, J., Tilford, S., & Whyte, P. (2014). *The economic consequences of leaving the EU.* London: Centre for European Reform. Available via: http://www.cer.org.uk/sites/default/files/smc_final_report_june2014.pdf.

Times Higher Education (THE). (2016). *Times higher education world university rankings.* Available via: https://www.timeshighereducation.com/world-university-rankings/2017/world-ranking#!/page/0/length/-1/sort_by/rank_label/sort_order/asc/cols/scores.

The UK in a Changing Europe. (2016). *Brexit and beyond: How the United Kingdom might leave the European Union.* London: Political Studies Association. Available via: http://ukandeu.ac.uk/wp-content/uploads/2016/11/Brexit-and-Beyond-how-the-UK-might-leave-the-EU.pdf.

Thirlwall, A. P., & Hussain, M. N. (1982). The balance of payments constraint, capital flows, and growth rate differences between developing countries. *Oxford Economic Papers, 34*(10), 498–509.

Traxler, F., & Woitech, B. (2000). Transnational investment and national labour market regimes: A case of "regime shopping"? *European Journal of Industrial Relations, 6*(2), 141–159.

Tudor, O. (2013). Unions and the EU. In A. Hug (Ed.), *Renegotiation, reform and referendum: Does Britain have an EU future?* 20–22. London: Foreign Policy Centre. Available via: http://fpc.org.uk/fsblob/1616.pdf.

Tybout, J. R. (2000). Manufacturing firms in developing countries: How well do they do, and why? *Journal of Economic Literature, 38*(1), 11–44.

UK Border Agency. (2013). *Working in the UK.* available via: http://www.ukba.homeoffice.gov.uk/visas-immigration/working/ (accessed 18 May 2013).

United Nations Conference on Trade and Development (UNCTAD). (2016). *Foreign direct investment: Outward flows, annual.* Available via: www.unctad.org/fdistatistics.

UUK. (2014). *The Impact of universities on the UK economy.* London: Universities UK. Available via: http://www.universitiesuk.ac.uk/policy-and-analysis/reports/Documents/2014/the-impact-of-universities-on-the-uk-economy.pdf.

Vargas-Silva, C., & Markaki, Y. (2015). *EU migration to and from the UK.* University of Oxford, Centre on Migration, Policy and Society (COMPAS), Migration Observatory Briefing. Available via: http://www.migrationobservatory.ox.ac.uk/sites/files/migobs/Briefing%20-%20Long%20Term%20Migration%20Flows%20to%20and%20from%20the%20UK_0.pdf.

Wacziarg, R. (2001). Measuring the dynamic gains from trade. *World Bank Economic Review, 15*(3), 393–429.

Walmsley, S. (2016). *Brexit: Where next for UK fisheries?* London: ABP MER (Marine Environmental Research). Available via: http://www.sff.co.uk/wp-content/uploads/2016/07/Scottish-Fishing-Synopsis-of-actions.pdf.

Whyman, P. B. (2007). The case for the Swedish wage-earner funds: A post keynesian solution to the dynamic inefficiency of capitalism through the socialisation of investment. *Journal of Post Keynesain Economics, 30*(2), 83–115.

Whyman, P. B. (2016). Food and the EU. In K. Hickson & J. Miles (Eds.), *The socialist case for Brexit* (pp. 31–36). London: Labour Leave.

Willis, G. (2016). *New model farming: Resilience through diversity.* London: Campaign to Protect Rural England. Available via: http://www.cpre.org.uk/resources/farming-and-food/farming/item/4347-new-model-farming.

Winters, L. A. (1984). British imports of manufactures and the common market. *Oxford Economic Papers, 36*(1), 103–118.

World Bank. (2016). *World development indicators.* Available via: http://databank.worldbank.org/data/reports.aspx?source=2&series=NY.GDP.PCAP.CD&country.

World Bank. (2016). *Gross domestic product 2015—Country rankings.* Available via:http://data.worldbank.org/data-catalog/world-development-indicators. Last updated 16 December 2016. Accessed 20 January 2017.

World Data Bank series on Portfolio Investment and FDI. (2016). World development indicators. Various series. Available via: http://databank.worldbank.org/data/reports.aspx?source=2&series=NE.TRD.GNFS.ZS&country=GBR.

Wray, L. R. (2011). *Minsky's money manager capitalism and the global financial crisis* (Levy Institute Working Paper No. 661). Available via: http://www.levyinstitute.org/pubs/wp_661.pdf.

Subject Index

Index of Places

© The Editor(s) (if applicable) and The Author(s) 2017
P.B. Whyman and A.I. Petrescu, *The Economics of Brexit*,
DOI 10.1007/978-3-319-58283-2

Made in the USA
Middletown, DE
20 August 2020